D0829656

Information Literacy: Essential Skills for the Information Age

Second Edition

Michael B. Eisenberg

Carrie A. Lowe

Kathleen L. Spitzer

Foreword by
Patricia Senn Breivik

LIBRARIES

UNLIMITED

A Member of the Greenwood Publishing Group

Westport, Connecticut • London

Library of Congress Cataloging-in-Publication Data

Eisenberg, Michael.

    Information literacy : essential skills for the information age.—2nd ed. / Michael B. Eisenberg, Carrie A. Lowe, and Kathleen L. Spitzer ; foreword by Patricia Senn Breivik.

      p. cm.

    Spitzer's name appears first on the earlier edition.

    Includes bibliographical references and index.

    ISBN 1–59158–143–5 (alk. paper)

    1. Information literacy. 2. Information literacy—Study and teaching—United States 3. Information literacy—Study and teaching (Elementary)—United States. 4. Information literacy—Study and teaching (Secondary)—United States. 5. Education—Standards—United States. 6. Education—Aims and objectives—United States. I. Lowe, Carrie A. II. Spitzer, Kathleen L. III. Title.

ZA3075.E385 2004

028.7—dc22   2003060591

British Library Cataloguing in Publication Data is available.

Copyright © 2004 by Michael B. Eisenberg, Carrie A. Lowe, and Kathleen L. Spitzer

All rights reserved. No portion of this book may be reproduced, by any process or technique, without the express written consent of the publisher.

Library of Congress Catalog Card Number: 2003060591

ISBN: 1–59158–143–5

First published in 2004

Libraries Unlimited, 88 Post Road West, Westport, CT 06881

A Member of the Greenwood Publishing Group, Inc.

www.lu.com

Printed in the United States of America

The paper used in this book complies with the Permanent Paper Standard issued by the National Information Standards Organization (Z39.48-1984).

10 9 8 7 6 5 4 3

Every reasonable effort has been made to track down the owners of copyright materials in this book, but in some instances this has proven impossible. The editors and publisher will be glad to receive information leading to more complete acknowledgments in subsequent printings of the book and in the meantime extend their apologies for any omissions.

To our #1 supporters—our spouses
Carol Eisenberg, Mark Hancock, and Gary Spitzer

Contents

Acknowledgments

This book is the based on two earlier books on the topic of information literacy published by the ERIC Clearinghouse on Information & Technology. The first was Christina S. Doyle's *Information Literacy in an Information Society: A Concept for the Information Age* (Doyle, 1994). [Published under U.S. Government contract RR93002009.] The second, authored by Kathy Spitzer with Mike Eisenberg and Carrie Lowe, built upon and extended Doyle's work. This new book, in turn, is a major revision and extension of the Spitzer, Eisenberg, and Lowe book.

As before, we are keenly aware of the contributions others have made to this volume. From across the country, professional colleagues submitted documents for consideration and answered our questions via telephone, fax, and e-mail. We are particularly grateful to Patricia Breivik, Dean of the University Library, San Jose State University; Brian Bannon from the Seattle Public Library; and Julie Walker, Executive Director of the American Association of School Librarians. We also wish to thank Eric Plotnick and others at the Information Institute of Syracuse for their encouragement and assistance in building on the earlier works. Particular thanks go to Jennifer Barth and Kelly Black from the AskERIC team for their excellent work on the annotated bibliography.

Thanks also to Cris Mesling, Assistant to the Dean at the University of Washington's Information School, and Sarah Zabel, graduate student in the master's of library science program. And finally, a very special thanks to Sue Wurster, formerly Publications Coordinator of the Information Institute of Syracuse, currently Executive Manager of Big6 Associates.

Michael B. Eisenberg
Carrie A. Lowe
Kathleen L. Spitzer
July 2003

Foreword

As this publication makes so clear, information literacy is not the product of any single profession or country. It is in many ways an amazingly successful grassroots effort of people around the world. Moreover, it remains a much-needed commonsense approach for addressing the very real challenge of providing equity of opportunity within today's Information Society.

There are a growing number of publications on information literacy. This book, however, remains one of the most definitive on the topic. As such, it shall be of much use to educators, librarians, and policy leaders who care about people and who are committed to empowering individuals for quality of life. In addition, it will save these proponents and practitioners of information literacy much time and effort by bringing together in one place so much information on the topic.

Dr. Patricia Senn Breivik
Dean, Library, San Jose State University and Chair,
National Forum on Information Literacy
June 2003

To be information literate, a person must be able to recognize when information is needed and have the ability to locate, evaluate, and use effectively the needed information.—American Library Association Presidential Committee on information Literacy (1989, p. 1)

Introduction

A chief financial officer returned home from vacation and found 2,000 e-mail messages waiting for him. He was so overwhelmed that he simply deleted them, thereby eliminating potentially valuable information (Kunde, 1997).

Scientists who needed to record the eclipse of the star Aldebaran from a multitude of viewpoints issued a call to amateur astronomers via the International Occultation Timing Association's Internet Web page. Those who answered the call were asked to tune to the Weather Channel to synchronize the starting of their camcorders to record the event. Videotapes were then forwarded to scientists for analysis (Kluger, 1997).

In October 1987, high winds assaulted the southern half of England, destroying more than 15 million trees and damaging almost one out of every six British houses. British weather forecasters, who were perhaps overconfident in relying on their computerized models, failed to predict the worst storm in England in 300 years. French weather forecasters were successful in predicting the severity of this same storm in their geographical area by combining information from computerized prediction models with satellite data and upper-air charts (Norton & Gotts, 1991).

In 1998, over 100,000 students became scientists as they participated in the Journey North, a Web-based initiative co-sponsored by the Annenberg/CPB Math and Science Project. Students tracked the migration of monarch butterflies, American robins, hummingbirds, right whales, and other species, and reported the latitude and longitude of their sightings, along with other descriptive information, via the Internet. They then manipulated the raw data to create maps and conduct other projects demonstrating the migration of these species (The Annenberg/CPB Projects, 1998).

As these examples illustrate, information can empower and enable us or overwhelm and confuse us. We are challenged on a daily basis to negotiate through vast amounts of information in a variety of formats. The basic information literacy skills of efficiently and effectively accessing, evaluating, and using information from a variety of sources are essential for survival in the Information Age.

In this book we trace the history and development of the term "information literacy". We examine the economic necessity of being information literate, and we explore the research related to the concept. We include reports on the National Education Goals (1991) and on the report of the Secretary's Commission on Achieving Necessary Skills (SCANS, 1991). We examine recent revisions in national subject matter standards that imply a recognition of the process skills included in information literacy. We outline the impact information literacy has on K–12 and higher education. And finally, we provide examples of information literacy in various contexts. Let's begin our journey by defining information literacy in Chapter 1.

Information Literacy:
Essential Skills for the Information Age

Second Edition

Defining Information Literacy

In this chapter, we will see how information literacy has been defined by various groups and individuals since its first mention in 1974. We will also briefly examine other literacies that are implicit in information literacy.

In 1974, Paul Zurkowski, president of the Information Industry Association, introduced the concept of "information literacy" in a proposal submitted to the National Commission on Libraries and Information Science (NCLIS). The proposal recommended that a national program be established to achieve universal information literacy within the next decade. According to Zurkowski, "People trained in the application of information resources to their work can be called information literates. They have learned techniques and skills for utilizing the wide range of information tools as well as primary sources in molding information-solutions to their problems" (p. 6).

Two years later, Burchinal (1976), in a paper presented at the Texas A & M University library's symposium, suggested: "To be information literate requires a new set of skills. These include how to locate and use information needed for problem-solving and decision-making efficiently and effectively" (p. 11). That same year, Owens (1976) tied information literacy to democracy, stating, "Beyond information literacy for greater work effectiveness and efficiency, information literacy is needed to guarantee the survival of democratic institutions. All men are created equal but voters with information resources are in a position to make more intelligent decisions than citizens who are information illiterates" (p. 27).

Behrens (1994) points out that these and other definitions of the 1970s were developed in response to the rapidly increasing amount of information available and to the fact that it was becoming more difficult to negotiate the complex world of information. During the 1980s, there was a recognition that computers and related technologies were becoming increasingly powerful tools for retrieval and manipulation of information. At the end of the decade, the *Final Report* of the American Library Association Presidential Committee on Information Literacy (1989) not only recognized the importance of information literacy to a democratic society, but provided a definition in terms of requisite skills: "To be information literate, a person must be able to recognize when information is needed and have the ability to locate, evaluate, and use effectively the needed information" (p. 1). This definition has been widely accepted by those within the library field and forms the basis of subsequent definitions.

> *To be information literate, a person must be able to recognize when information is needed and have the ability to locate, evaluate, and use effectively the needed information.*—American Library Association Presidential Committee on Information Literacy, *Final Report*, 1989, p. 1.

In 1992, Doyle published the results of a Delphi study that expanded this definition. Participants in the Delphi study agreed on the attributes of an information literate person, proposing that such a person is one who:

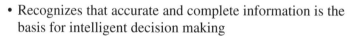

- Recognizes that accurate and complete information is the basis for intelligent decision making
- Recognizes the need for information
- Formulates questions based on information needs
- Identifies potential sources of information
- Develops successful search strategies
- Accesses sources of information including computer-based and other technologies
- Evaluates information
- Organizes information for practical application
- Integrates new information into an existing body of knowledge
- Uses information in critical thinking and problem solving. (1992, p. 8)

Since 1992, information literacy has been the topic of scores of publications and has been examined by educational institutions, professional organizations, and scholarly individuals. Many higher education institutions have formed campuswide committees to work toward including information literacy as a graduation outcome. Some are even calling it a new liberal art. As each group or individual has explored information literacy, new definitions have been offered:

> Implicit in a full understanding of information literacy is the realization that several conditions must be simultaneously present. First, someone must desire to know, use analytic skills to formulate questions, identify research methodologies, and utilize critical skills to evaluate experimental and experiential results. Second, the person must possess the skills to search for answers to those questions in increasingly diverse and complex ways. Third, once a person has identified what is sought, be able to access it. (Lenox & Walker, 1992, p. 314)

Information literate students are competent, independent learners. They know their information needs and actively engage in the world of ideas. They display confidence in their ability to solve problems and know what is relevant information. They manage technology tools to access information and to communicate. They operate comfortably in situations where there are multiple answers, as well as those with no answers. They hold high standards for their work and create quality products. Information literate students are flexible, can adapt to change, and are able to function independently and in groups (Colorado Educational Media Association, 1994, p. 1):

> [Information literacy includes] the abilities to recognize when information is needed and to locate, evaluate, effectively use, and communicate information in its various formats. (State University of New York [SUNY], 1997)

> [Information literacy is] a new liberal art that extends from knowing how to use computers and access information to critical reflection on the nature of information itself, its technical infrastructure, and its social, cultural and even philosophical context and impact. (Shapiro & Hughes, 1996)

Individuals are information literate if they: recognize that they have a need for information; possess the knowledge and skills that enable them to discover where and how to find the information they are seeking; are comfortable using the necessary tools to find, modify and assimilate that information into another work; and can critically evaluate and synthesize the information they find to understand the social, economic, and political implications of the information. (University of Arizona Library, 1996)

Information competence is the fusing or the integration of library literacy, computer literacy, media literacy, technological literacy, ethics, critical thinking, and communication skills. (Work Group on Information Competence, 1995, p. 5)

[Information literacy is] the ability to find, evaluate, use, and communicate information in all of its various formats. (Work Group on Information Competence, 1995, p. 4)

[Information literacy is] the ability to effectively identify, access, evaluate and make use of information in its various formats, and to choose the appropriate medium for communication. It also encompasses knowledge and attitudes related to the ethical and social issues surrounding information and information technology. (California Academic and Research Libraries Task Force, 1997)

Whether information comes from a computer, a book, a government agency, a film, a conversation, a poster, or any number of other possible sources, inherent in the concept of information literacy is the ability to dissect and understand what we see on the page or the television screen, in posters, pictures, and other images, as well as what we hear. If we are to teach information literacy, we must teach students to sort, to discriminate, to select, and to analyze the array of messages that are presented (Lenox & Walker, 1992, pp. 4-5).

These definitions are examples of the ways information literacy extends into the realms of critical thinking and ethical usage of information. The definitions also include the recognition that information may be presented in a number of formats, from the simple to the complex, and may include printed words, illustrations, photographs, charts, graphs, tables, multimedia, sound recordings, computer graphics, or animation. In the future, there may be other formats for presenting information—formats not yet imagined. It is important that we consider all of these possibilities when we use the term "information" and that we not be tied to the mental image of printed words and numbers. Using information in a variety of formats requires literacies beyond the basic ones of reading and writing. To negotiate complex information formats, we must also be skilled in other literacies: visual, media, computer, network, and, of course, basic literacy. Let's examine these in turn.

Visual Literacy

When we look at visual information such as photographs, illustrations, or computer graphics, we rely on our previous perceptions of the world to make sense of the visual images. Visual literacy is defined as the ability "to understand and use images, including the ability to think, learn, and express oneself in terms of images" (Braden & Hortin, 1982, p. 41). Visual literacy may be divided into three constructs:

- Visual learning
- Visual thinking, and
- Visual communication (Randhawa & Coffman, 1978).

Visual learning refers to "the acquisition and construction of knowledge as a result of interaction with visual phenomenon" (Moore & Dwyer, 1994, p. 107). Visual thinking involves the ability to "organize mental images around shapes, lines, colors, textures, and compositions" (Wileman, 1980, p. 13). Visual communication is defined as "using visual symbols to express ideas and convey meaning" (Moore & Dwyer, 1994, p. 109). Visual thinking and visual learning may come more easily than visual communication. Although many are born with talents for visualization and artistic expression, others are not. For those with less innate artistic ability, visual communication may be accomplished by using a camera or a computer graphics program.

Media Literacy

In 1992, representatives of the media literacy movement met at the National Leadership Conference on Media Literacy and agreed to define media literacy as the ability of a citizen to "access, analyze, and produce information for specific outcomes" (Aufderheide, 1993, p. 6). Those who advocate media literacy recognize the influence television, motion pictures, radio, recorded music, newspapers, and magazines have on us daily. The media literacy movement also recognizes the fact that educators have traditionally spent a preponderance of time teaching reading and little time focusing on media literacy.

In reference to the teaching of media literacy, Cortes (1992) notes that both fictional and nonfictional media provide information; help organize information and ideas; help create, reinforce, and modify values and attitudes; help shape expectations; and provide models for action. By developing lessons organized around these five assumptions, teachers can help students to be critical viewers and listeners who realize that all media are constructions that contain implicit messages.

Computer Literacy

Computer literacy is generally thought of as familiarity with the personal computer and the ability to create and manipulate documents and data via word processing, spreadsheets, databases, and other software tools. Often these skills are taught out of context in special computer classes. Eisenberg and Johnson (2002), however, believe that the computer is a tool that facilitates and extends our abilities to learn and to process information. For example, students can use e-mail to contact their classmates or their teacher to clarify an assignment, or they can use presentation software to present information to the class. As such, computer literacy is seen as an integral part of education and not as a separate entity.

The Computer Science and Telecommunications Board of the National Research Council are redefining computer literacy as *fluency with information technology* (FITness) in the higher education arena (1999). We address this distinction further in Chapter 9.

Digital Literacy

Digital literacy considers the broad range of resources that are accessible online and underscores the importance of looking at each of these resources with a critical eye. Emphasis is placed on the format of the information presented and the special considerations that each type of resource presents. For instance, according to digital literacy expert Paul Gilster, information received though e-mail might raise the following issues:

> An electronic mail address is the most basic clue to authorial experience and intentions; it allows you to probe more deeply into what the author has put on-line. The ability to engage in a dialogue with the source of your material is largely unique to the Internet. A friendly note will often lead to further material, as the author can cite his or her sources or suggest other sites with information that might be valuable to you. (1997b)

Many educational institutions are recognizing in digital literacy a practical way to teach information skills through primers and tutorials. Humboldt State University Library has created the Digital Literacy Closet, a resource center where students and faculty can receive expert assistance as they learn to manipulate new information resources. Syracuse University's School of Information Studies recently established the Center for Digital Literacy, an interdisciplinary research and development center encouraging the development of digital literacy skills across generations.

Network Literacy

Closely related to computer literacy is "network literacy," a term that is still evolving. To locate, access, and use information in a networked environment such as the World Wide Web, users must be network literate. McClure (1993), noting that the following can be the basis for discussion and research, describes network literacy in terms of knowledge and skills for the general public. A network literate person is one who:

- [Has] an awareness of the range and uses of global networked information resources and services

- [Has] an understanding of the system by which networked information is generated, managed, and made available

- [Can] retrieve specific types of information from the network using a range of information discovery tools

- [Can] manipulate networked information by combining it with other resources, enhancing it, or otherwise increasing the value of information for particular situations

- [Can] use networked information to analyze and resolve both work and personal related decisions and obtain services that will enhance their overall quality of life

- [Has an] understanding of the role and uses of networked information in problem solving and in performing basic life activities. (p. 160)

Table 1.1, "Elements of Information Literacy" (page 10) analyzes visual, media, computer, and network literacy in terms of information literacy. These literacies, as well as others discussed in the literature (e.g., cultural, scientific, technical, global and mathematical), focus on compartmentalized aspects of literacy. Information literacy is, in contrast, an inclusive term. Through information literacy, the other literacies can be achieved.

Table 1.1 Elements of Information Literacy

Information Literacy	Visual Literacy	Media Literacy	Computer Literacy	Digital Literacy	Network Literacy
An information literate person is one who:	Visual literacy is:	Media literacy is:	Computer literacy is:	Digital literacy is:	A network literate person is one who:
• recognizes that accurate and complete information is the basis for intelligent decision making,					
• recognizes the need for information,					
• formulates questions based on information needs,					
• identifies potential sources of information,					has an awareness of the range and uses of global networked information resources and services;
• develops successful search strategies,					has an understanding of the system by which networked information is generated, managed, and made available;
• accesses sources of information,		the ability to access,			can retrieve specific types of information from the network using a range of information discovery tools;
• evaluates information,	the ability to understand	analyze,		the ability to understand	
• organizes information for practical application,	and use images,	and produce information for specific outcomes. (Aufderheide, 1993)	the ability to create and manipulate documents and data via software tools.	and use information in multiple formats from a wide range of sources when it is presented via computers. (Gilster, 1997b)	can manipulate networked information by combining it with other resources, enhancing it, or otherwise increasing the value of information for particular situations;
• integrates new information into an existing body of knowledge, and	including the ability to think, learn, and express oneself in terms of images. (Braden & Hortin, 1982)				can use networked information to analyze and resolve both work and personal related decisions and obtain services that will enhance [his or her] overall quality of life;

Summary

Whatever our personal definition of information literacy may be, it is likely to stem from the definition offered in the *Final Report* of the American Library Association Presidential Committee on Information Literacy, "To be information literate, a person must be able to recognize when information is needed and have the ability to locate, evaluate, and use effectively the needed information" (1989, p. 1). As we have seen, this definition is reflective not only of the work of Zurkowski but of others who have sought to shape the concept. Let's summarize the key points of this chapter:

- The concept of "information literacy" was first introduced in 1974 by Paul Zurkowski.

- The American Library Association definition of information literacy, "To be information literate requires a new set of skills. These include how to locate and use information needed for problem-solving and decision-making efficiently and effectively" (1989, p. 11), forms the basis for expansion of the concept.

- Alternative definitions for information literacy have been developed by educational institutions, professional organizations, and individuals.

- Because information may be presented in a number of formats, the term "information" applies to more than just the printed word. Other literacies such as visual, media, computer, digital, network, and basic are implicit in information literacy.

Chapter

The Evolution of a Concept

2

The Final Report of the American Library Association Presidential Committee on Information Literacy (1989) provided the springboard for the development of the concept of information literacy. In this chapter we explore how information literacy has developed in both K–12 and higher education in the United States. We also examine other constituencies that embrace the concept and provide examples of the importance of information literacy in other countries.

The evolution of the concept of information literacy, since Zurkowski first used the term in 1974, has taken place both within and outside of the field of library science, not only in the United States but also throughout the world. Librarians have been especially sensitive to the so-called information explosion and its resultant repercussions. The concept of information literacy, which advocates the preparation of people to be successful users of information, addresses the concerns librarians have with the evolving nature of information sources and the overwhelming amount of information available. Those outside of the field of library science have also acknowledged the effects of the exponential growth of information.

Development of National Importance

The seminal event in the development of the concept of information literacy was the establishment of the American Library Association (ALA) Presidential Committee on Information Literacy in 1987. The committee, established by ALA President Margaret Chisholm, consisted of seven national leaders from the field of education and six from the field of librarianship. Their final report, released in January 1989, provided a definition of information literacy to which all could refer, and precipitated the dissemination of the concept of information literacy beyond the field of library science. The committee asserted that information literacy was a necessary skill for everyday life, for the business world, and for democracy:

> How our country deals with the realities of the Information Age will have enormous impact on our democratic way of life and on our nation's ability to compete internationally. Within America's information society, there also exists the potential of addressing many long-standing social and economic inequities. To reap such benefits, people as individuals and as a nation must be information literate. To be information literate, a person must be able to recognize when information is needed and have the ability to locate, evaluate, and use effectively the needed information. Producing such a citizenry will require that schools and colleges appreciate and integrate the concept of information literacy into their learning programs and that they play a leadership role in equipping individuals and institutions to take advantage of the opportunities inherent within the information society. Ultimately, information literate people are those who have learned how to learn. They know how to learn because they know how knowledge is organized, how to find information, and how to use information in such a way that others can learn from them. They are people prepared for lifelong learning, because they can always find the information needed for any task or decision at hand. (American Library Association Presidential Committee on Information Literacy, 1989, p. 1)

Six recommendations were outlined:

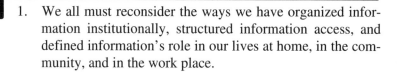

> 1. We all must reconsider the ways we have organized information institutionally, structured information access, and defined information's role in our lives at home, in the community, and in the work place.

2. A Coalition for Information Literacy should be formed under the leadership of the American Library Association, in coordination with other national organizations and agencies, to promote information literacy.

3. Research and demonstration projects related to information and its use need to be undertaken.

4. State Departments of Education, Commissions on Higher Education, and Academic Governing Boards should be responsible to ensure that a climate conducive to students' becoming information literate exists in their states and on their campuses.

5. Teacher education and performance expectations should be modified to include information literacy concerns.

6. An understanding of the relationship of information literacy to the themes of the White House Conference on Library and Information Services should be promoted. (pp. 11-12)

National Forum on Information Literacy (NFIL)

Based on the recommendation of the American Library Association, a coalition for information literacy was "strategized" at an ALA-sponsored meeting in April 1989 in Leesburg, Virginia. The first meeting of the National Forum on Information Literacy (NFIL) took place on November 9, 1989, with Patricia Senn Breivik serving as chair. The NFIL is a coalition of more than 65 national organizations from business, government, and education, all sharing an interest in, and a concern for, information literacy. The NFIL has met regularly since 1989 to promote the concept of information literacy as an imperative for the Information Age and to spread the concept to all professions.

Since then, under Breivik's leadership the NFIL has played an essential role in identifying trends in information literacy and bringing together key constituencies. The NFIL has no formal organizational structure; it is inclusive and open to representatives from any organization recognizing the relevance of information literacy to its work. NFIL member associations are diverse, including representatives from the American Association for Higher Education, American Association of Colleges for Teacher Education, American Association of School Administrators, Association for Supervision and Curriculum Development, College Board, EDUCAUSE, Hispanic Policy Development Project, International Visual Literacy Association, National Association of Secondary School Principals, National Consumers League, National Council for Social Studies, National Education Association, National Forum for Black Public Administrators, National School Boards Association, and the U.S. Small Business

Administration. Early meetings of the NFIL focused on definitions and procedure. Gradually, supporting member associations have included the topic of information literacy on their individual conference agendas. Dissemination from NFIL has been in the form of publications, especially association journals and in-house newsletters from NFIL members.

The NFIL is committed to fostering public awareness of the need for information literate people. Breivik summarized the coalition's activities in a 1998 progress report. The coalition is

- identifying organizations whose purposes can be enhanced through the promotion of information literacy and inviting membership in or affiliation with the coalition;

- encouraging member organizations and individuals to advocate appropriate actions to promote information literacy;

- providing a national forum for the exchange of ideas and programs so as to create public awareness of the need for information literacy and to collect specific examples of how information literacy may affect individual Americans;

- developing a public awareness program using press releases, public service announcements, and other means to alert citizens to the importance of information literacy;

- monitoring emerging trends and patterns and encouraging research and demonstration projects; and

- promoting the establishment of a clearinghouse to gather and disseminate information on programs in information literacy and on efforts to promote information literacy.

In *A Progress Report on Information Literacy: An Update on the American Library Association Presidential Committee on Information Literacy: Final Report*, written on behalf of the NFIL, Breivik, Hancock, and Senn (1998) examine progress made since the 1988 *Final Report* was issued and examine the future of information literacy. The authors state that "Forum members—after monitoring America's progress in addressing the issues raised in the Report of the Information Age—believe that there needs to be a national reevaluation of the seemingly exclusive emphasis on and enormous investments in computers and networks. They believe that the technology alone will never allow America to reach the potential inherent in the Information Age in not only its schools but also in its businesses. In fact, they believe that the dreams of a new and better tomorrow will only begin to be realized when all young people graduate into the workforce with strong information literacy skills" (1998, p. 7).

The progress report states that Forum members have agreed upon the following five recommendations for priority action in the new millennium:

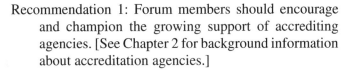

> Recommendation 1: Forum members should encourage and champion the growing support of accrediting agencies. [See Chapter 2 for background information about accreditation agencies.]
>
> Recommendation 2: Teacher education and performance expectations need to include information literacy skills.
>
> Recommendation 3: Librarian education and performance expectations need to include information literacy.
>
> Recommendation 4: Forum members need to identify ways to illustrate to business leaders the benefits of fostering an information literate workforce.
>
> Recommendation 5: There needs to be more research and demonstration projects related to information literacy and its use." (1998, pp. 7-8)

The NFIL recognizes the valuable contributions of individuals in the development and dissemination of the concept of information literacy. The Forum invites individuals to send in reports of their information literacy efforts so that progress can be monitored. The NFIL maintains a listserv at http://infolit@ala1.ala.org.

When asked to consider recent developments and trends for the future of information literacy, Breivik identifies three key areas receiving increasing attention: health literacy, information literacy within the context of business, and the development of information literacy skills in developing countries (Breivik, personal correspondence, May 14, 2003).

Development in K–12 Education

The history of information literacy in K–12 education began in April 1983, when the National Commission on Excellence in Education issued a report decrying the lack of rigorous education in America's schools. The commission's report, *A Nation at Risk* (1983), noted that American education standards had declined to the point where, "If an unfriendly foreign power had attempted to impose on America the mediocre educational performance that exists today, we might well have viewed it as an act of war" (p. 5). Although the report identified the management of complex information in electronic and digital forms as an important skill in a "learning society," it did not contain recommendations on the role of the library or on the role of information resources in K–12 education. In response to this report, The National Commission on Libraries and Information Science (NCLIS) unanimously advocated "the importance of the role of library and information resources to underpin all learning and . . . the essential skills and proficiencies involved in finding and using information effectively. A basic objective of education is for each student to learn how to identify needed information, locate and organize it, and present it in a clear and persuasive manner" (Hashim, 1986, p. 17).

NCLIS members, in the process of responding and developing strategy, agreed that a concept paper should be written to define what is meant by "information skills," as well as to identify the issues, questions, and problems related to the development of these skills. In "Educating Students to Think: The Role of the School Library Media Program" (Mancall, Aaron & Walker, 1986), three relevant components of a school library media program were described:

1. the role of school library media programs in helping students develop thinking skills,

2. the theoretical implications of current research on how children and adolescents process information and ideas, and

3. the practical implications and applications of the concepts as a basis for developing an information skills program in all curricular areas.

As the concept of information literacy developed, an empirical and logical base for the concept needed to be identified. In 1987, Kuhlthau's *Information Skills for an Information Society: A Review of the Research* carved out a niche for information literacy—a base to which all could refer in the next stages of development and implementation.

In this monograph, Kuhlthau included library skills and computer literacy in the definition of information literacy. It is important to note that library skills were described as "proficiency in inquiry" to correct the misconception that such skills are reserved only for the library. The library is an effective wellspring for these skills, but the larger focus is on student learning. Kuhlthau addressed two major themes:

• Library media programs should integrate information literacy across curricular areas to develop students' proficiency in inquiry.

• Information technologies provide access to information resources that are critical to student learning.

Kuhlthau's work pointed the way to the integration of information literacy with curriculum, and presages current development of the concept of information literacy where the library media program is the starting platform.

Information Power

In 1988, the American Association of School Librarians (AASL), a branch of the American Library Association (ALA), published *Information Power: Guidelines for School Library Media Programs*. These guidelines were significant because they were developed using an innovative approach.

First, the guidelines were developed cooperatively with the Association for Educational Communications and Technology (AECT), another national professional organization with similar concerns. Second, the guidelines were stated in qualitative, rather than in quantitative, terms. The vision presented in *Information Power* is of a school library media program that significantly expanded the access to and use of information and ideas by students, teachers, and parents.

The stated mission of *Information Power* is "to ensure that students and staff are effective users of ideas and information" (AASL & AECT, 1988, p. 1). This mission is accomplished by

- providing intellectual and physical access to materials in all formats;

- providing instruction to foster competence and stimulate interest in reading, viewing, and using information and ideas; and

- working with other educators to design learning strategies to meet the needs of individual students. (p. 1)

Information Power called for a shift in the role of the library media specialist from a passive "keeper of materials" to a key participant in the learning process. Library media specialists were to be perceived as change agents in the restructuring of the educational process (Eisenberg & Berkowitz, 1988). Accepted roles of the library media specialist included providing a variety of resources as the basis for experiential learning, sharing the process by which students acquire needed information skills with teachers, and encouraging students to pursue individual interests.

Development of *Information Literacy Standards for Student Learning*

In 1994, the American Association of School Librarians (AASL) published a position statement that identified the steps of the information problem-solving process as the key elements of an information literacy curriculum. The position statement was based on "Information Literacy: A Position Paper on Information Problem-Solving" (Wisconsin Educational Media Association, 1993), developed by the Wisconsin Educational Media Association (WEMA). These steps, which were based on the Eisenberg and Berkowitz Big6™ model (Eisenberg & Berkowitz, 1988) and also endorsed by the NFIL, include

- defining the need for information,

- initiating the search strategy,

- locating the resources,

- accessing and comprehending the information,

- interpreting the information,

- communicating the information, and

- evaluating the product and process.

The position statement advocates the importance of information literacy skills in the school restructuring movement:

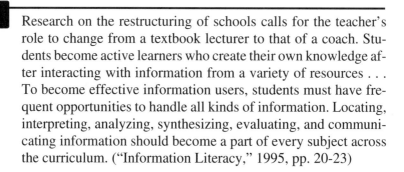

> Research on the restructuring of schools calls for the teacher's role to change from a textbook lecturer to that of a coach. Students become active learners who create their own knowledge after interacting with information from a variety of resources . . . To become effective information users, students must have frequent opportunities to handle all kinds of information. Locating, interpreting, analyzing, synthesizing, evaluating, and communicating information should become a part of every subject across the curriculum. ("Information Literacy," 1995, pp. 20-23)

The position statement envisions the library media specialist as a collaborator who works with teachers to integrate information literacy skills into the curriculum and to facilitate the change from textbook-based learning to learning that incorporates a variety of resources.

Throughout the next few years, information literacy standards and indicators were developed by AASL and AECT as part of the process of revising *Information Power*, the national guidelines for school library media programs. Input on information literacy standards was sought from members of the field and other educators throughout the development process via electronic mail and through formal hearings held at AASL and AECT conferences. During 1996–1997, a panel of 57 educators from within and outside the school library media field took part in a national Delphi study designed to formally validate the standards and indicators. Four rounds of the study were conducted, with panelists reacting to drafts that incorporated the suggestions and insights of the participants. The *Information Literacy Standards for Student Learning*, published in *Information Power: Building Partnerships for Learning* (AASL & AECT, 1998), are the result of this extensive process.

The *Information Literacy Standards for Student Learning* are articulated in three categories: information literacy, independent learning, and social responsibility. Within the three categories are nine standards and 29 indicators to describe the content and processes students need to achieve to be information literate (see Appendix A; ALA & AECT, 1998). Three levels of proficiency for each indicator are outlined: basic, proficient, and exemplary. Examples of the standards in action are given to show how each could be integrated with the curriculum. Each information literacy standard is also cross-correlated with selected examples from the content-area standards demonstrating how information literacy is inherent in each. The nine standards follow:

Category I: Information Literacy

> Standard 1: The student who is information literate accesses information efficiently and effectively.

> Standard 2: The student who is information literate evaluates information critically and competently.

> Standard 3: The student who is information literate uses information accurately and creatively.

Category II: Independent Learning

> Standard 4: The student who is an independent learner is information literate and pursues information related to personal interests.

> Standard 5: The student who is an independent learner is information literate and appreciates and enjoys literature and other creative expressions of information.

> Standard 6: The student who is an independent learner is information literate and strives for excellence in information seeking and knowledge generation.

Category III: Social Responsibility

> Standard 7: The student who contributes positively to the learning community and to society is information literate and recognizes the importance of information to a democratic society.

Standard 8: The student who contributes positively to the learning community and to society is information literate and practices ethical behavior in regard to information and information technology.

Standard 9: The student who contributes positively to the learning community and to society is information literate and participates effectively in groups to pursue and generate information. (ALA & AECT,1998)

In addition to their inclusion in *Information Power: Building Partnerships for Learning,* the standards are available as a separate publication designed for disseminating them to teachers, principals, parents, school boards, and administrators. The standards have been further disseminated in the American Library Association's *Indicators of Schools of Quality, Volume 1: Schoolwide Indicators of Quality,* developed by the National Study of School Evaluation (NSSE) in cooperation with Alliance for Curriculum Reform (ACR). The publication is intended to assist schools in self-assessing the quality of their efforts in improving student learning (ALA & AECT, 1998).

Information Power: Building Partnerships for Learning notes that the mission of the library media program remains the same as in 1988's *Information Power:* ensuring that students and staff are effective users of ideas and information. The publication points out that the achievement of that mission depends on school library media programs and services focused on information literacy. The essential elements of the library media program that support this mission are identified as: learning and teaching, information access, and program administration. Each element denotes a number of principles upon which an effective school library media program is based. Among the Learning and Teaching Principles of School Library Media Programs that fully support the integration of information literacy skills with the curriculum are:

Principle 1: The library media program is essential to learning and teaching and must be fully integrated into the curriculum to promote students' achievement of learning goals.

Principle 2: The information literacy standards for student learning are integral to the content and objectives of the school's curriculum. (AASL & AECT, 1998, p. 58)

The library media specialist's role in bringing the school library media program to fruition involves collaboration, leadership, and technology. *Information Power: Building Partnerships for Learning* (1998b) notes that "collaboration is essential as library media specialists work with teachers to plan, conduct, and evaluate learning activities that incorporate information literacy" (p. 50). As such, the library media specialist must be conversant with the curriculum, be able to connect learning objectives with information literacy, and establish a good relationship with teachers. The library media specialist provides leadership in changing from textbook-based learning to information-based learning and acts as a technologist who can collaborate to design instructional experiences that fully integrate technology. Materials such as an implementation kit and a slide show are available from the AASL Web site; these materials are designed for library media specialists presenting the information literacy standards to audiences of parents, teachers, and administrators (AASL, 2003).

Information Power: Building Partnerships for Learning is a powerful tool that can have a profound influence at the district, building, and classroom level. Julie Walker, executive director of the AASL, describes its impact as follows:

> *Information Power: Building Partnerships for Learning*, like any new framework, has served as a catalyst for school library media specialists to reflect on their practice. The two greatest areas of impact have been in teacher/SLMS collaboration and the awareness of the need for "hand and glove" teaching of information literacy skills and subject matter content. The emphasis on student learning—especially information literacy—has resulted in a framework that provides students with much richer learning experiences. (Walker, personal correspondence, May 5, 2003)

Information Power: Building Partnerships for Learning provides a basis for the school library media program to take the lead in educating students to be information literate, thereby providing them with the basic skills they will need to succeed in the Information Age.

Canadian School Libraries

The Association for Teacher-Librarianship in Canada created the *Students' Bill of Information Rights* in 1995; it has much in common with the *Information Literacy Standards for Student Learning*. It states:

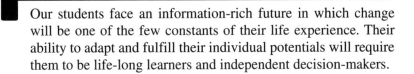

> Our students face an information-rich future in which change will be one of the few constants of their life experience. Their ability to adapt and fulfill their individual potentials will require them to be life-long learners and independent decision-makers.

We believe that all students should have the opportunity to:

- Master the skills needed to access information in print, non-print and electronic sources
- Understand and master effective research processes and reporting skills
- Develop the ability to evaluate, extract, synthesize and utilize information from a variety of sources and media
- Utilize data and information to expand their own knowledge base
- Explore the creative use of information
- Develop an understanding of our Canadian cultural heritage and history, as well as cultures and histories of other societies
- Enhance their own self knowledge through developing a love of reading
- Explore the values and beliefs of others by reading world literature
- Think critically, and make decisions based on personal needs and values as well as upon factual evidence, and
- Actively participate in decisions about their own learning.

Information is a vital component in the development of critical thought and independent decision-making, and, consequently, access to the ever-increasing body of available information is vital to the development of students' potentials. (Association for Teacher-Librarianship in Canada, 1995)

In November 1997, the Association for Teacher-Librarianship in Canada and the Canadian School Library Association issued a joint document referring to the *Students' Bill of Information Rights* (1995). The document, *Students' Information Literacy Needs in the 21st Century: Competencies for Teacher-Librarians* (1997), focuses on the need for highly skilled and educated teacher-librarians who will have an impact on students' development of information literacy skills:

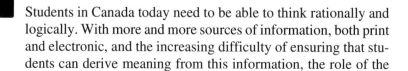

Students in Canada today need to be able to think rationally and logically. With more and more sources of information, both print and electronic, and the increasing difficulty of ensuring that students can derive meaning from this information, the role of the teacher-librarian becomes central. Teacher-librarians are skilled in accessing and evaluating information regardless of delivery system, book or computer, and providing leadership in the appropriate use of new information technologies. (Association for Teacher-Librarianship in Canada & Canadian School Library Association, 1997)

Noting that there is a body of research that points to the positive impact of the teacher-librarian on student achievement, and that teachers collaborate more in schools where there is a teacher-librarian, the document points out that

information literacy is incorporated into school and classroom programs because:

- The program is recognized as a partnership of the principal, teacher and teacher-librarian, supported by the school district and community

- The district insists on flexible scheduling. The teacher-librarian is not the preparation time or 'relief' for classroom colleagues

- The principal encourages collaboration and team teaching through this flexible schedule

- Teachers acknowledge that the processing and use of information is a school-wide concern, for integration with classroom content instruction, and

- The teacher-librarian takes the initiative, places a priority on cooperative program planning with colleagues and encourages team planning. (1997)

Through this document, the Canadian School Library Association and the Association for Teacher-Librarianship in Canada highlight the professional and personal competencies of teacher-librarians and provide practical examples of the roles and tasks that they perform.

Development in Higher Education

Academic librarians have played an integral part in the development of the concept of information literacy. The 1986 Carnegie Foundation Report on colleges outlined the importance of an academic library program to the undergraduate experience: "The quality of a college is measured by the resources for learning on the campus and the extent to which students become independent, self-directed learners" (Prologue and Major Recommendations of Carnegie Foundation's Report on Colleges, 1986, p. 21). Calling for undergraduates to spend "at least as much time in the library . . . as they spend in classes" (p. 21), the report recommended that academic institutions establish basic books libraries, and that academic librarians provide undergraduates with instruction in the use of information resources both inside and outside of the library.

This broader view of information skills instruction was the focus of a symposium co-sponsored by Columbia University and the University of Colorado in March 1987. The symposium, Libraries and the Search for Academic Excellence, brought together academic leaders and leaders in the field of librarianship to examine the role of libraries in academia. The outcomes and action recommendations resulting from the symposium institutionalized the importance of information literacy skills and formed the basis for current information literacy efforts in higher education:

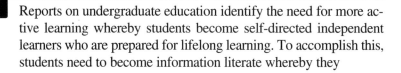

Reports on undergraduate education identify the need for more active learning whereby students become self-directed independent learners who are prepared for lifelong learning. To accomplish this, students need to become information literate whereby they

- Understand the process and systems for acquiring current and retrospective information, e.g., systems and services for information identification and delivery.

- Are able to evaluate the effectiveness and reliability of various information channels and sources, including libraries, for various kinds of needs.

- Master certain basic skills in acquiring and storing their own information, e.g., database skills, spreadsheet skills, word and information processing skills, books, journals, and report literature.

- Are articulate and responsible citizens in considering current and future public policy issues relating to information, e.g., copyright, privacy, privatization of government information, and those issues yet to emerge.

To make possible the above, information gathering and evaluation skills need to be mastered at the undergraduate level, and learning opportunities should be integrated within the existing departments, analogous, to writing across the curriculum, rather than as standalone bibliographic instruction programs. Administrators, faculty and librarians should be engaged in creative new partnerships which transmit to students the value and reward of research in their lives as students and beyond. Information literacy should be a demonstrable outcome of undergraduate education. (Breivik & Wedgeworth, 1988, pp. 187-188)

Information Literacy, published in 1989, outlined the challenges posed to academic institutions to reform instruction and meet the information demands of students and faculty as outlined in the outcomes and action recommendations of the symposium. Co-authored by Patricia Senn Breivik, who was at the time the library director at the University of Colorado at Denver, and Gordon Gee, then president of the Colorado University system, *Information Literacy* noted that academic institutions realize that it is important to train graduate students who can analyze information and think effectively. To develop these important information skills, Breivik and Gee suggested that faculty initiate library-based instruction that would require students to use a wide range of materials from the campus library, as well as from outside sources.

Academic institutions have been engaged in efforts to define information competencies and to develop and integrate information skills instruction (see Chapter 8). In *Student Learning in the Information Age* (1998), Breivik notes that information skills instruction is usually delivered through stand-alone courses, course-related instruction, and course-integrated instruction. Suggesting that information literacy skills are best taught through the course-integrated approach, Breivik provides numerous examples of information literacy initiatives that academic librarians and institutions could use to develop similar efforts on their own campuses.

One significant achievement in the development of information literacy instruction in higher education is the Association of College and Research Libraries' *Information Literacy Competency Standards for Higher Education* (2000) and the accompanying document, *Objectives for Information Literacy Instruction: A Model Statement for Academic Librarians* (2001). These tools provide a structured and logical way for academic librarians and university faculty to work together to integrate information literacy skills across the curriculum. Both documents are discussed at length in Chapter 8.

Development in Industry

Recently, business leaders have taken a greater interest in the development of information literacy skills in tomorrow's workers and citizens. One example of a large-scale, industry-based information literacy effort is the AOL Time Warner Foundation's 21st Century Literacy Initiative, which is "dedicated to helping young people acquire the 21st Century Literacy skills they need to succeed at school, at work and in their communities" (http://www.aoltimewarnerfoundation. org/whatwedo/whatwedo.html). The foundation strives to achieve this goal with several different programs, including

- a tutoring program to develop basic literacy in both children and adults;
- a teacher training institute to encourage the integration of technology in the classroom;
- media literacy tools, including broadcast, print, and Web resources;
- support services for new teachers;
- a summit for experts in the field, designed to shape public policy on information literacy; and
- a network connecting volunteers to mentoring opportunities.

Together, these efforts are designed to develop literacy skills in teens and increase public awareness of the importance of these skills.

Other industry efforts place greater emphasis on individual components of information literacy. "Don't Buy It," a Web site produced by KCTS and hosted by PBS (http://pbskids.org/dontbuyit/) develops media literacy skills in students ages nine through eleven. The site presents advertising tricks, consumer advice, and the truth about entertainment media in a fun and accessible way. It also includes a section on media activism and encourages kids to get involved in their own communities. The critical thinking skills developed with this resource relate directly to those necessary for information literacy.

Accreditation

Accreditation agencies have been influential in fostering the concept of information literacy as a means of creating a more active undergraduate learning environment. The Commission on Higher Education (CHE), Middle States Association of Colleges and Schools, which accredits institutions of higher education in Delaware, the District of Columbia, Maryland, New Jersey, New York, Pennsylvania, Puerto Rico, the Republic of Panama, and the U.S. Virgin Islands, was the first such agency to become a member of the National Forum on Information Literacy (NFIL).

The CHE developed the following standard on information literacy in 1994:

Each institution should foster optimal use of its learning resources through strategies designed to help students develop information literacy—the ability to locate, evaluate, and use information in order to become independent learners. It should encourage the use of a wide range of non-classroom resources for teaching and learning. It is essential to have an active and continuing program of library orientation and instruction in accessing information, developed collaboratively and supported actively by faculty, librarians, academic deans, and other information providers. (Commission on Higher Education, 1995, p. v)

The CHE was also involved in sponsoring a 1994–1995 national survey of 3,236 accredited U.S. colleges and universities, conducted to determine the extent to which information literacy had been assimilated into the curriculum of institutions of higher education. The decision to conduct the survey resulted from a meeting of the National Forum on Information Literacy (NFIL); involved the Association of College & Research Libraries (ACRL), the Commission on Higher Education (CHE) of the Middle States Association of Colleges and Schools, and the Western Association of Schools and Colleges' (WASC) Accrediting Commission for Senior Colleges and Universities; and was strongly supported by the American Association for Higher Education. Participants were asked to respond to five questions:

1. Does your campus have a functional information literacy program?

2. Does your campus offer a course that focuses on the development of information literacy abilities?

3. Are information literacy experiences integrated into courses in all majors?

4. Are there formal assessments of students' information literacy performance?

5. Are there faculty and staff development efforts provided to undergird the information literacy program on your campus?

Of the 3,236 surveys distributed, 834 surveys were returned. While noting that there may be limitations to the data due to the possible ambiguity of the respondents' interpretation of the term *information literacy*, the survey report stated that schools in the Middle States region were leading the way toward the integration of information literacy in the curriculum. The results showed that

- 22% of the respondents had a functional information literacy program

- 25% offered a course that focuses on the development of information literacy abilities

- 17% integrated information literacy experiences into courses in all majors

- 17% stated that there were formal assessments of students' information literacy performance

- 29% of the respondents noted that there were faculty and staff development efforts provided to undergird the information literacy on their campus. (Ratteray & Simmons, 1995)

Building on the information acquired from the survey, the Commission on Higher Education of the Middle States held two symposia in 1995 to bring together educators who had successfully integrated information literacy into their curricula. The conclusions of these symposia follow:

- Institutions should concentrate on developing effective processes to achieve information literacy and share with other institutions the results, both good and bad, of those efforts.

- Information literacy does not cease when the degree is achieved, but it must be viewed as a lifelong learning commitment. (Commission on Higher Education, 1995, p. 16)

Ralph A. Wolff, associate executive director of the Accrediting Commission for Senior Colleges and Universities of the Western Association of Schools and Colleges (WASC), echoes Middle States and adds:

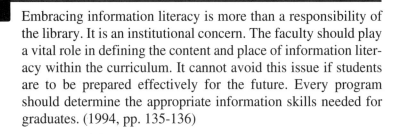

Embracing information literacy is more than a responsibility of the library. It is an institutional concern. The faculty should play a vital role in defining the content and place of information literacy within the curriculum. It cannot avoid this issue if students are to be prepared effectively for the future. Every program should determine the appropriate information skills needed for graduates. (1994, pp. 135-136)

The WASC, which accredits public and private schools, colleges and universities in California, Hawaii, and several territories, is currently reviewing its standards for accreditation, and will consider the inclusion of a standard on information competence.

In 1997, the California Academic and Research Libraries (CARL) established a Task Force to Recommend Information Literacy Standards to the WASC. A draft version of the task force's recommendations includes *Statement of Principles for Information Literacy Criteria,* which focuses on institutions' roles in developing information literate graduates:

> An institution ensures that all graduating students are information literate through a systematic and course-integrated campus-wide information literacy program. Information literacy learning opportunities are part of general education, academic majors, and graduate/professional programs. Educational program requirements or goals include statements about students' use of libraries, computing, information and learning resources and how course assignments contribute to their becoming information literate. Professional staffs with appropriate expertise are available to teach information literacy skills and develop collections, learning resources and information literacy curricula and learning experiences. The institution provides support for maintaining and improving the quality of information literacy instruction. (1997)

Support for Information Literacy from the Field of Education

Groups representing educators deem the concept of information literacy important. For example, the American Association of Higher Education (AAHE), an organization with over 8,700 members including faculty, administrators, and students, has an Action Community on Information Literacy, and sponsors the theme at each of its annual conferences. The National Education Association (NEA) has been active in support of information literacy as well. Sylvia Seidel, assistant director of Teacher Education Initiatives for the National Education Association (NEA), states: "The NEA recognizes the importance of information literacy and is presently pursuing strategies for embedding information literacy in their teacher education initiatives" (personal correspondence, December 8, 1997).

The Association for Supervision and Curriculum Development (ASCD) has been a member of the National Forum on Information Literacy (NFIL) from the beginning. ASCD's resolutions for 1991 demonstrate commitment to the importance of information literacy:

Resolution on Information Literacy

Today's information society transcends all political, social, and economic boundaries. The global nature of human interaction makes the ability to access and use information crucial. Differences in cultural orientation toward information and symbol systems make the management of information complex and challenging. Current and future reform efforts should address the rapidly changing nature of information and emerging information technologies. Information literacy, the ability to locate, process, and use information effectively, equips individuals to take advantage of the opportunities inherent in the global information society. Information literacy should be a part of every student's education experience. ASCD urges schools, colleges, and universities to integrate information literacy programs into learning programs for all students. (cited in Doyle, 1994, p. 12)

Articles on information literacy have been published in the *Educational Leadership* and *Education Update*, both publications of the ASCD, and an ERIC Digest (Hancock, 1993) on information literacy was written by the ASCD representative to NFIL. In addition, several information literacy related presentations have been on the schedule of ASCD's annual conferences since 1992.

In 1988, the National Council for the Social Studies (NCSS) Ad Hoc Committee on Scope and Sequence developed Essential Skills for Social Studies, a K–12 scope and sequence that included acquiring information, organizing and using information, and interpersonal relationships and social participation. The Essential Skills are included in the NCSS Curriculum Standards published in 1993. The NCSS publication *From Information to Decision Making: New Challenges for Effective Citizenship* (1989) focuses on information literacy skills and provides "ideas about ways social studies teachers may become effective in an information age with its ever increasing gap between what we understand and what we need to understand" (p. vii). The council is an active member of the NFIL and has endorsed the AASL position statement on information literacy.

Information Literacy Embraced Around the World

A review of the literature demonstrates that the concept of information literacy is embraced throughout the world. Both rich and poor countries recognize that education in information literacy skills is essential to produce a workforce of flexible, lifelong learners, which is increasingly a prerequisite to economic development.

Namibia

Despite the fact that there is a great disparity in educational resources in schools in Namibia, basic information science is a compulsory subject (Jacobs, 1995). This disparity was taken into account when a committee appointed by the minister of Basic Education and Culture developed the syllabus. Teachers instruct students in information skills by using the natural environment, the village, and historical and cultural sites, as well as friends, leaders, and elders, as sources of information. Skills taught include being alert, observation, interpretation, describing observations, making inquiries, appropriate communication techniques, attentive listening, formulation of questions, taking notes, and presenting information. The basic information science subject is intended to foster "an appreciation of the value of information in the context of the information age as a necessity to develop intellectually, socially, politically and economically and to make informed decisions" (Jacobs, 1995, p. 74).

South Africa

A paper presented by Olen at the 1995 Annual Conference of the International Association of School Librarianship details an information skills project for teachers in South Africa. The focus of the endeavor was to help teachers create projects that would allow pupils to "develop the information skills necessary to locate, select, organize and present information in a systematic way" (Olen, 1995, p. 59). Olen, a member of the Department of Information Science at the University of South Africa, reports that a literature survey shows that "subject teachers in secondary schools and lecturers in tertiary institutions should be role models for their pupils and students with regard to reading and information literacy development" (p. 57). Because many South African teachers lack experience with a school library in their own educational backgrounds, they have difficulty creating projects that use a variety of resources or provide students with opportunities to develop information literacy skills. Olen suggests that the information skills project, created to mediate this lack of experience, could be replicated and used as a model for teacher education programs in South Africa.

Australia

Information literacy is a well-developed and accepted concept in Australia, where the third national conference on information literacy was held in December 1997. The Australian Library and Information Association (ALIA) has an Information Literacy Forum, whose central principle asserts: "A thriving national and global culture, economy and democracy will be best advanced by people able to recognise their need for information, and identify, locate, access, evaluate and apply the needed information" (ALIA, 1997).

A number of Australian universities have embraced the information literacy concept; among them Griffith University, whose Web site (http://www. gu.edu.au:80/ins/training/computing/web/blueprint/content_blueprint.html) links to an information literacy blueprint developed by Christine Bruce. This document examines the theory of information literacy, identifies the characteristics of an information literate person, and presents a strategic plan for integrating information literacy into the curriculum.

Canada

The University of Calgary (Canada) Information Literacy Group was formed to develop an action plan to help the university develop information literacy strategies. The group provides a definition of information competency:

Within the context of lifelong learning and the broad information continuum, which ranges from data to knowledge to wisdom, information literacy competency focuses on five broad abilities:

- To recognize the need for information

- To know how to access information

- To understand how to evaluate information

- To know how to synthesize information

- To be able to communicate information

An information literate person recognizes the different levels, types and formats of information and their appropriate uses. The ability to place information in a context and an awareness of information access issues (copyright, privacy, globalization, currency of information, etc.) are key to information literacy. (University of Calgary Information Literacy Group, undated)

Rader (1996) notes that the importance of having an information literate population is supported by the Canadian government's information policy, and that Canadian librarians hold an annual conference to focus on the topic of information literacy.

Finland

In 1994, the Ministry of Education in Finland formed an Expert Committee to prepare a strategy for education, training, and research in the information society of the twenty-first century. Among the elements of *Education, Training, and Research in the Information Society: A National Strategy,* published in 1995, are information skills for

- "Students: It is the task of general education to provide every girl and boy with the versatile basic skills in acquiring, managing and communicating information which are necessary in the information society and essential for successful further study" (p. 38).

- "Adults: The opportunities for adults to learn the basic skills of acquiring and managing information, communicating and using information technology, and to subsequently upgrade these skills, must be improved" (p. 40).

- "Teachers: All teachers need new knowledge, skills and competencies (sic.) in order to be able to use information technology as a tool in their teaching work. They must also become familiar with applications in their respective fields. Teachers of all subjects need to know how to utilize information technology and take account of the requirements of the information society in their work" (p. 40).

- "Business: In the information society, the skills related to the acquisition and management of information are an increasingly essential part of professional competence in every field. In addition to basic general skills, mastery of the working methods and equipment essential for the practice of a chosen profession is essential. For all persons, information technology skills become increasingly important as a factor affecting employability" (p. 41).

Each administrative branch of the government will make action plans to implement the strategy, which will provide every citizen with the opportunity to acquire new skills and access to information.

Summary

In this chapter we have seen that although the concept of information literacy emanated from the library profession, it has been embraced by those within and outside the library profession throughout the world. Key points in this chapter include the following:

- The seminal event in the development of the concept of information literacy was the establishment of the American Library Association (ALA) Presidential Committee on Information Literacy in 1987, whose final report outlines the importance of the concept.

- The Presidential Committee on Information Literacy precipitated the formation of the National Forum on Information Literacy, a coalition of more than 65 national organizations, which seeks to disseminate the concept.

- The development of information literacy in K–12 education began with the publication of *A Nation at Risk* in 1983. *A Nation at Risk* identified the management of complex information in electronic and digital forms as an important skill in a "learning society," but it did not contain recommendations on the role of the library or on the role of information resources in K–12 education. In response, NCLIS members agreed that a concept paper should be written to define what is meant by "information skills." As a result, "Educating Students to Think: The Role of the School Library Media Program" was published in 1986 by Mancall, Aaron, and Walker.

- Kuhlthau's *Information Skills for an Information Society: A Review of Research*, published in 1987, included library skills and computer literacy in the definition of information literacy. Library skills were described as "proficiency in inquiry" to correct the misconception that such skills are reserved only for the library.

- The American Association of School Librarians has fully embraced information literacy as an essential component of K–12 education. AASL and AECT's 1988 publication, *Information Power: Guidelines for School Library Media Programs*, states that the mission of the school library media program is "to ensure that students and staff are effective users of ideas and information" (p. 1). AASL and AECT's newest guidelines, *Information Power: Building Partnerships for Learning*, published in 1998, reiterate this mission and include the Information Literacy Standards for Student Learning.

- Both the Canadian School Library Association and the Association for Teacher-Librarianship in Canada confirm the importance of information literacy in education and the role of the school library in educating students to be information literate.

- The 1986 Carnegie Foundation Report on colleges outlined the importance of an academic library program to the undergraduate experience. A symposium co-sponsored by Columbia University and the University of Colorado in March 1987, Libraries and the Search for Academic Excellence, resulted in outcomes and action recommendations that institutionalized the importance of information literacy skills and form the basis for current information literacy efforts in higher education.

- Accreditation agencies such as the Western Association of Schools and Colleges (WASC) and the Commission on Higher Education (CHE)

Middle States Association of Colleges and Schools have been influential in elevating the importance of information literacy in higher education.

- Other groups have been active in their support of information literacy. These groups include the American Association of Higher Education (AAHE), the National Education Association (NEA), the Association for Supervision and Curriculum Development (ASCD), and the National Council for the Social Studies (NCSS).

- Examples from around the world demonstrate that information literacy is deemed an important concept, most frequently tied to concerns about citizens becoming lifelong learners and promoting economic development.

Chapter

Information Literacy Research

3

Information literacy skills are the necessary tools that help us successfully navigate the present and future landscape of information. In this chapter we examine the body of research relating to information literacy in terms of three themes: the nature and scope of information literacy, the value of information literacy, and effective methods of information literacy skills instruction.

Research efforts in information literacy have yielded a number of useful insights for teachers and librarians and have helped us understand how students look for, use, and present information. Research has validated models that define information literacy and outline the information-seeking process and has demonstrated some of the benefits of these models.

Research from other fields also supports the relevance and importance of information literacy. For example, Loertscher and Woolls (2002) found that one step in the research process, "thinks and creates," is supported by research from fields including mathematics, gifted education, and general education theory.

Figure 3.1 (pages 40–42) is an updated version of Eisenberg and Brown's (1992) original comparison of information models. Using this figure, we can compare several widely known models of information literacy that have been developed through research and evaluation. This side-by-side view of information literacy models shows that there are many similarities among them. In

Kuhlthau
Information Seeking

Eisenberg/Berkowitz
Information Problem-Solving
(The Big6 Skills)

1. Initiation	1. Task Definition
2. Selection	1.1 Define the problem
	1.2 Identify information requirements

4. Formulation (of focus)	

3. Exploration	5. Collection	2. Information-Seeking Strategies
		2.1 Determine range of sources
		2.2 Prioritize sources
(Investigate information on the general topic)	(Gather information on the focused topic)	3. Location and Access
		3.1 Locate sources
		3.2 Find information
		4. Information Use
		4.1 Engage (read, view, etc.)
		4.2 Extract information

6. Presentation	5. Synthesis
	5.1 Organize
	5.2 Present

7. Assessment (of outcome/process)	6. Evaluation
	6.1 Judge the product
	6.2 Judge the process

Figure 3.1 Comparison of Information Skills Process Models (Adapted from Eisenberg & Brown [1992]).

Irving Information Skills	**Stripling/Pitts Research Process**	**New South Wales Info. Process**
1. Formulation/analysis of information need	1. Choose a broad topic	Defining
	2. Get an overview of the topic	
	3. Narrow the topic	
	4. Develop thesis/ purpose statement	
2. Identification /appraisal of likely sources	5. Formulate questions to guide research	Locating
	6. Plan for research and production	
3. Tracing/locating indiv. resources	7. Find, analyze, evaluate resources	Selecting
4. Examining, selecting, and rejecting individual resources		
5. Interrogating/using individual resources	8. Evaluate evidence/ take notes/compile bibliography	Organizing
6. Recording/storing information		
7. Interpretation, analysis, synthesis and evaluation of information	9. Establish conclusions/ Organize information in outline	Presenting
8. Shape, presentation, and communication of information	10. Create and present final product	Assessing
9. Evaluation of the assignment	(Reflection point—is the paper/project satisfactory)	

Figure 3.1 (*cont.*)

**ACRL Standards
The Information-Literate Student**

**AASL Information Literacy
Standards for Student Learning**

1. Determines the nature and extent of the information needed.

1. The student who is information literate accesses information efficiently and effectively.

2. Accesses needed information effectively and efficiently.

2. The student who is information literate evaluates information critically and competently

3. Evaluates info. and its sources critically and incorporates selected information into his or her knowledge base and value system.

3. The student who is information literate uses information accurately and creatively.

4. Individually or as a member of a group, uses information effectively to accomplish a specific purpose.

5. Understands many of the economic, legal, and social issues surrounding the use of information and accesses and uses information ethically and legally.

Figure 3.1 (*Cont.*)

fact, there is more agreement than disagreement among the models, as is true of information literacy research itself. For example, the driving force behind almost all of the models, and many of the findings, is "process": the understanding that information skills are not isolated incidents but rather are connected activities that encompass a way of thinking about and using information.

Four primary research themes pervade the literature and research in the field of information literacy (Eisenberg & Brown, 1992; Eisenberg & Lowe, 1997):

1. The nature and scope of information literacy.

2. The value of information literacy.

3. Effective methods of information literacy skills instruction.

4. The impact of information literacy skills instruction.

Research centering on the nature and scope of information literacy examines the information problem-solving process, the research process, and the specific skills within these processes. Research on the effect of information skills on performance in both academic and professional situations demonstrates the value of information literacy skills instruction. Finally, research on the impact of information literacy skills instruction focuses on the value of an integrated approach.

Examining the Themes

Theme 1: The Nature and Scope of Information Literacy

The nature of the concept itself provides a good starting point for those interested in studying information literacy. One of the great truths about modern society is that "information is everywhere." Information is a pervasive and essential part of our society and our lives. Humans are, at their essence, processors and users of information. This is not a recent development. Humans have always been dependent upon information to help them make decisions and guide their actions. Increases in the sheer volume of information and the complexity of information systems have come about largely because of advances in information technology and the accelerated rate at which we live our lives. Information literacy is the set of skills and knowledge that not only allows us to find, evaluate, and use the information we need, but perhaps more important, allows us to filter out the information we don't need. Information literacy skills are the necessary tools that help us successfully navigate the present and future landscape of information.

Doyle provided a valuable addition to the body of information literacy research with a Delphi study that led to a definition of information literacy. Doyle organized a diverse panel of experts, primarily drawn from members of the National Forum on Information Literacy, and asked them a series of questions concerning a working definition for information literacy. The experts engaged in a reiterative and structured communication process to develop and then fine-tune a definition. After creating an initial list of attributes of information literacy, the experts then ranked the relative importance of the various attributes included in the definition.

When Doyle's Delphi panel reached consensus, they had created both a definition of information literacy and a group of attributes the information literate person would possess. The definition the group agreed upon was: "Information literacy is the ability to access, evaluate, and use information from a variety of sources" (Doyle, 1992, p. 2). As we saw in Chapter 1, the group also defined 10 attributes of an information literate person. By identifying the essential components of information literacy, Doyle's study provides a research-based framework for developing practical applications and for implementing information literacy in curriculum across grade levels and educational situations.

Kuhlthau also contributed to the theoretical foundation of information literacy. Her series of empirical studies leading to theoretical conclusions comprise the most extensive body of work related to information literacy. Kuhlthau's research into the information-seeking behavior of students points directly to her philosophy about information literacy—that information literacy is not a discrete set of skills but rather a way of learning (1993). Kuhlthau concludes that by having students learn to be flexible thinkers and perpetual learners, we prepare them for the new challenges awaiting them in the Information Age.

Perhaps the most widely publicized and used model of information literacy is Eisenberg and Berkowitz's (1988) Big6™ Skills for Information Problem-Solving model. In their textbook on the Big6, Eisenberg and Berkowitz argue that the Big6 gives students a systematic framework for solving information problems, and that it can be used with students of all levels, from elementary school to corporate training. While the Big6 Skills model was developed largely through experience and reflection, Eisenberg points to Kuhlthau's findings, and the similarities among process models, as research support for the various models including the Big6 (see Eisenberg & Brown, 1992). More recently, Eisenberg has engaged in research to investigate the sufficiency and necessity of the Big6 in solving information problems (Eisenberg & Lowe, 1997). In interviewing participants about their information problem-solving behavior, the researchers found that most people use the Big6 strategy to solve information problems without even knowing it. After they learned the Big6 approach, most participants believed it would be a useful tool for solving future information problems. The study emphasized the importance of using information problem-solving skills across situations.

The New South Wales (NSW) (Australia) Information Process model closely matches the Big6 Skills model. The six steps of the NSW Information Process model are (1) defining, (2) locating, (3) selecting, (4) organizing, (5) presenting, and (6) assessing. The New South Wales Department of Education presents the information process as "a philosophical basis and working tool" for planning and teaching information problem-solving skills. The authors believe that this process should include parents and administrators as well as teachers and library media specialists.

The goal of the NSW information process is to develop "successful information users." This goal is achieved by having students develop information skills and by fostering positive information attitudes and values. These are taught in school and reinforced in family and community settings. The authors of the information process place information skills in two categories: skills concerned with locating information (for instance, finding information in a variety of forms and sources, and then finding information within sources), and skills concerned with understanding and using information (including evaluating information found, synthesizing information, and presenting relevant information). By recognizing the skills necessary for successful information problem solving, and also the positive attitude that makes it possible, the NSW model sends the message that schools should strive to produce well-rounded citizens of the Information Age.

Stripling and Pitts (1988) created a model of information literacy from the perspective of the school library media field. Having observed that most students who attempted to do research chose the same topics, used the same sources, and ended up with essentially the same products, Stripling and Pitts determined that students were not truly engaged in the research process. In response, they created a 10-step process (1988) that defined various points in the research process where students could stop and reflect. These reflection points emphasize research that is a thinking process requiring the active engagement of the researcher.

Students need to stop and reflect on their research as soon as they begin to choose and narrow a topic. Since students often lack background knowledge to pursue research on their assigned topics, the first steps of the Stripling and Pitts research model are designed to walk students through selecting a topic, gaining an initial overview through research and reading, forming a focus by narrowing the topic, and then researching the narrower topic in depth. This process, which is recursive, is shared by several models of information literacy, including Kuhlthau, Eisenberg and Berkowitz, and New South Wales.

The American Association of School Librarians' *Information Power* (1998) and the Association of College and Research Libraries' *Information Literacy Competency Standards for Higher Education* (2000) are standards documents, but each provides a model of the competencies of an information literate student. *Information Power's Information Literacy Standards for Student Learning* place an emphasis on demonstrated competency in the area of information literacy, the ability

- to access information efficiently and effectively,
- to evaluate information critically and competently, and
- to use it accurately and creatively.

These points suggest an iterative process that moves the student though an information problem-solving exercise.

ACRL's *Information Literacy Competency Standards for Higher Education* takes an approach similar to that of *Information Power*. According to this document, the information literate student in a higher education setting possesses the same basic information literacy skills identified by the AASL work, but with the addition of a global perspective. The document specifies that beyond solving the information problem, the student uses information to accomplish a specific outcome, and understands global issues of the legality and ethics of information use. According to the ACRL standards, the information literate student

- Determines the nature and extent of the information needed
- Accesses needed information effectively and efficiently
- Evaluates information and its sources critically and incorporates selected information into his or her knowledge base and value system
- Individually or as a member of a group, uses information effectively to accomplish a specific purpose
- Understands many of the economic, legal, and social issues surrounding the use of information and accesses and uses information ethically and legally. (ACRL, 2000)

Viewed together, *Information Power's Information Literacy Standards for Student Learning* and *Information Literacy Competency Standards for Higher Education* provide an ideal representation of the intellectual growth and maturation of an information literate student.

Bruce (1997), an Australia-based researcher, offers a unique approach to researching and defining information literacy. Bruce emphasizes the importance of understanding the way the concept of information literacy is conceived by information users themselves. She suggests a "relational" model for information literacy to accompany the "behavioral" models, which she believes dominate this field of research. The approach that Bruce used for her research is phenomenography; a form of descriptive analysis that attempts to explain how people conceive of topics such as information literacy. Rather than attempting to seek consensus, as Doyle did in her Delphi study, Bruce's phenomenographic study strove to provide an explanation and description of the differences in the ways people conceive of information literacy.

Bruce's study targeted a group of Australian higher educators. She asked them to describe their conceptions of their own information literacy, asking such questions as, "What does information literacy mean to you?" and "Describe your picture of an information literate person." She reported finding seven conceptions of information literacy among her sample of higher educators:

- The information technology conception—information literacy is seen as using information technology for information retrieval and communication.

- The information sources conception—information literacy is seen as finding information.

- The information process conception—information literacy is seen as executing a process.

- The information control conception—information literacy is seen as controlling information.

- The knowledge construction conception—information literacy is seen as building up a personal knowledge base in a new area of interest.

- The knowledge extension conception—information literacy is seen as working with knowledge and personal perspectives adopted in such a way that novel insights are gained.

- The wisdom conception—information literacy is seen as using information wisely for the benefit of others.

Bruce's work is significant in that it provides insight into what people think information literacy is. Figure 3.2 (page 48) provides a visual representation of Bruce's model of information literacy.

Theme 2: The Value of Information Literacy

As previously noted, Kuhlthau has emerged as a key researcher in establishing the relationship between library and information skills and student success. Some of her most important work has been in the identification and documentation of the affective side of the information process.

Starting in the mid-1980s, Kuhlthau conducted five research studies on the information-seeking and search behavior of library users (1993). These studies were designed to observe the actions the subjects took to solve their information problems and also to record the feelings they experienced throughout the process. The first study was a modest qualitative study of 25 high school seniors as they completed a research project. Kuhlthau used various instruments such as learning logs, questionnaires, and short writing assignments to collect data on the students' experiences. She explored the subject at greater length in detailed case studies of six participants. The patterns that emerged from her study prompted Kuhlthau to create a seven-stage information-seeking model, The Process of Learning from Information (see Figure 3.3, pages 50–51).

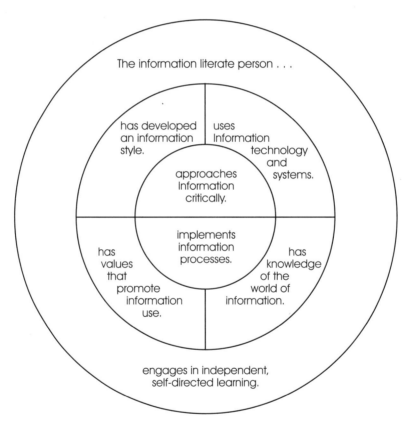

Figure 3.2. Seven Key Characteristics of an Information Literate Person.
Bruce, C. (1995). Information literacy: A framework for higher education. *The Australian Library Journal,* 44(3), 158-170. Reprinted with permission.

Early in the information-seeking process, students tend to feel anxious and uncertain about what they are doing. This anxiety and uncertainty can be exacerbated by the students' lack of focus in the search process and their lack of knowledge of technology and information resources. As students continue their research and narrow their focus, this uncertainty gives way to greater confidence. When the research is complete and the product is presented, students are left with a feeling of satisfaction or dissatisfaction, depending on their perception of their own success.

Kuhlthau's next two studies focused on a larger group of high school seniors and were conducted to verify the findings from her first study. This group of students represented a more diverse population with different levels of academic achievement. Kuhlthau used process surveys to capture the students' thoughts, feelings, and experiences at three points in the research process. The results of this study showed that information seeking is a process affecting, and being affected by, the feelings of the information seeker. Kuhlthau notes that the study revealed "a process of learning that began with vague thoughts and low confidence, and closed with significant clarification of thoughts and increased confidence" (Kuhlthau, 1993, p. 57). Kuhlthau provided further verification of her model by conducting another large-scale study of diverse users, this time in public and academic libraries.

Two longitudinal studies of students from the original group of high school seniors confirmed Kuhlthau's model of the information search process. Using the same instrument she had used five years earlier, Kuhlthau surveyed the students about the research process after they had completed four years of college. She found that her original search process model remained applicable for these students. Further evidence of the model was provided by case study analyses of four students.

Kuhlthau's thoughtful and thorough research has given us an important glimpse into students' experiences and feelings throughout the research process. Her research shows that it is especially important that instructors be aware of the anxiety students experience when embarking on research projects. Uncertainty is an important component of information problem solving and can compel individuals to engage in information problem-solving activities. However, uncertainty can also cause students to experience a great deal of anxiety.

Pitts et al.'s (1995) examination of the mental models of secondary students as they work through information problems also provides valuable insight into the ways students think about information problem solving. Pitts observed a class of eleventh and twelfth graders in a science class as they faced the task of producing a video documentary about marine biology. She learned that when the students began an information problem, they relied on their prior learning to help them solve it. In this situation, Pitts observed that the students used four domains of knowledge: subject matter, information seeking and use, life skills, and video production. When the students faced a problem as part of the assignment (such as not knowing how to locate information in the library), they first categorized the problem in terms of its domain, then checked for helpful prior learning. If they couldn't find any helpful prior learning, they either "finessed" the problem by using knowledge from another domain or produced a substandard product using their own inadequate knowledge. In other words, a lack of knowledge in one domain limited learning in another.

Todd's research reinforces Pitts's conclusion that students' limits in information seeking and use skills restrict their acquisition of subject matter understanding. Todd investigated the importance of associating instruction in library and information skills with students' overall success in school. He found that when information and library skills are taught in the context of information problem solving, and within subject areas, a positive effect on the learning process and on students' attitudes is created. Todd's results found evidence of improvement in test scores, recall, concentration and focus, and reflective thinking (Todd, 1995). These findings provide a compelling argument for including library and information skills instruction both in the library and as part of schoolwide curricula.

Tasks	Initiation	Selection	Exploration
Feelings (affective)	uncertainty	optimism	confusion/ frustration/ doubt
Thoughts (cognitive)	vague -		
Actions (physical)	seeking relevant information - exploring		

Figure 3.3. "The Process of Learning from Information." From C. C. Kuhlthau. (1995, January). *School Libraries Worldwide*, 1(1), p. 5.

Irving (1985) was one of the first researchers to highlight how important it is for students to have information skills when they complete classroom assignments. Irving noted that such skills are not just important for students when they are completing schoolwork, but are essential skills that can be used for all aspects of life: academic, professional, and personal. Irving believes that the information retrieval and processing skills, practiced and acquired through the completion of classroom assignments, will transfer to other areas of a student's life.

Irving identifies nine essential steps for successfully solving an information problem:

1. Formulation and analysis of the information need.

2. Identification and appraisal of likely sources of information.

3. Tracing and locating individual resources.

4. Examining, selecting, and rejecting individual resources.

5. Interrogating, or using, individual resources.

Formulation	Collection	Presentation
clarity	sense of direction/confidence	satisfaction or disappointment

focused

increased interest

seeking pertinent information documenting

6. Recording and storing information.

7. Interpretation, analysis, synthesis, and evaluation of information.

8. Shape, presentation, and communication of information.

9. Evaluation of the assignment.

Although Irving's process is outlined as a series of steps, the steps need not be negotiated in linear fashion. Some steps may be skipped, and some may be negotiated more than once.

Goodin (1991) examined the transferability of information literacy skills from high school to college in a study involving two groups of high school students. One group received instruction in library research skills in the context of information literacy, and the other group did not. The students were given pre- and post-tests on college-level library and information skills. The participants in the study wrote research papers that were subsequently evaluated by college-level instructors. Goodin found that the students who received library skills instruction scored significantly higher on the post-test than students who did not receive instruction. She also found that the research papers produced by the high school students who received such instruction were at a level of performance acceptable for college freshmen.

The *Impact of School Library Media Centers on Academic Achievement* study, undertaken by Lance, Welborn, and Hamilton-Pennell (1992) for the Colorado Department of Education, is a widely cited study on the impact of school library media programs on student learning. The study revealed some very important findings. Among these are the following:

- Where library media programs are better funded, academic achievement is higher, whether their schools and communities are rich or poor and whether adults in the community are well or poorly educated.

- Better funding for library media programs fosters academic achievement by providing students access to more library media staff and larger and more varied collections.

- Among predictors of academic achievement, the size of the library media program staff and collection is second only to the absence of at-risk conditions, particularly poverty and low educational attainment among adults.

- Students whose library media specialists participate in the instructional process are higher academic achievers.

Although Lance et al. do not address the issue of information literacy directly, the findings speak to the importance of the issue in no uncertain terms. A well-run, well-funded library media center has a significant positive impact on student achievement in public schools.

Lance, Rodney, and Hamilton-Pennell reexamined Colorado in 2000, in *How School Librarians Help Kids Achieve Standards: The Second Colorado Study* (2000a). This time, the researchers focused on Colorado Student Assessment Program (CSAP) reading scores, comparing these to characteristics of a school's library media program. They found that improvement in a school's library media program—defined as increases in program development, information technology, teacher/library media specialist collaboration, and visits to the library media center—aligned with improved scores on the CSAP. The study provides specific steps schools can implement to improve their library media programs.

Measuring Up to Standards: The Impact of School Library Programs & Information Literacy in Pennsylvania Schools (2000b), Lance, Rodney, and Hamilton-Pennell's look at Pennsylvania's library media programs, provides similar findings. In this study, the researchers found that Pennsylvania System of School Assessment (PSSA) reading scores improve with increases in

- professional and support staff hours in the library media center,

- technology and connectivity improvements, and

- the integration of information literacy across the curriculum.

The researchers have found similar results in their examinations of Alaska and Iowa's library media programs.

Theme 3: Effective Methods of Information Literacy Skills Instruction

Bibliographic instruction, the teaching of discrete sets of information and searching skills within the library setting, has served traditionally as the classic model for information skills instruction. In an information society, the ability to access, evaluate, and use information will be necessary in all aspects of our lives. As such, educators must provide opportunities for students to learn information skills throughout the curriculum. This can be facilitated with the collaboration of teachers and librarians (Eisenberg & Berkowitz, 1988). Similarly, for higher education, Breivik (1998) advocates collaboration among faculty and academic librarians in the development of a course-integrated approach to information literacy instruction.

Gratch et al. (1992) recognized the importance of information literacy skills in the curriculum, and she and others created a document outlining essential information literacy skills for students in teacher training programs. For information literacy instruction to be truly effective, the skills must be integrated throughout the curriculum. Gratch also emphasizes another principle of information literacy instruction: the need for collaboration among library media specialists and other teachers. Teachers and library media specialists can help students recognize the fact that information literacy skills will help them use information effectively in every area of their lives.

Despite the volume of research on the relative merits of different instructional approaches to information problem-solving skills, no study has ever been able to show one method to be superior over another (Eisenberg & Brown, 1992). What is clear, however, is that students do profit from library and information skills instruction, particularly when those skills are taught in context and across the curriculum (Todd, 1995).

Theme 4: The Impact of Information Literacy Skills Instruction

Related directly to the themes of value of information literacy instruction and effective methods of information literacy skills instruction is Dr. Ross Todd's extensive work in evidence-based practice. Evidence-based practice gives form and substance to the work of library media specialists:

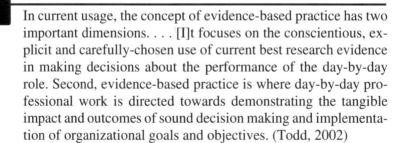

In current usage, the concept of evidence-based practice has two important dimensions. . . . [I]t focuses on the conscientious, explicit and carefully-chosen use of current best research evidence in making decisions about the performance of the day-by-day role. Second, evidence-based practice is where day-by-day professional work is directed towards demonstrating the tangible impact and outcomes of sound decision making and implementation of organizational goals and objectives. (Todd, 2002)

Evidence-based practice serves two purposes. It gives library media specialists and classroom teachers a body of research to consult when making curricular, instructional, and material decisions, and it also creates a legacy of evidence of the impact that information literacy instruction has on individual students' performances.

The implications of this type of evidence-based practice are manifold. In the current political climate of outcome-based learning, standards, and the No Child Left Behind Act of 2001, collecting indicators of impact on student learning proves a library media specialist's worth in a valuable way. Todd suggests that collecting evidence of impact is an excellent way to win the support of administrators, faculty, and parents, and can play a role in budgetary decisions that affect the library (Todd, 2003).

Conclusion: Information Literacy As a New Way of Thinking

Investigations by researchers in the field of information literacy have created an impressive body of research. The ideas represented in that literature are as diverse and creative as the researchers themselves, but there are common themes and ideas throughout.

First, information literacy is a process rather than a discrete set of skills. Doyle's (1994) definition of information literacy articulates this idea, and information problem-solving models such as those of Kuhlthau, Eisenberg and Berkowitz, Pitts and Stripling, AASL, and ACRL legitimize it. Educators must remember to provide students with opportunities to learn how to find information within sources and how to evaluate information for credibility and usefulness within the context of the larger information problem-solving process.

Second, information literacy represents a shift in thinking. For students to be successful in the Information Age, information literacy skills must be integrated throughout the curriculum, as well as being reinforced outside of school. The New South Wales model makes this commitment clear, assigning responsibility for helping students to develop their information literacy skills not only to teachers and library media specialists but also to community members. Gratch et al. (1992) concur by urging teachers to collaborate with library media specialists to create a curriculum that is rich in information literacy concepts.

Finally, information literacy is valuable. The various state studies conducted by Lance et al. link library media programs that have adequate programs, staff, and funding to student success. Goodin's (1991) findings reinforce how important it is for students to have information literacy skills to attain success, by concluding that high school students who possess information literacy skills will be more successful in the realm of higher education. Todd's work underscores the importance of evidence-based practice in how it informs decisions by the library media specialist and in proving impact on student learning. Clearly, information literacy is an essential key to student success, both today and in the information society of the future.

Summary

A comparison of information literacy skills models shows that there is more agreement than there is disagreement. Further examination of the studies reveals that there are three common themes throughout:

- Information literacy is a process. Information literacy skills must be taught in the context of the overall process.

- Information literacy skills instruction must be integrated with the curriculum and reinforced both within and outside of the educational setting to be successful.

- Information literacy skills are vital to future success.

Chapter

An Economic Perspective

4

Noted author Peter Drucker (in Harris, 1993), management guru, states that although knowledge is taking the place of capital, many people confuse data with knowledge. In other words, people lack the skills to analyze and convert data into knowledge. In this chapter we examine the economic ramifications of information literacy and explore the connections of information literacy to the skills of the workplace of the future as first identified by the Secretary's Commission on Achieving Necessary Skills (SCANS) report in 1991 and since expanded upon by groups such as the AOL Time Warner Foundation and the Partnership for 21st Century Skills.

The nature of information is changing the nature of the world's economy. Haeckel and Nolan (1993) state that codified information and knowledge are replacing capital and energy as the primary wealth-creating assets, just as capital and energy replaced land and labor 200 years ago. Research by Merrifield (in Haeckel and Nolan, 1993) of the Wharton School shows that "90% of the codified information that has been created since the ice age was created in the last 30 years and that this will double in the next 15 years" (p. 11). The effect of this transformation is that physical laborers are being replaced by knowledge workers—workers who are information literate.

In a knowledge economy, businesses will not succeed based on how well they manage materials or products but on how well they respond to their customers, to changes in governmental regulations, and to scientific breakthroughs (Ives & Jarvenpaa, 1993). To thrive in this environment, a business must not only use technology to store, retrieve, transfer, manage, and manipulate information but also employ information literate workers who will know how to interpret the information and transform it into knowledge. Such a transformation requires workers to be able to reason and make conjectures based on prior knowledge (see Figure 4.1).

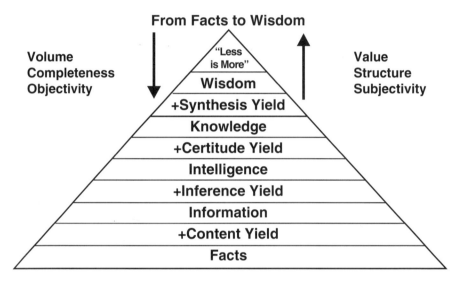

Information Hierarchy: An Example

Facts:	Observations with an assumed truth value (e.g., "Sales are down in Pittsburgh and Indianapolis.")
Context:	(Facts about facts)
Information:	Facts in context (e.g., "Sales fell off only in the two cities where these four things happened in the same period: We raised prices, a competitor entered with an introductory special offer, the weather was unseasonably cold, and sales of new houses fell off sharply.")
Inference:	(Reasoning)
Intelligence:	Inference applied to information (e.g., "Multiple linear regression analysis shows that sales volumes are highly correlated with the price differential between us and our nearest competitor.")
Certitude:	(Conviction—both objectively and subjectively based)
Knowledge:	Certitude about intelligence (e.g., "Sales fell off in Pittsburgh and Indianapolis because we raised our prices at the same time a competitor entered with an introductory low price. The same thing happened three times in the last four years in other cities.")
Synthesis:	(Integration of multiple types of knowledge)
Wisdom:	Synthesized knowledge (e.g., "Insist on forecasts of competitive price and promotional actions as a formal part of our pricing process.")

Figure 4.1. From Facts to Wisdom. Excerpted and reprinted from "The Role of Technology in an Information Age," by Stephen H. Haeckel and Richard L. Nolan. Reprinted with the permission of the authors and the Aspen Institute.

There is widespread recognition that students need a different set of skills to succeed today than they did 20 years ago. A study of 1,000 American adults sponsored by the AOL Time Warner Foundation found that 91 percent of respondents felt that it is important to prepare young people with twenty-first-century literacy skills, defined as the basics plus

- technology

- communications

- critical thinking

- adaptability

- decision-making, and

- problem-solving skills (AOL Time Warner Foundation, 2003).

Although the need for a new set of skills seems to be widely recognized, most Americans don't appear to feel that students have attained these necessary skills. The same research study found that less than half of responders think schools are doing a good job teaching students the twenty-first-century literacy skills they need. Perhaps the most telling aspect of this data set is the strong belief shared by business executives that schools are not producing the workforce they will need in the future; half of the executives responded that they feel American youth are behind those in other industrialized countries (AOL Time Warner Foundation, 2003).

How will the workplace change in the years ahead? To answer this question, Barner (1996) conducted literary research, formed focus groups, and interviewed more than 200 professionals representing diverse industries. He identified seven trends that will transform the workplace:

1. The virtual organization: The workforce will be decentralized.

2. The just in time workforce: There will be an increase in the number of temporary workers.

3. The ascendancy of knowledge workers: There will be a shift from producing products to managing information .

4. Computer coaching and electronic monitoring: There will be an increase in the use of electronic systems for learning, decision making, and performance monitoring.

5. The growth of worker diversity: The workforce will become more multicultural and will include more women.

6. The aging workforce: Fewer people will retire early.

7. The birth of the dynamic workforce: Companies will be less stable and more fluid.

Five of these trends that will demand increased information skills are described below:

- *The virtual organization:* The growth of technologies and computer networks that allow rapid transfer of voice, video, and data will make it increasingly possible for the workforce to access information from decentralized work sites. The instantaneous nature of communication will allow sales representatives to provide customers with up-to-the-minute information about a company's products and services. Barner believes that one implication of this trend is that workers will need to develop their communication and planning skills to keep pace with the virtual environment and the tremendous amount of information available in such an environment.

- *The just in time workforce:* According to Barner, there has been a 240 percent increase in the number of individuals employed by temporary agencies in the last 10 years. These employees need immediate access to information about a company's policies, work procedures, and practices, so that they can contribute to the company's success.

- *The ascendancy of knowledge workers:* As the workforce shifts from producing products to managing information, there will be less need for managers who do nothing but manage. Barner notes that such managers will have to contribute technical expertise that will require them to be lifelong learners able to keep pace with technological developments.

- *The growth of worker diversity:* The diversity of the U.S. labor force reflects national demographics for race and gender. The fact that companies are also setting up more plants in other countries adds to the multicultural nature of the workforce. According to Barner, organizations and managers will need information on how to communicate with people from other cultures to prevent a cross-cultural communication breakdown.

- *The birth of the dynamic workforce:* A need for continuous improvement will be recognized as companies and organizations become more fluid and less static. A commitment to lifelong learning and an ability to seek out and identify innovations will be needed to keep pace with, or outpace, changes.

It is clear that the workplace is being transformed by the knowledge economy and the globalization of industry. The next section looks at a government-sponsored commission that was formed to examine the changing nature of the economy and the skills that employees would need to keep pace.

The SCANS Report

In 1990 then Secretary of Labor Elizabeth Dole formed the Secretary's Commission on Achieving Necessary Skills (SCANS) to create a dialogue among workers, parents, and educators to examine the changes taking place in the working world and to determine the skills needed for employment. During a 12-month period, six panels analyzed jobs in both the private sector and the government. Researchers also conducted in-depth interviews with workers in 15 diverse occupations. The Commission concluded that due to the global nature of the economy and the impact of technology, "good jobs will increasingly depend on people who can put knowledge to work" (SCANS, 1991, p. xv).

In comparing the attributes of the traditional workforce with the high performance workforce needed to ensure success in the future, the Commission noted many differences (see Figure 4.2, page 62). In the traditional model, workers who perform the routine tasks of mass production are viewed as a cost. The training needed for such work is minimal, and authority is delegated to supervisors. In contrast, the high performance workforce that will participate in multiskilled work teams to envision and carry out flexible and customized production is seen as an investment. To enter such a workforce, basic skills and abilities are necessary, and training must be updated on a regular basis.

As a result of the analysis of changes taking place in the workplace, the SCANS report suggests and recommends skills that all Americans will need for entry level employment. These recommendations are phrased as outcome measures and include both foundation skills and practical competencies. The three-part skills foundation includes basic skills, thinking skills, and personal qualities (see Appendix B). The five competencies relate to the management of resources, interpersonal skills, information, systems, and technology (see Appendix C).

Although information literacy is not explicitly mentioned in the SCANS report, the five competencies mentioned in the report fit well with the comprehensive definition of information literacy. The extension of the three-part foundation beyond reading, writing, and arithmetic into listening/speaking skills and critical thinking skills, including knowing how to learn, implies skills that are included in the process of information literacy. A direct comparison of the third competency with the expanded definition of information literacy emphasizes the importance of information literate workers (see Figure 4.3, page 63).

Characteristics of Today's and Tomorrow's Workplace: SCANS Chart

Traditional Model	High Performance Model
Strategy	
• mass production • long production runs • centralized control	• flexible production • customized production • decentralized control
Production	
• fixed automation • end-of-line quality control • fragmentation of tasks	• flexible automation • on-line quality control • work teams, multiskilled workers
Hiring and Human Resources	
• labor-management confrontation • minimal qualifications accepted • workers as a cost	• labor-management cooperation • screening for basic skills abilities • workforce as an investment
Job Ladders	
• internal labor market • advancement by seniority	• limited internal labor market • advancement by certified skills
Training	
• minimal for production workers • specialized for craft workers	• training sessions for everyone • broader skills sought

Figure 4.2. Characteristics of Today's and Tomorrow's Workplace: SCANS Chart. From "Competing in the New International Economy." Washington: Office of Technology Assessment, 1990.

The Partnership for 21st Century Skills

Much of the groundwork laid by the SCANS report has been built upon by a new public–private organization, the Partnership for 21st Century Skills. This group—which includes members from the U.S. Department of Education, the AOL Time Warner Foundation, the National Education Association, and others—seeks to define twenty-first-century skills and find successful ways to integrate them into the curriculum.

Competency Three:	Information Literacy— Expanded Definition
Information: Acquires and uses information • acquires and evaluates information • organizes and maintains information • interprets and communicates information • uses computers to process information.	• recognizes that accurate and complete information is the basis for intelligent decision making • recognizes the need for information • formulates questions based on information needs • identifies potential sources of information • develops successful search strategies • accesses sources of information including computer-based and other technologies • evaluates information • organizes information for practical application • integrates new information into an existing body of knowledge • uses information in critical thinking and problem solving.
(SCANS, p. xvii)	(Doyle, 1992)

Figure 4.3. Correlation of SCANS Report Competency Three with the Expanded Definition of Information Literacy

A 2003 report from the Partnership lays out the organization's vision and its road map for implementation. According to the report, there are six key elements for fostering twenty-first-century learning:

1. Emphasize core subjects.

2. Emphasize learning skills.

3. Use 21st century tools to develop learning skills.

4. Teach and learn in a 21st century context.

5. Teach and learn 21st century content.

6. Use 21st century assessments that measure 21st century skills. (Partnership for 21st Century Skills, 2003)

Much of the work of the Partnership for 21st Century Skills is still in the planning stages. It can be expected that this important project will grow in scope and visibility over the next few years as it works toward preparing today's students for tomorrow's workplace.

Summary

The change from an economy based on labor and capital to one based on information requires information literate workers who will know how interpret information. Let's summarize the key points of this chapter:

- Barner's (1996) study of the new workplace indicates significant changes will take place in the future. Information technology is decentralizing the workplace. The workforce will be more diverse, and the economy will increasingly be more global. The use of temporary workers will increase. These changes will demand that workers possess information literacy skills.

- The SCANS report (1991) identifies the skills necessary for the workplace of the future. Rather than report to a hierarchical management structure, workers of the future will be required to actively participate in the management of the company and contribute to its success. The workplace will demand workers who possess skills beyond those of reading, writing, and arithmetic.

- The Partnership for 21st Century Skills (2003) project continues much of the work begun by the SCANS report as it seeks to redefine workplace preparation for the new millennium.

Chapter

K–12 Education: Information Literacy in the Context of National and State Standards

5

The SCANS report recognized that the quality of our children's education is linked to the success of our economy. Our nation's governors sought to raise the quality of education with the Goals 2000: Educate America Act, which outlines eight National Education Goals. This chapter explores information literacy in the context of the National Education Goals, the No Child Left Behind Act of 2001, content area standards, and state standards that seek to improve our children's education.

In the mid-1950s, the launch of the Russian satellite *Sputnik* stimulated the refocusing of American educational goals. Schools emphasized the academic and scientific aspects of education, and preparing students for college became a primary national goal. The acquisition of theoretical knowledge by academicians and researchers became valued by society.

As we saw in Chapter 2, *A Nation at Risk* was one of the most publicized top-down efforts to improve education. Other reports followed, and states jumped onto educational reform "bandwagons," expending dollars from state income and sales tax revenues. The impetus for these reforms was the need, perceived by state governments, for improved schooling to encourage economic growth (Cuban, 1990).

National Education Goals

A major effort toward improving the nation's education was set into motion by President George H.W. Bush and the nation's governors in September 1989 at an "Education Summit." The state of American education was the focus of the summit's discussion. As a result of the summit, six goals for the improvement of education were outlined. The governors committed their states to the achievement of these goals through restructuring education. President Bush met with the National Governors' Conference in Charlottesville, Virginia, in 1990, and together they publicly announced the National Education Goals. Bill Clinton, who was then governor of Arkansas, led the governors' task force in making the announcement. This marked the second time that national education goals had been established. In 1975, the National Governors' Conference publicized a list of national education goals, but little was done to implement them.

The aim of the National Education Goals was expressed as "individually, to promote higher levels of individual student achievement, and collectively, to build a globally competitive American work force" (America 2000, 1991, p. 2). As in the SCANS report, the importance of education to the development of a quality workforce was recognized. Six goals were proposed, each having several subgoals that specified the issues to be addressed. Broadly, the six goals covered issues ranging from the education of preschool aged children to adult literacy. The underlying theme was the importance of lifelong learning, with particular emphasis placed on schooling and preparation of students.

President Bush's administration created a plan to implement the National Education Goals. On May 22, 1991, President Bush submitted The America 2000 Excellence in Education Act to Congress. This proposed bill outlined a number of legislative initiatives to:

- Create and fund exemplary schools
- Reward schools that have made outstanding progress towards the achievement of the National Education Goals
- Focus on teacher training to foster leadership and instructional skills
- Allow parents to make educational choices for their children
- Provide greater authority to the National Assessment of Education Progress to collect data to measure achievement
- Establish Regional Literacy Resource Centers to support the goal that every American be literate by the year 2000. (America 2000, 1991)

Congress did not pass The America 2000 Excellence in Education Act. Instead Congress initiated the National Council on Education Standards and Testing (NCEST), which recommended that states participate in a voluntary program based on world class standards, and, coupled with assessment systems, measure student performance.

National Education Goals Passed as Legislation

During the Clinton administration, two additional goals focusing on teacher education and parental participation were added to the six goals that had been announced by President Bush and the nation's governors. The Goals 2000: Educate America Act was signed into law on March 31, 1994, by President William J. Clinton. The eight goals as they were incorporated into law follow:

Goal 1: School Readiness

> By the year 2000, all children in America will start school ready to learn.

Goal 2: School Completion

> By the year 2000, the high school graduation rate will increase to at least 90%.

Goal 3: Student Achievement and Citizenship

> By the year 2000, all students will leave grades 4, 8, and 12 having demonstrated competency over challenging subject matter including English, mathematics, science, foreign languages, civics and government, economics, arts, history and geography, and every school in America will ensure that all students learn to use their minds well, so they may be prepared for responsible citizenship, further learning, and productive employment in our nation's modern economy.

Goal 4: Teacher Education and Professional Development

> By the year 2000, the nation's teaching force will have access to programs for the continued improvement of their professional skills and the opportunity to acquire the knowledge and skills needed to instruct and prepare all American students for the next century.

Goal 5: Mathematics and Science

By the year 2000, United States students will be first in the world in mathematics and science achievement.

Goal 6: Adult Literacy and Lifelong Learning

By the year 2000, every adult American will be literate and will possess the knowledge and skills necessary to compete in a global economy and exercise the rights and responsibilities of citizenship.

Goal 7: Safe, Disciplined, and Alcohol- and Drug-free Schools

By the year 2000, every school in the United States will be free of drugs, violence, and the unauthorized presence of firearms and alcohol and will offer a disciplined environment conducive to learning.

Goal 8: Parental Participation

By the year 2000, every school will promote partnerships that will increase parental involvement and participation in promoting the social, emotional, and academic growth of children. (United States Department of Education, 1994)

No Child Left Behind

In January, 2002, President George W. Bush signed the No Child Left Behind Act of 2001 into law. This sweeping educational reform effort is based on four principles: increased accountability for students' results, an emphasis on research-based decision making, opportunities for parental involvement, and increased local control over the schools.

Although many of the specifics of the No Child Left Behind Act of 2001 are still in the process of being enacted, the framework of the legislation provides a key opportunity for information literacy instruction. The increased emphasis on accountability for schools and the related importance of high-stakes testing to demonstrate learning makes information literacy skills paramount. Information literacy skills help students manage preparing for comprehensive exams, offer test-taking strategies, and give teachers guidance for prioritizing the material to be learned. Information literacy researchers have begun to examine the significant aspects of No Child Left Behind, and the next few years will provide additional illumination of the ties between the legislation and information literacy instruction.

A Study to Examine the Information Literacy Aspects of the National Education Goals

In 1992, a national panel of experts from the organizational memberships comprising the National Forum for Information Literacy (NFIL) collaborated in a Delphi study that examined the original six National Education Goals. The purpose of the study, was to

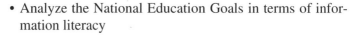

- Analyze the National Education Goals in terms of information literacy

- Create a comprehensive definition of information literacy

- Develop outcome measures for the information literacy concept, and

- Create policy recommendations for each goal for the National Forum on Information Literacy. (Doyle, 1992)

Through the Delphi study, the National Education Goals were used as a framework to demonstrate the critical nature of information literacy in realizing information society goals.

As a preliminary task, the group rated those education goals that members thought could be attained through information literacy skills. Goals 1, 3, and 6 (formerly 5) were rated well above the others and were the subjects for further consideration. The common theme of all three goals was lifelong learning:

- children starting school ready to learn (Goal 1);

- students leaving grades 4, 8, and 12 demonstrating competency with subject matter and able to use their minds well (Goal 3); and

- all adults being literate and equipped with skills necessary to survive in the global economy (Goal 6).

Goal 1 stresses the preschool, formative, and affective aspects of developing a value for information. Goal 3, concerned with schooling, points to the attainment of skills necessary for lifelong learning. Goal 6 addresses the widespread application of skills to employment and citizenship. The study demonstrated that information literacy skills are at the heart of successful attainment of these three goals.

Focus of Each Education Goal

Goal 1

Goal 1 calls for all children to start school ready to learn. The panelists agreed that this might be interpreted as

- acquiring skills such as knowing how to learn,

- valuing information, and

- having a positive and enthusiastic attitude.

Preschool children learn to value information by watching their parents—their first teachers. Other adults, including preschool teachers, are also role models. Children's motivation to read and access information begins with these first role models. Parents should value information and be able to demonstrate to their children effective strategies for accessing, evaluating, and using information. Many parents have yet to acquire these skills, so Goal 5, adult literacy, applies to them as learners. The continuum of lifelong learning is a circle. Adults' need for resources and skills development in turn affects future generations. (See Figure 5.1.)

Goal 3

Goal 3 is concerned with the way students learn how to use their minds to make informed decisions. During their years of general education (K–12), all students need to learn how to process information as they apply problem-solving and critical thinking skills to their school and personal lives. Learning these skills requires an active learning format in which students can process information to meet specific needs at a level that is developmentally appropriate for them. This inquiry approach is basic to active learning. An information rich environment is needed, in which many resources are available, including computer-based and other technologies. Teachers will need skills of their own to facilitate resource-based learning.

Panel members concluded that teachers are important keys to student attainment of information literacy. Because active learning represents a major shift in instructional strategy, a shift not often addressed in teacher preparation programs, extensive staff development programs for teachers will be needed. Such staff development must be ongoing, over a period of years, as teachers build confidence and develop applications suitable for their own classes. Teachers will have to become information literate themselves. They will need to be comfortable with a variety of resources, as well as with the processes of accessing, evaluating, and using information. It's also important that assessments be developed that integrate the process of information literacy into meaningful final projects, portfolios, or performances.

A library/media center containing a wide variety of print and nonprint resources was identified as being critical to the integration of information literacy into the curriculum. The library/media center should be staffed with a trained library media specialist who collaborates with classroom teachers in carrying out classroom objectives. The library/media center should become the hub of a school, where equity of access to resources is ensured. (See Figure 5.2, page 72.)

Goal 1. By the year 2000, all children in America will start school ready to learn.

- All disadvantaged and disabled children will have access to high quality and developmentally appropriate preschool programs that help prepare children for school.

- Every parent in America will be a child's first teacher and devote time each day to helping their child learn; parents will have access to the training and support they need.

- Children will receive the nutrition and health care needed to arrive at school with healthy minds and bodies, and the number of low weight babies will be significantly reduced through enhanced prenatal health systems. (*National Goals for Education,* 1990, p. 3)

Interpretation of Goal 1 from the Information Literacy Perspective

---

Parents are a child's first teachers. They provide the most important role models of the value of information to make decisions. In addition, they set an example for motivation to read and to access information.

Policy recommendations for the National Forum on Information Literacy (NFIL).

In order for children to start school ready to learn, a policy must include:

- A national commitment to the access of information for every American

- Community support through library facilities/community services for information rich resources, both print and non-print, and

- Parents' acceptance of their responsibility to develop a value for information by reading to children and discussing what has been read (Doyle, 1992, pp. 9-10).

Figure 5.1. Goal 1 of the National Education Goals of 1990

Goal 3.   By the year 2000, American students will leave grades 4, 8, and 12 having demonstrated competency over challenging subject matter including English, mathematics, science, history, and geography, and every school in America will ensure that all students learn to use their minds well, so that they may be prepared for responsible citizenship, further learning, and productive employment in our modern economy. (*National Goals for Education,* 1990, p. 3)

Interpretation of Goal 3 from the Information Literacy Perspective

The basic focus of education should be to prepare students to be lifelong learners, to know how to learn. Developing the competencies of information literacy requires an active learning process, which represents a paradigm shift for education.

Policy recommendations for the National Forum on Information Literacy (NFIL).

In order for students to become self-motivated, policy must include:

- National/state governments will make a commitment to ensure all students have equal and regular access to information by assuring adequate resources at each site.

- State Departments of Education/local school systems will develop and implement a resource-based learning curriculum.

- Curriculum standards that reflect a resource-based learning approach will be developed.

- Ongoing inservices will be conducted to ensure that teachers have the skills necessary to facilitate resource-based learning.

- Library/media centers will be recognized as key to successful implementation of resource-based learning.

- Parental support and participation in their children's learning will be considered integral. (Doyle, 1992, pp. 11-13)

Figure 5.2. Goal 3 of the National Education Goals of 1990

Goal 6

Goal 6 focuses on adult literacy and the skills necessary for gainful employment and good citizenship. In terms of information literacy, all Americans should be lifelong learners, able to access a variety of resources, proficient with various types of technologies, and able to evaluate and use information to meet personal and job-related needs. With more than 80 percent of American jobs somehow related to services, information has become the most important commodity in the marketplace. Those who can access information will be empowered with the skills necessary to be successful as employees and citizens.

The importance of addressing information literacy at the college level was recognized, although no specific outcome measures were suggested. Several panel members commented that this required immediate attention so that college students could be encouraged to learn and/or reinforce information processing skills.

In this research, the panel members reached consensus on 45 outcome measures for information literacy in the context of selected National Education Goals. These results were, in effect, cross-validated by the SCANS report discussed previously. There appears to be a rapid increase in public awareness of the need for information literacy skills, although there may not yet be a conscious connection between the concept and the inherent or needed skills.

SCANS, Goals 2000, and No Child Left Behind are national policy statements, the latter two having legal status. But it takes more than policy pronouncements to bring about the kind of change that will restructure the American educational system and produce students who are equipped for the Information Age. Both the SCANS report and Goals 2000 agree on much of what is needed: greater focus on teaching all students to become independent lifelong learners, to become critical thinkers, to use a variety of technologies proficiently, and to work effectively with others. Implicitly, all students must be prepared to use information literacy to solve problems in their personal lives as well as in school and in the workplace. We argue that it is more important for students to know how to find needed information than to try to memorize and store facts for future reference. (See Figure 5.3, page 74.)

National Subject Matter Association Curriculum Standards

Following the passage of the Goals 2000: Educate America Act, subject matter organizations were able to obtain funding to develop standards in their respective subject areas. Realizing that subject matter content is ever expanding, professional organizations developed national standards that emphasize a process approach. An analysis of these national standards documents shows that they all focus on lifelong learning, the ability to think critically, and the use of

Goal 6.   By the year 2000, every adult will be literate and will possess the knowledge and skills necessary to compete in a global economy and exercise the rights and responsibilities of citizenship.

- Every major American business will be involved in strengthening the connection between education and work.

- All workers will have the opportunity to acquire the knowledge and skill, from basic to highly technical, needed to adapt to emerging new technologies, work methods, and markets through public and private educational vocation, technical, workplace, and other programs.

- The number of quality programs, including those at libraries, that are designed to serve more effectively the needs of the growing number of part-time and mid-career students will increase substantially.

- The proportion of college graduates who demonstrate an advanced ability to think critically, communicate effectively, and solve problems will increase substantially. (*National Goals for Education,* 1990, p. 5)

Interpretation of Goal 6 from the Information Literacy Perspective

All Americans need to be lifelong learners.

Policy recommendations for the National Forum on Information Literacy (NFIL).

In order for Americans to be lifelong learners, policy must state that:

- National/state governments will be actively involved in improving the information literacy of citizens.

- Communities will promote lifelong learning.

- Businesses will promote the acquisition of information literacy skills by all.

- All Americans will be able to seek information to solve problems and make informed decisions.

- A wide variety of print and non-print resources will be available to all Americans at no/low cost through public libraries, national online networks, and shared resources with business and public institutions.

- Colleges will recognize that information literacy skills must be mastered by all college graduates. (Doyle, 1992, p. 17)

Figure 5.3. Goal 6 of the National Education Goals of 1990

new and existing information for problem solving. The sections that follow discuss each subject area standards document in general terms, whereas Appendix E examines selected specific elements within each document in relation to information literacy skills.

The No Child Left Behind Act of 2001 places even greater emphasis on standards, requiring each state to develop its own reading, math, and science standards. The groundwork created by the national association standards created in the wake of Goals 2000 can help guide these states as they frame their own content standards.

Mathematics Standards

The National Council of Teachers of Mathematics (NCTM) paved the way for all national standards curriculum reform efforts. They published national standards prior to the passage of the Goals 2000: Educate America Act. The Council accomplished its task by asking for input, reaction, and buy-in from the widest possible audience of teachers and practitioners. It also developed a companion document concerning revision of teacher certification.

Principles and Standards for School Mathematics (2000)—an update of the original *Curriculum and Evaluation Standards for School Mathematics* (1989)—states:

> The requirements for the workplace and for civic participation in the contemporary world include flexibility in reasoning about and using quantitative information. Conceptual understanding is an essential component of the knowledge needed to deal with novel problems and settings. Moreover, as judgements change about the facts or procedures that are essential in an increasingly technological world, conceptual understanding becomes even more important. . . . Change is a ubiquitous feature of contemporary life, so learning with understanding is essential to enable students to use what they learn to solve the new kinds of problems they will inevitably face in the future. (NCTM, p. 20)

Information literacy, as presented within this curriculum area, involves problem solving; the use of estimation; thinking strategies for basic facts; formulating and investigating questions from problem situations; and using computers, calculators, and other technologies. Assessment of mathematics also fits within the larger picture of information literacy because the focus of evaluation here is on using information in meaningful ways to demonstrate understanding.

Social Studies Standards

The National Council for Social Studies published *Curriculum Standards for Social Studies* (1993), which identifies 10 standards: culture; time, continuity, and change; people, places, and environments; individual development and identity; individuals, groups, and institutions; power, authority, and governance; production, distribution, and consumption; science, technology, and society; global connections; and civic ideals and practice. In the book information literacy is integrated with the achievement of the 10 standards. Categories of the essential skills include:

- Skills related to acquiring information.
- Skills related to organizing and using information.
- Skills related to interpersonal relationships and social participation. (1993, pp. 148-149)

The first two clearly parallel the process of information literacy, and the last relates the importance of information skills and access to information and democracy.

Science Standards

The National Committee on Science Education Standards and Assessment (NCSESA) of the National Research Council first met in May 1992. Attending the meeting were representatives from the National Science Teachers Association, the American Association for the Advancement of Science, American Association of Physics Teachers, American Chemical Society, Council of State Science Supervisors, Earth Science Education Coalition, and the National Association of Biology Teachers. The group decided early on to integrate curriculum, teaching, and assessment standards into a single volume, so that each standard would reinforce the others and produce a solid and complete vision for change.

The science standards include basic understandings of the physical, earth, and life sciences, divided into grade categories K–4, 5–8, and 9–12. Among the eight content standards is "Science as Inquiry," which focuses on students' abilities to conduct scientific experiments and use scientific reasoning and critical thinking skills to analyze results. This is an excellent application of information literacy using a hands-on approach appropriate to a particular subject matter.

The Science and Technology standard requires students to

- identify a problem or a need to change a current technological design;
- gather information and generate and evaluate alternative solutions;

- choose and test solutions and communicate results orally or in writing as well as through diagrams, models, and demonstrations. (National Research Council, 1993)

This process requires students to use a full range of information literacy skills.

Foreign Language Learning Standards

An 11-member task force representing a variety of languages, instructional levels, program models, and geographic areas coordinated the development of the foreign language standards. Rather than focusing on the memorization of vocabulary, verb conjugation, and grammar rules, the standards for foreign language learning reflect a philosophy that the study of a second language "increases enormously one's ability to see connections. Since the content of a foreign language course deals with history, geography, social studies, science, math, and the fine arts, it is easy for students to develop an interdisciplinary perspective at the same time they are gaining intercultural understandings" (National Standards in Foreign Language Education Project, 1999, p. 12). The task force identified five broad goal areas:

- communication,
- cultures,
- connections,
- comparisons, and
- communities.

Within each goal area, two or three content standards are specified, and within these, lists of sample progress indicators for grades 4, 8, and 12 are presented.

Learning a foreign language centers on an understanding of the relationship between culture and communication and involves the communicative processes of speaking, reading, and writing. Students acquire cultural understanding by studying the perspectives (meaning, attitudes, values, ideas), practices (patterns of social interactions), and products (books, tools, foods, laws, music, games) of the speakers of the native language. The information literacy skills of identifying potential sources of information, accessing sources of information including computer-based and other technologies, organizing information for practical application, integrating new information into an existing body of knowledge, and using information in critical thinking and problem solving are all necessary to the study of a foreign language.

National Geography Standards

Geography for Life: National Geography Standards 1994 (Geography Education Standards Project, 1994) identifies six categories of geography skills:

- the world in spatial terms,
- places and regions,
- physical systems,
- human systems,
- environment and society, and
- uses of geography.

Geography helps us to understand the relationships among people, places, and environment. A geographically informed person is able to make sense of not only the local environment (for example, the reasoning behind the location of business establishments in relation to consumers) but also the global environment (for example, the possible effects of global warming). Knowledge of geography requires the information literacy skills of identifying, using, and analyzing information in a variety of forms (maps, charts, and satellite photos) for the purposes of decision making, and critical thinking.

Increasingly sophisticated geographic information systems (GIS) are used to collect and manipulate data to answer questions and solve problems. Geographic information systems can provide data, but people who are capable of asking the right questions are necessary so that data may be analyzed and interpreted for decision making. Information literacy skills are needed to evaluate information and use it for critical thinking and problem solving.

English Language Arts Standards

The development of the *Standards for the English Language Arts* was co-directed by the International Reading Association and the National Council of Teachers of English (1996). There are 12 standards related to literacy growth. Among these, several correlate directly with information literacy:

3. Students apply a wide range of strategies to comprehend, interpret, evaluate, and appreciate texts. They draw on their prior experience, their interactions with other readers and writers, their knowledge of word meaning and of other texts, their word identification strategies, and their understanding of textual features.

5. Students employ a wide range of strategies as they write and use different writing process elements appropriately to communicate with different audiences for a variety of purposes.

7. Students conduct research on issues and interests by generating ideas and questions, and by posing problems. They gather, evaluate, and synthesize data from a variety of sources (e.g. print and non-print texts artifacts, people) to communicate their discoveries in ways that suit their purpose and audience.

8. Students use a variety of technological and informational resources (e.g., libraries, databases, computer networks, and video) to gather and synthesize information and to create and communicate knowledge. (IRA & NCTE, 1996, p. 3)

These four standards correlate very closely with Doyle's definition of information literacy. It is evident that the basic literacy of reading and writing involves the entire range of information literacy skills. In fact, the English Language Arts standards document points out that the definition of literacy has changed greatly. It was once defined as the ability to read and write one's own name; the National Literacy Act of 1991 now defines literacy as "an individual's ability to read, write, and speak in English and compute and solve problems at levels of proficiency necessary to function on the job and in society, to achieve one's goals, and to develop one's knowledge and potential" (IRA & NCTE, 1996, p. 4). As discussed previously in relation to the SCANS report, the skills needed to function on the job have changed considerably, and information literacy skills are a necessity.

National History Standards

The *National Standards for History* (National Center for History in the Schools, 1996) connect the knowledge of history with the ability to fully participate in a democratic society and state that

knowledge of history is the precondition of political intelligence. Without history, a society shares no common memory of where it has been, of what its core values are, or of what decisions of the past account for present circumstances. Without history, one cannot undertake any sensible inquiry into political, social, or moral issues in society. And without historical knowledge and the inquiry it supports, one cannot move to the informed, discriminating citizenship essential to effective participation in the democratic processes of governance and the fulfillment for all our citizens of the nation's democratic ideals. (p. 1)

Information literacy skills are essential to analyze the past and to make informed decisions about the future.

The standards identify four topics for grades K–4, ranging from living and working together in families and communities to the history of the United States and the cultures of the world. The standards for grades 5–12 are divided into United States History and World History, and are thematically grouped by eras. The document also identifies five standards of historical thinking: chronological thinking, historical comprehension, historical analysis, historical research capabilities, and historical issues analysis and decision making. The standards of historical thinking are interwoven with the outcome measures of the topics and eras.

The standards of historical thinking correlate closely with information literacy. For example, "the ability to interpret data presented in timelines" (p. 15) requires the information literacy skill of evaluating information. To "hypothesize influences of the past" (p. 15), one would have to use information skills in critical thinking and problem solving. The "formulation of a position or course of action on an issue" (p. 16) implies the need to use a range of information literacy skills, including recognizing that accurate and complete information is the basis for intelligent decision making, critical thinking, and problem solving.

Economics Standards

Economics is one of the nine core subject areas identified by the Goals 2000: Educate America Act. The *Voluntary National Content Standards in Economics* (National Council on Economic Education, 1997) define 20 content standards with benchmarks, so that students will learn basic economics and become productive and informed workers, consumers, savers, investors, and citizens. The standards focus on the practical application of knowledge. For example, content standard 1 states:

Students will understand that:

> Productive resources are limited. Therefore, people cannot have all the goods and services they want; as a result, they must choose some things and give up others.

Students will be able to use this knowledge to:

> Identify what they gain and what they give up when they make choices. (p. 1)

Benchmark for Grade 12:

At the completion of Grade 12, students will use this knowledge to:

> Explain how a high school senior's decision to work 20 hours per week during the school year could reduce her lifetime income. Also, explain how an increase in the legal minimum wage aimed at improving the financial condition of some low-income families could reduce the income of some minimum wage earners. (p. 3)

Economic decision making requires complex thinking skills because the variables involved are interdependent. Students need to use the whole range of information literacy skills to identify needed information, evaluate and analyze information, and use information for critical thinking and problem solving.

Physical Education Standards

The seven content standards for physical education serve to promote a healthy lifestyle and encourage physical activity for emotional well-being. The physical education standards address such basics as the development of motor skills, the ability to demonstrate responsible personal and social behavior in physical activity settings, and the ability to include others of diverse physical abilities in group physical activities. The physical education standards emphasize the application of knowledge to the creation of a personal fitness program. Students need to be able to identify the relationship between physical activity and its effect on the body and a healthy lifestyle. The information literacy skills of evaluating information and organizing information for practical application are particularly important for the creation of a personal physical fitness program.

National Health Standards

The *National Health Education Standards* (Joint Committee on National Health Standards, 1997) define a health-literate person as one who is

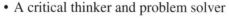

- A critical thinker and problem solver
- A responsible, productive citizen
- A self-directed learner, and
- An effective communicator. (p. 5)

The standards note that (as critical thinkers and problem solvers) health literate individuals can "identify and creatively address health problems and issues at multiple levels, ranging from personal to international. They can utilize a variety of sources to access the current, credible, and applicable information required to make sound health-related decisions" (p. 6). The ability to access and analyze information to make informed decisions about one's health is important particularly as advances in technology and science present a variety of care and treatment options.

National Arts Education Standards

The *National Standards for Arts Education* define art as "(1) creative works and the process of producing them, and (2) the whole body of work in the art forms that make up the entire human intellectual and cultural heritage" (Consortium of National Arts Education Associations, 1994, Preface). The arts education standards encompass dance, music, theater, and visual arts, and state that a secondary student should be able to "communicate at a basic level in the four arts disciplines and communicate proficiently in at least one art form, including the ability to define and solve artistic problems with insight, reason, and technical proficiency" (Introduction). The ability to solve artistic problems requires knowledge and understanding of art processes, as well the ability to analyze and evaluate information.

States Recognize the Importance of Information Literacy

The preceding sections show how information literacy fits within the national standards for the content areas. Individual states are now creating initiatives to ensure that students attain information literacy skills by the time they graduate from high school.

California

The California Media and Library Educators Association (1997) created a resource for educators seeking information on how to integrate the goals of information literacy into the curriculum. *Library Skills to Information Literacy: A Handbook for the 21st Century* takes the position that it is the responsibility of educators to prepare students for the challenges they will face in the Information Age. Although the handbook is based on several California programs and documents and was prepared by an educational association that represents that state, it is applicable to educators and curricula nationwide.

The handbook treats information literacy as a process: "Information literacy has been defined as 'the ability to access, evaluate, and use information from a variety of sources' " (California Media and Library Educators Association,

1997, p. 2). This definition gives the authors a standard upon which to base their model of information literacy. They believe information literacy can be viewed from three perspectives: the searcher's thinking process, the stages of the research process, and instructional strategies. All three of these interdependent components must be addressed in an information literacy curriculum to ensure that students will be properly prepared for success in the Information Age.

The handbook provides concrete examples and strategies to help educators create successful curricula that incorporate information literacy in content area contexts. Library media specialists must work together with teachers to integrate the goals of information literacy into every subject area. The handbook states:

> Why take the time and effort to combine the talents of the teacher with various specialists or other teachers on instructional units? There is only one reason: to improve the educational experience for every learner. The teacher could have stayed in the classroom using existing resources and technology there, but as the resources and technology of the library media center are added, new possibilities arise. (California Media and Library Educators Association, 1997)

The handbook provides information for teachers who wish to use an integrated, process-oriented curriculum in the classroom. It defines five steps for creating a fully integrated unit informed by the precepts of information literacy. The document provides specific strategies for each step of the process and defines roles for teachers, library media specialists, and students in the development and implementation of an information literacy curriculum.

Colorado

Colorado has made great strides in the field of information literacy. As discussed in Chapter 3, Lance, Wellborn, and Hamilton-Pennell's (1992) study, *The Impact of School Library Media Centers on Student Achievement*, firmly established how important a well-funded and professionally staffed library/media center is to a student's education. Following the publication of this study, in the summer of 1993 a team of state level personnel, library media specialists, representatives of higher education and public libraries, and content area specialists met at the invitation of Nancy Bolt and the Colorado State Library. The team sought to establish a philosophical base upon which to build a library media program that would reflect outcomes-based education and school restructuring (Walster, 1995).

Five broad areas for student development were identified, and writing teams were assigned. Over a period of a year, the teams created the *Model Information Literacy Guidelines* (Colorado Department of Education, 1994) from these five broad areas. The guidelines focus on student outcomes in each of the five following areas:

- students as knowledge seekers,

- students as quality producers,

- students as self-directed learners,

- students as group contributors, and

- students as responsible information users.

Each standard specifies a list of actions that students complete to accomplish the standard. The focus of the guidelines is on student improvement through the integration of processes across content areas.

Funding was obtained to develop and offer statewide training to implement the information literacy guidelines. Throughout 1994–1995, Colorado library media specialists participated in institutes, teleconferences, workshops, and mentoring that resulted in "a majority of media specialists in the state beginning to integrate information literacy guidelines with content-area standards" (Walster, 1995, p. 49).

Colorado has also led the way in developing assessment measures for information literacy. The *Rubrics for the Assessment of Information Literacy* (Colorado Department of Education, 1996) specify four levels of achievement for each of the five areas of the *Model Information Literacy Guidelines* (see Chapter 6) and can be used by educators in all content areas.

Kentucky

Kentucky's information literacy initiative, titled *Beyond Proficiency: Achieving a Distinguished Library Media Program* (Kentucky Department of Education, 2001), was developed in recognition of the importance of information literacy skills in the marketplace of an information-based society. The program emphasizes the vital role of the library media program in developing and promoting these skills, and thus places central importance on the schools' library media program and library media specialist. The Kentucky Department of Education (2001) writes in the program's handbook:

> One of the national education goals is for all adult Americans to be literate and to possess the knowledge and skills to compete in a global economy. Library media specialists promote informa-

tion literacy as they help students access, synthesize, produce, and communicate information. This goal is accomplished more effectively when teachers and library media specialists collaborate in providing opportunities for students to think critically. (Foreword)

Beyond Proficiency emphasizes the collaboration between library media specialists and teachers. Teachers bring to the classroom their own strengths and areas of expertise. In the case of the library media specialist, this strength is knowledge of information skills and resources. The Kentucky Department of Education believes the strength of a school's library/media center and the amount of experience students have with its collection of resources are the best indicators of student success: "Adequate library media facilities, with appropriate resources and professional personnel, are key components to success. The library media program should provide an inviting, accessible and stimulating environment for meeting the information needs of the total school community" (p. 6).

Beyond Proficiency delineates two specific sets of goals for a fully functioning library media program. Under this program, students will

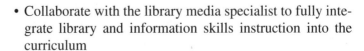

- Use a variety of library media resources and technologies to locate, organize, and present information relevant to a specific need or problem

- Evaluate, interpret, and select information that meets their needs

- Function as independent learners by using library media resources as well as resources beyond the school site, and

- Pursue areas of personal interest through reading and research in the library media center and beyond. (2001, p. 6)

Similarly, the school community will

- Collaborate with the library media specialist to fully integrate library and information skills instruction into the curriculum

- Consult with the library media specialist about resources required for units of study

- Provide individualized and independent learning opportunities for students through the use of the library media center

- Enhance their personal knowledge and educational expertise by accessing professional information through the library media center, and

- Assess students collaboratively. (2001, p. 6)

Beyond Proficiency outlines strategies schools can employ to improve existing library media programs. It also defines the essentials of an effective library media program. According to *Beyond Proficiency*, an effective library media program uses flexible scheduling, integrates concepts of information literacy throughout the curriculum, provides technology, provides an appropriate learning environment, has adequate staffing, places an emphasis on resources, and has a mechanism in place for governance and management. Accompanying each of these goals are ideas and strategies for library media specialists and administrators to use to implement them in the school, as well as the impact of each. *Beyond Proficiency* also reviews how information literacy skills reinforce Kentucky's Learning Goals and provides a tool for evaluating a library program.

Beyond Proficiency is an excellent example of a winning statewide information literacy curriculum. The goals that it defines are key to educating a generation of information literate citizens, and perhaps more important, the strategies it recommends make the achievement of those goals feasible.

Utah

The Utah State Office of Education (1996) developed an information literacy curriculum for secondary schools titled *Library Media/Information Literacy Core Curriculum for Utah Secondary Skills*. The curriculum emphasizes information literacy. Utah recognizes the profusion of information and the importance of information skills to Utah's students' success in school and life.

Similar to the Kentucky *Beyond Proficiency* effort, the *Library Media/Information Literacy Core Curriculum* emphasizes the importance of collaboration. The library media specialist and the classroom teacher must collaborate to create an effective information literacy curriculum. The program defines three roles for the library media specialist within the school: information specialist, curriculum consultant, and teacher. When the library media specialist's role is defined in this way, it is possible for the library media specialist to move beyond the walls of the library and become a dynamic and important figure—essential to the development of an information literacy curriculum for the school.

The *Library Media/Information Literacy Core Curriculum* specifies the Big6™ Skills approach to information problem solving (Eisenberg & Berkowitz, 1988) as the structure on which to build an information literacy skills curriculum. The Big6 is a highly useful approach to solving information problems and can be integrated throughout the curriculum. The steps in the Big6 are

1. Task Definition,

2. Information Seeking Strategies,

3. Location & Access,

4. Use of Information,

5. Synthesis, and

6. Evaluation.

According to the *Library Media/Information Literacy Core Curriculum*, "the Big6 Information Problem-Solving Process places the secondary library media/information literacy core curriculum, not in isolation, but as an integral part of all the other subject area core curricula" (Utah State Office of Education, 1996, p. ii).

The Utah State Office of Education states that the mission of the Utah *Library Media/Information Literacy Core Curriculum* is, "to ensure that all students are effective users of ideas and information in all formats" (p. ii). This is enacted through the program's interdisciplinary approach, which places an emphasis on process, and promotes confidence in students' problem-solving abilities.

The Utah *Library Media/Information Literacy Core Curriculum* provides clear direction and specific strategies for schools wishing to create an effective information literacy curriculum. The Big6 Skills process gives educators an excellent model for the development of curriculum and skills. The curriculum envisioned in this program could also easily be extended to the primary and post-secondary level.

Washington

The Office of the Superintendent of Public Instruction (OSPI) and the Washington Library Media Association (WLMA) (2001) worked together to produce *WLMA and OSPI Essential Skills for Information Literacy*. This document is designed as a tool for classroom teachers and library media specialists when planning collaboratively or in curriculum development.

The *Essential Skills* are foundationally different from many other state information literacy documents in that besides outlining characteristics of an information literate student they also constitute a research process model. As defined by WLMA and OSPI, the key information literacy skills are

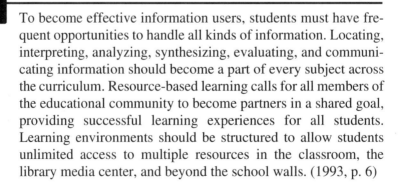

- The student recognizes a need for information.

- The student constructs strategies for locating information.

- The student locates and accesses information.

- The student evaluates and extracts information.

- The student organizes and applies information.

- The student evaluates the process and product. (OSPI & WLMA, 2001)

The *Essential Skills* outline benchmarks for each component of the information literacy skills at the fourth, seventh, and tenth grade levels.

Wisconsin

In 1993, the Wisconsin Educational Media Association (WEMA) released "Information Literacy: A Position Paper on Information Problem-Solving." This document, adopted by the American Association of School Librarians (AASL) in 1994, states that information literacy skills are absolutely necessary for student success in an information economy. The position paper describes what is required to make an information literacy curriculum a reality, outlines information problem-solving skills based on the Eisenberg and Berkowitz Big6 model, argues that resource-based learning provides opportunities for the development of these skills, and suggests that all educators participate in the information literacy process:

> To become effective information users, students must have frequent opportunities to handle all kinds of information. Locating, interpreting, analyzing, synthesizing, evaluating, and communicating information should become a part of every subject across the curriculum. Resource-based learning calls for all members of the educational community to become partners in a shared goal, providing successful learning experiences for all students. Learning environments should be structured to allow students unlimited access to multiple resources in the classroom, the library media center, and beyond the school walls. (1993, p. 6)

The ideas presented in WEMA's position paper are incorporated in and extended by the State of Wisconsin Department of Public Instruction's Model Academic Standards for Information and Technology Literacy, published in 1998. The document is one of nine standards documents developed by the Department of Public Instruction. The definition of information and technology literacy presented in the standards is both visionary and practical: "Information and Technology Literacy is the ability of an individual, working independently or with others, to use tools, resources, processes, and systems responsibly to access and evaluate information in any medium, and to use that information to solve problems, communicate clearly, make informed decisions and construct new knowledge, products, or systems" (State of Wisconsin Department of Public Instruction, 1998, p. 1). Four content standards are incorporated within the Information and Technology Literacy Standards: Media and Technology, Information and Inquiry, Independent Learning, and The Learning Community. Each contains detailed performance standards students should reach before graduating from grades 4, 8, and 12.

The "Media and Technology" standard states that students must be able to use a variety of technologies to find, organize, and synthesize information. Students will

- Use common media and technology terminology and equipment

- Identify and use common media formats

- Use a computer and productivity software to organize and create information

- Use a computer and communications software to access and transmit information

- Use media and technology to create and present information

- Evaluate the use of media and technology in a production or presentation. (1998, pp. 4-5)

Students graduating from high school are expected to have comprehensive experience with a variety of technologies and applications.

The second content standard, "Information and Inquiry," argues that students must be able to "access, evaluate, and apply information efficiently and effectively from a variety of sources in print, non-print, and electronic formats to meet personal and academic needs" (1998, p. 8). The performance standards associated with "Information and Inquiry" are similar to the steps in the information problem-solving model of the Big6 approach and presented in the WEMA position paper. Students will

- Define the need for information

- Develop information seeking strategies

- Locate and access information sources

- Evaluate and select information from a variety of print, non-print, and electronic formats

- Record and organize information

- Interpret and use information to solve the problem or answer the question

- Communicate the results of research and inquiry in an appropriate format

- Evaluate the information product and process. (1998, pp. 8-9)

"Independent Learning," the third content standard, requires students to use their technology and information skills independently to pursue personal and academic goals. This standard includes characteristics of media literacy and directs students to be discriminating consumers of a variety of media. To demonstrate mastery of the "Independent Learning" standards, students will

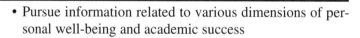

- Pursue information related to various dimensions of personal well-being and academic success

- Appreciate and derive meaning from literature and other creative expressions of information

- Develop competence and selectivity in reading, listening, and viewing

- Demonstrate self-motivation and increasing responsibility for their learning. (1998, p. 12)

The final content standard is "The Learning Community." The importance of being able to work as a part of a group and to respect intellectual property rights is emphasized. To meet these performance standards, students must

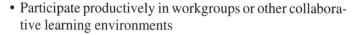

- Participate productively in workgroups or other collaborative learning environments

- Use information, media, and technology in a responsible manner

- Respect individual property rights

- Recognize the importance of intellectual freedom and access to information in a democratic society. (1998, pp. 14)

As a whole, these standards give educators a comprehensive guide for providing their students with skills necessary for life in an information society. The *Information and Technology Literacy Standards* document was distributed to all schools in the state of Wisconsin, along with rubrics, sample lessons, and strategies for integrating information literacy skills into the curriculum. With the publication of the Standards, the State of Wisconsin Department of Public Instruction has shown its dedication to preparing students for the workplace of the future.

Combining Information Literacy and National Content Standards

As we learned in Chapter 4, information literacy skills must not be taught in isolation but as integral components of the investigative and learning process. Efforts to combine subject area standards with information literacy standards show how this goal may be achieved.

Minnesota's Inquiry Process

Dalbotten (1998) examined the similarities among Minnesota's Inquiry Process, the national content standards of 12 disciplines, and information literacy skills as defined by the Big6™ information problem-solving process. The Inquiry Process, specified as the ability to conduct research and communicate findings, is one component of Minnesota's Graduation Standards in the High Standards section of the Profile of Learning. Minnesota's Inquiry Process involves the ability to

- Generate questions

- Determine feasibility

- Collect data

- Reduce and organize data

- Display data

- Compile conclusions/more questions. (Dalbotten, 1998, p. 32)

Noting that the national content standards "affirm the shift from learning isolated facts to becoming a self-directed learner who uses inquiry skills throughout life" (p. 48), Dalbotten created a series of charts to cross-correlate the inquiry process with specific components of national content standards (see Appendix F). These charts illustrate that inquiry skills are present within the national content standards of the 12 disciplines. Library media specialists may use these charts to help students transfer the inquiry process from one discipline to another (Dalbotten, 1998).

Oregon Common Curriculum Goals

The Oregon Educational Media Association published draft information literacy guidelines that connect and correlate the Oregon Common Curriculum Goals and the *Information Literacy Standards for Student Learning* developed by AASL and AECT. The guidelines were developed by an ad hoc committee of the Oregon Educational Media Association. The introduction to the document compares the learning process and the information search process.

The learning process and the information search process mirror each other: students actively seek to construct meaning from the sources they encounter and to create products that shape and communicate meaning effectively. Core elements in both learning and information theory converge to suggest that developing expertise in accessing, evaluating, and using information is the authentic learning that modern education seeks to promote (Steinke, 1997).

The ad hoc committee created benchmark statements that relate the library media program to the Oregon Common Curriculum Goals for English media and technology, reading, writing, and literature. In four areas—science, the social sciences, health education, and the arts—the committee went a step further, creating benchmark statements as well as content standards. A draft of the committee's work may be accessed at http://www.oema.net/infolit/infolit.html.

The *Information Literacy Guidelines: Scientific Inquiry* (see Table 5.1) demonstrate how these elements can be brought together to create an integrated instructional program.

Table 5.1 Oregon Educational Media Association (OEMA), Information Literacy Guidelines: Scientific Inquiry (2000)

Common Curriculum Goals	Content Standards	AASL/AECT National Standards
Design and conduct scientific investigations using knowledge of unifying concepts and processes, appropriate tools and techniques.	Use information resources to design and conduct scientific investigations using knowledge of unifying concepts and processes, appropriate tools and techniques.	Access information efficiently and effectively . . . 1. recognizes the need for information; 2. recognizes that accurate and comprehensive information is the basis for intelligent decision making; 3. formulates questions based on information needs; 4. identifies a variety of potential sources of information; 5. develops and uses successful strategies for locating information. AASL/AECT #1.
Use analysis and interpretation to formulate explanations and draw reasonable conclusions based on the results of an investigation.	Use information resources to formulate explanations and draw reasonable conclusions based on the results of an investigation.	Evaluates information critically and competently. . . 1. determines accuracy, relevance and comprehensiveness; 2. distinguishes among facts, point of view, and opinion; 3. identifies inaccurate and misleading information; 4. selects information appropriate to the problem or question at hand. AASL/AECT #2
Communicate investigations, explanations and conclusions.	Use information resources to communicate investigations, explanations and conclusions.	Uses information effectively and creatively . . . 1. organizes information for practical application; 2. integrates new information into one's own knowledge; 3. applies information in critical thinking and problem solving; 4. produces and communicates information and ideas in appropriate formats. AASL/AECT #3
Describe the role of science and technology in local, national and global issues.	Use information resources to understand the role of science and technology in local, national and global issues.	Practices ethical behavior in regard to information and information technology . . . 1. respects the principles of intellectual freedom; 2. respects intellectual property rights; 3. uses information technology responsibly. AASL/AECT #8

Reprinted with permission from OEMA from http://www.oema.net/infolit/sci.html.

Summary

National and state efforts are focusing on improving education. With the passage of the Goals 2000: Educate America Act, subject matter organizations were able to obtain funding to develop standards in their respective subject areas. The No Child Left Behind Act of 2001 places even greater emphasis on standards, requiring each state to develop core subject area standards for grades K–12. Analysis shows that information literacy skills are implicit in the National Education Goals and national content standards documents. Let's summarize the key points:

- The Goals 2000: Educate America Act, signed into law on March 31, 1994, by President Clinton, contains eight National Education Goals. Members of the organizations represented in the NFIL formed a panel to participate in a Delphi study that examined these goals in terms of information literacy. The Delphi panel agreed that three of the goals demonstrate the critical nature of information literacy to our information society: Goal 1: School Readiness; Goal 3: Student Achievement and Citizenship; and Goal 6: Adult Literacy and Lifelong Learning.

- An analysis of national content standards documents reveals that they all focus on lifelong learning, the ability to think critically, and the use of new and existing information for problem solving.

- Individual states are creating initiatives to ensure that students attain information literacy skills by the time they graduate from high school. Kentucky's *Beyond Proficiency: Achieving a Distinguished Library Media Program*, Utah's *Library Media/Information Literacy Core Curriculum for Utah Secondary Skills*, and California's *From Library Skills to Information Literacy: A Handbook for the 21st Century* are all examples of what states are doing to focus on the importance of information literacy skills for their students.

- National content standards, state standards, and information literacy skills terminology may vary; however all have common components relating to information literacy. Library media specialists and teachers may use these analyses to integrate information literacy skills with subject area instruction.

Chapter

K–12 Education: Restructuring and Information Literacy

6

Educational philosophies are shifting to place more emphasis on a process approach to learning. Costa (1993) states: "As we abandon traditional views of education, the skills of thinking and problem solving will replace discrete subject areas as the core of the curriculum and will lead to changes in instruction and assessment" (p. 50). In this chapter we discuss the relationship between information literacy and the restructuring of K–12 education.

Many educational institutions place emphasis on acquisition and retention of prescribed content and encourage students to work individually to achieve those ends. Unfortunately, this type of learning doesn't always prepare students to transfer and apply knowledge. Gardner (1993) points out that students who learn content through exercises and drills are able to do well on tests by giving correct answers. However, many "A" students fail miserably at applying their knowledge to real problems once they are outside the classroom. Through a restructuring process, educators are now placing emphasis on lifelong learning, on process as well as content, and on cooperative learning. Content is important, but students will "learn from the content rather than of the content" (Costa, 1993, p. 50).

As a result of restructuring, the roles of the teacher and the learner are shifting. At one time, the teacher was seen as the possessor of knowledge and the students as empty containers to be filled. To prepare students for the challenges of the workplace of the future, teachers are now taking on new roles as facilitators, instructional designers, and collaborative researchers. The teacher is viewed less as the "sage on the stage" and more as the "guide on the side."

To focus on process and learning from the content, educators are turning to various forms of resource-based learning: authentic learning, problem-based learning, and work-based learning.

Resource-Based Learning

Resource-based learning is often confused with resource-based teaching. When a teacher selects and uses a variety of resources such as newspapers, magazines, Web sites, or multimedia in addition to the textbook to construct a lesson, the teacher is using resource-based teaching. The students benefit from this approach since their learning experience is enriched beyond the textbook; however, the focus remains on the teacher. In resource-based learning, a variety of resources is also used, but the focus is shifted to the student, and the learner is at the center of the environment. Resource-based learning emphasizes the inquiry approach to learning, with the teacher taking on the role of facilitator (Haycock, 1991). Breivik and Senn (1998) further clarify the difference by referring to a 1977 *International Dictionary of Education* definition of resource-based learning as "a learning mode wherein the pupil learns from his own interaction with a range of learning resources rather than from class expository" (p. 12).

For example, a semester-long research project is a major requirement of the environmental science course taught at Cicero-North Syracuse High School (Cicero, New York). The class is run in seminar fashion, and students present their research results to the class. Topics are individually selected on the basis of the students' personal interests and are approved by the teacher. The teacher has collaborated with library media specialists to develop a rubric for assessing the project. Library media specialists also meet with students on an individual basis throughout the semester to assist them with information literacy skills. The library media specialists

- help students create and carry out search strategies,

- assist students in assessing whether their information resources are appropriate to the topic,

- suggest additional resources if they are needed,

- help students locate appropriate information within resources, and

- assist in the creation of multimedia presentations.

Authentic Learning

Students engaged in authentic learning construct meaning through disciplined inquiry and work toward products or performances that have meaning beyond success in school (Newmann & Wehlage, 1993). Through authentic learning, students address and investigate real world problems or personal situations.

An example of an interdisciplinary authentic learning approach linking biology, U.S. history, and American literature is described by Krovetz et al. (1993). The interdisciplinary team of teachers who developed the assignment agreed that through authentic learning, all students would be able to

1. articulate the purpose of activity;

2. analyze and practice what they do know;

3. acknowledge what they do not know;

4. formulate questions that lead to further knowledge;

5. synthesize connections between knowledge and life experience now and in the future; and

6. evaluate what was learned, how it was learned, and how it could be more effectively learned as a formal part of the assignment.

An authentic task relating to immigration and genealogy is reprinted in Figure 6.1 (page 98). Students completing this task use a variety of information literacy skills such as gathering information by interviewing and by observation, synthesizing information, and drawing conclusions.

Schack (1993) provides a less-structured example of authentic learning in her description of a personal scenario in an elementary school setting. A student remarked to her teacher that her mother had been feeding the family's house plants with water and gelatin. The teacher wondered out loud if feeding house plants with water and gelatin was advantageous. The student seemed interested in making a determination. Together, the student and teacher brainstormed and decided that a controlled experiment might be a way to find out. The teacher helped the student formulate a research question (Do rye seeds grow better with plain water, sugar water, salt water, gelatin and water, or no water?) and carry out the experiment. Throughout this process, the student learned information literacy skills:

• identifying a need for information (Is gelatin advantageous?),

• determining and accessing a source of information (designing and carrying out the experiment),

• organizing information (recording the data), and

• presenting information (analyzing and interpreting the data and presenting it to her Mom).

Purpose
1. To learn about the inheritance of specific genetic traits in your family,
2. To learn more about your family's immigration experience,
3. To increase your awareness of and tolerance for unrelated present-day immigrants.

History and Biology Section
Collect as much of the following information as possible:
- Names and relationships to you for as many family members as possible;
- Birth dates and places;
- Dates and locations of mating relationships (married or unmarried);
- Dates, causes, and locations of deaths;
- Nationalities (indicate fractions, if possible);
- Genetic family traits—select two from the list that you can trace through three generations. Select only traits that exist in both dominant and recessive form within your family tree.

History and English Section
Overall directions: Interview a member of your family who is the most knowledgeable and/or charming regarding your family's arrival in the United States. Write your questions ahead of time to elicit the required information. In addition, compose at least five of your own questions, based on the peculiar specifics of your personal situation. Remember, as you interview, to ask good follow-up questions based on the answers given to you. If you submit a taped interview along with your write-up, you will receive extra credit (in both history and English). The evaluation form is due with the assignment.

Required Information from Interview
WHEN: when the first member of your family arrived in the United States (circa OK);
WHO: name(s), age(s), relationship to one another, name changes upon/after arrival;
WHERE: from where they came, where they settled initially and later;

WHY: motivation for leaving native country (for example, hunger, unemployment, persecution. Explore the Push/Pull theory: What forced them to leave, and once they were established here did they pull other family members here as well?);
HOW: method of arrival in United States, how easy/hard the journey was;
EXPECTATIONS vs. REALITY: what differences did they find between their preconceived notions of the United States and reality.

To complete the assignment, you must first finish the interview. You have two options.

Option #1: Based on your interview, create a fictionalized account of the original immigrant experience of your family. This account must include some of the emotions felt by the family member(s) during the immigration experience. If these emotions don't come out in the interview, speculate what they might have been. Make sure you include any challenges or adventures that actually or might have occurred.

Option #2: Make your interview an observational experience. This means you must record the interview because your note-taking will largely focus on observational strategies. These include: complete character description focusing on physical traits, body language, tone of voice, language used, personality quirks; complete description of surrounding environment (show, don't tell); your own feelings (apprehension, excitement, curiosity) before, during, and after the interview. G

Dominant Traits	Recessive Traits
Dark eyes	Light eyes
Curl tongue	Can't curl tongue
Curly or wavy hair	Straight hair
Right-handed	Left-handed
Type A-B-AB blood	Type O blood
Near- or farsighted	Normal vision
Free earlobes	Attached earlobes
Normal hearing	Deafness from birth
Normal color vision	Color blind
Migraine headaches	No migraines

Figure 6.1. Authentic Task: Immigration and Genealogy. From M. Krovetz, D. Casterson, C. McKowen, & T. Willis, "Beyond Show & Tell," *Educational Leadership* 50, no. 7 (April 1993): 73-76. Reprinted with permission of the Association for Supervision and Curriculum Development. Copyright © 1993 by ASCD. All rights reserved.

The student also learned about treatment and control groups, how to mix and measure solutions, and how to use a graduated cylinder. Because she enlisted the help of another student who acted as a research assistant, she also learned about cooperating and working with others. Perhaps best of all, the student viewed herself as a competent researcher able to find solutions to problems.

Problem-Based Learning

Problem-based learning is closely related to authentic learning because the problems posed are real. Problem-based learning was developed by medical educators in the late 1960s and is used in more than 60 medical schools as a replacement for traditional lectures in the first two years of study. It has also been implemented in business schools; schools of education, architecture, law, engineering, and social work; and high schools (Barrows, 1996; Savery & Duffy, 1995).

To begin the process, teachers analyze the curriculum and pose a real problem reflective of the content area being taught. For example, students studying earth science might be asked "Can global warming be stopped?" This is a real problem and one on which National Oceanic and Atmospheric Administration (NOAA) scientists are presently working. The problem-based process would proceed as shown in Figure 6.2 (page 100).

The problem-based learning process as developed by Barrows (see Figure 6.3, pages 102–103) emphasizes critical thinking, linking old knowledge to new knowledge, application of knowledge, cooperative learning, and information literacy skills. Interestingly, a study has shown that students who learned content through problem-based learning and those who learned content in a more traditional manner scored equally well on standardized tests measuring their content acquisition (Gallagher & Stepien, 1996).

Work-Based Learning

In an effort to apply academic learning to the real world, a growing number of schools are forming partnerships with businesses. These partnerships are encouraged by the School-to-Work Opportunities Act of 1994. More than simple field trips or informal observation sessions, effective work-based learning programs foster technical competence, an understanding of the nature of work within a larger context, an ability to apply practical knowledge, and a recognition of the value of lifelong learning (Hamilton & Hamilton, 1997). Through structured partnerships with businesses and manufacturers, student apprentices also gain social skills, personal confidence, and an understanding of the expectations of the workplace.

Introduction:

To introduce the concept, the teacher shows a short video on global warming.

Discussion: (to propose hypotheses, identify facts, identify learning issues, and propose an action plan)

Following the video, students, in small groups, generate hypotheses based on their prior experiences and knowledge and list any pertinent facts. Students also discuss and identify learning issues—areas where they need to expand their knowledge in order to propose solutions to the problem. Each student has a chance to reflect verbally on the problem and take responsibility for specific learning issues. Students work as a team to develop an action plan. Throughout this process, the teacher acts as a facilitator.

Research and Resource Evaluation:

Students conduct research. They might interview a scientist, consult Web sites, use the library, or contact the National Oceanic and Atmospheric Administration (NOAA). Students meet to evaluate resources and discuss what was useful and what was not. The teacher acts as a consultant.

Problem Reexamination:

Students reexamine their original hypotheses and decide whether they want to change their hypotheses based on the facts they've gathered and learned. They identify additional learning issues and may formulate another action plan. Following this, the research and problem reexamination cycle repeats itself. The teacher acts as a facilitator.

Performance Presentation:

Student teams present possible solutions to the problem to the class. A discussion period follows each presentation. Again, the teacher acts as a facilitator.

Knowledge Abstraction:

Students summarize what they have learned.

Self Assessment:

Students reflect on their reasoning skills, information skills, group process skills, and learning skills.

Figure 6.2. Problem-Based Learning Example: Global Warming

One example of a school to work partnership involved a student at Binghamton (New York) High School and his work site coach at a company called Anitec. As a culminating activity to the student's apprenticeship, the coach gave him an architectural layout for a new silver analysis laboratory and asked him to prepare a functional design package for its electrical services. The following is a summary of the student's project, in terms of information literacy:

Identifies needed information and potential sources, develops successful search strategies and accesses sources of information including computer-based and other technologies:

The student interviewed lab technicians and engineers and read equipment specifications to identify and gather information about power requirements for test equipment, chemical exhaust fans, and general room power and lighting.

Evaluates information and organizes information for practical application:

The student analyzed the gathered information to determine the size of electrical circuits according to the National Electrical Code and to specify the various electrical components needed for the design.

Integrates new information into an existing body of knowledge and uses information in critical thinking and problem solving:

The design package developed by the student included several architectural auto-cad plan-view drawings, schematics, diagrams, a bill of materials, standard construction notes, and a scope of work. Through the project, the student demonstrated his ability to apply knowledge acquired through his apprenticeship and through his regular academic courses. (Hamilton & Hamilton, 1997)

Assessment of Information Literacy Skills

The emphasis on a process approach to education requires a concomitant shift in forms of assessment. Instead of completing a teacher-prepared examination requiring rote memorization of facts, students are asked to demonstrate and assess their own learning. Through authentic assessment, students reflect on their own learning, growth, and the processes by which skills have been achieved. Some of the forms of authentic assessment include portfolios, learning and research logs, and rubrics.

FACILITATING THE GROUP PROCESS

◆ **Guide students through the PBL Process**
- Proper sequence of phases
- Proper attention to each phase

◆ **Communicate at metacognitive level**
- Do not provide information
- Do not respond evaluatively

◆ **Probe student's knowledge/reasoning deeply**
- Challenge terms, opinions, "facts" (whether you agree or not)
- "Why? Why? Why?"

◆ **Involve all students in PBL process**

◆ **Modulate the challenge/flow of the process**
- Avoid overwhelming students
- Avoid student boredom

◆ **Monitor/manage interpersonal dynamics**
- Encourage group responsibility

◆ **Make educational diagnoses**
- Attend to problems of
- Knowledge/understanding
- Reasoning/critical thinking
- Self-directed study
- Initiative/diligence
- Ask students to reflect on these areas

◆ **Model, support, then fade from the process by encouraging students to:**
- Take responsibility for the PBL process
- Interact with each other
- Become independent learners

◆ **When in doubt:**
- Opt for student-centered action
- Let the process work (hold back)
- Ask for problem synthesis
- Ask "Why?"

Department of Medical Education
Southern Illinois University
School of Medicine   5/97

Figure 6.3. Problem-Based Learning Chart Developed by Barrows. ©1993. Reprinted with the author's permission. Problem-based Learning Institute, Lamphier High School/PBL Laboratory School, 1300 N. 11th Street, Springfield, IL.

FACILITATING THE GROUP PROCESS

◆ **Introductions**
◆ **Climate Setting**
  • Tutor's role/students' role
  • Open thinking; everyone contributes
  • Silence is assent

STARTING A NEW PROBLEM

◆ **Encountering the problem**
  • Establish objectives
  • Present the problem situation and assign tasks appropriate to problem format
  • Bring the problem home if necessary
  • Describe the product/performance required
◆ **Reasoning through the problem**
  • Hypothesis generation/inquiry
  • Analysis/synthesis

Hypotheses	Facts	Learning Issues	Action Plan
Brain-storming about: causation, effect &/or résolution	Syntheses of information obtained through hypotheses guided inquiry	List of what needs to be learned in order to complete the problem task	Things that need to be done in order to complete the problem task

◆ **Commitment as to probable outcome**
◆ **Learning issue shaping and distribution**
◆ **Resource identification**

STARTING A NEW PROBLEM

PROBLEM FOLLOW-UP

◆ **Resources used and their critique**
◆ **A summary of the problem**
◆ **Reassess the problem**
  • Start with changes needed in hypotheses column

Hypotheses	Problem Information	Learning Issues	Action Plan
Revise in light of new knowledge	Apply new information. Inquire for additional information. Summarize problem and its possible resolution.	Identify new (if necessary) or refine old.	Actions needed to complete performance/ presentation

◆ **Knowledge abstraction and summary**
  • Articulate definitions, concepts, abstractions, principles
  • Use diagrams, lists, flow charts, concept maps, lists
◆ **Self- and peer-evaluation**
  • Reasoning through the problem
  • Digging out information using appropriate resources
  • Assisting the group with its tasks
  • Gaining and refining knowledge
◆ **Tutor and group evaluation**

PERFORMANCE PRESENTATION

Figure 6.3. (*cont.*)

Portfolio Assessment

Portfolios allow students to demonstrate learning and growth over a period of time. The portfolio should be a "deliberate compilation, gathered according to a plan, for use by an identified reader or readers for specific needs or purposes" (Callison, 1993, p. 32). It may contain not only a student's final products or best work but also items that provide evidence of the processes used in the development of such items. Gardner refers to these as "process-folios" and suggests that they contain brainstorming strategies, drafts, critiques, journal entries identifying new understandings, and suggestions for future study (Gardner, 1993). As a starting point for information literacy skills self-assessment, Callison expanded questions originally developed by Marland (see Figure 6.4).

To show evidence of information literacy skills development, the portfolio may include references to, and reflections on, resources that have influenced the student's learning. For example, students working on term papers may incorporate the actual articles they read while researching their papers—including articles that were rejected. Students can reflect on these articles and provide reasons for including some references and excluding others. They can describe the processes they used to identify and gather the resources, and they can reflect on how and what they learned about their information-searching skills.

Learning and Research Logs

Reflection allows students to assimilate new information and identify processes that are helpful in completing the task at hand. Learning logs are especially useful in extracting information (Stripling, 1993). When students take notes, they divide their paper into two columns: one column for the actual information they are extracting from the source, and one column for their reflection, reactions, and comments. Students may note their feelings about the information, questions for further research, connections to known information, or comments about usage of that particular information.

A research log may be used to document the processes used in completing a particular project. Students may note their accomplishments, as well as any problems, questions, or frustrations they encountered. The library media specialist may comment by offering suggestions, giving encouragement, or asking questions for further exploration.

Rubrics for the Assessment of Information Literacy

Rubrics describe what learners should know and be able to do. Designed in the form of a matrix, rubrics contain target indicators and key behavior skills. Information literacy rubrics were designed by the Colorado State Department of Education (1996) to help educators assess students' progress toward achieving the goals of that state's *Model Information Literacy Guidelines* (1994). (See Chapter 5.)

What do I need to do?
Demonstrate your ability to:
- analyze the information task;
- analyze the audience's information need or demand;
- describe a plan of operation;
- select important or useful questions and narrow or define the focus of the assignment;
- describe possible issues to be investigated.

Where could I go?
Demonstrate your ability to:
- determine the best initial leads for relevant information;
- determine possible immediate access to background information (gaining the larger picture);
- consider information sources within and beyond the library.

How do I get to the information?
Demonstrate your ability to:
- identify relevant materials;
- sense relationships between information items;
- determine which resources are most likely to be authoritative and reliable;
- consider and state the advantages and disadvantages of bias present in resources;
- consider discovered facts and search for counterfacts;
- consider stated and personal opinions and search for counteropinions;
- determine extent of need for historical perspective.

How shall I use the resources?
Demonstrate your ability to:
- determine if information is pertinent to the topic;
- estimate the adequacy of the information;
- test validity of the information;
- focus on specific issues within the boundaries of the information obtained;
- group data in categories according to appropriate criteria;
- determine the advantages and disadvantages of different information formats and intellectual levels.

Of what should I make a record?
Demonstrate your ability to:
- extract significant ideas and summarize supporting, illustrative details;

- define a systematic method to gather, sort, and retrieve data;
- combine critical concepts into a statement of conclusions;
- restate major ideas of a complex topic in concise form;
- separate a topic into major components according to appropriate criteria;
- sequence information and data in order to emphasize specific arguments or issues.

Have I got the information I need?
Demonstrate your ability to:
- recognize instances in which more than one interpretation of material is valid and necessary;
- demonstrate that the information obtained is relevant to the issues of importance;
- if necessary, state a hypothesis or theme and match evidence to the focused goal of the paper or project;
- reflect, edit, revise, and determine if previous information search and analysis steps should be repeated.

How should I present it?
Demonstrate your ability to:
- place data in tabular form using charts, graphs, or illustrations;
- match illustrations and verbal descriptions for best impact;
- note relationships between or among data, opinions, or other forms of information;
- propose a new plan, create a new system, interpret historical events, and predict likely future happening;
- analyze the background and potential for reception of ideas and arguments of the intended audience;
- communicate orally and in writing to teachers and among peers.

What have I achieved?
Demonstrate your ability to:
- accept and give constructive criticism;
- reflect and revise again;
- describe the most valuable sources of information;
- estimate the adequacy of the information acquired and the need for additional resources;
- state future questions or themes for investigation;
- seek feedback from a variety of audiences.

Figure 6.4. Information Literacy Portfolio Questions. Adapted and reprinted from Daniel Callison, "The Potential for Portfolio Assessment," *School Library Media Annual* (Englewood, CO: Libraries Unlimited, 1994. Reprinted with the author's permission.

The Colorado *Rubrics for the Assessment of Information Literacy* (see Appendix G) tool allows teachers to identify what their students already know and what they need to learn in several broad areas of information literacy, including

- constructing meaning from information,

- creating a quality product,

- learning independently,

- participating as a group member, and

- using information and information technologies responsibly and ethically.

The benchmarks for these five areas are indicated along with measures for competence (In Progress, Essential, Proficient, Advanced). Educators need not expect that students will achieve advanced proficiency in each and every area. Rubrics are helpful in that they assess students' strengths and weaknesses and identify tangible goals for improvement.

Another form of information literacy rubric is presented by those designed around the Big6™ Skills. Since the Big6 is a process model, it lends itself well to rubrics measuring a student's achievement in any subject area. It can be expanded to include subject area standards, information literacy standards, and technology skills. One example of a rubric designed around the Big6 was presented by Janet Murray at the 2001 Big6 conference, available online at http://fp3e.adhost.com/big6/enewsletter/archives/e2_n4_conf/murray_ho.html.

Standardized Testing and Information Literacy

Standardized testing is a controversial topic in educational policy, but one that is a growing reality for American schools. The No Child Left Behind Act of 2001 places unprecedented emphasis on standardized tests; among its many reforms is the requirement that students in grades 3 through 8 be tested each year in reading and math. While implementing these tests presents a challenge for classroom teachers, school districts, states, and students, it creates an excellent opportunity for proponents of information literacy.

One key aspect of the bill's reforms is its directive that tests must be based on challenging state standards and must be comparable from year to year to ensure student progress. This creates a process model for the tests, which will need to show a student's grasp of higher level thinking skills rather than rote facts. This relates directly to the development of information literacy skills, and it is likely that as the No Child Left Behind reforms are implemented nationwide, researchers and policymakers will underscore the importance of these skills.

Research has proven that active, involved library media specialists have a positive impact on student achievement on standardized tests. A recent study of

Pennsylvania school libraries, *Measuring Up to Standards: The Impact of School Library Programs & Information Literacy in Pennsylvania Schools* (Lance et al, 2000b), found that Pennsylvania System of School Assessment reading scores rose with increases in support for the school library:

> The success of any school library information program in promoting high academic achievement depends fundamentally on the presence of adequate staffing—specifically each library should have at least one, full-time, certified school librarian with at least one full-time aide or other support staff member. For all three tested grades, the relationship between such staffing and PSSA reading scores is both positive and statistically significant. (p. 35)

Similar studies in Colorado (Lance et al., 2000a) and Alaska (Lance et al., 1999) found similar results. Clearly, there is an important role for information literacy specialists in an era of school reform, and it is now up to researchers and policymakers to grasp the promise for student achievement implicit in information literacy skills.

Summary

Educational restructuring makes information literacy skills a necessity as students seek to construct their own knowledge and create their own understandings. Key points in this chapter include the following:

- Educators are selecting various forms of resource-based learning (authentic learning, problem-based learning, and work-based learning) to help students focus on the process and to help students learn from the content. Information literacy skills are necessary components of each.

- The process approach to education is requiring new forms of student assessment. Students demonstrate their skills, assess their own learning, and evaluate the processes by which this learning has been achieved by preparing portfolios and learning and research logs, and using rubrics.

- The new era of standardized testing ushered in by the passage of the No Child Left Behind Act of 2001 presents both challenges and opportunities for information literacy instruction. Research has shown that an active, well-funded library media program positively affects student achievement on standardized tests.

Chapter

K–12 Education: Information Literacy Efforts

7

In this chapter we provide a number of examples of information literacy efforts in K–12 education. Examples range from those created on a state or regional level to those created in schools or districts by teams or individual classroom teachers or library media specialists.

A variety of examples of information literacy efforts in K–12 education are described in the print literature and found on the Internet. They range from state and regional ventures designed to coordinate information literacy standards within the curriculum to local efforts carried out by individual library media specialists and teachers to integrate information literacy skills with specific lessons or units of study.

Individual districts and schools, often through their library media programs, ultimately implement national and state information literacy guidelines. As noted earlier, the Colorado Study (Lance et al., 1992) makes it clear that library media programs make a difference in the quality of a student's education. It is up to school districts and individual schools to ensure that their library media programs are adequately funded and staffed to provide information literacy education.

Bellingham Schools

During the 1995–1996 school year, teachers at Bellingham Schools (Bellingham, Washington) worked in teams to create experiences that would engage their peers in the same type of integrated learning they hoped to offer their students. Teams selected topics from curriculum guides and designed learning experiences that incorporated technology and higher order thinking skills from Bloom's Taxonomy (Bloom, 1956). One project challenged teachers to use information found on the Internet to select an endangered species, investigate the habitat of the species, and suggest an alternate location where the species might thrive.

In an effort to extend teachers' understandings further, a team of 12 teachers and library media specialists under the leadership of Jamie McKenzie, then director of libraries, media, and technology, designed Bellingham Schools Course Online: Information Literacy and the Net (http://www.bham.wednet. edu/studentgal/onlineresearch/oldonline/literacy.htm) during the fall of 1997. This eight-hour online staff development course incorporates information literacy, visual literacy, textual literacy, and numerical literacy, as well as Gardner's Seven Intelligences as teachers investigate online resources (J. McKenzie, personal communication, March 28, 1998) (see Figure 7.1).

Bellingham Schools
Course Outline:
Information Literacy
and the Net

This eight hour staff development course emphasizes student investigations as vehicles to explore the information available over the Internet. The course engages participants in learning the **Research Cycle,** several types of literacy, **Gardner's Seven Intelligences** and much more.

This course is primarily about Information Literacy and Information Problem-Solving. Learning to use the software is secondary.

If you would like to download these lessons to use them locally, please contact Jamie McKenzie for permission.

Module 1

Question: What is Information Literacy? How many other literacies exist?

Achievement Targets: Construct a working definition of the concept "information literacy" and gain an overview of class goals and content.

Continued on next page

Delivery Strategy: This is an opportunity for small group discussion and the introduction of "learning journals" which participants will keep open throughout all the sessions on a word processor.
Go to Module One

Module 2

Question: What is Visual Literacy?

Achievement Targets:
1) Construct a definition of visual literacy
2) Explore some visual resources on the Net
3) Learn to save graphics
4) Learn to navigate: the Back button, the Go menu, the Stop button

Delivery Strategy: Visit the Library of Congress site and explore its great collections of photographs, stopping to analyze one photograph in considerable depth. For this lesson go to Visual Literacy

Module 3

Question: What is Textual Literacy?

Achievement Targets:
1) Construct definition of text literacy
2) Explore electronic text resources on the Net
3) Learn more about how to navigate with Netscape: parts of the URL (address)
4) Learn to save text files by copying and pasting text or saving a file to the "H" drive

Delivery Strategy: Participants will visit Project Bartleby at Columbia in order to see how electronic text differs from hard copy. For this lesson go to Textual Literacy

Module 4

Question: What is Numerical Literacy?

Achievement Targets:
1) Construct definition of numerical literacy
2) Explore some numerical resources on the Net
3) Learn how to save and then use datasets with a spreadsheet
4) File Management: anticipating the need for directories

Delivery Strategy: Visit the U.S. Census site and compare two counties in Connecticut using the data found there. For this lesson Go to Numerical Literacy

Module 5

Question: How might we use the Research Cycle to achieve literacy and build insight?

Achievement Targets: Review the steps of the **Research Cycle**.

Delivery Strategy: Readings and (ultimately) a video showing students working through the steps.

For this lesson go to: Research Cycle!

Continued on next page

Module 6

Question: In what ways do we gather information?

Achievement Targets: Gather information from the Web in order to make a decision on Which City is Best?

Delivery Strategy: Compare and contrast parks and recreation information about three cities using Mapquest

For this lesson go to: Gathering Information

Module 7

Question: How might we Sort, Analyze and Synthesize Information most effectively?

Achievement Targets: Experience the challenge of creating an answer from the information gathered.

Delivery Strategy: Synthesize findings recorded in Works during Module 6

For this lesson go to: Sorting, Analyzing and Synthesizing Information

Module 8

Question: How do we provide the social foundations and group skills needed to make this kind of research work? How will we measure student progress with literacy?

Achievement Targets: Work with ESL's and various documents for information literacy and assessment throughout the research cycle.

Delivery Strategy: Review and consider use of assessment documents

For this lesson go to: Assessment, Teamwork, and Essential Student Learnings

Module 9

Question: In what ways could this type of learning support multiple intelligences and different learning styles?

Achievement Targets: Brainstorm strategies for different learning styles and intelligences.

Delivery Strategy: Explore a page of definitions outlining and explaining Gardner's Multiple Intelligences.

For this lesson go to: Multiple Intelligences

Module 10

Question: Where are the good curriculum resources on the Web and how might I use them?

Achievement Targets: Bookmarks

Delivery Strategy: Visit sites on District Curriculum Pages. Go to Curriculum Page lesson.

Continued on next page

Module 11

Question: Where are the good teacher resources on the Web and how might I use them?

Achievement Targets: Bookmarks (continued)

Delivery Strategy: Visit, evaluate and consider the value of teacher sites. Go to Teacher Sites lesson.

Module 12

Question: Where are the good information sites for virtual field trips, weather and daily news? How might I use them?

Achievement Targets: Bookmarks (continued)

Delivery Strategy: Visit, evaluate and consider the value of virtual field trips, weather and daily news sections of the district home page. Go to Real Time Research Resource lesson.

Module 13

Question: Now that I've visited a variety of good sites, how will I use this information to design an effective learning experience for students?

Achievement Targets: Importance of using pre-selected sites

Delivery Strategy: Pick one site that has potential to develop the research cycle, and create a lesson involving an essential question to use with a specific group of students.

Module 14

Question: How do we use indexes and search engines to find information efficiently on the Web?

Go to lesson.

Achievement Targets: Search Engines, Indexes

Delivery Strategy: Participants will test the features of two different search engines in order to see which one returns the best information in the top ten "hits." They will also learn how indexes differ from search engines.

Module 15

Question: How do I connect globally using Telecommunications and Mail?

Achievement Targets: Global activities, Mail

Delivery Strategy: With you and your partner's classroom needs in mind, review five or more activities from each of these groups: Problem Solving Projects, Information Collections, and Interpersonal Exchanges. During the second half of the module, in small groups, explain how you could use the lessons effectively with your students. Internet Projects

Continued on next page

Module 16

Question: How does your lesson plan support the district policy?

Achievement Targets: Familiarity with the Bellingham School District Board Policy as it pertains to Internet Policy and Procedures for Students.

Delivery Strategy: Scan the District Policy to see its main components. Relate the policy to lesson plans.

Go to the Policy lesson . . .

Credits: This class was invented by the following Bellingham staff members: Tara Felder, John Schick, Carolyn Hinshaw, Linda Lamb, Eileen Andersen, Dar New, Jamie McKenzie, and Mary Gilson. Return to Bellingham Schools Home Page, Copyright Notice Copyright, 1996, Bellingham Public Schools. All rights reserved. These lessons may be copied by non-profit, public learning institutions only for use with their own staff. If they are used in this manner, proper credit must be given on each page citing the source. All other purposes are expressly prohibited without explicit permission. Revised 4/1/99.

Figure 7.1. Bellingham Schools Course Outline. Reprinted with the author's permission from http://www.bham.wednet.edu/studentgal/onlineresearch/oldonline/literacy.htm.

Big6 for Kids Web Site

The Big6's Web presence has long been a trusted tool for educators seeking a logical way to integrate information literacy and technology skills into the curriculum. Recently, the creators of the Big6 launched a section of the Web site especially for students, including games, activities, and pointers that encourage information literacy skills and reinforce Big6 concepts.

The Big6 for Kids Web site is divided by grade level. The section for kindergarten through second grade students includes more games and informal activities to develop basic skills. An example of this is "Go Fishing with the Super3," a game designed by Barbara A. Jansen (see Figure 7.2). This activity reviews the Super3, an information literacy model for very young students, as kids design and create a fishing game out of household objects.

While the resources for younger students focus on having fun with information literacy, the section designed for high school students presents useful tools to help secondary students succeed. Writing tips, ideas for choosing research projects, and an excellent research paper organizer are included on the site, as well as resources for teachers and parents.

Figure 7.2. Go Fishing with the Super3. By Barbara A. Jansen. Reprinted with permission from
http://www.big6.com/kidsshowarticle.php?id=224.

California Technology Assistance Project—Region VII

The Information Literacy Task Force of Region VII California Technology Assistance Project, encompassing Fresno, King, Madera, Mariposa, Merced, and Tulare Counties, developed information literacy guidelines for grades kindergarten through 12. The introduction to the guidelines states:

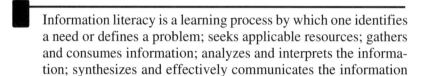

Information literacy is a learning process by which one identifies a need or defines a problem; seeks applicable resources; gathers and consumes information; analyzes and interprets the information; synthesizes and effectively communicates the information to others and evaluates the process.

Information literate people are avid readers and consumers of artistic and cultural information. They are critical and creative thinkers, interested learners, and organized investigators. They use the information responsibly and are effective communicators. They collaborate with others, both in person and through technologies in designing, developing and evaluating information projects or products. As they do so, their skill in using information technology increases.

Information literacy skills are lifelong learning skills which require a student to apply higher level thinking. Information literacy skills are not to be taught in isolation but rather continuously integrated throughout the curriculum. They are most meaningful when taught within an inter-disciplinary unit or within a unit addressing an authentic, real-life need or problem. (Undated)

The Information Literacy Task Force consisted of a teacher/principal, a teacher, two library media teachers, a library media specialist, and Dr. David Loertscher, professor at the School of Library and Information Science at San Jose State University. The information literacy model focuses on the investigative process and contains seven categories divided into subskills:

- identifies a need or a problem,
- seeks applicable resources,
- gathers information,
- analyzes information,
- interprets and synthesizes information,
- communicates information, and
- evaluates process and product.

A unique element offered by the task force is a chart describing information literacy development (see Table 7.1).

Table 7.1 California Technology Assistance Project (CTAP): Information Literacy Development

Student Characteristics	Types of Information	Help and Guidance
Beginner: 1. Has little or no experience using a wide variety of information sources. 2. Requires a great deal of teacher direction and support. 3. Has limited skill in defining, organizing and carrying out a project. 4. Has little experience in analyzing and interpreting information. 5. Lacks critical thinking skills. 6. Developing as an avid reader. 7. Requires skill development in technology tools.	**Sources Beginner:** 1. Guided to a limited number of pre-selected sources. 2. Simple, straight forward, clear and concise, and readily available. 3. Appropriate reading, viewing, listening, and conceptual levels. 4. Format and appearance of information is inviting. 5. Simple searching mechanisms or structure: student can easily find information (one-step lookup).	**Beginner:** 1. Conduct mini-lessons about specific sources. 2. Closely monitor students as they encounter information. 3. Introduce information literacy components. 4. Introduce simple presentation models.
Intermediate: 1. Takes on a project with enthusiasm, but topic is often too general. 2. Has experience using a few information sources well. 3. Is easily frustrated as the project develops. 4. Lacks skill in gathering relevant information. 5. Is developing skills of information analysis and interpretation. 6. Is an independent and interested reader. 7. Is developing more independent technology tool skills.	**Intermediate:** 1. Both simple and a few complex information sources are accessible. 2. Complex enough that persistence and skill are required to yield results (may require two-step lookup). 3. The conceptual level of the source requires better reading, viewing, listening and thinking skills. 4. The source may use coding or unfamiliar symbols that must be translated by the user. 5. Number and variety of information sources and technologies are expanding.	**Intermediate:** 1. Ensure access to a variety of resources. 2. Conduct mini-lessons about locating and searching a variety of information sources. 3. Assist students in recognizing and filtering for relevant information. 4. Introduce analysis and interpretation of information. 5. Support and guide students as they encounter information. 6. Help students refocus or expand their thinking as they encounter difficulties. 7. Teach the information literacy components and technology skills. 8. Introduce a wider variety of presentation models.
Advanced: 1. An avid reader. 2. A critical thinker. 3. An interested learner. 4. An organized investigator. 5. An effective communicator. 6. A responsible information user. A skilled user of technology tools.	**Advanced:** 1. Complex and sophisticated information sources are accessible. 2. Contain a variety of view points and perspectives. 3. Persistence in searching exploits the richness of a source. 4. Complex arrangement, format, appearance, or coding is not considered a major barrier. 5. Emphasize primary sources as well as secondary sources. 6. Provide a full range of information technologies.	**Advanced:** 1. Encourage use of the full range of information sources and technologies. 2. Provide more sophisticated searching strategies. 3. Challenge student's critical thinking. 4. Provide feedback as the project progresses. 5. Support the creation of quality and sophisticated presentations.

Reprinted with the author's permission from http://www.ctap.fcoe.k12.ca.us/ctap/Info.Lit/Benchmarks.html.

The chart helps teachers identify students' information literacy development by comparing the students' characteristics with the chart. Teachers can then use the chart to suggest information sources to the students and use appropriate instructional strategies.

Project SCORE History Social Science

The Schools of California Online Resources for Education (SCORE) provides teachers and students with quality resources on the Web. The SCORE History Social Science site notes:

> A major goal of SCORE History-Social Science is to provide a resource to build the information literacy of students so that they are more able to function as effective workers and citizens in an era when everyone is continuously bombarded by data. Information literacy helps people deal with this data glut by developing the ability to plan a resource-based project, think critically about data, research for needed information and create and present a new synthesis to others using technology. (Undated)

The site provides a chart coordinating information literacy skills with the "Domains of History Social Science Thinking" (see Figure 7.3).

A major goal of SCORE History-Social Science is to provide a resource to build the information literacy of students so that they are more able to function as effective workers and citizens in an era when everyone is continuously bombarded by data. "Information literacy" helps people deal with this data glut by developing the ability to plan a resource-based project, think critically about data, research for needed information and create and present a new synthesis to others using technology. The following is a first draft identifying the skills that our students will need. These skills are closely related to the intellectual processes that teachers have long identified as the "Domains of History-Social Science Thinking." I would appreciate your comment and feedback.—Peg Hill, San Bernardino County Superintendent of Schools Office

INFORMATION LITERACY SKILLS
"Access, evaluate and use information from a variety of sources."—Chris Doyle

Planning Skills Related to Information Literacy
- Recognizes when there is a need for information to solve a problem or develop an idea
- Formulates questions based on information needs
- Brainstorms multiple strategies for approaching a problem or issue

Continued on next page

- Identifies, organizes and sequences tasks to complete an information based project
- Creates and organizes an effective research team
- Identifies tasks which need to be accomplished and assigns them to and manages their completion by various members of the research team

Domains of H/SS Thinking Related to Information Literacy
- Interprets history-social science data
    - Puts data into own words
    - Puts information in context
    - Reads and creates a logical interpretation of data derived from many different kinds of sources, such as media, charts, graphs, timelines, maps, etc.
- Relates historical events, people and eras
    - Shows similarities and differences
    - Compares and contrasts
    - Draws logical conclusions
    - Relates past to present
    - Uses social, political, economic concepts to understand the context in which information was created or used
- Analyzes cause and effect
    - Puts events in sequence
    - Shows multiple and related causes and effects
    - Distinguishes between correlation and cause and effect in related events
- Uses multiple perspectives
    - Takes the role or position of another and examines issues from that point of view
    - Makes multiple interpretations from the same evidence
    - Points out present assumptions, especially those that were not present in the past
    - Points out social norms of a home culture which are not present in another culture
- Supports a thesis
    - Takes a position or point of view based on evidence
    - Creates a logical argument in writing or speaking supported with relevant evidence

Other Thinking Skills Related to Information Literacy
- Evaluates the quality of information
    - Establishes authority
    - Determines accuracy, authenticity and relevance of information
    - Distinguishes among opinion, reasoned argument and fact
- Analyses messages from various sources for their design, form, structure and sequence
- Identifies the effects of camera angles, lighting, music, special effects, layout and sequence in a presentation
- Creates new information by synthesizing data from primary and secondary sources

Continued on next page

Searching/Researching Skills Related to Information Literacy
- Identifies potential sources of information
- Reads competently
- Locates, selects and analyzes information from multiple sources
- Integrates new information to existing knowledge
- Uses keywords effectively to search for information related to a topic
- Uses Boolean logic to narrow a database search
- Organizes and stores data in searchable formats

Presenting Skills Related to Information Literacy
- Knows many different kinds of presentation formats and the type of information they are best at conveying
- Selects a presentation format which matches the information being conveyed and the audience for which it is intended
- Organizes information for practical application
- Uses writing, speaking, drama and layout as needed to make an effective presentation

Resources on the SCORE pages were evaluated by history-social science leaders in California. Going beyond these links allows student access to unknown material. Each school site is responsible for evaluating resources for appropriateness in the local school community.

Figure 7.3. Domains of History Social Science Thinking. Reprinted with permission from http://score.rims.k12.ca.us/infolit.html.

According to Peg Hill, SCORE director, lessons and activities on the site ask students to access, evaluate, and use data from the Web to create meaning and support positions on issues. Problem-based lessons are marked with a score target addressing information literacy skills that require students to create and present new knowledge.

Forest Creek Elementary School

Students at Forest Creek Elementary School (Round Rock, Texas) engage in Big6™ Skills activities on developmentally appropriate levels (B. Jansen, personal communication, January 25, 1998). The information skills process is included in the prescribed Round Rock ISD Curriculum Standards. These skills are always integrated into the subject content standards—usually language arts, science, and social studies.

In all grades, the library staff collaborates with teachers to design lesson sequences that are based on the Big6 steps, beginning with the first level of the process—presenting the Curriculum Standard(s) as an information problem to solve. This provides motivation and rationale for the students to study content and a reason for them to use the Big6 to solve the problem. The librarian and the teachers try to create authentic problems to make the Curriculum Standards relevant to the students' needs and interests.

Beginning with kindergarten, the librarian works with the teachers to introduce the Big6 process to students. She uses puppets and a song she wrote to introduce a problem and each of the steps it takes to work through it. The six steps of the Big6 are presented in basic question form for kindergarten through second grade. The subskills are not presented in writing, but only in concept, as the teacher introduces the Big6 Skills. Primary sources (observation, survey, and interview) are used as much as possible. Print sources are used when appropriate, but young learners are never required to take notes independently. Note taking is accomplished through the use of Big6 buddies (older student or adults) who help the younger children find and record relevant information, or through note-taking triads (adult reading from information source, students critically listening and identifying relevant information, and adult taking relevant notes in words students can understand). Students are instructed to create developmentally appropriate products that best show results. Self-evaluation takes place beginning with simple peer evaluation in kindergarten, and written evaluation begins in the first grade.

Students in grades 3 through 5 begin defining tasks based on given information problems. The librarian and teachers develop the problem statements and give the students the opportunity to define the tasks to solve the problems. Very specific instruction is given for using each of the Big6 Skills, including the subskills, so those students will learn appropriate strategies to use the Big6 to acquire and use information. Independent use of the Big6 is not required at this grade level, but by the time students are in middle school and high school, they will have internalized the Big6 process enough to be able to use it independently. The use of technology is integrated in each of the Big6 Skills in grades K–5 whenever effective and appropriate and is taught at the point of need.

Kenneth R. Olson Middle School

Students at Olson Middle School (Tabernacle, New Jersey), and students from anywhere else in the world, can learn about information literacy skills by going to the Big6™–Dig It! Internet Web site developed by Shayne Russell, the school's educational media specialist. Students are asked to think about how they could find information about an archaeological dig and are taught information literacy skills along the way (see Figure 7.4, pages 122–124).

The Web pages are an abbreviated version of a 40-minute Hyperstudio lesson on the Big6 that can be used to research ancient civilizations of the Southwest. The media specialist wanted the students to know that people in the field were doing original research and making discoveries just as the students do in their research projects. The Hyperstudio lesson was a collaborative project among several schools that participated in an Earthwatch expedition to Arizona. Student projects are posted at http://home.earthlink.net/~s.russell/bigsixdigit.html.

The Big6™–Dig it!

Did you know that the process you use to do research in the school media center is very much like the process scientists use in the field? The "BIG SIX" is a step-by-step method for solving "information problems". If you follow these six important steps, when it comes time to pull that school research project together, you'll have all the pieces you need!

Here's what those six steps might involve if you were an archaeologist working on the Casa Malpais/Earthwatch archaeological expedition in Springerville, Arizona, as well as what they mean for you in your school media center!

1. TASK DEFINITION

Before you can begin your research, you must first know what you are looking for!

What are you trying to find out? What question do you want to answer?

Here at Casa Malpais, archaeologists are trying to learn what this site was used for. Was it more than just a regular village? Was it a ceremonial site? A place where people came to trade?

2. INFORMATION SEEKING STRATEGIES

Because the archaeologists know what they want to learn from the site, they will be able to recognize the clues that will help them to answer their questions. But where should they begin digging? First they think about all the possible places to look; then they decide where would be the BEST place to dig.

Think of all the sources of information that might help YOU to answer your question. Then try the one that you think will help you the most first!

3. LOCATION & ACCESS

So far, we've just been thinking about our research. Now it's time to get to work. Archaeologists have special tools they use to get to the information they are looking for—like trowels, brushes, dustpans, buckets, and screens—because their information is usually buried!

Continued on next page

You may have to dig for your information, too—but don't bring your trowel to the media center! You'll be using different tools—like MacCatalog, SIRS Discoverer, the Reader's Guide for Young People, and the indexes and tables of contents in books to find your information. Or you might be looking for video tapes, or even people who can answer your questions!

4. USE OF INFORMATION

To find the artifacts that will help them answer their questions, the archaeologists have to sift through a lot of dirt they've removed from the site.

While you're doing your research you will also need to be looking, listening, and watching very carefully to find the facts that relate to your question—you'll need to "sift out" a lot of information that isn't relevant or that doesn't help you. This step is where you'll be reading the books or articles you found in step 3 above, or watching video tapes or interviewing people, and deciding which information you can actually use.

Don't forget to keep track of where you found your information! A good archaeologist always carefully records where each artifact was found. Make sure you collect that information, too—you'll need it for your bibliography!

5. SYNTHESIS

Here's the important step where you piece together all the information you've found to see if it answers the question you asked back in step 1! First you'll need to get your information organized. Archaeologists do this by keeping each type of artifact they find in separate bags that are organized according to what room they were found in and where in the room they were found. You might want to use an outline, or a "graphic organizer" (a drawing), or lists to organize the facts you find.

Once you're all organized, you can use your facts to answer the question you asked way back in step #1. Then, you'll need to think about how to present your information so that others can learn from it too. What will your final project be—a report? a model? a demonstration? Whatever type of presentation you choose, do your very best work!

Lastly, archaeologists label and catalog each artifact they find, so that other scientists will know where each one was found if they want to learn more about it. In a way, you will be doing this too when you write your bibliography. Your bibliography lets people who read (or see, or hear . . .) your presentation know where you got your information. That way, if they'd like to learn more about your topic, they could go to the same resources you used and read more about it!

Continued on next page

6. EVALUATION

Our last step is a "thinking" step! Sit back and admire your work and think about what you've done. Are you happy with what you found? The Earthwatch volunteers who found this beautiful Pinedale pot (it's around 700 years old!) sure were!

Think about whether you were able to answer the question you asked back in step 1. What things did you do that were very helpful in finding the answer? Are there things you would do differently the next time you have a research project to do?

If you take the time to evaluate your work, you will become a better researcher (or maybe even . . . someday . . . an archaeologist)!

The "Big Six" was developed and copyrighted by Michael B. Eisenberg and Robert E. Berkowitz.

Resources:
Eisenberg, Michael B. and Robert E. Berkowitz. Information Problem-Solving: the Big Six Skills Approach to Library & Information Skills Instruction. Norwood, NJ: Ablex Publishing Co., 1990. Visit the Big Six Skills website! http://big6.syr.edu/

Figure 7.4. The Big6™–Dig it! Web site, Olson Middle School. Reprinted with the author's permission from http://home.earthlink.net/~s.russell/bigsixdigit.html.

Kindred Public School

Verna LaBounty, the library media specialist at the Kindred Public School (Kindred, North Dakota), serving students in grades K–1, maintains a Big6™ information page on the Internet for students and staff. An explanation of how the Big6 model incorporates technological skills is included on the Web site (available at http://www.kindred.k12.nd.us/CyLib/overview.html). Sample student projects and assignments are listed on the site, including a rain forest portfolio project. For this project, the library media specialist created an assignment guide using the Big6 Skills model as a framework (refer to http://www.kindred.k12.nd.us/CyLib/rainf.html). Students are able to access the assignment guide from home and use the links to find information (see Figure 7.5).

Mankato, Minnesota

The Mankato Schools have developed an excellent information literacy curriculum for the primary grades. The curriculum is built on two common projects undertaken by every grade level during the school year. Mankato's information literacy curriculum highlights the district's commitment to the establishment of information literacy skills for every student:

RAIN FOREST PORTFOLIO

Big 6 #1 Task Definition:
Each student will become an expert on an assigned animal that lives in the tropical rain forest.

Information needed:
- Common and scientific name of the animal
- Range or location of the animal
- What animal eats and what eats the animal
- Drawing of the animal and a picture of the animal
- Description of the animal's habitat (canopy, mid- layers, floor, etc.)
- How the animal lives: in groups, alone, etc.
- Is the animal endangered? If so, how can individuals help preserve it?
- Other important information about the animal

Big Six #2 Information-seeking Strategies
Encyclopedias, geographic magazines, non-fiction and picture books on the rain forest, videos, Internet

Big Six #3 Location and Access
LMC, ILL, Internet access in LMC and computer lab LMC Resources:
Vid Rec 333 Rain forest
599 Sch Animals in danger
574.5 Laz Endangered species
574.5 Las The last rain forests
591 M Animals in their worlds
574.5 Ban Conserving rain forests
591.03 Fe Animal encyclopedia for children
599.09 Joh Animals of the tropical forests
574.5 Ham Tropical rain forests

Internet Links
Biome Studies
Rain Forest
Rain Forest Action Network Home Page
Exotic Birds
Local High School Students Study Rain Forest
Sumatran Rain Forests Photos
How to Save the Rain Forest
Olympic National Park

Big Six #4 Use of Information
Note taking
Credit sources

Big Six #5 Synthesis
Decorated folder that contains research notes and finished materials which may be stories, poems, cartoons, T-shirt or button designs, bumper sticker or personalized license plate. Presentation will be in "poster form." One-third of the class will set up stations and the other two-thirds will rotate to each poster station taking notes and asking questions. Then the next third of the class sets up and so forth until all poster stations have been visited.

Big Six #6 Evaluation
Finished assignment fulfills task.

____ Information found matches information needed.

____ Sources credited, even the textbook.

____ Work is neat, accurate, and creative.

____ Work completed by due date and includes name and date.

Figure 7.5. Rain Forest Portfolio Project, Kindred Public School. From The Big Six © Eisenberg/Berkowitz, 1990. Reprinted with the author's permission from http://www.kindred. k12.nd.us/CyLib/rainf.html.

■
Potential employers of Mankato public school graduates should be confident that their new employees will know how to identify information needs, locate relevant information in an efficient manner, understand and evaluate information, and use the information to solve a problem, complete a task, or be able to communicate that information clearly to others. Graduates will be able to use technology effectively in the information problem solving process. (Mankato Area Public Schools, 2003)

Mankato's information literacy curriculum, assignment links, and rubrics for assessment are available online at http://www.isd77.k12.mn.us/resources/infocurr/infolit.html.

South Carolina

South Carolina has developed the South Carolina Information Literacy and Technology Education Integration Plan to assist all educators in the implementation of information literacy skills in the curriculum. The South Carolina State Department of Education sees information literacy and technology integration as nothing short of a revolution in the classroom. According to the site, students "will be engaged in their learning and voluntarily move from just 'doing school,' employing such unethical behavior as plagiarism, to actively participating, analyzing information, and assisting their fellow students in learning. Student-centered learning in an inquiry-based instructional atmosphere will provide the infrastructure necessary to meet the No Child Left Behind legislation requirement that every student function at the 'proficient' level by 2014" (2003).

The Information Literacy and Technology Education Integration Plan is based on the Big6 and includes curriculum examples, planning guides and templates, a matrix, and presentations. It emphasizes the importance of collaboration between classroom teachers and library media specialists and places an emphasis on standards and evaluation. The Plan is a scalable, flexible resource for K–12 teachers and is available online at http://www.myscschools.com/offices/technology/ms/lms/getpage.cfm?ID=1354.

Information Literacy After School

Parents can foster information literacy at home by helping their children with their homework. However, many parents are dismayed at the prospect of this task. They do not look forward to nagging their children about completing their homework, nor do they look forward to their children's complaints. In *Helping with Homework: A Parent's Guide to Information Problem-Solving*, Eisenberg and Berkowitz (1996) present a win-win solution for this age-old problem.

Eisenberg and Berkowitz present a strategy that parents can use to empower their children with information literacy skills rather than completing the children's homework for them or becoming stuck in the blame-complain cycle. In their book, the authors state that parents can use the Big6 Information Problem-Solving strategies to help their children by:

- Examining the task

- Trouble-shooting when problems arise

- Brainstorming alternatives

- Reflecting on the finished product. (p. 37)

As we suggested in Chapter 3, reinforcement of such skills at home helps students understand the value of information literacy in their lives. Access ERIC has prepared a brochure for parents highlighting the importance of information literacy skills and offering advice for parents who wish to make information literacy a part of informal instruction at home. Among other key points, it encourages parents to help children explore their interests using a variety of information resources (Access ERIC, 2000). By encouraging students to explore topics that are of keen interest while thinking critically about the types of resources they use, parents can help their children develop a set of skills that will serve them throughout their lives.

Homeschoolers and Information Literacy

Homeschoolers are growing in number and influence in the United States. According to the most recent statistics from the United States Department of Education, National Center for Education Statistics (2001), there are nearly one million children being homeschooled in this country. Since homeschooling parents are largely responsible for choosing curriculum and information resources for their students, it is essential that they develop information literacy skills for their own benefit and that of their children.

Many homeschoolers rely on their local public library for materials and curriculum ideas, and public libraries present an opportunity for homeschoolers to learn information literacy skills. The American Library Association has created a special suite of resources for parents and students that address central ideas of information literacy. These resources—part of the ALA's "@ Your Library" campaign—provide advice and instruction for parents and students. *Information Literacy—Unlocking Your Child's Door to the World* states:

■
True information problem solving activities involve identifying
a plan of action or a decision which is supported by a foundation
of facts, but given an original interpretation. An example would
be asking students to draft and deliver a speech defending how
they would vote as a senator on a bill designed to extend low cost,
government funded, flood insurance to individuals who continually rebuild communities in known flood plains. Participation in
this type of learning activities will help prepare students to succeed in the real world after their formal education is completed.
(Jay, 2003)

The parent resources are available from ALA's Web site, at https://cs.ala.org/
@yourlibrary/jointhemajorleagues/literacy/resources.shtml.

Summary

In this chapter we provided a number of examples of information literacy
efforts created on an individual, local, or regional basis. Through these examples
we learned that:

- Imaginative Web-based information literacy tutorials can be created and
  integrated with curriculum areas or can be used for staff development
  purposes.

- Library media programs can foster information literacy by integrating
  the presentation of information literacy skills with the curriculum presented at all grade levels.

- Information literacy efforts are not limited to the library field but are also
  employed by regional educational consortiums.

- Parents can encourage their students to develop information literacy at
  home by helping them work through the information problem-solving
  process as they assist their children with their homework. If the parent is
  responsible for educating his or her homeschooling child, it is important
  that information literacy become part of the curriculum.

Chapter

Information Literacy in Higher Education

8

Shapiro and Hughes state: "Information literacy should in fact be conceived more broadly as a new liberal art that extends from knowing how to use computers and access information to critical reflection on the nature of information itself, its technical infrastructure, and its social, cultural and even philosophical context and impact as essential to the mental framework of the educated information-age citizen as the trivium of basic liberal arts (grammar, logic and rhetoric) was to the educated person in medieval society" (1996).

Many higher education institutions are in the process of developing information literacy competencies for their students. In this chapter we explore the status of information literacy efforts in higher education. We examine information literacy skills instruction and present examples of information literacy competency development.

Recognizing that students and faculty need to learn to access, evaluate, and use information effectively and efficiently, academic librarians have been offering bibliographic instruction in the form of library orientation, library use instruction, information resources use, and a broad range of information literacy skills for some time. As early as 1880, academic librarians wrote about their role as educators, but the contemporary development of bibliographic instruction is about 25 years old (Farber, 1995). Bibliographic instruction, once concerned with teaching the use of the library itself, has been expanded to include educating users to access, evaluate, and use information from a variety of print and nonprint sources both within and outside of the library.

Information Literacy Standards

The baseline for most of the work of individual universities, colleges, and systems is *Information Literacy Competency Standards for Higher Education,* developed by the Association of College and Research Libraries (ACRL). Approved in 2000, their focus is on implementing concepts of information literacy across the higher education curriculum. In the standards document, the authors underscore the reasons why information literacy instruction is as valuable for college students as it is for their younger colleagues:

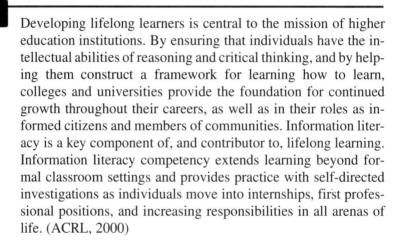

Developing lifelong learners is central to the mission of higher education institutions. By ensuring that individuals have the intellectual abilities of reasoning and critical thinking, and by helping them construct a framework for learning how to learn, colleges and universities provide the foundation for continued growth throughout their careers, as well as in their roles as informed citizens and members of communities. Information literacy is a key component of, and contributor to, lifelong learning. Information literacy competency extends learning beyond formal classroom settings and provides practice with self-directed investigations as individuals move into internships, first professional positions, and increasing responsibilities in all arenas of life. (ACRL, 2000)

The *Competency Standards* include performance indicators and outcomes, as well as the six standards, which are based on the ACRL's definition of an information literate student. The information literate student:

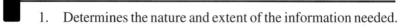

1. Determines the nature and extent of the information needed.

2. Accesses needed information effectively and efficiently.

3. Evaluates information and its sources critically and incorporates selected information into his or her knowledge base and value system.

4. Individually or as a member of a group, uses information effectively to accomplish a specific purpose.

5. Understands many of the economic, legal, and social issues surrounding the use of information and accesses and uses information ethically and legally. (ACRL, 2000)

Appendix I includes the three performance indicators and related outcomes for each standard.

According to the *ACRL Competency Standards* documentation, the *Standards* extend the work of the AASL Task Force on Information Literacy Standards, thereby "providing higher education an opportunity to articulate its information literacy competencies with those of K–12 so that a continuum of expectations develops for students at all levels" (ACRL, 2000). So while the *Competency Standards* are clearly written for an older and more sophisticated student, they share the basic principles of *Information Power: Building Partnerships for Learning* (ALA & AECT, 1998b).

A major strength of the ACRL's work is the document it released in 2001, *Objectives for Information Literacy Instruction: A Model Statement for Academic Librarians (IS Objectives)*. This tool underscores the necessity for information literacy to be shared across the campus, rather than confined to the library itself. Furthermore, the *IS Objectives* provide examples of terminal objectives (specific student learning outcomes) for the instructor who wishes to incorporate the *Competency Standards* into an instructional setting of any length or format.

The *Objectives* further refine the *Competency Standards'* Outcomes. For instance, for Competency Standard One (the information literate student defines and articulates the need for information), examples of outcomes include describing the difference between general and subject-specific information sources and demonstrating when it was appropriate to use each (ACRL, 2001).

The *IS Objectives* and the *Competency Standards* provide academic librarians with a way to demonstrate the importance of information literacy to faculty members, as well as a tangible plan for implementing it across the higher education curriculum.

Establishment of the Institute for Information Literacy

To initiate, develop, and teach information skills in higher education, it is important that academic librarians and administrators be knowledgeable in the theory and practice of information literacy. To meet this need, the Association of College and Research Libraries (ACRL) has established the Institute for Information Literacy (IIL). The Institute for Information Literacy is dedicated to playing a leadership role in assisting individuals and institutions in integrating information literacy throughout the full spectrum of the education process. The Institute for Information Literacy has three goals:

1. to prepare librarians to become effective teachers of information literacy programs.

2. to support librarians and other educators and administrators in playing roles in the development and implementation of information literacy programs.

3. to forge new relationships throughout the educational community to work towards information literacy curriculum development. (Institute for Information Literacy, 2003)

Cerise Oberman, dean of library and information services, conceived the idea for the Institute for Information Literacy. Oberman introduced IIL in her keynote speech at the 1997 Library and Orientation Exchange (LOEX) Conference as one possibility for meeting the demand for information skills instruction in higher education. Response to the idea was enthusiastic, and ACRL embraced the idea.

Oberman helped form the Institute for Information Literacy and continues to serve as chair of the Advisory Committee, which includes representatives from other academic institutions and higher education organizations. The four program initiatives of the Institute for Information Literacy are

1. Annual Immersion Programs: four-and-a-half-day professional development education that provides intensive information literacy training and education for new librarians, librarians new to teaching, and mid-career librarians who will assume a leadership role in information literacy in their institutions or communities;

2. Institutional Strategies—Best Practices: assisting individual institutions in developing strategies for the implementation of effective information literacy programs;

3. Community Partnerships: helping community partners (e.g., academic and K–12; academic, K–12, and public, etc.) to work toward instituting "community-based" information literacy programs; and

4. Web Resources: linking to a wide variety of information literacy issues including best practices, assessment, and links to other information on information literacy resources.

In the summer of 2003, IIL sponsored its fifth immersion program. This intensive training program is designed to provide academic librarians with tools and techniques to develop their school's information literacy curriculum.

Immersion 2003 offered two tracks of study: "Librarian as Teacher" and "Librarian as Program Developer." Additional information about the Institute for Information Literacy may be obtained by visiting the IIL Web site at http://www.ala.org/Template.cfm?Section=ACRLs_Institute_for_Information_ Literacy.

Fluency with Information Technology

Another important development in information as well as technology literacy for the college population is the Computer Science and Telecommunication Board, National Research Council's *Being Fluent with Information Technology*. This handbook outlines what college students should "know about information technology in order to use it more effectively now and in the future" (CSTB and NRC, 1999).

Being Fluent provides a guide for college curriculum planners to develop FITness (Fluency with Information Technology) in their college students and outlines the importance of this knowledge. We explore *Being Fluent* in greater depth in Chapter 9.

Information Literacy Instruction

A search of the print literature and the Internet reveals that information literacy instruction in higher education can take a variety of forms: stand-alone courses or classes, online tutorials, workbooks, course-related instruction, or course-integrated instruction. Course-integrated instruction differs from course-related instruction in that the information literacy instruction and assignment are built into the course. A number of examples illustrate each form of instruction.

Stand-Alone Courses or Classes

Stand-alone courses on information literacy may or may not be credit bearing, and may be in seminar format. Breivik (1998) notes that not all stand-alone courses are successful in outreach because students may not enroll in them if the courses are not required.

New Mexico State University

Information Literacy (LSC 311) is offered at New Mexico State University. The course is designed to develop students' critical thinking and technological skills. Students completing the course participate in electronic and in-class discussions, listen to lectures, and complete hands-on assignments and research projects (Beck, 2002).

Purdue University

The purpose of Purdue University's Information Strategies (GS 175) course is to introduce students to concepts of information retrieval that will be transferable to large computer networks or research libraries. Students learn how to find, analyze, organize, and present information through activities, lectures, homework, and a final project (Brandt, 2002).

University of Washington

University of Washington's INFO 220 is a credit course that is linked to an academic area; students must be co-enrolled in the related class. The course addresses specific information problems presented by the subject's discipline, presenting assignments from the academic area. The course description states that the course "focuses on identification of the information need, information seeking, evaluation and presentation of information, and selection of the appropriate information sources" (2003). The course is sponsored by the UW Information School but is taught by the university's librarians.

University of Wisconsin-Parkside

Students at the University of Wisconsin-Parkside are required to fulfill an information literacy requirement either by enrolling in a university seminar or by completing a self-paced instruction program. An information literacy skills workbook is available online that includes instruction in using the library catalog, using periodical indexes, citing sources, exploring the Internet, and using reference sources. Skills learned through the seminar are reinforced through class assignments (University of Wisconsin-Parkside, 2003).

Online Tutorials

Academic libraries have developed a number of online tutorials. Tutorials range from the simple to the complex and focus on issues such as online searching, evaluating Web sites, citing sources, information ethics, and broader information literacy topics.

Cornell University

The Olin*Kroch*Uris libraries at Cornell University have an Internet Web-based tutorial that teaches seven steps to effective library research: identifying and developing a topic, finding background information, using catalogs to find books, using indexes to find periodical articles, finding Internet resources, evaluating information, and citing sources. Students can also electronically access an ask-a-librarian feature (Division of Reference Services, 1997).

James Madison University

Students enrolled in the general education program at James Madison University are required to meet objectives relating to information-seeking and technology skills. To meet these objectives, the Carrier Library reference staff created "Go for the Gold," a Web-based tutorial in eight individually accessible modules. Each module contains learning objectives and interactive exercises relating to the world of information, searching electronic databases, finding information resources, using Internet sources, evaluating information, citing sources, and developing a search strategy (Carrier Library, undated).

University of Louisville

The Office of Information Literacy at the University of Louisville offers Web pages with information literacy links for faculty and students. The faculty page contains links to resources within and outside the university and includes tips for finding and evaluating information on the World Wide Web. The student page teaches students how to use the library, locate resources, use databases, use the Internet, evaluate Internet resources, write a paper, and cite sources (University of Louisville Office on Information Literacy, undated).

North Carolina State University

The Library Orientation Basic Orientation (LOBO), developed by North Carolina State University Library, is an example of a very extensive and elegantly designed information literacy online tutorial. The tutorial requires students to log in and keeps track of their progress, so they do not have to complete all the sessions in one sitting. Guests may also log in. The first session teaches students about the nature of the world of information and how information sources differ in their scope of coverage. Students are guided through two examples of topics that they might investigate, and they are shown the type of information resources that would be best for each example. Students interact with the tutorial by answering questions as they proceed through it. Other components teach students about choosing and searching databases and reading search results (North Carolina State University Library, undated).

University of Texas

The University of Texas has created Texas Information Literacy Tutorial (TILT), an interactive educational environment introducing basic principles of information literacy. TILT presents a variety of subjects—ranging from online commerce to security and privacy—in a creative and engaging manner. TILT was designed as an assignment to be used by writing instructors to reinforce proper research skills. TILT is available online at http://tilt.lib.utsystem.edu/.

Workbooks

Students at Temple University are required to complete a library skills workbook before starting their second semester. The workbook, aimed at helping students become independent users of information, is available in customized versions for the areas of business, criminal justice, education, humanities, science/technology, and the social sciences. Students are not required to complete any one particular version of the workbook but are encouraged to complete a version pertaining to their declared major or, if they are undecided, pertaining to an area they might declare as a major (Temple University Libraries, 2002).

Course-Related Instruction

The University of California at Berkeley library is typical of many academic libraries. It offers drop-in library research workshops, faculty instruction, Internet training workshops, collaboration with faculty to develop course-integrated assignments, and course-related instruction. Using this type of instruction, librarians highlight discipline specific resources related to particular courses (University of California at Berkeley Library, 2002).

Course-Integrated Instruction

Many academic library programs are turning to course-integrated instruction to provide users with information literacy skills in the context of actual information needs (Breivik, 1998). This approach makes information literacy skills instruction inherently more meaningful than when such skills are taught out of context.

The University of Arizona

The University of Arizona library's Web site, at http://www.library.arizona. edu/infolit/InfoLit2000/infolit.shtml, showcases a number of models of course-integrated instruction. Projects collaboratively designed by librarians and faculty have been developed for

- anthropology,
- art education,
- arts and sciences,
- educational psychology,
- English,
- French,
- geography,

- history,

- humanities,

- library science,

- linguistics,

- materials science engineering,

- political science,

- public administration,

- teaching and teacher education,

- theater arts, and

- women's studies.

A page for each project features the names of the developers, the course, the assignments, and the course-integrated information literacy instruction. For example, students in History 436–Civil War and Reconstruction track three different events in newspapers representing different political viewpoints during the 1860s and 1870s. Students create a portfolio of these articles and share their findings with their class. Librarians teach the students how to locate newspapers of the Civil War era (University of Arizona, Librarian–Faculty Teaching Technology Partnerships, undated-c).

Florida International University

The Florida International University Library Instruction Program tries to reach every student. Rather than requiring a separate course in information skills, the Library Instruction Program consists of classes linked to the curriculum throughout the university. The Library Certification Program is taught in conjunction with the Freshmen Composition Program and is required for all sections. Students learn about information search strategies and critical thinking. The program has been expanded to build on the foundation of the Library Certification Program. Librarians and faculty members collaborate to design assignments that are integrated into courses in a number of major fields of study, including engineering, biology, history, public speaking, and psychology (Florida International University, 2000).

Tri-County Technical College

Tri-County Technical College (Pendleton, South Carolina) is developing a curriculum-integrated information literacy program for students enrolled in its two-year associate degree programs. The program focuses on finding and evaluating information and on using information in context of the students' chosen career fields. The college offers degrees in business and human services, health education, and industrial and engineering technology (Tri-County Technical College, undated).

The Role of Faculty

Although most academic institutions see the necessity for information literacy skills instruction, budgetary constraints often dictate the number of library personnel assigned to such instruction. As academic librarians work with individual faculty members to integrate information skills instruction, they often find themselves overwhelmed by the task of working with every course taught by every faculty member to ensure that all students develop information literacy skills. To remedy this situation, some academic institutions are developing programs to prepare faculty to integrate information literacy skills into their courses. This places the academic librarian in the role of collaborator and mentor (Smith, 1997).

North Dakota State

The staff at the Mundt Library at North Dakota State has concluded that

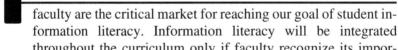

faculty are the critical market for reaching our goal of student information literacy. Information literacy will be integrated throughout the curriculum only if faculty recognize its importance, make it a goal as they develop their syllabi, and know how to teach information literacy themselves. (Smith, 1997)

To realize faculty instruction in information skills, the concept of information competence must be accepted by faculty as a component of undergraduate education. The Library Committee, consisting of general faculty, will review the Mundt Library's information literacy competencies, which will then be presented to the faculty. The library hopes that as the college is reviewing general education requirements in the near future, information literacy will be included as one component. Following this, the challenge to the staff at the Mundt Library will be to develop faculty training that will be convenient and frequent. Library staff members will develop handouts, Web documents, and other materials that can be adapted by faculty for teaching information literacy skills.

Oberlin College

Librarians at Oberlin College have presented extensive workshops to the faculty on topics such as

- Information sources and search strategies
- Standard reference sources
- How catalogs and databases are organized
- Effective database searching
- Electronic indexes
- Lexis/Nexis and other full-text databases
- Tools for searching the Web
- Government documents
- Information literacy in the curriculum. (Oberlin College Library, 2000)

The last workshop focuses on how to integrate information literacy skills into existing courses. Responses to the workshop include the following comments from faculty:

Having taken this workshop, I am in a better position to help our students become more information literate, instead of leaving the task entirely to the librarians. (Oberlin College Library, 2000)

I'm definitely going to structure research projects in my advance courses around teaching students what research is and how you go about it, rather than just sending them off to the library. (Oberlin College Library, 2000)

Information Competencies

In the introduction to this chapter we included a quote from Shapiro and Hughes, who believe that information literacy should be considered a new liberal art (1996). To ensure that all students who graduate from academic institutions are information literate, information literacy efforts need to be undertaken in a systematic way and must be embraced not only by the staff of academic libraries but also by the faculty and administration of the academic institution. In recognition of the importance of information literacy, statewide university systems and individual colleges and universities are undertaking strategic planning to determine information competencies, to incorporate instruction in information competence throughout the curriculum, and to add information competence as a graduation requirement for students. Such efforts are often initiated by librarians and spearheaded by committees that systematically examine programs at other colleges and universities, conduct surveys of students and faculty, arrive at and adopt a definition of information literacy, and create a plan for the dissemination of information competence information.

California State University System

In January 1993, the Council of Library Directors of the California State University (CSU) system, under the auspices of the Commission on Learning Resources and Instructional Technology (CLRIT), embarked on a planning effort to identify and foster information competence. Their charge was to recommend policy guidelines to the chancellor, who facilitates the effective uses of learning resources and instructional technology throughout the CSU system (University Library–Cal Poly Pomona, 1995). The result of the Council of Library Directors' efforts is presented in *Transforming CSU Libraries for the 21st Century: A Strategic Plan of the CSU Council of Library Directors.* Information competency for all students was identified as one of the action items. The Commission on Learning Resources and Instructional Technology (CLRIT) approved the strategic plan and requested that the Office of Academic Affairs form a work group to address the issue of information competence. The group was charged with recommending basic competence levels on the use of recorded knowledge and information, and processes for assessment of student competence (University Library–Cal Poly Pomona, 1995).

The CSU Work Group on Information Competence began its work in April 1995. Its investigation of information competence included an extensive literature review, consultation with experts, informal and formal surveys to determine what CSU campuses were already doing in the area of information competence, and a review of how other universities and colleges had defined information competence. As part of its effort, the Work Group sponsored a systemwide workshop to examine what is meant by "information competence". The definition agreed upon is that "information competence is the fusing or the integration of library literacy, computer literacy, media literacy, technological literacy, ethics, critical thinking, and communication skills" (University Library–Cal Poly Pomona, 1995).

After an examination of the literature, and as a result of the workshop, the Work Group defined a set of core competencies, revised in January 1997, which read:

Information Competence

A Set of Core Competencies

In order to be able to find, evaluate, use, communicate and appreciate information in all its various formats, students must be able to demonstrate the following skills:

1. Formulate and state a research question, problem or issue not only within the conceptual framework of a discipline, but also in a manner in which others can readily understand and cooperatively engage in the search.

2. Determine the information requirements for a research question, problem or issue in order to formulate a search strategy that will use a variety of resources.

3. Locate and retrieve relevant information, in all its various formats, using, when appropriate, technological tools.

4. Organize information in a manner that permits analysis, evaluation, synthesis and understanding.

5. Create and communicate information effectively using various media.

6. Understand the ethical, legal and socio-political issues surrounding information.

7. Understand the techniques, points of view and practices employed in the presentation of information from all sources. (Curzon, 1997)

An ambitious plan set forth by the Work Group to include information competence as a priority within the CSU includes four elements:

- to encourage the development of courses or programs, including assessment components, relating to information competence;

- to disseminate information about information competence;

- to collaborate between CSU and other universities, schools, or agencies to foster connection among programs within and beyond CSU; and

- to create and provide instructional tools to assist with the teaching and learning of information competence.

To carry out the goals set forth by the Work Group, several projects relating to information competence have been funded, including the following:

- Chico: Information Competence for Business Students: A Self-Paced Course

- Northridge: Information Competence: A Workshop Series for Area High Schools and Junior Colleges

- San Luis Obispo, Pomona, Monterey Bay, Fullerton, Los Angeles: Information Competency Implementation through Interactive Instructional

Materials: A Systemwide Collaboration, which will develop multimedia presentations, in class exercises, Web instructional modules, and an electronic workbook

- Dominguez Hills in cooperation with Northridge and San Marcos: Developing Information Competencies: A model list, activities and assessment instrument to develop a model list of information competencies for high school, community colleges, and lower division CSU student

The Information Competence Work Group recommended its continuance through the 1998–1999 fiscal year. The group proposed a capstone conference in 1999 to focus on what has been learned about information competence, and the group will publish the deliverables from all of the grant projects for use by all the campuses (Curzon, 1997).

State University of New York System

The State University of New York (SUNY) Council of Library Directors Information Literacy Initiative Committee has been working to identify information literacy competencies and promote their adoption across curricula. Their final report, issued on September 30, 1997, contains a detailed list of nine information competencies that can be applied to any discipline. They define information literacy as "the abilities to recognize when information is needed and to locate, evaluate, effectively use, and communicate information in its various formats" (SUNY 1997):

 SUNY Council of Library Directors Information Literacy Initiative Committee Information Literacy Competencies

Competency 1: To recognize the need for information.

Indicators:

- Recognizes that accurate and comprehensive information is the basis for intelligent decision making.

- Frames appropriate questions based on information needs.

- Defines a manageable focus and time line.

Competency 2: To access information from appropriate sources.

Indicators:

- Understands and can use the variety of information sources available, including: Internet, CD-ROM interfaces, electronic library catalogs, microformats and print materials.

- Identifies a variety of potential sources of information.

- Can select those sources that are appropriate to a given need.

- Develops efficient and effective search strategies.

- Consults experts for assistance/guidance when needed.

- Understands standard systems of information organization.

- Identifies and retrieves information relevant to the question/need.

Competency 3: To develop skills in using information technologies.

Indicators:

- Can access the campus information systems and understands how to access information networks.

- Can access the Internet, and can navigate the information highway to locate information appropriate to the need.

- Uses group communication methods, electronic mail, discussion groups for information gathering, feed back, and interaction.

- Can effectively expand or narrow a search as needed.

- Understands and can use word processing, spreadsheets, databases and computer file management.

- Can manipulate and transfer electronic information.

Competency 4: To critically analyze and evaluate information.

Indicators:

- Filters large amounts of information.

- Determines accuracy, relevance, and comprehensiveness of information.

- Assesses the reliability and accuracy of information.

- Distinguishes among facts, points of view, and opinion.

- Thinks critically about the content of information.

- Understands the process of knowledge generation and publication patterns in appropriate disciplines/fields.

Competency 5: To organize and process information.

Indicators:

- Synthesizes information from a variety of sources.

- Integrates new information into ones own knowledge base.

- Makes inferences, connections, and draws conclusions.

- Organizes information for practical application.

Competency 6: To apply information for effective and creative decision making.

Indicators:

- Applies information in critical thinking and problem solving.

- Creates new information or knowledge through synthesis.

- Produces quality products appropriate to specific needs.

Competency 7: To generate and effectively communicate information and knowledge.

Indicators:

- Produces and communicates information in effective and appropriate formats.

- Disseminates information in appropriate modes.

- Evaluates the effectiveness/success of products developed and presented.

Competency 8: To understand and respect the ethical, legal, and socio-political aspects of information and its technologies.

Indicators:

- Respects the principles of equitable access to information.

- Respects intellectual property rights.

- Applies principles of academic honesty in use of information.

- Acknowledges works of others through accurate citations and references.

Competency 9: To develop attitudinal objectives that lead to appreciation of lifelong learning.

Indicators:

- Understands that information searching requires time, diligence, and practice, and that skills are learned over time.

- Increases self-confidence with practice and experience in information seeking.

- Recognizes that the information search process is evolutionary and changes during the course of investigation.

- Knows that careful and attentive scrutiny of information tools and resources is essential to success.

- Appreciates that information literacy requires an ongoing involvement with learning and information technologies so that independent lifelong learning is possible. (SUNY, 1997)

The committee recommends an ambitious process for creating an awareness of the importance of information literacy and for integrating information literacy competencies into courses throughout the SUNY system. One means for implementation is similar to the Writing Across the Curriculum (WAC) initiative, which focuses on the integration of writing skills throughout disciplines other than English. The committee suggests that libraries form the locus of information competency efforts, and that librarians fulfill the leadership/support role for the integration of information literacy competencies, much as the campus writing centers provide this role for the Writing Across the Curriculum initiative.

University of Massachusetts System

The Information Literacy Project of the University of Massachusetts began in 1996 with funding from the Office of the President. Committee members included librarians from all five campuses, who consulted with academic computing personnel and faculty to develop information literacy competencies. Four discussion meetings covering the topics of defining information literacy, establishing competencies, developing outcome-based strategies, and implementing ideas were held beginning in October 1996 and concluding in May 1997. Between these sessions, an interactive Internet Web page focusing on the results of the discussions was created on the UMass at Dartmouth Web site. Participants and faculty throughout the UMass system were invited to add their comments to the discussions (University of Massachusetts, Dartmouth, 2000).

The committee decided to adopt the American Library Association definition of information literacy. In developing competencies, the committee referenced Stripling and Pitts's *Brainstorms and Blueprints: Teaching Library Research as a Thinking Process* (1988), which offers a taxonomy comprising six levels:

- Level 1: Fact finding
- Level 2: Asking questions
- Level 3: Organizing information
- Level 4: Evaluating/deliberating
- Level 5: Integrating/concluding
- Level 6: Conceptualizing

Because the committee decided that no assumptions could be made regarding the level of skills that entering students would bring to the university, the competencies include each aspect of the six taxonomies.

The competencies developed by the committee state that University of Massachusetts students will

1. Recognize the need for information

   - By articulating the assignment, project or information need
   - By stating the purpose of the information need
   - By initiating a search strategy
   - By relating the information needed to what is already known
   - By identifying appropriate and using general reference sources (including people, multimedia, WWW, and print)
   - By restating concepts in own words

2. Formulate questions based on information needs

- By using different types of questions (e.g., seeking information, analysis, opinion)

- By developing a central question that is the foundation of a thesis statement

- By noting key words, concepts, and phrases

3. Identify potential sources of information

- By identifying and using types of resources relevant to the research topic (including multimedia, people, WWW, and print, etc.)

- By developing an awareness of the structure of databases

- By understanding the limitation of databases and print resources (dates, errors, self-imposed, subject matter limits, timeliness, updates)

- By differentiating between primary and secondary sources

- By identifying possible databases to be searched

4. Develop and use successful search strategies

- By accessing print and technology based sources of information

- By using electronic resources to locate, retrieve and transfer information

- By knowing when and how to obtain assistance from a reference librarian, particularly when accessing library resources

- By systematically organizing information

- By understanding the advantages and disadvantages of different database search techniques (truncation, free text, fixed vocabulary, combined free text/fixed vocabulary, Boolean)

- By being able to broaden and narrow searches as necessary

- By recognizing that information is organized in one or a combination of ways (e.g., by date, by author, by geographic location, by type of product, etc.)

- By interpreting information found in reference sources, including electronic sources

- By revising or expanding the thesis statement as necessary

- By using subject headings or cross references to find additional resources

- By crediting sources

- By using electronic resources to locate, retrieve and transfer information

- By following established etiquette and local guidelines for using electronic resources

- By determining availability of resources and knowing how to obtain those not available locally

- By knowing how to print, photocopy, download, etc.

5. Evaluate information

- By differentiating between fact and opinion

- By identifying currency, authority (motive, point of view bias, scholarship, intended audience, objectivity, consistency)

- By eliminating irrelevant pieces of information

- By distinguishing between popular and scholarly resources

6. Use information

- By communicating clearly

- By paraphrasing accurately

- By determining the most effective means of presentation (decide purpose, audience process)

- By preparing an accurate bibliography

- By integrating information from a variety of sources. (University of Massachusetts, Dartmouth, 2000)

The Information Literacy Project committee received funding from the Office of the President to develop a generic WWW site that could be used by students in freshman level courses. Plans call for the site to be piloted in one course on each of the five University of Massachusetts campuses (Barnes, personal correspondence, March 4, 1998).

University of Arizona

The University of Arizona Library initiated an Information Literacy Project to determine what information skills students need, examine programs at other colleges and universities, and develop models for an information literacy program. The project charge states:

> Many University of Arizona students do not possess the information seeking or computer related skills to complete the assignments that are expected of them. Because of this wide variety of information skill mastery, faculty are limited in the types of interaction and assignments they can pursue. (University of Arizona Library, 1996)

An Education Action Planning Team was formed as the result of a 1996–1997 Information Literacy Project. The team was charged with the task of creating a campuswide, competency-based information literacy program. The team is working to formally adopt a set of information literacy competencies as the framework for the program. It will coordinate the creation of an information literacy Web tutorial, market the information literacy program to promote campuswide awareness, and coordinate the integration of information literacy competencies into the instructional activities of the library. Three Information Literacy colloquium classes were taught during the fall 1997 semester. Each one-hour class focused on a broad subject area: fine arts/humanities, science/ engineering, and social sciences.

Assessment of Information Literacy Skills

Assessing the information literacy skills possessed by higher education students presents another set of complicated issues. Several universities are engaging in early exploration of this topic, providing a glimpse of what the future might hold in this area of research.

Kent State University

Kent State's groundbreaking Project for Standardized Assessment of Information Literacy Skills (SAILS), funded in part by a grant from the Institute of Museum and Library Services (IMLS), seeks to develop a valid and credible assessment tool for measuring information literacy skills, thereby creating a set of data that could be presented to administrators and other decision makers to prove the validity and importance of strong libraries and information literacy instruction. Project SAILS is working with several other institutions as it moves through each phase of research and development. Project SAILS is available online at: http://sails.lms.kent.edu/index.php.

California State Polytechnic University Pomona

In the fall of 1998, Cal Poly Pomona created a Web-based assessment tool to measure the information competency of incoming freshmen and transfer students. The goal behind the project was to establish a baseline of skills and knowledge for needy students to guide the development of instruction and the implementation of technology.

The assessment tool, a Web-based survey form, collected demographic information and asked students to respond to a number of information problem-solving scenarios. The results of the project provide a fascinating glimpse into information literacy for one incoming university class. The project development, tool, and results are available online at www.csupomona.edu/~library/InfoComp.

Washington State

The higher education institutions of Washington have created the inter-institutional Assessment of Information and Technology Literacy project in response to a Washington State legislature mandate to assess information and technology literacy among higher education students in the state. The program, implemented in the 2002–2003 school year, targets three areas of assessment: writing, quantitative and symbolic reasoning, and information and technology literacy (University of Washington, 2001). More information on the project is available at http://depts.washington.edu/infolitr/.

Conclusion: Information Literacy and the Higher Education Frontier

Information literacy is a key issue for America's higher education institutions. Vast amounts of staff time, resources, and effort are put toward building library and technology resources; it is vital that students possess the skills to get the most out of the array of resources presented to them.

Abby Kasowitz-Scheer and Michael Pasqualoni spoke to the complex array of issues facing colleges and universities in regard to information literacy in their 2001 ERIC digest: "Information literacy instruction is alive and well on campuses today. However, there is much work to be done before integrated ILI across the curriculum is standard practice."

They go on to identify some key challenges, including

■

- motivating students to learn information literacy skills;
- assessing student mastery of concepts and skills;
- training librarians to serve as instructors and instructional designers (Grassian & Kaplowitz, 2001);
- advocating the value of information literacy (Bawden, 2001) in an environment of competing literacies (Snavely & Cooper, 1997); [and]
- preparing students for business settings that demand a more specialized level of information fluency (Marcum, 2002).

The authors also note a clear need for discussion of information literacy instruction outside of the library field. A more multidisciplinary approach to information literacy research and instruction will create opportunities for more substantial, curriculum-integrated, and long-lasting instructional experiences that will benefit students throughout and beyond their academic careers.

Summary

The 1990s saw colleges and universities implement information literacy instruction in a number of ways. The inclusion of information competencies as a graduation requirement is the key that will fully integrate information literacy into the curriculum of academic institutions. Information literacy standards present a framework for further development of this area in higher education. Key points in this chapter include the following:

- The ACRL's Information Literacy Competency Standards for Higher Education and accompanying documentation present an important step in standardizing information literacy across higher education.

- Information literacy instruction in higher education can take a variety of forms: stand-alone courses or classes, online tutorials, workbooks, course-related instruction, or course-integrated instruction. The latter may be more effective since the information literacy instruction is part of the course.

- The Association of College and Research Libraries (ACRL) has established the Institute for Information Literacy (IIL) to play a leadership role in assisting individuals and institutions in integrating information literacy throughout the full spectrum of the education process.

- Statewide university systems and individual colleges and universities are undertaking strategic planning to determine information competencies, to incorporate instruction in information competence throughout the curriculum, and to add information and technology competence as a graduation requirement for students.

- As colleges and universities implement information literacy requirements, academic librarians may be overwhelmed by requests for instruction. Some academic library programs are preparing faculty to facilitate their students' mastery of information literacy skills so that the faculty can in turn provide information literacy learning experiences for the students enrolled in their classes.

- Of increasing interest and importance is assessment of information and technology skills—on entering as well as exiting higher education.

Chapter

Technology and Information Literacy

9

"Just as 16th century navigators were required to read the stars and understand tides to find their way, today's students must learn to become information navigators, finding their way through print, graphic, electronic, and visual media to discover and interpret relevant information. They must become critical thinkers and analyzers using technology to access, interpret, and evaluate the quality and appropriateness of the information they have discovered.

And, as navigators of old drew maps to share what they found with others, today's students must learn how to create and share knowledge using all the forms of media and telecommunications to communicate their ideas, engage in discourse, and solve problems." (Illinois State Board of Education, 1996, p. 27)

This statement eloquently details the need for students to be technology literate. In this chapter we examine technology and determine how information literacy and technology fit together in the K–12 and higher education environments.

Familiarity with computers is becoming a prerequisite for most jobs. Educators must prepare students for the future by teaching them computer skills. Educators and the general public widely accept the premise that students must be technologically competent to be successful today and in the future; however, competence with technology must be set within in the context of information literacy. As noted in Chapter 4, the U.S. Department of Labor Secretary's Commission on Achieving Necessary Skills (SCANS) (1991) states that the competencies for all entry-level employees must include the ability to (1) acquire and use information and (2) work with a variety of technologies.

Peter Drucker (1992), well-known management guru, argues that "executives have become computer-literate . . . but not many executives are information literate" (p. A16). Being able to use computers is not enough. Executives must be able to apply computer skills to real situations and real needs. They must be able to identify information problems and locate, use, synthesize, and evaluate information in relation to those problems.

Information technology affects everyone. Today's successful companies focus on meaningful uses of information technology and hire employees who are able to apply technology to a range of situations. It is the responsibility of our educational system to develop students who are not only technologically literate but also information literate. Students must know how to use technology to solve information problems.

Technology in K–12 Schools

A 2003 Corporation for Public Broadcasting (CPB) report on children's Internet use gives a fascinating glimpse of the ways technology is being used in America's schools. According to the report, 69 percent of children say that the computer lab is their main point of access to the Internet at school, as opposed to the classroom (29 percent) or the library/media center (43 percent). This suggests that for the most part, Internet resources are not integrated seamlessly into classroom instruction but rather stand alone as a research tool or peripheral technology.

When more fully realized, computer and communications technology can be used in education in a number of ways to

- Individualize instruction

- Increase the ability to access, evaluate and communicate information

- Increase the quantity and quality of students thinking and writing

- Improve students ability to solve complex problems

- Cultivate artistic expression

- Increase global awareness

- Create opportunities for students to share meaningful work with an audience other than the teacher and class

- Provide access to courses not available locally

- Make students feel comfortable with the tools of the Information Age

- Increase the productivity and efficiency of schools. (Peck & Doricott, 1994)

Two Approaches to Technology Education

There are two pedagogical approaches to technology in K–12 schools: technology as the object of instruction, and the process/skills in context approach—using technology as a tool. The latter approach is becoming more widely supported as being consistent with current pedagogy and preparing students for lifelong learning.

Technology as the Object of Instruction

Technology as an object of instruction in schools finds its roots in the business courses that have long been a staple in American high schools. Just as students were once taught how to type on electric typewriters, many are now taught principles of computing. They are taught important computer applications, basic architecture, and so forth. This approach teaches computers as an academic subject. Students learn about computers much as they do about biology or American history. There is no doubt that in today's world, all students need to learn about computers to succeed in the marketplace. Schools that teach technology as an object of instruction attempt to meet this need through the curriculum.

The Association of Computing Machinery *Model High School Computer Science Curriculum* (Task Force of the Pre-College Committee of the Education Board of the ACM, 1997), currently in its fourth draft, is an example of teaching technology as an object of instruction. The ACM Model outlines the skills necessary to succeed in an economy dependent upon information technology.

Computer technology has a profound effect on our society and world. Every citizen needs some familiarity with this technology and its consequences in the home, school, workplace, and community. Because the details of the technology change from day to day, keeping up with those details is difficult and often unproductive. Therefore the study of the subject must concentrate on the fundamental scientific principles and concepts of the field (Task Force of the Pre-College Committee of the Education Board of the ACM, 1997).

The ACM Model argues that computer science should be considered an integral part of the high school curriculum for all students, and that information technology should be taught as a subject in the core curriculum. The ACM Model focuses on competency in the following seven areas:

- algorithms;
- programming languages;
- operating systems and user support;
- computer architecture;
- social, ethical, and professional context;
- computer applications; and
- additional topics (artificial intelligence, graphics, etc.).

These topics can be approached through a variety of teaching styles. Although hands-on learning in a lab may benefit some students, others might learn better through an apprenticeship in a computer company. Rather than focusing on in-context instruction, the ACM approach to information technology instruction pushes skill sets and discrete concepts to the forefront of instruction.

The International Society for Technology in Education (ISTE) (2002) presents another model for technology instruction with its *National Educational Technology Standards for Students (NETS)*. The standards provide a set of goals demonstrating technology proficiency for K–12 students, and "provide a framework for preparing students to be lifelong learners who make informed decisions about the role of technology in their lives" (ISTE, 2002).

NETS is organized around basic principles that move K–12 students from rudimentary understanding of computers to relative proficiency with many forms of technology. These basic principles, the "Technology Foundation Standards for Students," follow:

1. Basic operations and concepts

- Students demonstrate a sound understanding of the nature and operation of technology systems.
- Students are proficient in the use of technology.

2. Social, ethical, and human issues

- Students understand the ethical, cultural, and societal issues related to technology.
- Students practice responsible use of technology systems, information, and software.

- Students develop positive attitudes toward technology uses that support lifelong learning, collaboration, personal pursuits, and productivity.

3. Technology productivity tools

  - Students use technology tools to enhance learning, increase productivity, and promote creativity.

  - Students use productivity tools to collaborate in constructing technology-enhanced models, prepare publications, and produce other creative works.

4. Technology communications tools

  - Students use telecommunications to collaborate, publish, and interact with peers, experts, and other audiences.

  - Students use a variety of media and formats to communicate information and ideas effectively to multiple audiences.

5. Technology research tools

  - Students use technology to locate, evaluate, and collect information from a variety of sources.

  - Students use technology tools to process data and report results.

  - Students evaluate and select new information resources and technological innovations based on the appropriateness for specific tasks.

6. Technology problem-solving and decision-making tools

  - Students use technology resources for solving problems and making informed decisions.

  - Students employ technology in the development of strategies for solving problems in the real world. (ISTE, 2002)

The "Technology Foundation Standards" provide the guiding principle for the performance indicators specified for each grade level. In this way, *NETS* presents a vision of technology proficiency for educators and students of all grade levels.

Technology As an Integral Tool:
The Process/Skills in Context Approach

As we saw in Chapter 6, current educational paradigms focus on

- the acquisition of higher-order thinking and problem-solving skills,
- the integration of basic skills with real world tasks,
- the availability of information resources for use at the time of need, and
- the active role of students as architects of their own education.

Using technology as an integral tool supports these constructs. Rather than teaching individual skills out of context as in the technology-as-the-object-of-instruction model, the technology-as-an-integral-tool model emphasizes the use of technology in context to accomplish goals and solve problems. Examples of this approach include

- a journalism class using a desktop publishing program to design and lay out the school newspaper;
- an art class using a digital camera to take pictures of students' artwork, then using a Web authoring program to create Web pages displaying their artwork to the world;
- a physical education class using software to record and analyze information from heart monitors worn while exercising; and
- a foreign language class using a videotape-editing program to edit a skit the students had previously written and videotaped.

Integration of technology throughout the curriculum is advocated in the 1997 *Report to the President on the Use of Technology to Strengthen K–12 Education in the United States,* which recommends that schools:

> Focus on learning with technology, not about technology. Although both are worthy of attention, it is important to distinguish between technology as a subject area and the use of technology to facilitate learning about any subject area. While computer-related skills will unquestionably be quite important in the twenty-first century, and while such skills are clearly best taught through the actual use of computers, it is important that technology be integrated throughout the K–12 curriculum, and not simply used to impart technology-related knowledge and skills. Although universal technological literacy is a laudable national goal, the Panel believes the Administration should work toward

the use of computing and networking technologies to improve the quality of education in all subject areas. (President's Committee of Advisors on Science and Technology Panel on Educational Technology, 1997)

Eisenberg and Johnson (2002) concur by arguing that teaching students a "laundry list" of technology skills and concepts does not give them adequate preparation for the information society of the future. The authors view technology skills in the context of the information problem-solving process which, in turn, is taught in the context of the curriculum. For example, searching the Web is viewed as a location and access skill, and brainstorming with classmates in a chat environment is seen as task definition. Eisenberg and Johnson demonstrate how technology skills can be viewed in an information literacy context by presenting scenarios of the use of technology skills throughout the Big6™ Information Problem-Solving process (see Figure 9.1, pages 159–162). Janet Murray's (1999) comparison of the Big6, *NETS*, and AASL/AECT's *Information Literacy Standards* provides another perspective on the interdependence of technology skills, information literacy skills, and information problem solving strategies (see Figure 9.2, pages 163–164).

Applications in a Big6™ Context

1. Task Definition
The first part in the information problem-solving process involves recognizing that an information need exists, defining the problem, and identifying the types and amount of information needed. In terms of technology, students will be able to:

- Communicate with teachers regarding assignments, tasks, and information problems using e-mail; online discussions (e.g., listservs, threaded Web-based discussions, newsgroups); real-time communications (e.g., instant messaging services, chat rooms, IP telephony); desktop teleconferencing; and groupware on the Internet, intranets, and local area networks.

- Generate topics, define problems, and facilitate cooperative activities among groups of students locally and globally using e-mail, online discussions, real-time communications, desktop teleconferencing, and groupware on the Internet and local area networks.

- Generate topics, define problems, and facilitate cooperative activities with subject area experts locally and globally using e-mail, online discussions, real-time communications, desktop teleconferencing, and groupware on the Internet and local area networks.

- Define or refine the information problem using computerized graphic organization, brainstorming or idea generating software. This includes developing a research question or perspective on a topic.

Continued on next page

2. Information Seeking Strategies

Once the information problem has been formulated, the student must consider all possible information sources and develop a plan for searching. Students will be able to:

- Assess the value of various types of electronic resources for data gathering, including databases, CD-ROM resources, commercial and Internet online resources, electronic reference works, community and government information electronic resources.
- Assess the need for and value of primary resources including interviews, surveys, experiments, and documents that are accessible through electronic means.
- Identify and apply specific criteria for evaluating computerized electronic resources.
- Identify and apply specific criteria for constructing meaningful original data gathering tools such as online surveys, electronic interviews, or scientific data gathering tools such as probes, meters, and timers.
- Assess the value of e-mail, online discussions, real-time communications, desktop teleconferencing, and groupware on the Internet and local area networks as part of a search of the current literature or in relation to the information task.
- Use a computer to generate modifiable flow charts, time lines, organizational charts, project plans (such as Gantt charts), and calendars which will help the student plan and organize complex or group information problem-solving tasks.
- Use handheld devices such as personal digital assistants (PDAs), electronic slates or tablet PCs to track contacts and create to-do lists and schedules.

3. Location and Access

After students determine their priorities for information seeking, they must locate information from a variety of resources and access specific information found within individual resources. Students will be able to:

- Locate and use appropriate computer resources and technologies available within the school library media center, including those on the library media center's local area network (e.g., online catalogs, periodical indexes, full-text sources, multimedia computer stations, CD-ROM stations, online terminals, scanners, digital cameras).
- Locate and use appropriate computer resources and technologies available throughout the school including those available through intranets or local area networks (e.g., full-text resources, CD-ROMs, productivity software, scanners, digital cameras).
- Locate and use appropriate computer resources and technologies available beyond the school through the Internet (e.g., newsgroups, listservs, WWW sites, ftp sites, online public access library catalogs, commercial databases and online services, and other community, academic, and government resources).
- Know the roles and computer expertise of the people working in the school library media center and elsewhere who might provide information or assistance.
- Use electronic reference materials (e.g., electronic encyclopedias, dictionaries, biographical reference sources, atlases, geographic databanks, thesauri, almanacs, fact books) available through intranets or local area networks, stand-alone workstations, commercial online vendors, or the Internet.

Continued on next page

- Use the Internet or commercial computer networks to contact experts and help and referral services.
- Conduct self-initiated electronic surveys through e-mail, listservs, newsgroups and online data collection tools.
- Use organizational systems and tools specific to electronic information sources that assist in finding specific and general information (e.g., indexes, tables of contents, user's instructions and manuals, legends, boldface and italics, graphic clues and icons, cross-references, Boolean logic strategies, time lines, hypertext links, knowledge trees, URLs, etc.) including the use of:
- Search tools and commands for stand-alone, CD-ROM, networked or Web-based online databases and services;
- Search tools and commands for searching the Internet, such as search engines, meta search tools, bots, directories, jump pages, and specialized resources such as those that search the Invisible Web;
- Specialized sites and search tool commands that limit searches by date, location, format, collection of evaluated sites or other criteria.

4. Use of Information
After finding potentially useful resources, students must engage (read, view, listen) the information to determine its relevance and then extract the relevant information. Students will be able to:

- Connect and operate the computer technology needed to access information, and read the guides and manuals associated with such tasks.
- Know and be able to use the software and hardware needed to view, download, decompress and open documents, files, and programs from Internet sites and archives.
- Copy and paste information from an electronic source into a personal document complete with proper citation.
- Take notes and outline with a word processor, database, presentation or similar productivity program.
- Record electronic sources of information and locations of those sources in order to properly cite and credit sources in footnotes, endnotes, and bibliographies.
- Use electronic spreadsheets, databases, and statistical software to process and analyze statistical data.
- Analyze and filter electronic information in relation to the task, rejecting information that is not relevant.
- Save and backup data gathered to secure locations (floppy disk, personal hard drive space, RW-CD, online storage, flash memory, etc.)

5. Synthesis
Students must organize and communicate the results of the information problem-solving effort. Students will be able to:

- Classify and group information using a word processor, database or spreadsheet.
- Use word processing and desktop publishing software to create printed documents, applying keyboard skills equivalent to at least twice the rate of handwriting speed.

Continued on next page

- Create and use computer-generated graphics and art in various print and electronic presentations.
- Use electronic spreadsheet software to create original spreadsheets.
- Generate charts, tables and graphs using electronic spreadsheets and other graphing programs.
- Use database software to create original databases.
- Use presentation software to create electronic slide shows and to generate overhead transparencies and slides.
- Create and use projection devices to show hypermedia and multimedia productions with digital video, audio and links to HTML documents or other programs. Convert presentations for display as Web pages.
- Create Web pages and sites using hypertext markup language (HTML) in a text document or using Web page creation tools and know the procedure for having these pages loaded to a Web server.
- Use e-mail, ftp, groupware, and other telecommunications capabilities to publish the results of the information problem-solving activity.
- Use specialized computer applications as appropriate for specific tasks, e.g., music composition software, computer-assisted drawing and drafting programs, mathematics modeling software, scientific measurement instruments, etc.
- Properly cite and credit electronic sources (text, graphics, sound and video) of information within the product as well as in footnotes, endnotes, and bibliographies.

6. Evaluation

Evaluation focuses on how well the final product meets the original task (effectiveness) and the process of how well students carried out the information problem-solving process (efficiency). Students may evaluate their own work and process or be evaluated by others (i.e., classmates, teachers, library media staff, parents). Students will be able to:

- Evaluate electronic presentations in terms of the content and format and design self-assessment tools to help them evaluate their own work for both content and format.
- Use spell and grammar checking capabilities of word processing and other software to edit and revise their work.
- Apply legal principles and ethical conduct related to information technology related to copyright and plagiarism.
- Understand and abide by telecomputing etiquette when using e-mail, newsgroups, listservs and other Internet functions.
- Understand and abide by acceptable use policies and other school rules in relation to use of the Internet and other electronic technologies.
- Use e-mail, real-time communications (e.g., listservs, newsgroups, instant messaging services, chat rooms, IP telephony) desktop teleconferencing, and groupware on the Internet and local area networks to communicate with teachers and others regarding their performance on assignments, tasks, and information problems.
- Thoughtfully reflect on the use of electronic resources and tools throughout the process.

Figure 9.1. Technology as a Tool. From Eisenberg & Johnson (2002). Reprinted with permission.

Big6 Skill: 1. Task Definition

Information Literacy Standards:
- 1.1 recognizes the need for information
- 1.3 formulates a question based on information needs

National Educational Technology Standards:
- 6.1 Students use technology resources for solving problems and making informed decisions.

Basic Activities:
- Concept Mapping

Advanced Activities:
- Graphic Organizers

Big6 Skill: 2. Information Seeking Strategies

Information Literacy Standards:
- 1.4 identifies a variety of potential sources of information
- 2.4 selects information appropriate to the problem or question at hand

National Educational Technology Standards:
- 5.3 Students evaluate and select new information resources . . . based on the appropriateness for specific tasks.

Basic Activities:
- Subject Directories, Evaluating Web sites

Advanced Activities:
- Web site evaluation

Big6 Skill: 3. Location & Access

Information Literacy Standards:
- 1.5 develops and uses successful strategies for learning information
- 7.1 seeks information from diverse sources, contents, disciplines, and cultures

National Educational Technology Standards:
- 5.1 Students use technology to locate, evaluate, and collect information from a variety of sources.

Basic Activities:
- Keyword Searching, Search Strategies

Advanced Activities:
- MetaSearch Engines Searching Tutorial

Big6 Skill: 4. Use of Information

Information Literacy Standards:
- 2.1 determines accuracy, relevance, and comprehensiveness
- 2.2 distinguishes among facts, point of view, and opinion

National Educational Technology Standards:
- 2.2 Students practice responsible use of technology systems, information, and software

Continued on next page

Basic Activities:
  • Analyze Sources
Advanced Activities:
  • Identify Point of View

Big6 Skill: 5. Synthesis

Information Literacy Standards:
  • 3.1 organizes information for practical application
  • 3.4 produces and communicates information and ideas in appropriate formats
  • 9.1 shares knowledge and information with others
National Educational Technology Standards:
  • 3.2 Students use productivity tools to collaborate in constructing technology-enhanced models, prepare publications, and produce other creative works.
  • 4.2 Students use a variety of media and formats to communicate information and ideas effectively to multiple audiences.
Basic Activities:
Critical Thinking Appropriate Product Bibliographic Citations Advanced Activities:
  • Classroom Applications

Big6 Skill: 6. Evaluation

Information Literacy Standards:
  • 6.1 assesses the quality of the process and products of one's own information-seeking
National Educational Technology Standards:
  • 3.1 Students use technology tools to enhance learning, increase productivity, and promote creativity.
Basic Activities:
  • Assessment Rubrics
Advanced Activities:
  • Information Power

Figure 9.2. Applying Big6™ Skills, Information Literacy Standards and ISTE NETS to Internet Research. Reprinted with permission from http://www.surfline.ne.jp/janetm/big6info.htm.

Many U.S. states embrace the idea of teaching technology skills in the context of information problem solving. Fulton (1997) provides details of efforts in Oregon, where technology standards are incorporated with information literacy standards, and in Illinois, where the standards call for students to become:

  • Information seekers, navigators, and evaluators
  • Critical thinkers, analyzers, and selectors of information and technologies appropriate to the task

- Creators of knowledge using information resources and technology
- Effective communicators using a variety of appropriate technologies/media
- Technical users
- Responsible citizens in a technological age. (p. 35)

Other state projects that include technology skills in the context of information literacy standards are the California Technology Assistance Project (CTAP) *Information Literacy Guidelines K–12* (undated). These standards, which follow a basic information problem-solving model, include appropriate technology skills at each step of the process. This reinforces the idea that technology skills are best learned in the context of information literacy.

Technology in Higher Education

The 2002 Campus Computing Survey reported that information technology has moved beyond the realm of classroom tools (e-mail, online databases, class Web sites, etc.) to assume a role as a key component of campus life. According to the survey, campus Web portals are gaining popularity across the country. Some 21.2 percent of reporting schools had a portal up and running by fall 2002, while 20.4 percent are in the final planning stages for such a tool. Similarly, Web site services for students are on the rise. Some of the services include undergraduate application, course reserves, registration, transcripts, and eCommerce (2002 Campus Computing Survey). Not only is technology changing life and instruction on campus, but it is also allowing colleges and universities to offer their courses to students all over the world through distance education. According to the Survey, 62 percent of participating higher education institutions offered distance education courses in 2001.

The Computer Science and Telecommunications Board of the National Research Council has authored an extremely important document outlining the need for technology education on campus: *Being Fluent With Information Technology* (1999). The book argues that college students must develop "FITness," which is characterized by knowledge in three areas:

- Contemporary skills, the ability to use today's computer applications, enable people to apply information technology immediately. In the present labor market, skills are an essential component to job readiness. Most importantly, skills provide a store of practical experience on which to build new competence.

- Foundational concepts, the basic principles and ideas of computers, networks, and information, underpin the technology. Concepts explain the how and why of information technology, and they give insight into its opportunities and limitations. Concepts are the raw material for understanding new information technology as it evolves.

- Intellectual capabilities, the ability to apply information technology in complex and sustained situations, encapsulate higher-level thinking in the context of information technology. Capabilities empower people to manipulate the medium to their advantage and to handle unintended and unexpected problems when they arise. The intellectual capabilities foster more abstract thinking about information and its manipulation. (1999, p. 3)

The handbook argues that the benefits of FITness are many and include personal rationales, a workforce rationale, an educational rationale, and a societal rationale.

The handbook moves beyond simply arguing for the importance of FITness to provide a framework for its implementation at the college level. It explores the intellectual framework for making FITness a part of university curriculum, examines collateral issues, and outlines methods of implementation.

The University of Washington is a leader in the development of FITness in the curriculum. In spring 2003, The Information School, Computer Science and Engineering, and Computing and Communications collaborated to offer the course "Fluency with Information Technology." According to instructor Grace Beauchane Whiteaker, the course consists of three multifaceted units—networks, programming, and database design. The university is also developing an unmoderated, public domain, distance learning version of the course, which will be released in spring 2004 (Whiteaker, personal correspondence, September 29, 2003).

Technology for Information

The Internet is a technology that presents a special set of problems and opportunities for educators in both the K–12 and post-secondary environments. The sheer volume of material on the Web easily leads to information overload, and the less-than-perfect searching tools it provides often lead to frustration. Eisenberg and Berkowitz (1996) advocate teaching students to use the Internet in the same way any technology is taught—from a process approach. Information technology skills, particularly those relating to the Internet, must be taught within two different contexts: the subject area curriculum and the overall information literacy process. By learning technology skills in context, students of all ages discover how to use technology to meet their information needs. They also learn the kind of mental flexibility they need to adapt to the changing information technology environment. The Big6 Web site (http://big6.com) provides more strategies, examples, and lessons for teaching students to get what they need from the Internet without suffering information overload.

Of course, other technologies used in schools, colleges, and universities provide access to information. Information is available on the World Wide Web, CD-ROMs, local networked full-text sources, and databases. These sources require a level of information literacy from users comparable to what is necessary for using the Internet. When using these resources, users must be able to select among sources to find the best resources to satisfy their information needs. There are several criteria for determining relevant sources:

- accuracy,
- completeness,
- reliability (Is it authoritative?),
- preciseness,
- validity (Is it on target?),
- availability,
- currency,
- ease-of-use,
- cost, and
- entertainment (Is it fun?).

The ability to judge the appropriateness of an information source, whether it is on CD-ROM or on the World Wide Web, is an information literacy skill that all students must develop.

The Benefits of Information Technology

Information technology integrated into the curriculum can enhance the development of students' information literacy skills. A Center for Applied Special Technology (2000) study of 500 fourth and sixth graders in seven large urban districts across the United States looked at students' use of the Internet in the context of a unit of study on Civil Rights. The study was co-sponsored by the Scholastic Network and the Council of the Great City Schools. Students were divided into two groups: those with online access and those without. An overview of the study states:

> The results show significantly higher scores on measurements of information management, communication, and presentation of ideas. It offers evidence that using Scholastic Network and the Internet can help students become independent, critical thinkers, able to find information, organize and evaluate it, and then effectively express their new knowledge and ideas in compelling ways. (Center for Applied Special Technology, 2000)

These are the information literacy skills we want for all of our children. The recent increase in the availability of technology in our schools at all levels affords teachers an opportunity to infuse technology into education, so that students will learn the essential information literacy skills they need to be successful in their future lives.

Summary

Information technology is the great enabler. It provides, for those who have access to it, an extension of their powers of perception, comprehension, analysis, thought, concentration, and articulation through a range of activities including "writing, visual images, mathematics, music, physical movement, sensing the environment, simulation, and communication" (Carpenter, 1989, p. 2).

As Carpenter (1989) has detailed, technology, in all of its various forms, offers us tools to access, manipulate, transform, evaluate, use, and present information. These technology skills are integral to the information problem-solving process taught in the context of the curriculum.

Let's review key points in this chapter:

- Technology in schools includes computers, televisions, video cameras, video editing equipment, and TV studios.

- Two approaches to technology in K–12 schools are technology as the object of instruction and the process/skills in context approach—using technology as a tool. The latter approach makes sense in terms of current pedagogy.

- Many U.S. states are starting to incorporate technology skills instruction in the context of information literacy skills. Examples from Oregon, Illinois, and California show how this may be achieved.

- Technology is changing the way higher education institutions are offering instruction and conducting campus life.

- The importance of information technology knowledge and skills is gaining the attention of colleges and universities.

- Use of the Internet should be taught within the contexts of the subject area curriculum and the overall information literacy process.

- One study suggests that students who use technology as a tool may become better at managing information and communicating and presenting ideas.

Chapter

Information Literacy: The Future and the Past

10

The broad educational and library communities are increasingly recognizing the value of information literacy and are in the process of integrating information literacy skills instruction with the curriculum. What began as an expansion of traditional library skills instruction in K–12 and bibliographic instruction (BI) in higher education is now a major focus of education and an increasing interest of societies worldwide, with organizations like the Partnership for 21st Century Skills and AOL Time Warner taking up the charge.

In this chapter we provide brief examples of areas where we believe information literacy efforts will expand in the future. We will also briefly reflect upon what we have learned about information literacy.

As we noted in previous chapters, efforts to infuse information literacy throughout the educational community are firmly established. These efforts are still expanding thanks to such endeavors as

- the inclusion of *Information Literacy Standards for Student Learning* in the publication *Information Power: Building Partnerships for Learning*, developed by the American Association of School Librarians (AASL) and the Association for Educational Communications and Technology (AECT);

- the development of information literacy skills standards by many states;

- the decision by some national accreditation agencies to include information competency as a component of accreditation;

- the development of information competencies by the Association of College and Research Libraries (ACRL) as well as individual colleges and universities; and

- the beginnings of societal attention through the work of groups like the Partnership for 21st Century Skills and AOL Time Warner.

Where Will We See Information Literacy Efforts Expand in the Future?

Challenges posed by new technologies and the rapidly increasing amount of information available from a variety of sources make it clear that information literacy skills are important for everyone. In this section we take a brief look at areas where information literacy programs have potential for growth.

K–12 and Higher Education

The K–12 arena has been one of the greatest success stories for information literacy integration thus far. In the future, K–12 and higher educators will continue building on current efforts described throughout this book, with an acceleration of information literacy efforts. Within five years, information literacy will be pervasive in most educational situations.

Particular contexts for the growth of information literacy will be in evaluation and standards (the latter particularly in K–12). As states respond to No Child Left Behind with the development and refinement of state subject standards, they will realize that the application of these standards will need to be broad and include concepts of information literacy. This will lead to a redoubled effort to find efficient and standardized ways to evaluate information literacy skills in students of all ages.

The various technology literacy efforts going on around the country will merge into more broad, information literacy-based efforts—whether called information literacy, information and technology literacy, information and communications technology (ICT) literacy, or fluency. There will be less of an emphasis on technology and computing skills education out of the context of curriculum and broader information skills.

Finally, the excellent groundwork of AASL/AE CT's *Information Literacy Standards for Student Learning*, ACRL's *Information Literacy Competency Standards for Higher Education*, and ISTE's *Technology Foundation Standards for All Students* will lead technology integration and information literacy experts to combine efforts to create the definitive information literacy and technology standards. These will help guide decisions from policy to purchasing as education enters a new era.

Public Libraries

The public library is still the place where anyone may have free access to information in both print and electronic formats. Public libraries teach information literacy skills to groups and in one-to-one sessions. The Deerfield (Illinois) Public Library, for example, is typical of public library programs that provide instruction to the public on how to use computers to access information in various formats including the World Wide Web. The library's basic computer searching classes are repeated several times each month, and there are special sessions designed specifically for home-based business owners who want to learn how to use the Internet.

The Science, Industry and Business Library (SIBL), located in Manhattan, and part of The New York Public Library, is the world's largest public information center devoted entirely to science and business. The library has an extensive research collection, a wealth of electronic resources, and more than 170 public workstations. To help and encourage the public to use both electronic and print resources, SIBL offers free classes. As many as five classes are offered each day in a state-of-the-art teaching facility. The library trains an average of 1,000 people each month. SIBLs Web workshops are particularly popular. Designed for both beginners and intermediates, they focus on the skills needed to search the World Wide Web. SIBL is developing a new course to teach the public how to evaluate information found on Web sites (Bentley, 1997).

Information literacy is a key component of user education at Seattle Public Library. The librarians use information literacy as a guiding principle in many interactions with users, from formal instruction to reference help.

Basic literacy instruction is also common in public libraries. However, basic literacy is no longer sufficient for survival in the Information Age. Along with learning to read, students must also learn information literacy skills. A project funded by the Lila Wallace Readers' Digest Fund and the American Library Association allowed the Onondaga County (New York) Public Library (OCPL) to develop such a course. The OCPL adult literacy/learner curriculum teaches basic literacy students how to search for information using a computer (both local and via the Internet), how to communicate via e-mail, how to read their search results, and how to analyze information found in print and electronic resources.

Community Technology Centers (CTCs) will play an increasingly large role in the future. These organizations—which make technology resources available to members of the community who are typically disenfranchised—will continue to have a major impact on the narrowing of the digital divide. There is a real opportunity for CTCs and public libraries to work together to provide integrated information literacy and technology instruction to people of all ages.

Adult Education

The skills needed to access, evaluate, and use information to maintain employment, or make personal decisions, are constantly changing. Adult learners need to commit to lifelong learning to improve their information skills. In a project sponsored by an NFIL Literacy Leader Fellowship, Cowles (1997) found that there was little difference between the Internet skills of literacy students and the rest of the adult population. Her project team conducted a needs assessment of 245 adult learners and 123 adult education instructors in Oregon. Survey results were used to develop and test curricular materials focusing on information skills for adult learners. Participants were instructors and learners in Oregon, Washington, North Carolina, Ohio, Illinois, and other states. A staff development team representing various educational settings such as corrections, family literacy, welfare reform, ESOL, adult basic education, and adult secondary education presented the curricular materials to the Adult Literacy and Technology Conference in Boise, Idaho, and to the Oregon Adult Basic Education Summer Conference. Cowles reports that the project is ongoing with additional support coming from the Northwest Regional Literacy Resource Center and some 353 additional funding sources (Cowles, personal communication, March 1998).

Education Programs in the Private and Public Sector

As noted previously, companies must have information literate workers to maintain a position in today's economy. Kanter (1996) reported on efforts by the Bank of Boston to teach its employees how to use technology and information. The bank has a long-range education plan that emphasizes information technology training and makes such training available when and where users need it by offering over 100 self-paced courses.

As the importance of information literacy reaches public consciousness (and as the cost of workplace technical infrastructure continues to mount), expect to see information literacy programs put in place throughout the government, with programs mirrored in public affairs schools. Analysis of global information issues will provide meaty content for a new generation of policymakers and politicians, and this issue will come to the fore in the next decade.

A similar movement will begin in information-rich professions like medicine and law. The overwhelming amount of information and wide range of resources lawyers and doctors are exposed to will point to a need for information literacy skills for these individuals. The medical informatics field shows enormous promise and will continue to grow and develop.

Conclusion: A Look Back

Throughout our examination of information literacy, we have shown how information literacy efforts have accelerated since Zurkowski first mentioned the concept in 1974. Because the *Final Report* of the American Library Association (ALA) Presidential Committee on Information Literacy was the seminal event in the definition, development, and dissemination of the concept of information literacy, it seems fitting to conclude this monograph by reprinting a portion of that report here:

How our country deals with the realities of the Information Age will have enormous impact on our democratic way of life and on our nation's ability to compete internationally. Within America's information society, there also exists the potential of addressing many long-standing social and economic inequities. To reap such benefits, people as individuals and as a nation must be information literate. To be information literate, a person must be able to recognize when information is needed and have the ability to locate, evaluate, and use effectively the needed information. Producing such a citizenry will require that schools and colleges appreciate and integrate the concept of information literacy into their learning programs and that they play a leadership role in equipping individuals and institutions to take advantage of the opportunities inherent within the information society. Ultimately, information literate people are those who have learned how to learn. They know how to learn because they know how knowledge is organized, how to find information, and how to use information in such a way that others can learn from them. They are people prepared for lifelong learning, because they can always find the information needed for any task or decision at hand. (American Library Association Presidential Committee on Information Literacy, 1989, p. 1)

Let's more closely analyze each section of this text, considering what we have learned throughout the book.

> How our country deals with the realities of the Information Age will have enormous impact on our democratic way of life and on our nation's ability to compete internationally.

An economy based on information requires workers who will know how to locate, analyze, manage, interpret, use, and present information in all of its formats. In identifying the skills necessary for the workplace of the future, the Secretary's Commission on Achieving Necessary Skills (SCANS) report published in 1991 notes that workers will need to be lifelong learners who possess skills beyond those of reading, writing, and arithmetic. The Commission concluded that due to the global nature of the economy, and the impact of technology, "good jobs will increasingly depend on people who can put knowledge to work" (SCANS, 1991, p. xv). The AOL Time Warner Foundation and the Partnership for 21st Century Skills are finding ways to implement the vision of SCANS in today's schools.

> Within America's information society, there also exists the potential of addressing many long-standing social and economic inequities. To reap such benefits, people as individuals and as a nation must be information literate. . . . Producing such a citizenry will require that schools and colleges appreciate and integrate the concept of information literacy into their learning programs and that they play a leadership role in equipping individuals and institutions to take advantage of the opportunities inherent within the information society.

Given that the economy will be based on information, it is incumbent upon our educational system, from kindergarten through adult education, to incorporate information literacy skills instruction within content areas. The publication of the *Information Literacy Standards for Student Learning* in the national guidelines for school library media programs, *Information Power: Building Partnerships for Learning*, fosters this process on the K–12 level as library media specialists and teachers work collaboratively to provide opportunities for students to learn information literacy from the content. Higher education institutions are well on their way to including information literacy competencies as a graduation requirement, while academic librarians and faculty members work together to make this a reality. The creation of the Institute for Information Literacy (IIL) helps the effort by providing models for information literacy skills instruction, and ACRL's *Information Literacy Competency Standards for Higher Education* create a tangible definition of information literacy in higher education.

> To be information literate, a person must be able to recognize when information is needed and have the ability to locate, evaluate, and use effectively the needed information.

Educators and librarians have used this definition of information literacy as a springboard for discussion of what information literacy entails. Many information literacy definitions, developed throughout the past decades, have expanded this definition to include information in its variety of formats. The *Information Literacy Standards for Student Learning* and ACRL's *Information Literacy Competency Standards for Higher Education* enumerate the skills inherent in becoming information literate. Among these skills is the use of technology. Technology is changing the way we learn and is making information instantaneously available in a variety of formats. Technology is a tool that allows us to access, manipulate, transform, evaluate, use, and present information. These technology skills are integral to the information literacy skills that are taught in the context of the curriculum.

> Ultimately, information literate people are those who have learned how to learn. They know how to learn because they know how knowledge is organized, how to find information, and how to use information in such a way that others can learn from them. They are people prepared for lifelong learning, because they can always find the information needed for any task or decision at hand.

Patricia Senn Breivik, noted information literacy advocate and author, states that "In this next century, an 'educated' graduate will no longer be defined as one who has absorbed a certain body of factual information, but as one who knows how to find, evaluate, and apply needed information" (1998, p. 2). Breivik's quote embodies the shift in our educational institutions to focus on process rather than content. However, we must realize that even after we graduate, our education is never complete. Our ability to be information literate depends on our willingness to be lifelong learners as we are challenged to master new, and as yet unknown, technologies that will surely alter the landscape of information in the future.

Summary

Although no one can predict the future, we believe that we are simply at the beginning of the information literacy movement. An explosion of interest in this topic is imminent, with libraries, K–12, higher education, and community groups leading the way.

Appendix A

Information Literacy Standards for Student Learning

Prepared by the American Association of School Librarians and the Association for Educational Communications and Technology

From *Information Power: Building Partnerships for Learning* by American Association of School Librarians and Association for Educational Communications and Technology. Copyright © 1998 American Library Association and Association for Educational Communications and Technology. Reprinted by permission of the American Library Association.

The following three categories, nine standards, and twenty-nine indicators describe the content and processes related to information that students must master to be considered well educated. The items related to information literacy describe the core learning outcomes that are most obviously related to the services provided by school library media programs. The items related to the other two other areas—independent learning and social responsibility—are grounded in information literacy and describe more general aspects of student learning to which school library media programs also make important contributions.

The latter two categories build upon the first so that, taken together and pursued to the highest levels, the standards and indicators present a profile of the information literate high school graduate: one who has the ability to use information to acquire both core and advanced knowledge and to become an independent, lifelong learner who contributes responsibly and productively to the learning community. The standards and indicators themselves are written at a level of generality that assumes that individual states, districts, sites, and school personnel must provide the level of detail necessary to apply them across multiple sources and formats of information and to the developmental, cultural, and learning needs of all the students they serve.

Information Literacy Standards
for Student Learning

Category I: Information Literacy

Standard 1: **The student who is information literate accesses information efficiently and effectively.**

Indicator 1: Recognizes the need for information

Indicator 2: Recognizes that accurate and comprehensive information is the basis for intelligent decision making

Indicator 3: Formulates questions based on information needs

Indicator 4: Identifies a variety of potential sources of information

Indicator 5: Develops and uses successful strategies for locating information.

Standard 2: **The student who is information literate evaluates information critically and competently.**

Indicator 1: Determines accuracy, relevance, and comprehensiveness

Indicator 2: Distinguishes among fact, point of view, and opinion

Indicator 3: Identifies inaccurate and misleading information

Indicator 4: Selects information appropriate to the problem or question at hand.

Standard 3: **The student who is information literate uses information accurately and creatively.**

Indicator 1: Organizes information for practical application

Indicator 2: Integrates new information into one's own knowledge

Indicator 3: Applies information in critical thinking and problem solving

Indicator 4: Produces and communicates information and ideas in appropriate formats.

Category II: Independent Learning

Standard 4: **The student who is an independent learner is information literate and pursues information related to personal interests.**

Indicator 1: Seeks information related to various dimensions of personal well-being, such as career interests, community involvement, health matters, and recreational pursuits

Indicator 2:   Designs, develops, and evaluates information products and solutions related to personal interests.

Standard 5:   The student who is an independent learner is information literate and appreciates and enjoys literature and other creative expressions of information.

Indicator 1:   Is a competent and self-motivated reader

Indicator 2:   Derives meaning from information presented creatively in a variety of formats

Indicator 3:   Develops creative products in a variety of formats.

Standard 6:   The student who is an independent learner is information literate and strives for excellence in information seeking and knowledge generation.

Indicator 1:   Assesses the quality of the process and products of personal information seeking

Indicator 2:   Devises strategies for revising, improving, and updating self-generated knowledge.

Category III: Social Responsibility

Standard 7:   The student who contributes positively to the learning community and to society is information literate and recognizes the importance of information to a democratic society.

Indicator 1:   Seeks information from diverse sources, contexts, disciplines, and cultures

Indicator 2:   Respects the principle of equitable access to information.

Standard 8:   The student who contributes positively to the learning community and to society is information literate and practices ethical behavior in regard to information and information technology.

Indicator 1:   Respects the principles of intellectual freedom

Indicator 2:   Respects intellectual property rights

Indicator 3:   Uses information technology responsibly.

Standard 9: **The student who contributes positively to the learning community and to society is information literate and participates effectively in groups to pursue and generate information.**

Indicator 1: Shares knowledge and information with others

Indicator 2: Respects others' ideas and backgrounds and acknowledges their contributions

Indicator 3: Collaborates with others, both in person and through technologies, to identify information problems and to seek their solutions

Indicator 4: Collaborates with others, both in person and through technologies, to design, develop, and evaluate information products and solutions.

Appendix B

SCANS: A Three-Part Foundation

Basic Skills: *Reads, writes, performs arithmetic and mathematical operations, listens, and speaks.*

> **Reading:** Locates, understands, and interprets written information in prose and in documents such as manuals, graphs, and schedules.
>
> **Writing:** Communicates thoughts, ideas, information, and messages in writing; and creates documents such as letters, directions, manuals, reports, graphs, and flow charts.
>
> **Arithmetic/Mathematics:** Performs basic computations and approaches practical problems by choosing appropriately from a variety of mathematical techniques.
>
> **Listening:** Receives, attends to, interprets, and responds to verbal messages and other cues.
>
> **Speaking:** Organizes ideas and communicates orally.

Thinking Skills: *Thinks creatively, makes decisions, solves problems, visualizes, knows how to learn and reason.*

> **Creative Thinking:** Generates new ideas.
>
> **Decision Making:** Specifies goals and constraints, generates alternatives, considers risks, and evaluates and chooses best alternative.
>
> **Problem Solving:** Recognizes problems and devises and implements plan of action.
>
> **Seeing Things in the Minds Eye:** Organizes and processes symbols, pictures, graphs, objects and other information.
>
> **Knowing How to Learn:** Uses efficient learning techniques to acquire and apply new knowledge and skills.

Reasoning: Discovers a rule or principle underlying the relationship between two or more objects and applies it in solving a problem.

Personal Qualities: *Displays responsibility, self-esteem, sociability, self-management, and integrity and honesty.*

Responsibility: Exerts a high level of effort and perseveres towards goal attainment.

Self-Esteem: Believes in own self-worth and maintains a positive view of self.

Sociability: Demonstrates understanding, friendliness, adaptability, empathy, and politeness in group settings.

Self-management: Assesses self accurately, sets personal goals, monitors progress, and exhibits self-control.

Integrity/Honesty: Chooses ethical courses of action.

Reprinted with permission from *What Work Requires of Schools: A SCANS Report for America 2000.*

Appendix C

SCANS Definitions: The Five Competencies

Resources:

Allocates Time: Selects relevant, goal-related activities, ranks them in order of importance, allocates time to activities, and understands, prepares, and follows schedules.

Allocates Money: Uses or prepares budgets, including making cost and revenue forecasts, keeps detailed records to track budget performance, and makes appropriate adjustments.

Allocates Material and Facility Resources: Acquires, stores, and distributes materials, supplies, parts, equipment, space, or final products in order to make the best use of them.

Allocates Human Resources: Assess knowledge and skills and distributes work accordingly, evaluates performance, and provides feedback.

Interpersonal:

Participates as a Member of a Team: Works cooperatively with others and contributes to group with ideas, suggestions, and effort.

Teaches Others: Helps others learn.

Serves Clients/Customers: Works and communicates with clients and customers to satisfy their expectations.

Exercises Leadership: Communicates thoughts, feelings, and ideas to justify a position. Encourages, persuades, convinces or otherwise motivates an individual or groups, including responsibly challenging existing procedures, policies, or authority.

Negotiates: Works towards an agreement that may involve exchanging specific resources or resolving divergent interests.

Works with Cultural Diversity: Works well with men and women and with a variety of ethnic, social, or educational backgrounds.

Information:

Acquires and Evaluates Information: Identifies need for data, obtains it from existing sources or creates it, and evaluates its relevance and accuracy.

Organizes and Maintains Information: Organizes, processes, and maintains written or computerized records and other forms of information in a systematic fashion.

Interprets and Communicates Information: Selects and analyzes information and communicates the results to others using oral, written, graphic, pictorial, or multi-media methods.

Uses Computers to Process Information: Employs computers to acquire, organize, analyze, and communicate information.

Systems:

Understands Systems: Knows how social, organizational, and technological systems work and operates effectively within them.

Monitors and Corrects Performance: Distinguishes trends, predicts impact of actions on system operations, diagnoses deviations in the function of a system/organization, and takes necessary action to correct performance.

Improves and Designs Systems: Makes suggestions to modify existing systems to improve products or services, and develops new or alternative systems.

Technology:

Selects Technology: Judges which set of procedures, tools, or machines, including computers and their programs, will produce the desired results.

Applies Technology to the Task: Understands the overall intent and the proper procedures for setting up and operating machines, including computers and their programming systems.

Maintains and Troubleshoots Technology: Prevents, identifies, or solves problems in machines, computers, and other technologies.

Reprinted with permission from *What Work Requires of Schools: A SCANS Report for America 2000* (ED 332 054).

Appendix D

A Chronology of the Development of Information Literacy

The following chronology was constructed by combining information from this publication with that explored by Shirley Behrens in "A Conceptual Analysis and Historical Overview of Information Literacy," College and Research Libraries, 55(4), 309-322. *It is not meant to be all inclusive, nor was it constructed to exclude any particular viewpoint or source. The reader is referred to Behrens's article for an excellent discussion and analysis of the development of information literacy.*

1974   Zurkowski introduces the concept of information literacy in a proposal submitted to the National Commission on Libraries and Information Science (NCLIS):

> People trained in the application of information resources to their work can be called information literates. They have learned techniques and skills for utilizing the wide range of information tools as well as primary sources in molding information-solutions to their problems. (Zurkowski, 1974, p. 6)

1976   Burchinal presents a paper at the Texas A & M University library's symposium that further refines information as a set of skills:

> To be information literate requires a new set of skills. These include how to locate and use information needed for problem-solving and decision-making efficiently and effectively. (Burchinal, 1976, p. 11)

1979   The Information Industry Association (IIA) defines an information literate as:

> a person who knows the techniques and skills for using information tools in molding solutions to problems. (Garfield, 1979, p. 210)

1979   Taylor suggests the elements of information literacy in *Library Journal*:

> an approximate definition of [information literacy] would include the following elements:
>
> - That solutions to many (not all) problems can be aided by the acquisition of appropriate facts and information
> - That knowledge of the variety of information resources available (who and where) is a requisite of this literacy
> - That the information process, which is continual, is as important as the spot information process, which is occasional, and
> - That there are strategies (when and how) of information acquisition. (Taylor, 1979, p. 1875)

1982   *Time* magazine names the computer as the Man of the Year.

1983   April—National Commission on Excellence in Education issues *A Nation at Risk*, a report decrying the lack of a rigorous education in the nation's schools. Despite identifying the management of complex information in electronic and digital forms as an important skill in a learning society, the report makes no recommendations on the role of the library or information resources in K–12 education.

1983   In an article in the *Bulletin of the American Society for Information Science*, Hortin refers to computer literacy, then to information literacy:

> Computer literacy has to do with increasing our understanding of what the machine can and cannot do. There are two major components of computer literacy: hardware and software. (Horton, 1983, p. 14)

> Information literacy, then, as opposed to computer literacy, means raising the level of awareness of individuals and enterprises to the knowledge explosion, and how machine-aided handling systems can help identify, access, and obtain data, documents and literature needed for problem-solving and decision-making. (p. 16)

1985   Irving's *Study and Information Skills Across the Curriculum* highlights the importance of information skills for students in completing classroom assignments and further asserts that such skills are essential skills for all aspects of life—academic, professional, and personal.

1985   A definition created for the Auraria Library at the Denver campus of the University of Colorado to investigate how the library could use its education program to ensure information literacy of its students states:

> General definition: Information literacy is the ability to effectively access and evaluate information for a given need. (Developed by Martin Tessmer, 1985)

> Characteristics of information literacy:

> - An integrated set of skills and knowledge skills (research strategy, evaluation) knowledge of tools and resources
> - Developed through acquisition of attitudes persistence attention to detail; caution in accepting printed word and single sources
> - Time and labor intensive
> - Need driven (a problem-solving activity)
> - Distinct but relevant to literacy and computer literacy
> - Information literacy is *not*:
> - (Only) knowledge of resources
> - Library dependent (as a sole source)
> - Information finding (also understanding and evaluating). (in Breivik, 1985, p. 723)

1986   Mancall, Aaron, and Walker publish "Educating Students to Think: The Role of the School Library Media Program," which describes the role of school library media program in helping students develop thinking skills and the need to develop an information skills program in all curricular areas.

1987   Kuhlthau publishes *Information Skills for an Information Society: A Review of the Research,* which points the way toward the inclusion of information literacy with the curriculum. In this publication she states:

What does it mean to be literate in an information society? Information literacy is closely tied to functional literacy. It involves the ability to read and use information essential for everyday life. It also involves recognizing an information need and seeking information to make informed decisions. Information literacy requires the abilities to manage complex masses of information generated by computers and mass media, and to learn throughout life as technical and social changes demand new skills and knowledge. (Kuhlthau, 1987, p. 2)

1987   March—Libraries and the Search for Academic Excellence, a symposium co-sponsored by Columbia University and the University of Colorado, brings together academic leaders and leaders in the field of librarianship to examine the role of libraries in academia. The outcomes and action recommendations resulting from the symposium establish the importance of information literacy skills and form the basis for current information literacy efforts in higher education:

Reports on undergraduate education identify the need for more active learning whereby students become self-directed independent learners who are prepared for lifelong learning. To accomplish this, students need to become information literate whereby they:

- Understand the process and systems for acquiring current and retrospective information, e.g., systems and services for information identification and delivery

- Are able to evaluate the effectiveness and reliability of various information channels and sources, including libraries, for various kinds of needs

- Master certain basic skills in acquiring and storing their own information, e.g., database skills, spreadsheet skills, word and information processing skills, books, journals, and report literature, and

- Are articulate and responsible citizens in considering current and future public policy issues relating to information, e.g., copyright, privacy, privatization of government information, and those issues yet to emerge.

To make possible the above, information gathering and evaluation skills need to be mastered at the undergraduate level, and learning opportunities should be integrated within the existing departments, analogous, to writing across the curriculum, rather than as standalone bibliographic instruction programs. Administrators, faculty and librarians should be engaged in creative new partnerships which transmit to students the value and reward of research in their lives as students and beyond. Information literacy should be a demonstrable outcome of undergraduate education. (Breivik & Wedgeworth, 1988, pp. 187-188)

1987   Margaret Chisholm, president of ALA, appoints a Presidential Committee on Information Literacy including leaders in the fields of education and librarianship.

1988   AASL & AECT publish *Information Power,* which states that the mission of the school library media program is "to ensure that students and staff are effective users of ideas and information" (AASL & AECT, 1988, p. 1).

1988   Eisenberg and Berkowitz publish *Curriculum Initiative: An Agenda and Strategy for Library Media Programs,* which presents the Big6™ Skills Model of Information Problem Solving, a model that gives students a systematic framework for solving information problems.

1988   The National Council for the Social Studies Ad Hoc Committee on Scope and Sequence develops *Essential Skills for Social Studies*, a K–12 scope and sequence that includes acquiring information, organizing and using information, and interpersonal relationships and social participation.

1988   Stripling and Pitts (1988) publish *Brainstorms and Blueprints*, a model of information literacy from the perspective of the school library media field.

1989   January—The American Library Association Presidential Committee on Information Literacy asserts that information literacy is a necessary skill for everyday life, for the business world, and for democracy:

How our country deals with the realities of the Information Age will have enormous impact on our democratic way of life and on our nation's ability to compete internationally. Within America's information society, there also exists the potential of addressing many long-standing social and economic inequities. To reap such benefits, people—as individuals and as a nation—must be information literate. To be information literate, a person must be able to recognize when information is needed and have the ability to locate, evaluate, and use effectively the needed information. Producing such a citizenry will require that schools and colleges appreciate and integrate the concept of information literacy into their learning programs and that they play a leadership role in equipping individuals and institutions to take advantage of the opportunities inherent within the information society. Ultimately, information literate people are those who have learned how to learn. They know how to learn because they know how knowledge is organized, how to find information, and how to use information in such a way that others can learn from them. They are people prepared for lifelong learning, because they can always find the information needed for any task or decision at hand. (American Library Association Presidential Committee on Information Literacy, 1989, p. 1)

1989   April—Based on the recommendation of ALA, a coalition for information literacy is "strategized" at an ALA-sponsored meeting in Leesburg, Virginia.

1989   May—Olsen and Coons, in a paper presented at the Seventeenth National LOEX Library Instruction Conference, state that:

We define information literacy as understanding the role and power of information, having the ability to locate it, retrieve it, and use it in decision making, and having the ability to generate and manipulate it using electronic processes. In short, information literacy is a necessary expansion of the traditional notion of literacy, a response to the revolution in which we are living. (Olsen & Coons, 1989, p. 8)

1989   September—President Bush and the nation's governors meet at an Education Summit to discuss the state of American education. As a result of the summit, six goals for the improvement of education are outlined.

1989   November 9—The first meeting of the National Forum on Information Literacy (NFIL), a coalition of organizations from business, government, and education, takes place, with Patricia Senn Breivik serving as chair.

1989   The National Council for the Social Studies (NCSS) publishes *From Information to Decision Making: New Challenges for Effective Citizenship* (1989), which focuses on information literacy skills and "provides . . . ideas about ways social studies teachers may become effective in an information age with its ever increasing gap between what we understand and what we need to understand" (NCSS, 1989, p. vii).

1989   Breivik and Gee publish *Information Literacy* (1989), a monograph fo-
        cusing on the role of the academic library in developing lifelong learners:

> Information literacy is a survival skill in the information age. In-
> stead of drowning in the abundance of information that floods
> their lives, information-literate people know how to find, evalu-
> ate, and use information effectively to solve a particular problem
> or make a decision, whether the information they select comes
> from a computer, a book, a government agency, a film, or any of
> a number of other possible resources. Students have long relied
> on the knowledge of teachers and the information skills of librar-
> ians. In fact, when the volume of information was modest, they
> could often manage without becoming information literate them-
> selves. What the information explosion has done is turn an old
> problem—functional illiteracy—into a new crisis. To address
> this crisis, we need a new educational philosophy based on a
> fuller understanding of the information explosion and a redefini-
> tion of literacy that includes information skills. (p. 12)

1990   President Bush meets with the National Governors' Conference in Char-
        lottesville, Virginia, and together they publicly announce the National
        Education Goals.

1990   The Secretary's Commission on Achieving Necessary Skills (SCANS)
        is formed by Secretary of Labor Elizabeth Dole to create a dialogue among
        workers, parents, and educators to examine the changes taking place in the
        working world and determine the skills needed for employment.

1991   May 22—President Bush submits the America 2000 Excellence in Edu-
        cation Act to Congress. This represents the Bush administration's plan to
        implement the National Education Goals.

1991   The SCANS report concludes that due to the global nature of the econ-
        omy and the impact of technology, "good jobs will increasingly depend
        on people who can put knowledge to work" (SCANS, 1991, p. xv).

1991   The Association for Supervision and Curriculum Development (ASCD)
        adopts a resolution on information literacy:

Resolution on Information Literacy
Today's information society transcends all political, social, and
economic boundaries. The global nature of human interaction
makes the ability to access and use information crucial. Differences
in cultural orientation toward information and symbol systems

make the management of information complex and challenging. Current and future reform efforts should address the rapidly changing nature of information and emerging information technologies. Information literacy, the ability to locate, process, and use information effectively, equips individuals to take advantage of the opportunities inherent in the global information society. Information literacy should be a part of every student's education experience. (Doyle, 1994, p. 12)

1991   One of the recommendations of the second White House Conference on Library and Information Services (WHCLIS) calls for the U.S. government to establish a National Coalition for Information Literacy (including schools, libraries, labor and industry, government, parents, and the general public), with the intention of developing a strategic plan for the general development of skills required for information literacy.

1991   Goodin's research shows that the students who receive library skills instruction in the context of information literacy scored significantly higher on a post-test than students who did not receive instruction.

1991   National Literacy Act of 1991 defines literacy as "an individual's ability to read, write, and speak in English, and to use the computer and solve problems at levels of proficiency necessary to function on the job and in society, to achieve one's goals, and to develop one's knowledge and potential" (National Institute for Literacy, undated).

1992   Eisenberg and Brown publish "Current Themes Regarding Library and Information Skills Instruction: Research Supporting and Research Lacking," comparing several widely known models of information literacy that have been developed through research and evaluation. The authors conclude that there are more similarities than there are differences among these models.

1992   Gratch et al. publish *Information Retrieval and Evaluation Skills for Education Students*, a document outlining essential information literacy skills for students in teacher training programs.

1992   Lance, Welborn, and Hamilton-Pennell's *The Impact of School Library Media Centers on Academic Achievement* (1992) reveals some very important findings:

> • Where library media programs are better funded, academic achievement is higher, whether their schools and communities are rich or poor and whether adults in the community are well or poorly educated.

- Better funding for library media programs fosters academic achievement by providing students access to more library media staff and larger and more varied collections.

- Among predictors of academic achievement, the size of the library media program staff and collection is second only to the absence of at-risk conditions, particularly poverty and low educational attainment among adults.

- Students whose library media specialists participate in the instructional process are higher academic achievers.

1992 Doyle publishes the results of a Delphi study analyzing the National Goals for Education and expands the definition of information literacy. An information literate person is one who:

- Recognizes that accurate and complete information is the basis for intelligent decision making

- Recognizes the need for information

- Formulates questions based on information needs

- Identifies potential sources of information

- Develops successful search strategies

- Accesses sources of information including computer-based and other technologies

- Evaluates information

- Organizes information for practical application

- Integrates new information into an existing body of knowledge

- Uses information in critical thinking and problem solving. (Doyle, 1992, p. 8)

1992 The State University of New York Task Force on College Entry Level Knowledge and Skills recommends the inclusion of strong information literacy components in teacher education and library school curricula.

1992 The term "information literacy" is added as a descriptor to the ERIC Thesaurus.

1993 January—The Council of Library Directors of the California State University (CSU) system begins a planning effort to identify and foster information competence under the auspices of the Commission on

Learning Resources and Instructional Technology (CLRIT). The Council's charge was to recommend to the Chancellor policy guidelines that facilitate the effective uses of learning resources and instructional technology throughout the CSU (University Library–Cal Poly Pomona, 1995).

1993   Wisconsin Educational Media Association publishes "Information Literacy: A Position Paper on Information Problem-Solving."

1993   Middle States Association of Colleges and Schools Commission on Higher Education adds assessment of information literacy in the curriculum to its agenda.

1993   Kuhlthau publishes her research into the information-seeking behavior of students, noting that information literacy is not a discrete set of skills but rather a way of learning.

1994   March 31—The Goals 2000: Educate America Act specifying the eight National Education Goals is signed into law by President Clinton.

1994   The American Association of School Librarians publishes a position paper outlining seven basic elements of information literacy.

1994   The Commission on Higher Education (CHE), Middle States Association of Colleges and Schools, which accredits institutions of higher education, develops the following standard on information literacy:

> Each institution should foster optimal use of its learning resources through strategies designed to help students develop information literacy—the ability to locate, evaluate, and use information in order to become independent learners. It should encourage the use of a wide range of non-classroom resources for teaching and learning. It is essential to have an active and continuing program of library orientation and instruction in accessing information, developed collaboratively and supported actively by faculty, librarians, academic deans, and other information providers. (Commission on Higher Education, 1995, p. v)

1994   Breivik and Senn publish *Information Literacy: Educating Children for the 21st Century* (1994), a monograph focusing on the integration of information literacy with the K–12 curriculum via resource-based learning.

1994
to
1995   As the result of a meeting of the National Forum on Information Liter-
       acy, a national survey of 3,236 accredited U.S. colleges and universities
       is conducted to determine the extent to which information literacy had
       been assimilated into the curriculum of institutions of higher education.
       The survey involves the Association of College and Research Libraries
       (ACRL), the Commission on Higher Education (CHE) of the Middle
       States Association of Colleges and Schools, and the Western Association of
       Schools and Colleges, Accrediting Commission for Senior Colleges and
       Universities. Analysis of the 834 surveys that were returned shows that 22
       percent of the respondents had a functional information literacy program
       and 25 percent offered a course that focuses on the development of informa-
       tion literacy abilities (Ratteray & Simmons, 1995).

1995   April—The California State University (CSU) Work Group on Information
       Competence begins to investigate information competence by conducting
       an extensive literature review, consulting with experts, and undertaking in-
       formal and formal surveys to determine what CSU campuses were already
       doing in the area of information competence. They also review how other
       universities and colleges have defined information competence.

1995   The Commission on Higher Education of the Middle States holds two sym-
       posia to bring together educators who had successfully integrated informa-
       tion literacy into their curricula. The conclusions of these symposia are:

           • Institutions should concentrate on developing effective pro-
             cesses to achieve information literacy and share with other
             institutions the results, both good and bad, of those efforts.

           • Information literacy does not cease when the degree is
             achieved, but it must be viewed as a lifelong learning com-
             mitment. (CHE, 1995, p. 16)

1995   Pitts' examination of the mental models of secondary students as they
       work through an information problem shows that when students begin an
       information problem, they rely on their prior learning to help them solve it.

1995   The Ministry of Education in Finland Expert Committee, formed in
       1994, prepares a strategy for the twenty-first century. *Education, Train-
       ing, and Research in the Information Society: A National Strategy* identi-
       fies information skills for students, adults, teachers, and businesses.

1995   Todd's research finds that when information and library skills are taught to
       students in the context of information problem solving and within subject ar-
       eas, a positive effect on the learning process and on students' attitudes is
       created.

1995   The Association for Teacher-Librarianship in Canada (ATLC) creates a
        Student's Bill of Information Rights:

> Our students face an information-rich future in which change
> will be one of the few constants of their life experience. Their
> ability to adapt and fulfill their individual potentials will require
> them to be life-long learners and independent decision-makers.
>
> We believe that all students should have the opportunity to:
>
> - Master the skills needed to access information in print,
>   non-print and electronic sources
>
> - Understand and master effective research processes and
>   reporting skills
>
> - Develop the ability to evaluate, extract, synthesize and uti-
>   lize information from a variety of sources and media
>
> - Utilize data and information to expand their own knowl-
>   edge base
>
> - Explore the creative use of information
>
> - Develop an understanding of our Canadian cultural heri-
>   tage and history, as well as cultures and histories of other
>   societies
>
> - Enhance their own self knowledge through developing a
>   love of reading
>
> - Explore the values and beliefs of others by reading world
>   literature
>
> - Think critically, and make decisions based on personal
>   needs and values as well as upon factual evidence, and
>
> - Actively participate in decisions about their own learning.
>
> Information is a vital component in the development of critical
> thought and independent decision-making, and, consequently,
> access to the ever-increasing body of available information is vi-
> tal to the development of students' potentials. (Association for
> Teacher-Librarianship in Canada, 1995)

1996   Eisenberg and Johnson publish *Computer Skills for Information Prob-
        lem Solving: Learning and Teaching Technology in Context,* noting that
        teaching students a "laundry list" of technology skills and concepts does

not give students adequate preparation for the information society of the future. The authors view technology skills in the context of the information problem-solving process which, in turn, is taught in the context of the curriculum.

1996   The Information Literacy Project of the University of Massachusetts begins with funds from the Office of the President.

1996   The University of Arizona Library initiates an Information Literacy Project to determine what information skills students need, to examine programs at other colleges and universities, and to develop models for an information literacy program.

1996   AASL and AECT National Guidelines Vision Committee publishes a draft of *Information Literacy Standards for Student Learning*, stating that "the learning process and the information search process mirror each other: students actively seek to construct meaning from the sources they encounter and to create products that shape and communicate that meaning effectively" (1996).

1997   Cerise Oberman, Dean of Library and Information Service at the Plattsburgh State University of New York, delivers the keynote speech for the Library and Orientation Exchange (LOEX) Conference and proposes a National Information Literacy Institute (later to be renamed the Institute for Information Literacy) as one possibility for meeting the demand for information skills instruction in higher education.

1997   In *The Seven Faces of Information Literacy*, Bruce (1997), an Australia based researcher, proposes a unique approach to researching and defining information literacy by emphasizing the importance of understanding the way that the concept of information literacy is conceived by information users themselves.

1997   September 30—The State University of New York (SUNY) Council of Library Directors Information Literacy Initiative Committee issues a final report containing a detailed list of nine information competencies that can be applied to any discipline and defines information literacy as "the abilities to recognize when information is needed and to locate, evaluate, effectively use, and communicate information in its various formats" (SUNY Information Literacy Initiative, 1997).

1997   The California Academic and Research Libraries (CARL) establishes a Task Force to Recommend Information Literacy Standards to the Western Association of Schools and Colleges (WASC). A draft version of the task force's recommendations includes a "Statement of Principles for Information Literacy Criteria" that focuses on institutions' roles in developing information literate graduates:

An institution ensures that all graduating students are information literate through a systematic and course-integrated campus-wide information literacy program. Information literacy learning opportunities are part of general education, academic majors, and graduate/professional programs. Educational program requirements or goals include statements about students' use of libraries, computing, information, and learning resources and how course assignments contribute to their becoming information literate. Professional staffs with appropriate expertise are available to teach information literacy skills and develop collections, learning resources and information literacy curricula and learning experiences. The institution provides support for maintaining and improving the quality of information literacy instruction. (1997)

1997   November—The Canadian School Library Association and the Association for Teacher-Librarianship in Canada issue *Students' Information Literacy Needs in the 21st Century: Competencies for Teacher-Librarians,* pointing out the necessity of highly skilled and educated teacher- librarians who influence students' development of information literacy skills:

Students in Canada today need to be able to think rationally and logically. With more and more sources of information, both print and electronic, and the increasing difficulty of ensuring that students can derive meaning from this information, the role of the teacher-librarian becomes central. Teacher-librarians are skilled in accessing and evaluating information regardless of delivery system, book or computer, and proving leadership in the appropriate use of new information technologies. (Association for Teacher Librarianship in Canada & Canadian School Library Association, 1997)

1998   March—Breivik, Hancock, and Senn publish *A Progress Report on Information Literacy: An Update on the American Library Association Presidential Committee on Information Literacy: Final Report* on behalf of the NFIL. This progress report examines the six original recommendations identified in the original report and outlines five recommendations that the NFIL has prioritized for action in the future.

1998   National Study of School Evaluation (NSSE) in cooperation with Alliance for Curriculum Reform (ACR) publishes *Indicators of Schools of Quality, Volume 1: Schoolwide Indicators of Quality.* The publication is intended to assist schools in self-assessing the quality of their efforts in improving student learning and includes the information literacy standards developed by AASL and AECT.

1998   Breivik publishes *Student Learning in the Information Age* (1998), which provides numerous examples of information literacy initiatives that other academic librarians and institutions can use to develop similar efforts on their own campuses.

1998   Breivik and Senn publish *Information Literacy: Educating Children for the 21st Century, Second Edition* (1998), focusing on the integration of information literacy with the K–12 curriculum via resource-based learning.

1998   *Information Power: Building Partnerships for Learning* (1998) is published by the American Library Association. The national guidelines for school library media programs include the "Information Literacy Standards for Student Learning." Implementation and supplementary materials are available on the AASL Web site.

1999   The Computer Science and Telecommunications Board of the National Research Council publishes *Being Fluent with Information Technology* (1999), which provides a call to action to develop "fluency with information technology" (FITness) in college students.

1999   February—Fitness in Information Technology Summit held in Seattle, Washington. Topics include the integration of FITness modules into course CSE 100 at the University of Washington. Summaries of presentations and discussions are available online at http://depts.washington.edu/itlit/.

2000   The AASL Information Power Action Research Project begins pilot studies to show the correlation between school library programs and academic achievement. Information on participating in the study, instruments, and guidelines for collecting data are available online at http://www.ala.org/Content/ NavigationMenu/AASL/Professional_Tools10/ Information_Power/Action_Research_Project/Action_Research_Project_ Manual.htm.

2000   The Association of College and Research Libraries publishes *Information Literacy Competency Standards for Higher Education,* available online at http://www.ala.org/Content/NavigationMenu/ACRL/Standards_ and_Guidelines/Information_Literacy_Competency_Standards_for_ Higher_Education.htm.

2000   The International Society for Technology in Education introduces the *Educational Technology Standards and Performance Indicators for All Teachers.*

2001   February—Claremont McKenna College begins three-year plan to implement FITness. Goals, student learning objectives, departmental projects, and more are available online at http://ets.academic.claremontmckenna.edu/fit/default.html.

2001   The International Society for Technology in Education introduces the *Educational Technology Standards for Administrators.*

2002   The Big6 Web site relaunches, with information literacy and information problem-solving resources for students, parents, teachers, and librarians, available at http://www.big6.com.

2002   University of Memphis's FedEx Technology Institute receives grant in support of Fluency in Information Technology program.

2002   President Bush signs the No Child Left Behind Act into law, increasing accountability for America's public schools.

2002   In response to the No Child Left Behind Act, businesses, educators, and government agencies form the Partnership for 21st Century Skills to identify key skills for success in the twenty-first century.

2003   ICT Literacy Summit convened in Washington, D.C. Summit seeks to identify how technology can support students in preparing for twenty-first-century work and life. Web site at http://www.ictliteracy.info/.

Chronology Bibliography

American Association of School Librarians. (Undated). *Information power* [Online]. Available: http://www.ala.org/aaslTemplate.cfm?Section=Information_ Power. (Accessed June 4, 2003).

American Association of School Librarians. (Undated). *AASL information power action research project manual* [Online]. Available: http:// www.ala.org/Content/NavigationMenu/AASL/Professional_Tools10/ Information_Power/Action_Research_Project/Action_Research_Project_ Manual.htm. (Accessed June 4, 2003).

American Association of School Librarians (AASL) and Association for Educational Communications and Technology (AECT). (1988). *Information power: Guidelines for school library media programs.* Chicago: Author.

American Association of School Librarians and Association for Educational Communications and Technology National Guidelines Vision Committee. (1996, October). *Information literacy standards for student learning* [Online]. Available: http://www.ala.org/aaslTemplate.cfm?Section=Information_Power& Temlate=/ContentManagement/ContentDisplay.cfm&ContentID=12972. (Accessed June 21, 2003).

American Library Association and Association for Educational Communications and Technology. (1998). *Information power: Building partnerships for learning.* Chicago: Author.

American Library Association Presidential Committee on Information Literacy. *Final report.* (1989). Chicago: Author.

Association for Teacher-Librarianship in Canada. (1995). *Students' bill of information rights* [Online]. Available: http://www.atlc.ca/AboutATLC/studrigh.htm. (Accessed May 7, 2003).

Association for Teacher-Librarianship in Canada and Canadian School Library Association. (1997, November). *Students information literacy needs in the 21st century: Competencies for teacher-librarians* [Online]. Available: http://www.atlc.ca/Publications/competen.htm. (Accessed May 7, 2003).

Behrens, S. J. (1994, July). A conceptual analysis and historical overview of information literacy. *College and Research Libraries, 55*(4), 309-322.

Breivik, P. S. (1985). Putting libraries back in the information society. *American Libraries, 16* (723).

Breivik, P. S. (1998). *Student learning in the information age.* Phoenix, AZ: Oryx Press.

Breivik, P. S., & Gee, E. G. (1989). *Information literacy.* New York: Macmillan.

Breivik, P. S., Hancock, V., & Senn, J. (1998). *A progress report on information literacy: An update on the American Library Association Presidential Committee on information literacy: Final report.* Chicago: ALA, Association of Research Librarians.

Breivik, P. S., & Senn. J. (1994). *Information literacy: Educating children for the 21st century.* New York: Scholastic. *Second Edition* (1998).

Breivik, P. S., & Wedgeworth, R. (1988). *Libraries and the search for academic excellence.* Metuchen, NJ: Scarecrow Press.

Bruce, C. (1997). *The seven faces of information literacy.* Adelaide (AU): Auslib Press.

Burchinal, L. G. (1976, September 24). The communications revolution: America's third century challenge. In *The future of organizing knowledge: Papers presented at the Texas A & M University library's centennial academic assembly, Sept. 24, 1976.* College Station, TX: Texas A & M University.

California Academic and Research Libraries Task Force. (1997, September 29). *Draft recommendations to WASC on an information literacy standard* [Online]. Available: http://www.carl-acrl.org/Archives/DocumentsArchive/Reports/rectoWASC.html. (Accessed May 13, 2003).

Commission on Higher Education (CHE). Middle States Association of Colleges and Schools. (1995). *Information literacy, lifelong learning in the middle states region. A summary of two symposia.* Philadelphia: Middle States Association.

Computer Science and Telecommunications Board, National Research Council. (1999). *Being fluent with information technology.* Washington, DC: National Academy Press.

Doyle, C. S. (1992). *Final report to National Forum on Information Literacy.* Syracuse, NY: ERIC Clearinghouse on Information Resources.

Doyle, C. S. (1994). *Information literacy in an information society: A concept for the information age.* Syracuse, NY: ERIC Clearinghouse on Information and Technology.

Eisenberg, M., & Berkowitz, R. (1988). *Curriculum initiative: An agenda and strategy for school library media programs.* Norwood, NJ: Ablex Publishing.

Eisenberg, M. B., & Brown, M. K. (1992). Current themes regarding library and information skills instruction: Research supporting and research lacking. *School Library Media Quarterly , 20*(2), 103-109.

Eisenberg, M. B., and Berkowitz, R. (2002). *The Big6: An information problem-solving process* [Online]. Available: http://www.big6.com. (Accessed June 4, 2003).

Eisenberg, M. B., & Johnson, D. (1996). *Computer skills for information problem solving: Learning and teaching technology in context.* ERIC Digest. (Report no. EDO-IR-96-04). Syracuse, NY: ERIC Clearinghouse on Information and Technology.

Garfield, E. (1979). 2001: An information society? *Journal of Information Science, 1,* 210.

Goodin, M. E. (1991). The transferability of library research skills from high school to college. *School Library Media Quarterly , 19*(1), 33-42.

Gratch, B., et al. (1992). *Information retrieval and evaluation skills for education students.* Chicago: ACRL.

Horton, F. W. (1983). Information literacy vs. computer literacy. *Bulletin of the American Society for Information Science, 9*(14).

Information competence in the CSU: A report submitted to the Commission on Learning Resources and Instructional Technology (CLRIT) by the CLRIT Information Competence Work Group; revised: 1/97. In *A set of core competencies* [Online]. Available: http://library.csun.edu/susan.curzon/corecomp.html. (Accessed May 7, 2003).

International Society for Technology in Education. (2000). *Educational technology standards and performance indicators for all teachers* [Online]. Available: http://cnets.iste.org/teachers/t_stands.html. (Accessed June 4, 2003).

International Society for Technology in Education. (2001). *Educational technology standards and performance indicators for administrators* [Online]. Available: http://cnets.iste.org/administrators/a_stands.html. (Accessed June 4, 2003).

Irving, A. (1985). *Study and information skills across the curriculum.* London: Heinemann Educational Books.

Kuhlthau, C. C. (1987). *Information skills for an information society: A review of research.* Syracuse, NY: ERIC Clearinghouse on Information Resources. (ED 297 740).

Kuhlthau, C. C. (1993). *Seeking meaning: A process approach to library and information services.* Greenwich, CT: Ablex.

Lance, K. C., Welborn, L., & Hamilton-Pennell, C. (1992). *The impact of school library media centers on academic achievement.* Denver: Colorado Department of Education.

Malsed, M. (Undated). *FITness* [Online]. Available: http://ets.academic.claremontmckenna.edu/fit/default.html. (Accessed June 4, 2003).

Mancall, J. C., Aaron, S. L., & Walker, S. A. (1986). Educating students to think: The role of the library media program. A concept paper written for the National Commission on Libraries and Information Science. *School Library Media Quarterly, Journal of the American Association of School Librarians, 15*(1), 18-27.

Ministry of Education, Helsinki (Finland). (1995). *Education, training, and research in the information society: A national strategy.* Helsinki (Finland): Author.

National Commission of Excellence in Education. (1983). *A Nation at risk: The imperative for educational reform.* Washington, DC: U.S. Government Printing Office.

National Council for the Social Studies. (1989). *From information to decision making: New challenges for effective citizenship.* Washington, DC: NCSS. (ED 310 956).

National Institute for Literacy. (Undated). *Fast facts on literacy* [Online]. Available: http://www.nifl.gov/nifl/facts/facts_overview.html. (Accessed May 13).

National Study of School Evaluation. (1997). *Indicators of schools of quality vol. 1: Schoolwide indicators of quality.* Shaumberg, IL: Author.

New South Wales Department of Education. (Undated) *Information skills in the school* [brochure]. New South Wales (AU): Author.

Olsen, J. K., & Coons, B. (1989). Cornell University's information literacy program. In *Coping with information illiteracy: Bibliographic instruction for the information age.* Papers presented at the seventeenth national LOEX library instruction conference held in Ann Arbor, Michigan, 4-5 May 1989.

Partnership for 21st Century Skills [Online]. (Undated). Available: http://www.21stcenturyskills.org/index.asp. (Accessed June 4, 2003).

Pitts, J., et al. (1995). Mental models of information: The 1993-1994 AASL/ Highsmith research award study. *School Library Media Quarterly, 23*(3), 177-184.

Ratteray, O. M., & Simmons, H. L. (1995). *Information literacy in higher education: A report on the middle states region.* Philadelphia: Middle States Association of Colleges and Schools.

Secretary's Commission on Achieving Necessary Skills. (1991). *What work requires of schools: A SCANS report for America 2000.* Washington, DC: U.S. Government Printing Office.

State University of New York (SUNY) Information Literacy Initiative [Online]. (1997, October 2). Available: http://www.sunyconnect.suny.edu/ili/Default.htm. (Accessed May 1, 2003).

Stripling, B., & Pitts, J. (1988). *Brainstorms and blueprints: Teaching library research as a thinking process.* Littleton, CO: Libraries Unlimited.

Taylor, R. S. (1979). Reminiscing about the future. *Library Journal, 104,* 1875.

Todd, R. Integrated information skills instruction: Does it make a difference? *School Library Media Quarterly 23*(2), 133-139.

University Library–Cal Poly Pomona. (1995). *Information competence in the CSU: A report* [Online]. Available: http://www.csupomona.edu/library/InfoComp/CLRIT.html. (Accessed May 1, 2003).

University of Arizona Library. (1996). *Information literacy project: Project charge* [Online]. Available: http://dizzy.library.arizona.edu/infolit/CHARGE.HTM. (Accessed May 1, 2003).

University of Massachusetts, Dartmouth. (2000). *Information literacy project: Defining competencies* [Online]. Available: http://www.lib.umassd.edu/infolit/infolit.html. (Accessed May 1, 2003).

University of Memphis. (Undated). *AT&T gives $200,000 grant to FedEx Technology Institute supporting "fluency in information technology"* [Online]. Available: http://fedex.memphis.edu/news/att120402.html. (Accessed June 4, 2003).

University of Washington. (1999). *FITness in information technology.* Available: http://depts.washington.edu/itlit/. (Accessed June 4, 2003).

U.S. Department of Education. (Undated). *No child left behind* [Online]. Available: http://www.nochildleftbehind.gov/. (Accessed June 4, 2003).

Wisconsin Educational Media Association. (1993). *Information literacy: A position paper on information problem-solving.* Appleton, WI: WEMA Publication.

Zurkowski, P.G. (1974). *The information service environment relationships and priorities.* Washington, DC: National Commission on Libraries and Information Sciences.

Appendix E

Correlation of Information Literacy Skills with Selected National Subject Matter Standards

Appendix E cross-correlates selected excerpts from National Standards documents with Doyle's attributes of an information literate person. This table does not cross-correlate all aspects of each National Subject Matter standard.

Doyle's Attributes	National Standards for Art Education	
An information literate person is one who:s	Music, Standard 6 Achievement Standard, Advanced: Students: f) analyze and describe uses of the elements of music in a given work that make it unique, interesting, and expressive (p. 61).	Theatre, Standard 5 Achievement Standard: Students: a) apply research from print and nonprint sources to script writing, casting, design, and directing choices (p. 47).
recognizes that accurate and complete information is the basis for intelligent decision making;		X
recognizes the need for information;		X
formulates questions as information needs;		X
identifies potential sources of information;		X
develops successful search strategies;		X
accesses sources of information including computer-bases and other technologies;		X
evaluates information;	X	X
organizes information for practical application;	X	X
integrates new information into an existing body of knowledge; and		X
uses information in critical thinking and problem solving. (Doyle, 1992)	X	X

Doyle's Attributes	National Standards for Art Education	
An information literate person is one who:	Standard 5 Voluntary exchange occurs only when all participating parties expect to gain. This is true for trade among individuals or organizations within a nation, and among individuals or organizations in different nations. Benchmark, Grade 4: At the completion of grade 4, students will: 3) describe a trade they have made, such as one with baseball cards, stickers, or lunch desserts, and explain why they agreed to trade (p. 9).	Standard 14 Entrepreneurs are people who take risks of organizing productive resources to make goods and services. Profit is an important incentive that leads entrepreneurs to accept the risks of business failure. Benchmark, Grade 8: At the completion of grade 8, students will: 4) Identify a restaurant that went out of business and give reasons why this might have occurred (p. 27).
recognizes that accurate and complete information is the basis for intelligent decision making;	X	
recognizes the need for information;		X
formulates questions as information needs;		X
identifies potential sources of information;		X
develops successful search strategies;		X
accesses sources of information including computer-bases and other technologies;		
evaluates information;	X	X
organizes information for practical application;	X	X
integrates new information into an existing body of knowledge; and	X	X
uses information in critical thinking and problem solving. (Doyle, 1992)	X	X

Doyle's Attributes	National Standards for Art Education	
An information literate person is one who:	8. Students use a variety of technological and informational resources (e.g., libraries, databases, computer networks, video) to gather and synthesize information and to create and communicate knowledge (p. 3).	5. Students conduct research on issue and interests by generating ideas and questions, and by posing problems. They gather, evaluate, and synthesize data from a variety of sources (e.g. print and non-print texts, artifacts, people) to communicate their discoveries in ways that suit their purpose and audience (p. 3).
recognizes that accurate and complete information is the basis for intelligent decision making;		
recognizes the need for information;		
formulates questions as information needs;		X
identifies potential sources of information;	X	X
develops successful search strategies;	X	X
accesses sources of information including computer-bases and other technologies;	X	X
evaluates information;	X	X
organizes information for practical application;	X	X
integrates new information into an existing body of knowledge; and	X	X
uses information in critical thinking and problem solving. (Doyle, 1992)	X	X

Doyle's Attributes	National Standards for Art Education	
An information literate person is one who:	Standard 1.1 Sample progress indicator, Grade 8 Students compare, contrast, and express opinions and preferences about the information gathered regarding events, experiences and other school subjects (p. 42).	Standard 5.1 Sample progress indicator, Grade 12 Students present information about the language and culture to others (p. 65).
recognizes that accurate and complete information is the basis for intelligent decision making;		
recognizes the need for information;		
formulates questions as information needs;		
identifies potential sources of information;	X	
develops successful search strategies;	X	
accesses sources of information including computer-bases and other technologies;	X	
evaluates information;	X	
organizes information for practical application;	X	X
integrates new information into an existing body of knowledge; and	X	
uses information in critical thinking and problem solving. (Doyle, 1992)	X	

Doyle's Attributes	National Standards for Art Education	
An information literate person is one who:	Human systems—Grades K-4 The student is able to describe the characteristics and locations of cities, as exemplified by being able to use maps and other graphics to locate major cities in North America and explain the processes that have caused them to grow (p. 129).	Human systems—Grades 9–12. The student is able to analyze and evaluate international economic issues from a spatial point of view, as exemplified by being able to formulate reasoned arguments regarding the causes and geographic consequences of an international debt crisis (p. 207).
recognizes that accurate and complete information is the basis for intelligent decision making;	X	
recognizes the need for information;	X	
formulates questions as information needs;		
identifies potential sources of information;		
develops successful search strategies;		
accesses sources of information including computer-bases and other technologies;	X	X
evaluates information;	X	X
organizes information for practical application;	X	X
integrates new information into an existing body of knowledge; and	X	X
uses information in critical thinking and problem solving. (Doyle, 1992)	X	X

Doyle's Attributes	National Standards for Art Education	
An information literate person is one who:	Performance indicator, Grades 9–11: Students will: 2) demonstrate the ability to evaluate resources from home, school and community that provide valid health information (p. 36).	Standard 4 Performance indicator, Grades 5–8: Students will: 2) analyze how messages from media and other sources influence health behaviors (p. 33).
recognizes that accurate and complete information is the basis for intelligent decision making;	X	
recognizes the need for information;		
formulates questions as information needs;		
identifies potential sources of information;		
develops successful search strategies;		
accesses sources of information including computer-bases and other technologies;		
evaluates information;	X	X
organizes information for practical application;	X	X
integrates new information into an existing body of knowledge; and	X	X
uses information in critical thinking and problem solving. (Doyle, 1992)	X	X

Doyle's Attributes	National Standards for Art Education	
An information literate person is one who:	Standard 3—Grades 5–12 How the United States changed from the end of World War I to the eve of the Great Depression. The student understands politics and international affairs in the 1920s. The student is able to assess the effects of woman suffrage on politics (p. 115).	Topic 4: The History of People of Many Cultures Around the World Standard 7—Grades K-4 The student is able to analyze the dance, music, and arts of various cultures around the world to draw conclusions about the history, daily life, and beliefs of the people in history (p. 36).
recognizes that accurate and complete information is the basis for intelligent decision making;	X	
recognizes the need for information;	X	
formulates questions as information needs;	X	
identifies potential sources of information;	X	
develops successful search strategies;	X	
accesses sources of information including computer-bases and other technologies;	X	
evaluates information;	X	X
organizes information for practical application;	X	X
integrates new information into an existing body of knowledge; and	X	X
uses information in critical thinking and problem solving. (Doyle, 1992)	X	X

Doyle's Attributes	National Standards for Art Education	
An information literate person is one who:	Communication Standard Instructional programs from prekindergarten through grade 12 should enable all students to organize and consolidate their mathematical thinking through communication; communicate their mathematical thinking coherently and clearly to peers, teachers, and others; analyze and evaluate the mathematical thinking and strategies of others; and use the language of mathematics to express mathematical ideas precisely (p. 60).	Connections Standard Instructional programs from prekindergarten through grade 12 should enable all students to recognize and use connections among mathematical ideas; understand how mathematical ideas interconnect and build on one another to produce a coherent whole; recognize and apply mathematics in contexts outside of mathematics. (p. 64).
recognizes that accurate and complete information is the basis for intelligent decision making;		
recognizes the need for information;		
formulates questions as information needs;		
identifies potential sources of information;		
develops successful search strategies;		
accesses sources of information including computer-bases and other technologies;		
evaluates information;		X
organizes information for practical application;		X
integrates new information into an existing body of knowledge; and	X	X
uses information in critical thinking and problem solving. (Doyle, 1992)	X	X

Doyle's Attributes	National Standards for Art Education	
An information literate person is one who:	Standard 5 Demonstrates responsible personal and social behavior in physical activity settings. Grade 8 Sample benchmark: Makes choices based on the safety of self and others (p. 70).	Standard 6 Demonstrates understanding and respect for differences among people in physical activity settings. Grade 12 Sample benchmark: Develops strategies for including persons of diverse backgrounds and abilities in physical activity (p. 99).
recognizes that accurate and complete information is the basis for intelligent decision making;	X	
recognizes the need for information;	X	X
formulates questions as information needs;		
identifies potential sources of information;		
develops successful search strategies;		
accesses sources of information including computer-bases and other technologies;		
evaluates information;	X	X
organizes information for practical application;	X	X
integrates new information into an existing body of knowledge; and	X	X
uses information in critical thinking and problem solving. (Doyle, 1992)	X	X

Doyle's Attributes	National Standards for Art Education	
An information literate person is one who:	Standard 3—High School Social studies programs should include experiences that provide for the study of people, places, and environments so that the learner can describe, differentiate, and explain the relationships among various regional and global patterns of geographic phenomena such as landforms, soils, climate, vegetation, natural resources, and population (p. 35).	Standard 6—Early Grades Social studies programs should include experiences that provide for the study of how people create and change structures of power, authority, and governance, so that the learner can: identify and describe factors that contribute to cooperation and cause disputes within and among groups and nations (p. 39).
recognizes that accurate and complete information is the basis for intelligent decision making;		
recognizes the need for information;		
formulates questions as information needs;		
identifies potential sources of information;		
develops successful search strategies;		
accesses sources of information including computer-bases and other technologies;		
evaluates information;	X	X
organizes information for practical application;	X	X
integrates new information into an existing body of knowledge; and	X	X
uses information in critical thinking and problem solving. (Doyle, 1992)	X	X

Doyle's Attributes	**National Standards for Art Education**	
An information literate person is one who:	Content Standard 4, Grades 9–12: Students should be able to: evaluate current criticisms of campaigns and proposals for their reform (p. 119).	Content Standard 2, Grades 5–8: Students should be able to: evaluate the influence of television, radio, the press, newsletters and emerging means of electronic communication on American politics (p. 69).
recognizes that accurate and complete information is the basis for intelligent decision making;	X	X
recognizes the need for information;	X	X
formulates questions as information needs;	X	
identifies potential sources of information;	X	
develops successful search strategies;	X	
accesses sources of information including computer-bases and other technologies;	X	X
evaluates information;	X	X
organizes information for practical application;	X	X
integrates new information into an existing body of knowledge; and	X	X
uses information in critical thinking and problem solving. (Doyle, 1992)	X	X

Appendix F

Dalbotten's Correlation of Inquiry Skills to National Content Standards*

Dalbotten's work examines all 12 National Content Standards and cross-correlates them with Minnesota's Inquiry Process and the Big6™ Skills. Appendix F presents three of these cross-correlations: English/Language Arts, Geography, and History.

*Reprinted with permission from M. S. Dalbotten "Inquiry in the National Content Standards," in D. Callison, J. McGregor, and R. Small, *Instructional Interventions for Information Use.* Proceedings of the Treasure Mountain Research Retreat VI, Troutdale, OR.

	Inquiry in General* **Information** **Problem-Solving****	**Generate Questions*** **Task Definitions****	**Determine Feasibility*** **Information Seeking****
English/ **Language Arts** *Source:* National Council of Teachers of English. (1996) *Standards for the English language arts.* Urbana, IL: Author.	Students need to be able to use language to pose significant questions, to become informed, to obtain and communicate information, and to think critically and creatively. p. 18	Use language to **pose significant questions**, to become informed, to obtain and communicate information, and to think critically and creatively. p. 18 Pose questions as they read, listen, and view: e.g. What inferences can I draw from this text? p. 21	Use language to pose significant questions, to **become informed**, to obtain and communicate information, and to think critically and creatively. p. 18
	Students conduct research on issues and interests by generating ideas and questions, and by posing problems. They gather, evaluate and synthesize data from a variety of sources (e.g. print and non-print texts, artifacts, people) to communicate their discoveries in ways that suit their purpose and audience. p. 25	Conduct research on issues and interests by generating ideas and questions, and by posing problems. p. 25	**Gather, evaluate,** and synthesize **data** from a variety of sources (e.g. print and non-print texts, artifacts, people) to communicate their discoveries in ways that suit their purpose and audience. p. 25
	Students use a variety of technological and informational resources (e.g. libraries, databases, computer networks, video) to gather and synthesize information and to create and communicate knowledge. p. 25		Use a variety of technological and informational resources (e.g. libraries, databases, computer networks, video) to **gather** and synthesize **information** and to create and communicate knowledge. p. 25

Collect Data* Location and Access**	Reduce and Organize Data* Information Use**	Display Data* Synthesis**	Compile Conclusions/ More Questions Evaluation**
Use language to pose significant questions, to become informed, to **obtain** and communicate **information**, and to think critically and creatively. p. 18	Use language to pose significant questions, to become informed, to obtain and **communicate information**, and to think critically and creatively. p. 18	Use language to pose significant questions, to become informed, to obtain and communicate information, and to **think critically and creatively.** p. 18 Use a wide range of strategies (including . . . synthesizing) to interpret and create various types of texts p. 20	Provide informed opinions about texts they encounter, and to support their interpretations with multiple forms of evidence. p. 21
Gather, evaluate and synthesize **data** from a variety of sources (e.g. print and non-print texts, artifacts, people) to communicate their discoveries in ways that suit their purpose and audience. p. 25	Gather, **evaluate,** and synthesize **data** from a variety of sources (e.g. print and non-print texts, artifacts, people) to communicate their discoveries in ways that suit their purpose and audience. p. 25	Gather, evaluate and **synthesize data** from a variety of sources (e.g. print and non-print texts, artifacts, people) to communicate their discoveries in ways that suit their purpose and audience. p. 25 Use a variety of technological and informational resources (e.g. libraries, databases, computer networks, video) to gather and **synthesize information** and to create and communicate knowledge. p. 25	Gather, evaluate and synthesize data from a variety of sources (e.g. print and non-print texts, artifacts, people) to **communicate their discoveries in ways that suit their purpose and audience.** p. 25 Use a variety of technological and informational resources (e.g. libraries, databases, computer networks, video) to gather and synthesize information and **to create and communicate knowledge.** p. 25

	Inquiry in General* **Information Problem-Solving**	**Generate Questions*** **Task Definitions**	**Determine Feasibility*** **Information Seeking**
Geography *Source:* Bednarz, S. W., and others. (1994). *Geography for life; national geography standards.* Washington, DC: Department of Education, National Endowment for the Humanities, and the National Geographic Society.	The Five Sets of Geographic Skills 1 Asking Geographic Questions 2. Acquiring Geographic Information 3. Organizing Geographic Information 4. Analyzing Geographic Information 5. Answering Geographic Questions. p. 54	Skill Set 1 Asking Geographic Questions Plan and organize a geographic research project (e.g. specify a problem, pose a research question or hypothesis and identify data sources) (Grades 9-12). p. 54	Skill Set 2 Acquire Geographic Information Systematically locate and gather geographic information from a variety of primary and secondary sources (Grades 9-12). p. 54
	The Five Sets of Geographic Skills 1 Asking Geographic Questions 2. Acquiring Geographic Information 3. Organizing Geographic Information 4. Analyzing Geographic Information 5. Answering Geographic Questions. p. 54		

Collect Data* Location and Access**	Reduce and Organize Data* Information Use**	Display Data* Synthesis**	Compile Conclusions/ More Questions Evaluation**
Skill Set 2 Acquire Geographic Information Systematically locate and gather geographic information from a variety of primary and secondary sources (Grades 9-12). p. 54	Skill Set 2 Acquire Geographic Information Systematically locate and gather geographic information from a variety of primary and secondary sources (Grades 9-12). p. 54	Skill Set 3 Organize Geographic Information Select and design appropriate forms of maps to organize geographic information (Grades 9-12). p. 54 Select and design appropriate forms of graphs, diagrams, tables, and charts to organize geographic information (Grades 9-12). p. 54 Use a variety of media to develop and organize integrated summaries of geographic information (Grades 9-12). p. 54	
		Skill Set 4 Analyze Geographic Information Use quantitative methods of analysis to interpret geographic information (Grades 9-12). p. 54 Make inferences and draw conclusions from maps and other geographic representations (Grades 9-12). p. 54 Use the processes of analysis, synthesis, evaluation, and explanation to interpret geographic information from a variety of sources (Grades 9-12). p. 54	Skill Set 5 Answer Geographic Questions Formulate valid generalizations from the results of various kinds of geographic inquiry (Grades 9-12). p. 54 Evaluate the answers to geographic questions (Grades 9-12). p. 54 Apply geographic models, generalizations, and theories to the analysis, interpretation, and presentation of geographic information (Grades 9-12). p. 54

	Inquiry in General* Information Problem-Solving**	Generate Questions* Task Definitions**	Determine Feasibility* Information Seeking**
Geography *Source:* Bednarz, S. W., and others. (1994). *Geography for life; national geography standards.* Washington, DC: Department of Education, National Endowment for the Humanities, and the National Geographic Society.	Standard 1 The World in Spatial Terms How to use maps and other geographic representations, tools, and technologies to acquire, process, and report information from a spatial perspective. p. 144	Standard 1 The World in Spatial Terms Use geographic tools and technologies to **pose and answer questions** about spatial distributions and patterns on Earth by being able to use maps to understand patterns of movement in space and time. p. 145	Standard 1 The World in Spatial Terms Use maps and other geographic representations, tools, and technologies to **acquire**, process, and report **information** from a spatial perspective. p. 144
	Standard 6 Places and Regions How culture and experience influence people's perceptions of places and regions. p. 117		

Collect Data* Location and Access**	Reduce and Organize Data* Information Use**	Display Data* Synthesis**	Compile Conclusions/ More Questions Evaluation**
Standard 1 The World in Spatial Terms Use maps and other geographic representations, tools, and technologies to **acquire**, process, and report **information** from a spatial perspective. p. 144	Standard 1 The World in Spatial Terms Use maps and other geographic representations, tools, and technologies to acquire, **process**, and report **information** from a spatial perspective. p. 144	Standard 1 The World in Spatial Terms Use maps and other geographic representations, tools, and technologies to acquire, process, and **report information** from a spatial perspective. p. 144 Show spatial information on geographic representations by being able to construct diagrams or charts to display spatial information (e.g. construct a bar graph that compares the populations of the five largest cities in a U.S. state). p. 109	
Standard 6 Places and Regions Compare the different ways in which people view and relate to places and regions by being able to conduct interviews to collect information on how people of different age, sex, or ethnicity view the same place or region, . . . then organize the information by subject (e.g. medical facilities) type of interviewee (e.g. Africa-American male teenager) and response. p. 117	Standard 6 Places and Regions Compare the different ways in which people view and relate to places and regions by being able to conduct interviews to collect information on how people of different age, sex, or ethnicity view the same place or region, . . . then organize the information by subject (e.g. medical facilities) type of interviewee (e.g. Africa-American male teenager) and response. p. 117		

	Inquiry in General* **Information** **Problem-Solving****	**Generate Questions*** **Task Definitions****	**Determine Feasibility*** **Information Seeking****
Geography	Standard 18 The Uses of Geography		Standard 18 The Uses of Geography
Source: Bednarz, S. W., and others. (1994). *Geography for life; national geography standards.* Washington, DC: Department of Education, National Endowment for the Humanities, and the National Geographic Society.	How to apply geography to interpret the present and plan for the future. p. 181		Integrate multiple points of view to analyze and evaluate contemporary geography issues by being able to **do research on both the student's own point of view and other people's perceptions** of a controversial social, economic, political, or environmental issue that has a geographic dimension and then write a report on that subject, which includes an informed judgment as to what solution should be implemented. pp. 181-182

Collect Data* Location and Access**	Reduce and Organize Data* Information Use**	Display Data* Synthesis**	Compile Conclusions/ More Questions Evaluation**
	Standard 18 The Uses of Geography Integrate multiple points of view to analyze and evaluate contemporary geography issues by being able to do research on both the student's own point of view and other people's perceptions of a controversial social, economic, political, or environmental issue that has a geographic dimension and then **write a report** on that subject, which includes an informed judgment as to what solution should be implemented. p. 181-182	Standard 18 The Uses of Geography Integrate multiple points of view to analyze and evaluate contemporary geography issues by being able to do research on both the student's own point of view and other people's perceptions of a controversial social, economic, political, or environmental issue that has a geographic dimension and then write a report on that subject, which **includes an informed judgment as to what solution should be implemented. p.** 181-182	

	Inquiry in General* Information Problem-Solving**	Generate Questions* Task Definitions**	Determine Feasibility* Information Seeking**
History *Source:* National Center for History in the Schools. (1996). *National standards for history.* Los Angeles, CA: Author.	Historical thinking skills that enable students to evaluate evidence; develop comparative and causal analyses, interpret the historical record; and construct sound historical arguments and perspectives on which informed decisions in contemporary life can be based. p. 2	Standard 3. The student engages in historical analysis and interpretation. A. Formulate questions to focus their inquiry and analysis. p. 21	
		Standard 4: The student conducts historical research. A. Formulate historical questions. p. 22	

Collect Data* Location and Access**	Reduce and Organize Data* Information Use**	Display Data* Synthesis**	Compile Conclusions/ More Questions Evaluation**
Standard 2 The student comprehends a variety of historical sources. F. Draw upon data in historical maps . . . p. 19 G. Draw upon the visual and mathematical data presented in graphs, including charts, tables, pie and bar graphs, etc. p. 19 H. Draw upon the visual data presented in photographs, paintings, cartoons, and architectural drawings in order to clarify, illustrate or elaborate upon information presented in the historical narrative. p. 19-20			
Standard 4: The student conducts historical research. B. Obtain historical data from a variety of sources, including: library and museum collections, historic sites, historical photos, journals, diaries, . . . and so on. p. 22	Standard 4: The student conducts historical research. C. Interrogate historical data by . . . testing the data source for its credibility, authority and authenticity; and detecting and evaluating bias, distortion, and propaganda by omission, suppression or invention of facts. p. 22	Standard 4: The student conducts historical research. D. Marshal needed information of the time and place in order to construct a story, explanation, or historical narrative. p. 22	

Appendix G

An Explanation of Rubrics and Their Application in Standards Education

The Information Literacy Rubrics are an extension of the Model Information Guidelines (Colorado Department of Education, State Library and Adult Education Office, Colorado Educational Media Association, 1994).

A rubric is a descriptive measurement for defining what a learner should know, and can do. This document was created to define the knowledge and ability of every student in how they:

- Construct meaning from information

- Create a quality product

- Learn independently

- Participate as a group member, and

- Use information and information technologies responsibly and ethically

The rubrics are designed in a matrix, or grid of benchmarks which define the information literate student. The far left column contains the Target Indicators, or the individual components of each of the five information literacy guidelines. Each target indicator is followed by four qualities, or key behavior skills to be measured. These are written in student language, labeled In Progress, followed by Essential, Proficient, and Advanced. Page 1 is an overview for all five guidelines; pages 2-8 address specific benchmarks. the final page is a checklist for a student or teacher which may be used in the assessment process.

It should not be a goal to have each student attempt to achieve the Advanced level in each skill area on each project. Rather, the goal should be to assess students on the key points important to the specific content area task, and understand the process for applying that skill in other curricular work. [Example: In a task involving the knowledge seeking process, the student might first be assessed in determining information needs, and acquiring the information. In a

233

later task, they could be assessed in the organization, processing and evaluation of the information.]

The ideal application and use of these assessments is in a collaborative curriculum involving the student, teacher, media specialist and other stake holders in the school environment. These rubrics can be used as written to define information goals for the student, or as a framework for student/teacher-written assignments. They are applicable to all grades and content areas, but only through a cooperative effort between the key players will they be truly effective in ensuring student buy-in to understanding the information literacy process.

Knowing how to apply these skills is necessary for successful living in the twenty-first century and beyond.

Target Indicators	In Progress	Essential	Proficient	Advanced
Student as a Knowledge Seeker	• I need someone to tell me when I need information, what information I need, and help me find it.	• Sometimes I can identify my information needs. I ask for help finding and using information.	• I am able to determine when I have a need for information. I often solve problems by using a variety of information resources.	• I know my information needs. I am confident that I can solve problems by selecting and processing information.
Student as a Quality Producer	• Someone else sets the standards and I try to create a product to meet them.	• I may need help understanding what makes a good product, and support to create it.	• I compare my work to models and use them as an example for my product.	• I hold high standards for my work and create quality products.
Student as a Self-Directed Learner	• I have trouble choosing my own resources and I like someone to tell me the answer.	• I might know what I want, but need to ask for help in solving information problems.	• I choose my own resources and like being independent in my information searches.	• I like to choose my own information resources. I am comfortable in situations where there are multiple answers as well as those with no answers.
Student as a Group Contributor	• I need support to work in a group. I have trouble taking responsibility to help the group.	• I usually participate with the group. I offer opinions and ideas, but can not always defend them. I rely on others to make group decisions.	• I participate effectively as a group member. I help the group process, and evaluate and use information with the group.	• I am comfortable leading, facilitating, negotiating, or participating in a group. I work with others to create a product that fairly represents consensus of the group.

Target Indicators	In Progress	Essential	Proficient	Advanced
Students as a Responsible Information User	• If I find information I can use I copy it directly. I need to be reminded about being polite and about sharing resources and equipment with others.	• I usually remember to give credit when I use someone else's ideas. It is okay for others to have different ideas from mine. I try to be polite and share information resources and equipment with others.	• I do not plagiarize. I understand the concept of intellectual freedom. I am polite and share resources and equipment with others.	• I follow copyright laws, and help others understand the concept of intellectual freedom. I can defend my rights if challenged. I acknowledge and respect the rights of others to use information resources and equipment.
Determines Information Needs	• I need someone to tell me the topic and what information I need.	• I need someone to define the topic. I can identify, with help, some of the information I need.	• I determine a topic and identify the information I need.	• I determine a manageable topic and identify the kinds of information I need to support the topic.
Develops Information Seeking Strategies and Locates Information	• Someone else selects the information resources I need and shows me how to find the information. • Someone else develops my plan and timeline. • I do not know what to record when doing research, nor what bibliographic information is.	• I select resources but they are not always appropriate. • I have an incomplete plan. I have a timeline, but don't always stick to it. • I return to the same source to find the bibliographic details.	• I use a variety of information strategies and resources. • I have a complete plan and stay on my timeline. • I sometimes record bibliographic information.	• I always select appropriate strategies and resources. • I have a complete plan and can adjust my timeline when needed. • I always record bibliographic information for all my sources.

Target Indicators	In Progress	Essential	Proficient	Advanced
Acquires Information	• I don't understand how to use information resources. • Someone helps me extract details from information.	• I do not use a variety of information resources. • I can extract details and concepts from one type of information resource.	• I prefer to limit the number of information resources I use. • I extract details and concepts from different types of resources.	• I am comfortable using various information resources. • I extract details and concepts from all types of resources.
Analyzes Information	• I have no way to determine what information to keep, and what to discard. • Someone helps me decide what information to use.	• I sometimes apply appropriate criteria to decide which information to use. • I don't always know what criteria to use.	• I examine my information and apply criteria to decide what to use. • I usually know what criteria to use.	• I effectively apply criteria to decide what information to use. • I can match criteria with needs.
Organizes Information	• I try to organize information, but have trouble and have to ask for help. • I need to be reminded to credit sources.	• I know some ways to organize information. I can use one or two very well. • Sometimes I credit sources appropriately.	• I organize information in different ways. • I usually credit sources appropriately.	• I choose to organize information in a way that matches my learning style and/or to best meet my information needs. • I always credit sources appropriately.
Processes Information	• I put information together without processing it.	• I combine information to create meaning. I draw conclusions.	• I integrate information from a variety of sources to create meaning that connects with prior knowledge. I can draw conclusions on my own from my sources.	• I integrate information to create meaning that connects with prior knowledge and draw clear and appropriate conclusions. I provide specific and supportive details.

Target Indicators	In Progress	Essential	Proficient	Advanced
Acts on Information	• I am not sure what actions to take based on my information needs. • I ask for help to find everything I need.	• I know what to do with the information I find. • Some of the information I find is appropriate to my needs.	• I act based on the information I have collected and processed. • I do this in a way that is appropriate to my needs.	• I act independently of the information I have collected and processed. • I do this in a way that is appropriate to my needs. I can explain my actions so that others understand.
Evaluates Process and Product	• I don't know how I did. I need someone to help me figure out how to improve.	• I know how well I did and have a few ideas on how to improve next time.	• I know when I've done a good job, and know when there are things I could have done better. I make some revisions.	• I evaluate the product and the process throughout my work, and make revisions when necessary.
Recognizes Quality and Craftsmanship	• I need help understanding what makes a good product, and how to create it.	• I look at the available products and sometimes see what is needed to create my own.	• I look at several products, evaluate them and know what I need to do.	• I look at several products provided to me by my instructor, critique them, and see ways to make a better product.
Plans the Quality Product	• I need help to understand the steps needed to plan my work. I like someone to help me with each step in completing the product.	• I need to be shown the steps to make my plan, and then can work on my own.	• I know the steps necessary for completing my product and make a plan to complete it.	• I create a process and a timeline (with a back-up plan) for all the steps needed to complete my product.

Target Indicators	In Progress	Essential	Proficient	Advanced
Creates a Quality Product	• I need help to find which sources to use. I don't know how to use the facts to solve the problem. I have trouble creating the product..	• I use the minimum sources assigned. I just list the facts. I always use the same sources for other work.	• I create and improve my product by using a variety of resources from the media center or school.	• I compare and contrast facts from a variety of sources available both in and out of my community. I am comfortable using various media for products and audiences. I discover new sources on my own.
Presents a Quality Product	• My product is incomplete. I don't revise	• I complete, but need help with revisions to my product.	• I complete, practice, and revise my product.	• I complete, practice, and revise my product several times. I ask others to give me feedback.
Evaluates Quality Product	• I don't know how to make my product better.	• I need help to understand the best part of my product, and what could have been improved.	• I understand why my product is good, and what could make it better.	• I exceed my expectations when producing and improving a quality product.
Voluntarily Establishes Clear information Goals and Manages Progress	• Setting information goals is difficult for me. • I need help from someone to choose what I'm supposed to do. • I work best with problems that have only one answer.	• I can set some information goals by myself. • I can sometimes find what I'm supposed to do on my own. • I see that sometimes there may be more than one solution for any project or problem.	• I almost always set my own information goals. • I can usually find a variety of information resources o achieve those goals. • When there is more than one solution, I choose the appropriate one for my project or problem.	• I can set my own information goals, and choose the best way to achieve them. • I like to explore and evaluate various resources and solutions. I use them to create a new solution to the problem. • I'm comfortable in situations where there are multiple answers, or no "best" answer.

Target Indicators	In Progress	Essential	Proficient	Advanced
Voluntarily Consults Media Sources	• I usually use the easiest source, and only one source.	• I can do what is asked of me, and usually find answers to questions after consulting a few sources.	• I understand how different sources are organized, and look for the ones that best meet my needs.	• I look at may different sources to find those that meet my needs. I consider various point-of-view and the merits of the resources before choosing those that work best for me.
Explores Topics of Interest	• I have trouble enjoying my reading, and have a hard time staying with a book—or other reading material. • I tend to over-use certain information resources to the exclusion of others when I do read. • I have trouble exploring new topics. Someone needs to help me get started.	• I enjoy reading certain types of books and other information resources. • I usually read only about one subject, or stay with one author's work. • I explore new topics when required.	• I like reading several different types of literature. • I enjoy reading in a variety of formats (e.g. books, CD-ROM, and other media). • I read to explore and learn about a variety of topics.	• Reading is very important to me, and I enjoy reading and exploring may different topics. • I use information resources for information and personal needs, and actively seek answers to questions. • I consider alternative perspectives and evaluate differing points-of-view. • I read for pleasure, to learn, and to solve problems.
Identifies and Applies Personal Performance Guidelines	• I just do what I'm told. Someone tells me if it's good or not.	• I know when I've done a good job.	• I know when I've done a good job, and know why I was successful. I am satisfied with the results.	• I know how I learn best, and can choose the method(s) which guarantees my success. I can evaluate what I've done. I'm not always satisfied with my results.

Target Indicators	In Progress	Essential	Proficient	Advanced
Helps Group to Determine Information Needs	• I do not participate constructively in a group. • I sometimes distract the group. • I rely on others to decide what information is needed.	• I usually participate to determine the information needs of the group.	• I am willing to do what is needed to help determine the information needs of the group.	• I assume my appropriate role in the group. • I am comfortable leading, facilitating, negotiating, or participating in defining the information needs of the group.
Shares Responsibility for Planning and Producing a Quality Product	• I am not a part of the group, and/or rarely take responsibility to help plan the group's information needs.	• I help define the jobs, and assume some responsibility in assisting and task completion.	• I help to define jobs, and am actively responsible in helping to complete the task.	• I help the group go beyond the basic resources. • I am responsible for helping synthesize the ideas into a finished product.
Collaborates to Determine Relevant information	• I have trouble participating in a group, or take over and don't listen to the ideas of others.	• I sometimes participate in selecting, organizing, and integrating information for some sources.	• I work with others to select, organize, and integrate information from a variety of sources.	• I actively work with others and help the group select, organize, and integrate information from a variety of sources.
Acknowledges Diverse Ideas and Incorporates Them When Appropriate	• I need support to work in a group. I often do not respect input from others.	• I show respect for the ideas of others.	• I encourage team members to share ideas.	• I respect and help the group find and incorporate diverse ideas.

Target Indicators	In Progress	Essential	Proficient	Advanced
Offers Useful Information to the Group, Defends Information When Appropriate, and Seeks Consensus to Achieve a Stronger Product	• I sometimes make the group's progress difficult.	• I offer information or ideas, but am unable to defend my own ideas, or those of others.	• I offer and defend information that is brought to the group.	• I offer useful information to the group, defend that information when appropriate, and seek consensus to achieve a stronger product.
Clearly Communicates Ideas in Presenting the Group Product	• I choose not to participate in the presentation, or am unprepared to make a good presentation. • Sometimes I am disruptive	• I help in presenting the group product.	• I contribute to the group and demonstrate the ability to use a variety of presentation methods.	• I work hard in assuring that all contributions from the group are included in the final product. • I help the group present effectively using a variety of media.
Evaluates Product, Process, and individual Roles Continuously	• I don't work with a group and am not certain how to evaluate the process or product.	• I evaluate my own role, but need support to apply certain criteria to the group product. • I am more comfortable allowing others to do the work.	• I effectively evaluate my own role and the roles of others. • I continuously apply appropriate evaluation criteria to the group product.	• I work with the group to evaluate roles, and apply appropriate evaluation criteria to process the product. • I suggest improvements for the next project.

Target Indicators	In Progress	Essential	Proficient	Advanced
Practices Ethical Usage of Information and information Sources	• I don't give credit to others when I use their information. • I don't know why some things need quote marks, and have trouble putting information in my own words. • I don't know why I can't use other people's work (from books, or other information resources).	• I can usually put information in my own words. • If I use someone else's words, I usually remember to put them in quotes. • I can create a bibliography to credit my sources, and don't copy other people's work. • I know it's against the law to copy computer disks, tapes, or other materials.	• I follow copyright laws and guidelines by giving credit to all quotes and ideas, citing them in notes and bibliography properly. • I only make copies of print, software, or tapes when I can located permission from the author/publisher, or by locating permission on the materials.	• I understand and appreciate that copyright protects the creator of the resource, so I always follow and uphold copyright regulations. • I do not plagiarize. • I cite all my sources by following a format demonstrated to me by a teacher or other source. • When I need to copy something, I know how to, and do get permission from the copyright holder.
Respects Principle of Intellectual Freedom	• I usually don't pay attention to what others read, listen to, or view, and sometimes react inappropriately to them.	• I don't try to keep someone from expressing their own ideas, nor reading, listening to, or viewing what they want.	• I understand it is important to have many and differing perspectives on a subject. • I know I have the right to express my opinion, and usually offer my opinion in an appropriate manner.	• I can explain my First Amendment rights, and if challenged, know the process available to me to defend those rights. • I promote the rights of others, and defend them as well.

Target Indicators	In Progress	Essential	Proficient	Advanced
Follows Guidelines and Etiquette When Using Electronic Information Resources	• Someone tells me how to use the information resources, and works with me to get the information I need. • I spend so much time using the resources that I deny access for others. • I need to be reminded of the guidelines for using electronic resources responsibly.	• I have been trained to use electronic resources, can use them with minimal supervision, and can usually get the information I need without help. • I share electronic resources and try to follow appropriate guidelines for their use.	• I get the information I need in a reasonable amount of time so others can also use the materials. • I follow guidelines for the use of information resources and use them efficiently.	• I serve as a mentor for others who want to learn how to use electronic resources. • I use my skills to promote positive and ethical uses of those resources. • I use materials and equipment fairly and carefully.
Maintains the Physical Integrity of Information Resources and Facilities	• I know that information resources/facilities have rules and consequences, and sometimes I follow those rules.	• I usually follow the rules in my school for use of information resources, and accept the consequences when I occasionally break a rule. • I never intentionally cause damage to any materials or equipment.	• I respect the rights of others by following the rules, and never intentionally keep materials from being available to them. • I tell someone immediately about any damage I cause or discover.	• I appreciate the many resources and facilities that are available to me. • I help others follow the rules for the use of equipment and materials. • I use materials fairly, carefully, and equitably. • I suggest new rules when appropriate.

Target Indicators	In Progress	Essential	Proficient	Advanced
Recognizes the Need for Equal Access to Materials and Resources	• I use some information resources. • Sometimes I only use items from home or my classroom, but might go to the library media center during a scheduled class time. • I don't care if someone else needs to use the information I have. • I don't like to share.	• I go to the library media center when I need information resources. • When my library doesn't have what I need, I know I can ask the media specialist/librarian to help me find it from another source.	• I know it is important for others to have access to information resources, so I usually return items when they are due. • When I need other materials that are not in my school, I look for them on ACLIN, or other suitable networks, and work with my library media specialist to borrow from other sources.	• I use several libraries and on-line sources when necessary and appropriate to find information I need. • I share resources with others when it is helpful. • I follow the rules in all buildings, including returning all materials on time.

Information Literacy Guidelines

Students as Knowledge Seekers . . .	Students as Quality Producers . . .	Students as Self-Directed Learners . . .	Students as Group Contributors . . .	Students as Responsible Information Users . . .
• Decide what information is needed.	• Understand what a quality product is.	• Set goals.	• Work together to plan a project.	• Don't copy information.
• Develop a plan.	• Plan quality products.	• Read for pleasure.	• Decide together what information is needed.	• Give credit to sources.
• Locate information.	• Create quality products.	• Use media sources for information and personal needs.	• Respect the ideas of others and include different points of view.	• Understand others' rights to choose own reading materials.
• Analyze information to see if it's useful.	• Present quality products	• Seek answers to question.	• Offer useful information to the group.	• Allow others to have access to electronic sources.
• Combine information from different sources.	• Evaluate quality products.	• Explore topics of interest.	• Clearly communicate ideas.	• Take care of materials.
• Do something with the information.		• Ask for help.	• Help evaluate the group project.	
• Evaluate the results.				

Barbara Higgins, South Middle School, Aurora Public Schools (1995)

Guidelines Checklist

Guideline 1: Students as Knowledge Seekers	Guideline 2: Students as Quality Producers	Guideline 3: Students as Self-Directed Learners	Guideline 4: Students as Group Contributors	Guideline 5: Students as Responsible Information Users
• Decide what information is needed.	• Understand what a quality product is.	• Set goals.	• Work together to plan a project.	• Don't copy information.
• Develop a plan.	• Plan quality products.	• Read for pleasure.	• Decide together what information is needed.	• Give credit to sources.
• Locate information.	• Create quality products.	• Use media sources for information and personal needs.	• Respect the ideas of others and include different points of view.	• Understand others' rights to choose own reading materials.
• Analyze information to see if it's useful.	• Present quality products	• Seek answers to question.		• Allow others to have access to electronic sources.
• Combine information from different sources.	• Evaluate quality products.	• Explore topics of interest.	• Offer useful information to the group.	• Take care of materials.
• Do something with the information.		• Ask for help.	• Clearly communicate ideas.	
• Evaluate the results.			• Help evaluate the group project.	

Reprinted from Rubrics for the Assessment of Information Literacy. Based on the Information Literacy Guidelines for Colorado Students, Teachers and School Library Media Specialists, ©1996; published by Colorado Department of Education.

Appendix H

Being Fluent with Information Technology

Reprinted with permission from *Being Fluent with Information Technology* ©1999 by the National Academy of Sciences, courtesy of the National Academies Press, Washington, D.C.

EXECUTIVE SUMMARY

Information technology is playing an increasingly important role in the work and personal lives of citizens. Computers, communications, digital information, software—the constituents of the information age—are everywhere.

Between those who search aggressively for opportunities to learn more about information technology and those who choose not to learn anything at all about information technology, there are many who recognize the potential value of information technology for their everyday lives and who realize that a better understanding of information technology will be helpful to them. This realization is based on several factors:

- Information technology has entered our lives over a relatively brief period of time with little warning and essentially no formal educational preparation for most people.

- Many who currently use information technology have only a limited understanding of the tools they use and a (probably correct) belief that they are underutilizing them.

- Many citizens do not feel confident or in control when confronted by information technology, and they would like to be more certain of themselves.

- There have been impressive claims for the potential benefits of information technology, and many would like to realize those benefits.

- There is concern on the part of some citizens that changes implied by information technology embody potential risks to social values, freedoms or economic interests, etc., obligating them to become informed.

And, naturally, there is simple curiosity about how this powerful and pervasive technology works.

These various motivations to learn more about information technology raise the general question, What should everyone know about information technology in order to use it more effectively now and in the future? Addressing that question is the subject of this report.

The answer to this question is complicated by the fact that information technology is changing rapidly. The electronic computer is just over 50 years old, "PC," as in personal computer, is less than 20 years old, and the World Wide Web has been known to the public for less than 5 years. In the presence of rapid change, it is impossible to give a fixed, once-and-for-all course that will remain current and effective.

Generally, "computer literacy" has acquired a "skills" connotation, implying competency with a few of today's computer applications, such as word processing and e-mail. Literacy is too modest a goal in the presence of rapid change, because it lacks the necessary "staying power." As the technology changes by leaps and bounds, existing skills become antiquated and there is no migration path to new skills. A better solution is for the individual to plan to adapt to changes in the technology. This involves learning sufficient foundational material to enable one to acquire new skills independently after one's formal education is complete.

This requirement of a deeper understanding than is implied by the rudimentary term "computer literacy" motivated the committee to adopt "fluency" as a term connoting a higher level of competency. People fluent with information technology (FIT persons) are able to express themselves creatively, to reformulate knowledge, and to synthesize new information. Fluency with information technology (i.e., what this report calls FITness) entails a process of lifelong learning in which individuals continually apply what they know to adapt to change and acquire more knowledge to be more effective at applying information technology to their work and personal lives.

Fluency with information technology requires three kinds of knowledge: contemporary skills, foundational concepts, and intellectual capabilities. These three kinds of knowledge prepare a person in different ways for FITness.

- Contemporary skills, the ability to use today's computer applications, enable people to apply information technology immediately. In the present labor market, skills are an essential component of job readiness. Most importantly, skills provide a store of practical experience on which to build new competence.

- Foundational concepts, the basic principles and ideas of computers, networks, and information, underpin the technology. Concepts explain the how and why of information technology, and they give insight into its opportunities and limitations. Concepts are the raw material for understanding new information technology as it evolves.

- Intellectual capabilities, the ability to apply information technology in complex and sustained situations, encapsulate higher-level thinking in the context of information technology. Capabilities empower people to manipulate the medium to their advantage and to handle unintended and unexpected problems when they arise. The intellectual capabilities foster more abstract thinking about information and its manipulation.

For specificity, the report enumerates the ten highest-priority items for each of the three types of knowledge. (Box ES.1 lists these ten items for each type of knowledge.) The skills, linked closely to today's computer usage, will change over time, but the concepts and capabilities are timeless.

Concepts, capabilities, and skills—the three different types of knowledge of FITness—occupy separate dimensions, implying that a particular activity involving information technology will involve elements of each type of knowledge. Learning the skills and concepts and developing the intellectual capabilities can be undertaken without reference to each other, but such an effort will not promote FITness to any significant degree. The three elements of FITness are co-equal, each reinforcing the others, and all are essential to FITness.

FITness is personal in the sense that individuals fluent with information technology evaluate, distinguish, learn, and use new information technology as appropriate to their own personal and professional activities. What is appropriate for an individual depends on the particular applications, activities, and opportunities for being FIT that are associated with the individual's area of interest or specialization.

FITness is also graduated and dynamic. It is graduated in the sense that FITness is characterized by different levels of sophistication (rather than a single fluent / not fluent judgment). And, it is dynamic in that FITness entails lifelong learning as information technology evolves.

In short, FITness should not be regarded as an end state that is independent of domain, but rather as something that develops over a lifetime in particular domains of interest and that has a different character and tone depending on which domains are involved. Accordingly, the pedagogic goal is to provide students with a sufficiently complete foundation of the three types of knowledge that they can "learn the rest of it" on their own as the need arises throughout life.

Because FITness is fundamentally integrative, calling upon an individual to coordinate information and skills with respect to multiple dimensions of a problem and to make overall judgments and decisions taking all such information into account, a project-based approach to developing FITness is most appropriate.

Projects of appropriate scale and scope inherently involve multiple iterations, each of which provides an opportunity for an instructional checkpoint or intervention. The domain of a project can be tailored to an individual's interest (e.g., in the department of a student's major), thereby providing motivation for a person to expend the (non-trivial) effort to master the concepts and skills of FITness. In addition, a project of appropriate scope will be sufficiently complex that intellectual integration is necessary to complete it. Note also that much of the infrastructure of existing skills-based computer or information technology literacy efforts (e.g., hardware, software, network connections, support staff) will be important elements of efforts to promote FITness.

Although the essentials of FITness are for the most part not dependent on sophisticated mathematics, and should therefore generally be accessible in some form to every citizen, any program or effort to make individuals more FIT must be customized to the target population. Because the committee was composed of college and university faculty, the committee chose to focus its implementational concerns on the four-year college or university graduate as one important starting point for the development of FITness across the citizenry. Further, the committee believes that successful implementation of FITness instruction will require serious rethinking of the college and university curriculum. It will not be sufficient for individual instructors to revisit their course content or approach. Rather, entire departments must examine the question of the extent to which their students will graduate FIT. Universities need to concern themselves with the FITness of students who cross discipline boundaries and with the extent to which each discipline is meeting the goals of universal FITness.

In summary, FIT individuals, those who know a starter set of information technology skills, who understand the basic concepts on which information technology is founded, and who have engaged in the higher-level thinking embodied in the intellectual capabilities, should use information technology confidently, should come to work ready to learn new business systems quickly and use them effectively, should be able to apply information technology to personally relevant problems, and should be able to adapt to the inevitable change as information technology evolves over their lifetime. To be FIT is to possess knowledge essential to using information technology now and in the future.

Box ES.1 The Components of Fluency with Information Technology

NOTE: Readers are urged to read Chapter 2 for more elaboration of these items.

Intellectual Capabilities

1. Engage in sustained reasoning.
2. Manage complexity.
3. Test a solution.
4. Manage problems in faulty solutions.
5. Organize and navigate information structures and evaluate information.
6. Collaborate.
7. Communicate to other audiences.
8. Expect the unexpected.
9. Anticipate changing technologies.
10. Think about information technology abstractly.

Information Technology Concepts

1. Computers
2. Information systems
3. Networks
4. Digital representation of information
5. Information organization
6. Modeling and abstraction
7. Algorithmic thinking and programming
8. Universality
9. Limitations of information technology
10. Societal impact of information and information technology

Information Technology Skill

1. Setting up a personal computer
2. Using basic operating system features
3. Using a word processor to create a text document
4. Using a graphic and/or artwork package to create illustrations, slides, or other image-based expressions of ideas
5. Connecting a computer to a network
6. Using the Internet to find information and resources
7. Using a computer to communicate with others
8. Using a spreadsheet to model simple processes or financial tables
9. Using a database system to set up and access useful information
10. Using instructional materials to learn how to use new applications or features

Chapter 2 The Intellectual Framework of Fluency with Information Technology

2.1 What is Fluency with Information Technology?

Fluency with information technology (abbreviated as FITness) goes beyond traditional notions of computer literacy. As noted in Chapter 1, literacy about information technology might call for a minimal level of familiarity with technological tools like word processors, e-mail, and Web browsers. By contrast, FITness requires that persons understand information technology broadly enough to be able to apply it productively at work and in their everyday lives, to recognize when information technology would assist or impede the achievement of a goal, and to continually adapt to the changes in and advancement of information technology. FITness therefore requires a deeper, more essential understanding and mastery of information technology for information processing, communication, and problem solving than does computer literacy as traditionally defined. (Box 2.1 addresses the difference between literacy and FITness in more specific terms.) Note also that FITness as described in this chapter builds on many other fundamental competencies, such as textual literacy, logical reasoning, and knowledge of civics and society.

Information technology is a medium that permits the expression of a vast array of information, ideas, concepts, and messages, and FITness is about effectively exploiting that expressive power. FITness enables a person to accomplish a variety of different tasks using information technology and to develop different ways of accomplishing a given task.

Box 2.1 I Use Computers All Day—Am I FIT?

Many Americans use information technology daily in their work, but such contact does not automatically bestow fluency with information technology. Although many jobs—medical records data entry, submitting credit card transactions, building spreadsheets in an accounting department, designing homes using architectural computer-aided design tools, and numerous others—require facility with the tools provided by specific information technology systems, this kind of expertise is often restricted largely to the skills dimension of FITness. Developing FITness as described in this report requires more than sustained contact with information technology, though such experience can nevertheless provide a good point of departure. Common fears about "breaking something" will have been overcome, certain common protocols will have been learned, and unusual situations will have been encountered.

There are highly FIT individuals across America and the world, of course. Through a combination of classes, experience, reading, curiosity, and probably persistence, these individuals not only have acquired skills that make information technology useful in their work and personal lives, but they also have learned a base of concepts and intellectual capabilities sufficient to acquire new knowledge about information technology independently, allowing them to expand their use and to adopt to change. Some are "techies," but many are simply individuals who by various means have gained enough basic knowledge to become independent, lifelong learners. As they learn more, they become more FIT, more adept at applying information technology to personally relevant tasks.

FITness comes in degrees and gradations and is tied to different purposes. FITness is thus not an "end state" that is independent of domain, but rather develops over a lifetime in particular domains of interest involving particular applications. Aspects of FITness can be developed by using spreadsheets for personal or professional budgeting, desktop publishing tools to create or edit documents or Web pages, search engines and database management tools for locating information on the Web or in large databases, and design tools to create visualizations in various scientific and engineering disciplines.

The wide variety of contexts in which FITness is relevant is matched by the rapid pace at which information technology evolves. Most professionals today require constant upgrading of technological skills as new tools become useful in their work; they learn new word processing programs, new computer-assisted design environments, or new techniques for searching the World Wide Web. Different applications of information technology emerge rather frequently, both in areas with long traditions of using information and information technology and in areas that are not usually seen as being technology-intensive. Perhaps the major challenge for individuals embarking on the goal of lifelong FITness involves deciding when to learn a new tool, when to change to a new technology, when to devote energy to increasing technological competency, and when to allocate time to other professional activities.

The above comments suggest that FITness is personal, graduated, and dynamic. FITness is personal in the sense that individuals evaluate, distinguish, learn, and use new information technology as appropriate to their own sustained personal and professional activities. What is appropriate for an individual depends on the particular applications, activities, and opportunities for FITness that are associated with the individual's area of interest or specialization, and what is reasonable for a FIT lawyer or a historian to know and be able to do may well differ from what is required for a FIT scientist or engineer. FITness is graduated in the sense that it is characterized by different levels of sophistication (rather than a single FIT / not-FIT judgment), and it is dynamic in that it requires lifelong learning as information technology evolves.

Put differently, FITness should not be assessed according to whether a person "has/does not have" all ten capabilities, and is not a single "pass / fail judgment." People with different needs and interests and goals will have lesser or greater stakes in the various components of FITness—they will obviously have greater stakes in those components that are most directly linked to their own individual needs. Nevertheless, the committee believes that all of the elements discussed below are necessary for individuals to exploit effectively the power of information technology across even a relatively small range of interests and needs.

2.2 The Elements of FITness

FITness involves three types of knowledge. These types, described briefly below, interact to reinforce each other, leading to deeper understanding of information technology and its uses.

- Intellectual capabilities. The intellectual capabilities of FITness refer to one's ability to apply information technology in complex and sustained situations and to understand the consequences of doing so. These capabilities transcend particular hardware or software applications. Indeed, the items listed as capabilities in Section 2.4 have general applicability to many domains other than information technology. But a great deal of research (and everyday experience as well) indicates that these capabilities do not easily transfer between problem domains,[1] and in general, few individuals are equally adept with these capabilities in all domains. For this reason, these capabilities can be regarded as "life skills" that are formulated in the context of information technology.

- Fundamental concepts. Concepts refer to the foundations on which information technology is built. This is the "book learning" part of fluency, although it is highly doubtful that a decent understanding of the concepts described in Section 2.5 can be achieved strictly through the use of textbooks. The concepts are fundamental to information and computing and are enduring in the sense that new concepts may become important in the future as qualitatively new information technologies emerge, but the presented list of fundamental concepts will be augmented with rather than replaced by new concepts.

- Contemporary skills. Skills refer to the ability to use particular (and contemporary) hardware or software resources to accomplish information processing tasks. Skills embody the intent of the phrase "knowing how to use a computer" as that phrase is colloquially understood. Skills include (but are not limited to) the use of several common software applications. The "skills" component of FITness necessarily changes over time be-

---

[1] See for example, National Research Council. 1999. How People Learn: Brain, Mind, Experience, and School, Chapter 3, "Learning and Transfer," National Academy Press, Washington, D.C.

cause the information technology products and services available to citizens continually change. The enumeration given in Section 2.6 is appropriate for today, but the list would have been different five years ago and will surely be different five years from now.

Section 2.3 discusses the relationship of capabilities, concepts, and skills, as well as the role of knowledge in particular domains.

Intellectual capabilities and fundamental concepts of information technology are instantiated in or relevant to a wide variety of contexts. Intellectual capabilities and skills relate to very practical matters, getting at the heart of what it means to function in a complex technology-oriented world. And all have the characteristic that the acquisition of information technology skills, the understanding of information technology concepts, and the development of intellectual capabilities are lifelong activities. Over a lifetime, an individual will acquire more skills and develop additional proficiency with those skills, understand information technology concepts in a richer and more textured manner, and enhance his or her intellectual capabilities through engagement in multiple domains.

The discussion below proposes a "top ten" in each classification. (The ten are not listed in any order of priority.) Experts will doubtless recognize omissions and the list could easily be extended. But it is easy to generate longer lists, and at some point, the length of a list exceeds need, practicality, and even feasibility. The committee believes that it is important to identify the items of highest significance among possible alternatives, and the ten items in each category represent the committee's collective judgment of the most important. It is the committee's hope that all who draw from, build on, critique, or modify these lists will also impose a limit of ten on themselves.

2.3 A Tripartite Approach to FITness

Capabilities, concepts, and skills—the three different types of knowledge basic to FITness—occupy separate dimensions, implying that a particular activity involving information technology will involve elements of each type of knowledge. Learning information technology skills and concepts and developing the intellectual capabilities can be undertaken without reference to each other, but such an effort will not promote FITness to any significant degree. The three elements of FITness are co-equal, each reinforcing the others, and all are essential to FITness.[2]

- Study that emphasizes skills without fundamental concepts and intellectual capabilities meets some needs for utility in the short term. But although these skills enable one to perform basic tasks with a word processor (for example), they may not help much in countering the frustration felt when the computer freezes, the printer cannot be accessed, or

---

[2] The statement that "concepts, capabilities, and skills are co-equal" applies only to their epistemological importance to FITness. It does not argue that the appropriate pedagogies for each type of knowledge are, or should be, identical. This point is addressed at somewhat greater length in Section 4.3.

the paragraphs mysteriously develop new fonts. Similar frustration is often experienced by an individual learning a new word-processor. The fundamental concepts underlying information technology are the basis for a mental model of how a specific application is (or is not) working, a model that enables reflective thought about what might be done to fix a problem or how a new application might work. The capabilities of FITness enable a person to deal with unexpected consequences and make appropriate decisions about learning new features or new software, and they are necessary for one to engage in any kind of sustained effort using information technology.

- Study of information technology concepts in isolation from skills or capabilities is reminiscent of computer science education in the days before computers became abundant. The concepts represent abstract information about deep and interesting phenomena. They are worthy of study for their inherent interest, like studying sub-atomic particles and the structure of matter. But taught in the context of skills and capabilities, concepts also become the foundation on which one codifies one's experience, abstracts to new situations, and reasons about information technology. As information technology changes, concepts provide the basis for adapting to the change, inasmuch as the new systems adhere to the same principles the old systems did. Further, concepts provide the raw material needed to engage in capability-based action such as engaging in sustained reasoning and managing complexity.

- Study that emphasizes capabilities at the expense of concepts and skills will lack the essential connection to information technology. Although the intellectual capabilities are quite general, their development in the context of FITness requires a substantive connection to information technology that is provided by exposure to the concepts and skills. For example, to learn to "debug" a program or test an application, students need to understand the concepts implemented in the artifact. To implement their designs and work with others they need communication and search skills.

FITness integrates skills, concepts, and capabilities into an effective understanding of information technology, enabling citizens to use information technology to solve personally relevant problems and apply their knowledge of information technology to new situations. This integration is an essential element for individuals to learn over a lifetime. Thus, a pedagogical approach that balances the treatment of these three elements is essential—this is the subject of Chapter 4.

2.4 Intellectual Capabilities for FITness

Within the framework of FITness as described above, the intellectual capabilities integrate knowledge specific to information technology with problem domains of personal interest to individuals. Many of the capabilities on this "top ten" list might be familiar in other disciplines—engineering design, library science, or general education—or even from an understanding of what is needed to live a productive life. Indeed, no assertion is made that these capabilities are unique or "belong" to information technology. However, the prominence and importance of information technology in society today take them out of the world of the designer or engineering specialist and put them squarely in the lives and workspaces of us all.

The essential elements of FITness include the ability to:

1. Engage in sustained reasoning

Sustained reasoning starts with defining and clarifying a problem. Understanding exactly what problem is to be solved and knowing when it has been solved are often the most difficult aspects of problem solving. And, because information technology will in general operate in the way in which one directs it to operate, rather than the way in which one intends it to operate, precise specification of the problem to be solved with information technology is even more critical for solving other types of problems.

Once the problem has been defined, multiple attempts at formulating a solution are often required. An initial solution is often revised or improved by iteration, which often causes a refinement in the definition of the problem. Reasoning is used for planning, designing, executing, and evaluating a solution.

The "sustained" aspect of this capability is intended to convey an integrated effort that covers days or weeks rather than a one-time event. Thus, individuals might use desktop publishing programs, computer-assisted design tools, visualization and modeling environments, Web-search engines, or a variety of other technological resources to help implement a solution.

2. Manage complexity

Problems often have a variety of solutions, each with its advantages and disadvantages, and trade-offs are often necessary in determining the most appropriate solution. One solution may require extensive design but result in a relatively straightforward implementation; another may require the opposite—a simple design but a costly implementation. Furthermore, any given approach to a solution will often result in components of a system interacting in complex, unexpected ways.

A sustained activity involving information technology will typically be complex, involving a number of tasks, such as problem clarification, solution formulation, solution design and implementation, and testing and evaluation of the outcome. The solution developed for the problem will often contain several components, including both hardware and software. A person needs to be able to plan a project, design a solution, integrate the components, respond to unexpected interactions, and diagnose what is needed from each task. Some of the steps of the project may involve some type of computer programming. Such programming could entail configuring system control panels, using and adapting existing software packages for one's needs, or writing code in some programming language.

Another source of complexity is the need to manage the resources that technology provides, especially when the resources available are inadequate. Thus, a user of information technology needs to be able to manage resources: Do processes require too much time? Too much disk space? Is the bandwidth available to download what is offered? And of course, are there ways to perform necessary tasks that will not exceed the limits imposed by resource availability and / or adequacy?

A third source of complexity is the fact that large information technology-based systems often have interdependencies. That is, small changes in one part of the system can have large effects on another part of the system that is "apparently" separate from that part. Such interdependencies can be reduced by enforcing a rigid separation between different system parts, but this practice is much easier to describe than to implement.

3. Test a solution

Determining the scope, nature, and conditions under which a technological solution is intended to operate can be difficult. A solution to a problem must be tested in two ways—to determine that the design is correct or appropriate to the problem at hand (i.e., that the solution, when implemented correctly, will meet user needs) and to determine that the implementation of a given design is correct.

Testing entails determining whether a proposed solution meets design goals and works under diverse conditions, taking into account that most systems will be used in ways that were not intended, as well as in expected ways. Testing involves identifying the uses most likely to cause a failure, developing ways of testing for all normal modes of operation, determining typical misuses of the system, and designing the system so that it responds gracefully when misused. Furthermore, because some fixes to problems may introduce more problems, special care is necessary to fix (or manage) the initial flaws. Testing is also best seen as an activity concurrent with design, because the alternative is to implement a complete system before knowing whether the implementation is correct.

4. Manage problems in faulty solutions

When systems crash and technological tools fail, users need the ability to "debug," that is, to detect, diagnose, and correct problems and faults (i.e., bugs). Debugging is a complex process that often goes beyond the technology and includes the personal and social aspects of the undertaking (e.g., when a system has multiple interacting components, each of which is the responsibility of a different individual). Debugging also involves other capabilities, such as sustained reasoning, managing complexity, and testing.

Debugging is necessary because the best-designed and best-integrated systems will still exhibit unanticipated behavior. Bugs are inevitably encountered in any ongoing effort using information technology, and thus users must anticipate the need to identify them, diagnose their sources (e.g., by recognizing patterns in observations or in fault reports, distinguishing root causes from derivative but proximate causes, and designing systematic diagnostic experiments), understand the implications of eliminating those sources, and take steps to modify the system appropriately. Alternatively, the appropriate response to a faulty system that is vital to some application may well be to structure the environment in which the system operates to limit the risk associated with its use.

Testing reveals bugs, but once discovered, bugs need to be repaired cleanly and correctly. Good design also involves designing systems that are more easily fixed when something goes wrong (a process often known as "anti-bugging"). For example, a well-designed system has clear documentation. Well-designed systems avoid hidden dependencies, so fixes at one point do not create new flaws at another. The system design itself facilitates examination of what the system is doing and enables the reporting of unexpected events.

Debugging also involves making the everyday elements of technology work. When something goes wrong, it is desirable to be able to trace the chain of events upon which correct operation depends. A typical example today starts with a person who tries to print a document prepared with a word processor, and the printer doesn't produce any output. There could be a flaw anywhere along a chain of potential causes: the printer isn't plugged in or is turned off; the printer isn't connected to the computer; the wrong driver is selected; the printer queue is blocked; improper parameters were set in the print command; and many other possible events. A user needs to recognize that this is a solvable problem, find the broken link in the chain, and either solve the problem or call the appropriate expert.

5. Organize and navigate information structures and evaluate information

Most sustained activities involve the location, evaluation, use, and organization of information. Often searching for and locating information involve other aspects of FITness, including evaluating the validity of information and resolving conflicting accounts of situations. (Note also the connection to information literacy, discussed in Section 3.2.)

This capability also involves the ability to find and evaluate information at different levels of sophistication. Tasks range from reading a manual to finding and using online help. Web searches may be necessary to find more complex information. Of course, as the level of complexity rises, it becomes increasingly important (and more difficult) to ascertain accuracy. An individual must be prepared to evaluate the reliability of a source, understand the nature of a shared information space such as the Web, and regard with appropriate caution the quality of the information retrieved.

This capability also suggests that one must be able to structure information appropriately to make it useful. The information created must be retrievable and useful for the intended purpose. Thus, the design process for information structures involves elements of communication (and may involve programming of some sort).

6. Collaborate

When project responsibilities must be divided among a number of people, collaboration abilities are involved. Among other things, collaboration involves a strategy for dividing a task into pieces that can be worked on individually. In practice, how a problem is divided is based on both the structure of the problem and the organizational structure of the team that will solve it (e.g., different individuals may have different talents). In collaborating, individuals need to avoid duplication of effort as well as inconsistencies in the parts that they deliver for integration into the final product. Furthermore, each must have a clear sense for how the various parts of a solution are made to operate together as well as the expectations for his or her own part, the importance of clearly specified interfaces as a technique for increasing the likelihood that parts of a solution can operate together, and a strategy for ensuring that team members work on an appropriately recent version of the solution.

Information technologies used for collaboration do not change what is required of a collaboration, but they do change how a collaboration takes place. Information technologies such as telephones, e-mail, video-conferencing, shared Web pages, chat rooms, and so on enable collaborators to work together remotely and asynchronously, with relatively less reliance on face-to-face interactions. But learning how to cope with the limitations of technologically mediated interactions thus becomes essential. For example, if team members communicate by e-mail, they may well lose some ability to communicate clearly and unambiguously; at the very least, they may be forced to articulate things explicitly that a face-to-face interaction would not require.

7. Communicate to other audiences

In conveying information to others, it is often necessary to use technology. This may involve the use of images or processes as well as words. Effective communication requires familiarity with and understanding of the pros and cons of various means of communication, because the intervening technology may change the nature of the communication. For example, it is much more difficult to provide driving directions to a given location by using the telephone than by gesturing and pointing to a map.

But a deeper aspect of communication with other audiences is the nature of that communication, independent of media. For example, communicating problem statements or project outcomes to customers, interested individuals, and others requires an understanding of audience needs and background knowledge. An effective communication to experts might involve translating informal needs into formal requirements, for example, moving from a "wish list" expressed during a lunchtime conversation to a more formal tasking to a work team. These formal requirements form the basis for discussing whether or not a project performs correctly, and therefore underlie the ability to test and debug. Without communication that carries nuance and detail, it is impossible to know whether a project component is being built correctly.

A related dimension of communication with other audiences is documentation. Documentation is almost always a component of informing an "outsider" audience about the nature of a system, such as an office system, a manufacturing system, or an information technology system. Documentation makes content more explicit and provides many opportunities for someone to think through the structure of a project. The development of documentation can be regarded as a process of devising the minimum set of information and instructions needed for an unknown task to be performed with a specific tool by a non-expert.

8. Expect the unexpected

Even when a technological system works as intended to solve a problem as it was originally stated, its use may still have unexpected consequences, because the system is embedded in a larger social and technological context that may not have been properly anticipated. In some instances, these unexpected consequences may even overshadow the intended outcome (i.e., the solving of the original problem). Users should understand that such consequences are not uncommon and work to mitigate or exploit them as appropriate.

Unforeseen benefits or drawbacks may result when a technology deployed for one purpose is used for other purposes. For example:

- One of the original "primary" purposes of the ARPANET (the predecessor to the Internet) was to facilitate the use of computers many miles away from one's local desktop; as users learned how to use the ARPANET, they found that it was most useful for its e-mail capabilities.

- Making Web browsers in school libraries available to all students is intended to give students easy access to the rich information content of the Internet. But open access may unintentionally expose students to child molesters, hate speech, and pornography.

In other cases, unexpected side effects may occur because a technological system is deployed on a much larger scale than originally expected. For example:

- Introducing computers into schools on a large scale means that many teachers must be trained to use them effectively.[3]

- Introducing information technology into businesses on a large scale often results in unexpected recurring expenditures to keep hardware and software investments current with evolving applications.[4] Small applications of information technology can be funded on a shoestring (e.g., because problems can be solved in a "quick and dirty" manner). But on a large scale, maintenance, support, documentation, and training become big sources of expense.

Finally, technological systems may be designed for a particular intensity of usage, but may display unexpected behavior or may result in unexpected consequences when the actual intensity of usage is higher. For example:

- Acquisition of a cellular telephone "for emergency use only" for a low monthly payment often results in first-time bills that are much larger than expected, because the user finds the convenience of the cellular telephone irresistible.

- A server designed for a particular load may crash when subject to too many requests for service arriving at the same time, as often happens when access is sought to a popular Web site.[5]

9. Anticipate changing technologies

While no one can predict accurately the future course of technology, technology inevitably changes. FITness entails the capability to adapt to new technology efficiently and how to learn a new language or system, building on what

---

[3] See, for example, Panel on Educational Technology. 1997. Report to the President on the Use of Technology to Strengthen K-12 Education in the United States, President's Committee of Advisors on Science and Technology (PCAST), Washington, D.C., March, Chapter 5.

[4] Such experiences in the private sector are often reported in the trade press. See, for example, M. Lynne Markus and Robert I. Benjamin. 1997. "Are You Gambling on a Magic Bullet?", Computerworld, October 20; Clayton M Christensen. 1997. "Fatal Attraction: The Dangers of Too Much Technology," Computerworld, June 16; Vaughan Merlyn and Sheila Smith. 1997. "Be Careful What You Wish For: Managing Technology's Unintended Consequences," Computerworld, January 20.

[5] William Stallings. 1996. Data and Computer Communications, 5th Edition, Prentice-Hall, New York. See also Keynote Systems, Inc. 1998. "Top 10 Discoveries About the Internet," and "How Fast Is the Internet?" Available online at, respectively, <http://www.keynote.com/measures/top10.html> and <http://www.keynote.com/measures/howfast.html>

is already known about older, perhaps similar technologies and facilities. For example, new versions of technology and tools will almost certainly appear, and they may offer benefits over older versions (e.g., the new version may be faster or offer more features). At the same time, additional functionality often comes at a cost (e.g., the need to upgrade system resources such as memory, or the need to learn the new set of features). Users thus must be prepared to weigh whether the benefits of the inevitable new version outweigh its costs. Decisions as to when or whether to upgrade, which tool to use, and how many features to learn are examples of such adaptation.

10. Think about information technology abstractly

A person who effectively determines how to apply information technology to his or her needs will think about information technology abstractly. For example, she will reflect on her use of information technology, identifying characteristics and commonalities that cut across technological experiences. She will transfer the principles of technological solutions from one setting to another. She will recognize technological analogies, and use them to become adept with new technology quickly. She will have high expectations for technological solutions, and she will find work-arounds when technology falls short.

A second dimension of thinking abstractly about information technology is to consider what aspects of information technology affect a policy issue. For example, a person engaged in such thought will try to determine if and how the technology makes previous policy solutions inadequate. He or she will think deeply about proposed metaphors, such as assertions that putting up a Web page is equivalent to publishing.

2.5 Information Technology Concepts[6]

If information technology were unchanging, then most people would find it unnecessary to learn information technology concepts. The information technology skills could be taught once and for all, and the conceptual foundation underlying information technology would be of interest only to specialists. But information technology changes daily and often dramatically, rendering present-day skills obsolete but also offering new opportunities to solve personally relevant problems. How can one prepare for this inevitable change? How can one quickly upgrade one's skills to exploit new opportunities?

---

[6] The discussion in this section identifies various information technology concepts in a form that approximates that of a catalog description of a course. A full explanation of the concepts would be appropriate for a textbook, but not for a report attempting to outline a basic framework for understanding information technology. Some of these concepts may not be familiar to non-specialists, a point that previews a pedagogical approach discussed in Chapter 4 involving the joint teaching efforts of information technology specialists and domain experts.

The answer lies in understanding a few of the basic ideas and concepts underpinning information technology. These concepts are approximately independent of particular technology or applications, though they are instantiated in different ways in different technologies and applications. In particular, the new and improved information technology of the future will also depend on these concepts, and an understanding of the principles on which information technology rests will continue to enable a person to acquire information technology skills more easily. And, because these concepts are fundamental, they are far more enduring than information technology skills that are tied to specific technologies.

The topics given in the following list touch on ideas of computation, communication, and information that are deep and intellectually challenging. Although any of the topics could be the basis of years of graduate study for a specialist, the basic ideas are straightforward and accessible, having been regularly taught to nonspecialists for years. Note also that the time and effort required to teach and learn each concept may vary widely.

The concepts presented below reflect the committee's judgments about the most important conceptual foundations of information technology contributing to FITness. There is no intended order.

1. Computers

Key aspects of a stored-program computer, including:

- The program as a sequence of steps,

- The process of program interpretation,

- The memory as a repository for program and data (including notions of memory hierarchy and associated ideas of permanence / volatility), and

- Overall organization, including relationship to peripheral devices (e.g., I/O devices).

The appropriate emphasis is not necessarily a specific electronic realization such as a particular computer, but rather the idea of a computational task as a discrete sequence of steps, the deterministic interpretation of instructions, instruction sequencing and control flow, and the distinction between name and value. Computers do what the program tells them to do given particular input, and if a computer exhibits a particular capability, it is because someone figured out how to break the task into a sequence of basic steps, i.e., how to program it.

2. Information systems

The general structural features of an information system, including, among others, the hardware and software components, people and processes, interfaces (both technology interfaces and human-computer interfaces), databases, transactions, consistency, availability, persistent storage, archiving, audit trails, security and privacy and their technological underpinnings.

Most knowledge workers in the labor force interact with one or more information systems, becoming knowledgeable about their characteristics and idiosyncrasies. Understanding the abstract structure of such systems prepares students for employment, enhances job mobility, enables workers to adapt to new systems more quickly, and helps them to exploit more fully the facilities of a given system.

3. Networks

Key attributes and aspects of information networks, including their physical structure (messages, packets, switching, routing, addressing, congestion, local area networks (LANs), wide area networks (WANs), bandwidth, latency, point-to-point communication, multicast, broadcast, Ethernet, mobility), and logical structure (client/ server, interfaces, layered protocols, standards, network services).

Computers are generally much more useful when connected to each other and to the Internet. The goal is to understand how computers can be connected to each other and to networks, and how information is routed between computers. The appropriate emphasis is how the parameters of communication, such as latency and bandwidth, affect the responsiveness of a network from a user's point of view and how they might limit one's ability to work.

4. Digital representation of information

The general concept of information encoding in binary form. Different information encodings: ASCII, digital sound, images, and video / movies. Topics such as precision, conversion and interoperability (e.g., of file formats), resolution, fidelity, transformation, compression, and encryption are related, as is standardization of representations to support communication.

The appropriate emphasis is the notion that information that is processed by computers and communication systems is represented by bits (i.e., binary digits). Such a representation is a uniform way for computers and communication systems to store and transmit all information; information can be synthesized without a master analog source simply by creating the bits and so can be used to produce everything from Toy Story animations to forged e-mail; symbolic information in machine-readable form is more easily searchable than physical information.

5. Information organization

The general concepts of information organization, including forms, structure, classification and indexing, searching and retrieving, assessing information quality, authoring and presentation, and citation. Search engines for text, images, video, audio.

Information in computers, databases, libraries, and elsewhere must be structured to be accessible and useful. How the data should be organized and indexed depends critically on how users will describe the information sought (and vice versa), and how completely that description can be specified. In addition to locating and structuring information, it is important to be able to judge the quality (accuracy, authoritativeness, and so forth) of information both stored and retrieved. Section 3.2 provides some additional discussion.

6. Modeling and abstraction

The general methods and techniques for representing real-world phenomena as computer models, first in appropriate forms such as systems of equations, graphs, and relationships, and then in appropriate programming objects such as arrays or lists or procedures. Topics include continuous and discrete models, discrete time, events, randomization, and convergence, as well as the use of abstraction to hide irrelevant detail.

Computers can be made to play chess, predict the weather, and simulate the crash of a sports car by abstracting real-world phenomena and manipulating those abstractions using transformations that duplicate or approximate the real-world processes. One goal is understanding the relationship between reality and its representation, including notions of approximation, validity, and limitations; i.e., not all aspects of the real world are modeled in any one program, and a model is not reality.

7. Algorithmic thinking and programming

The general concepts of algorithmic thinking, including functional decomposition, repetition (iteration and / or recursion), basic data organizations (record, array, list), generalization and parameterization, algorithm vs. program, top-down design, and refinement. Note also that some types of algorithmic thinking do not necessarily require the use or understanding of sophisticated mathematics. The role of programming, which is a specific instantiation of algorithmic thinking, is discussed in Chapter 3.

Algorithmic thinking is key to understanding many aspects of information technology. Specifically, it is essential to comprehending how and why information technology systems work as they do. To troubleshoot or debug a problem in an information technology system, application, or operation, it is essential to have some expectation of what the proper behavior should be, and how it might fail to be realized. Further, algorithmic thinking is key to applying information technology to other personally relevant situations.

8. Universality

The "universality of computers" is one of the fundamental facts of information technology discovered by computing pioneers A.M. Turing and Alonzo

Church in the 1930s, before practical computers were created.[7] Shorn of its theoretical formalism and expressed informally, universality says that any computational task can be performed by any computer. The statement has several implications:

- No computational task is so complex that it cannot be decomposed into instructions suitable for the most basic computer.

- The instruction repertoire of a computer is largely unimportant in terms of giving it power since any missing instruction types can be programmed using the instructions the machine does have.

- Computers differ by how quickly they solve a problem, not whether they can solve the problem.

- Programs, which direct the instruction-following components of a computer to realize a computation, are the key.

Universality distinguishes computers from other types of machines (Box 2.2).

9. Limitations of information technology

The general notions of complexity, growth rates, scale, tractability, decidability, and state explosion combine to express some of the limitations of information technology. Tangible connections should be made to applications, such as text search, sorting, scheduling, and debugging.

Computers possess no intuition, creativity, imagination, or magic. Though extraordinary in their scope and application, information technology systems cannot do everything. Some tasks, such as calculating the closing price for a given stock on the NASDAQ exchange, are not solvable by computer. Other tasks, such as that of placing objects into a container so as to maximize the number that can be stored within it (e.g., optimally filling boxcars, shipping containers, moving vans, or space shuttles), can be solved only for small problems but not for large ones or those of practical importance.[8] Some tasks are so easily solved that it hardly matters which solution is used. And, because the programs that run on computers are designed by human beings, they reflect the assumptions that their designers build into them, assumptions that may be inappropriate or wrong. Thus, for example, a

---

[7] Alonzo Church. 1936. "An Unsolvable Problem of Elementary Number Theory," American Journal of Mathematics, 58:345–363; Alan M. Turing. 1936. "On Computable Numbers, with an Application to the Entscheidungsproblem," Proceedings of the London Mathematical Society, Ser. 2, 42:230–265, 43:544–546.

[8] In the case of the maximization problem above (often known as the "knapsack" problem), the proper arrangement can be determined by exhaustively trying all arrangements and orientations of the objects. But this calculation cannot be performed in any reasonable length of time when many objects can be placed into the container. Yet the penalty of not being able to find the maximizing arrangement can be high, as when shipping two containers rather than one or launching the Space Shuttle twice rather than once. When the problem is large enough that the maximizing arrangement cannot be practically computed, it is necessary to use "nearly maximal" arrangements that can be more easily determined.

computer simulation of some "real" phenomenon may or may not accurately reflect the underlying reality (and a naÏve user may be unable to tell the difference between a generally true simulation and one that is fundamentally misleading). Assessing what information technology can be applied—and when it should be applied—is essential in today's information age.

Box 2.2 On Universality—In Principle and in Practice

The universality property of computers is a theoretical result. Is it true in practice? The answer is yes, definitely, but there are complicating practical issues that can obscure the truth of this fact.

How can a computer without connection to a printer perform the computation, "print the report"? Of course, it cannot. But, the computer can without change perform the task, given a printer and the necessary software to format the report and drive the printer. Similarly, a computer embedded in an automobile's carburetor cannot print a report either, because, first, it does not have the proper input/output devices and, second, its software is permanently set to the task of mixing fuel. But the computer, i.e., the central processing unit, is not a limitation in these or other cases. Indeed, it is the universality of computers that explains why they are so ubiquitous in modern America: a computer chip with a program stored in read-only memory (ROM) is more convenient to design, cheaper to build, more reliable, and easier to maintain than specialized circuitry for controlling appliances, automobile subsystems, and other mechanical devices, as well as electronics like cell phones and Global Positioning System (GPS) devices.

Further, the observation that applications like word processing require different software to run on a Macintosh versus a PC seems to contradict the above claims and imply that the instruction set does matter. In a narrow sense it does, since the Mac cannot directly execute the binary encoding of a program specialized to the PC and vice versa. This is because the Mac and the PC use different microprocessor chips and the binary files for software applications are customized for each type of microprocessor. But those two different binary encodings can be created from a single source program by a translator (compiler) that specializes the computation to each instruction set. The two machines are literally running the same source program, i.e., performing the same word processing computation. And there is an indirect sense in which any PC software can run on a Mac and vice versa. A program can be written for one machine to emulate the instruction set of the other machine, allowing it to execute the actual binary encoding used by the other machine. Being indirect, this would be slower than a customized version, but it truly illustrates universality.

10. Societal impact of information and information technology

The technical basis for social concerns about privacy, intellectual property, ownership, security, weak/strong encryption, inferences about personal characteristics based on electronic behavior such as monitoring Web sites visited, "netiquette," "spamming," and free speech in the Internet environment.

Understanding social issues strongly connected to information technology goes beyond FITness to general principles of good citizenship. Policy issues that relate to information technology, including privacy, encryption, copyright, and related concerns, are increasingly common today, and informed citizens must have a basis for understanding the significance of those issues and for making reasoned judgments about them.

Information technology connects to the world at large in many ways, and characteristics of the technology have implications for everyday issues. Consider, for example, intellectual property. Copyright is accompanied by a well-established body of law, but now that the Web makes images and documents available to a huge audience, it has become much more important for Web users to understand that the ability to see an image on the Web does not automatically imply that the image can be copied or reused.

Numerous other issues are apparent today on which many non-technologists are asked to make judgments. Is the Internet just another form of publication, and therefore subject to the same First Amendment and copyright protections that newspapers enjoy? Is encryption a potential weapon that needs to be kept out of foreign hands? Why are standards important, and how do we promote the use of standards without permitting unregulated monopolies to stifle innovation? Does inviting technologically skilled workers from other countries create or destroy jobs? How do we encourage children to achieve the highest levels of technological competence? Does information technology cause job displacement and / or upskilling? How is it possible to promote social equity regarding access to information technology?

Discussion

These fundamental concepts represent major ideas underpinning information technology. The claim that FITness demands an understanding of these concepts is most frequently challenged by an analogy: If most people can drive without understanding how an automobile works, why should anyone need to know how a computer works?

The weakness in this analogy is embodied in the difference between the two kinds of machines. Automobiles perform essentially one task, transporting people and things from one location to another, and are incapable of other physical tasks, say, mixing concrete. Any computer can perform any information processing task—this is the concept of universality. It is not only a principle; it is a fact used every day. When one wants to manage a household budget, one doesn't buy a new computer for budgeting. Rather, one buys and installs software to add budgeting to the computer's other capabilities. Not being specialized like other machines that directly affect the physical world, computers may well affect our lives more than these other machines have, including automobiles. Knowing the conceptual foundations, then, is essential to understanding this impact—what information technology can do, what it cannot do, what risks computers and access to information bring, and so on. Armed with such knowledge, individuals can make informed choices ranging from personal decisions (like taking precautions against computer viruses) to matters of public policy such as protecting privacy interests.

An equally important motivation for learning information technology concepts is that they provide foundational knowledge to be used when acquiring and applying the intellectual capabilities. To perform the reasoning and thinking activities embodied in the capabilities, it is necessary to have some understanding of the range of possibilities. Furthermore, understanding these concepts enables an individual to be more versatile and more creative in his or her use of information technology tools.

Finally, Box 2.3 points out that even in a world in which the public's exposure to information technology is through specialized information appliances rather than desktop computers or through technologies that adapt to user needs and knowledge, the fundamental concepts of information technology will still be useful in understanding how to use such devices effectively.

2.6 Information Technology Skills

Skills such as managing a personal computer, using word processing, network browsers, mail, and spreadsheet software, or understanding an operating system are what are most usually subsumed under the label of "computer literacy."

Because information technology skills are closely tied to today's applications, the set of necessary skills can be expected to change at about the same rate that commercial information technology changes, i.e., quite rapidly. (Note, for example, that a list of skills developed five years ago would not have mentioned the Web or the Internet.) Changes in the specific interests and needs of the individual involved also have a significant effect on what skills are (or become) necessary. Over the course of a lifetime, individuals who use information technology must regularly evaluate their skills and determine which new skills they need for their workplace or personal success. FITness entails a continuing acquisition of new skills and adaptation of a set of skills to a changing environment.

Box 2.3 FITness, Personal Computers, Information Appliances, and Adaptive Technology

Today, desktop computers are a primary platform through which individuals interact with information technology. But whether this proposition will remain true in the future is an open question. Some reports suggest that information appliances—single-purpose devices that manipulate information—may become more common and ubiquitous in the future. Indeed, those making this prediction argue that information appliances can be made so easy to use that no knowledge of information technology will be necessary to operate them.

Predictions of the future technology environment are notoriously uncertain. It is likely that today's desktop computers (or their equivalents) will continue to be used by information workers. But the intellectual framework outlined in this chapter for FITness will continue to have applicability even to individuals dealing with information appliances. Of course, the specific skills needed will be different. But the basic concepts and intellectual capabilities of FITness will continue to be relevant. For example:

- An algorithm of some sort will be driving the operation of an information appliance. Understanding the general characteristics of algorithms will help the user to understand the limitations of a given device. For example, a navigation system for a car may provide the "best" route from Point A to B; the user may find it useful to know whether "best" refers to the most scenic route or the shortest route or the fastest route.

- Input to an information appliance is likely to remain "brittle," in the sense that the device will respond to the input that the user actually provides, not the input that the user intended to provide. This is a consequence of several concepts, including the digital representation of information and the nature of computational devices and information systems.

- A wireless information appliance that facilitates interaction with large amounts of date will require a local database for a fast response. The navigation system described above, for example, will in general not receive maps through the air, but rather will require maps "pre-stored" in some way that is local to the device.

- Identifying and correcting faults will always be necessary for the user to understand how he or she used the device improperly.

Furthermore, a knowledge of the basic concepts of FITness will enable a person to move more freely among information appliances. For example, a user will need to know to look for a way to correct mistaken input.

None of this is to argue the impossibility of operating an information appliance by the memorized application of a particular set of keystrokes—which today enables some individuals to obtain something useful from a computer. But gaining the full value from either a computer or an information appliance will require the full intellectual range of FITness.

In a similar vein, kit can be argued that information technology should be—and someday will be—designed to minimize what the individual must know in order to use it. For example, some information technology applications attempt to adapt to a particular user's style and needs. Other applications attempt to conceal their internal operation to reduce the burden on the user.

Such technological adaptations to the relatively naVve user are unquestionably helpful. But they do not—indeed, cannot—eliminate the need for FITness. For example, it is hard to imagine that a complex application has no operating faults in it, and thus users will always have to cope with things that don't work. All of the rationales articulated above for FITness in the context of information appliances equally apply to well-engineered and user-adaptive information technology applications.

The list of skills below is appropriate for today's technologies (circa 1999) and focuses on what one would need to know to buy a personal computer, set it up, use the principal software that comes with it, subscribe to an Internet service provider, and use its services. These items and other similar ones emerged from a question posed to attendees at the committee's January 1998 workshop about what an information technology-literate person should know.

This list of skills extends in one important way the content of "computer literacy" courses that teach individuals how to use specific software packages. It is true that students need to use specific software and hardware to acquire skills with information technology. But the skills involved in the committee's list are generic skills, rather than the specific skills needed to operate a particular vendor's product. For example, "word processing" refers to the use of functionality common to most or all word processors, rather than the specific commands, key-bindings, or dialog boxes of one vendor's software. Acquiring these skills includes understanding what similarities and differences to expect between different products for the same task.

Today's set of ten essential skills includes:

1. Setting up a personal computer

A person who uses computers should be able to connect the parts of a personal computer and its major peripherals (e.g., a printer). This entails knowing about the physical appearance of cables and ports, as well as having some understanding of how to configure the computer (e.g., knowing that most computers provide a way to set the system clock, or how to select a screen saver and why one may need to use a screen saver).

2. Using basic operating system features

Typical of today's operating system use is the ability to install new software, delete unwanted software, and invoke applications. There are many other skills that could reasonably be included in this category, such as the ability to find out from the operating system whether there is sufficient disk space.

3. Using a word processor to create a text document

Today, minimal skills in this area include the ability to select fonts, paginate, organize, and edit documents. Integration of image and other data is becoming essential. In the near future, requirements in this area will likely include the creation of Web pages using specialized authoring tools.

4. Using a graphics and/or artwork package to create illustrations, slides, or other image-based expressions of ideas

Today, this skill involves the ability to use the current generation of presentation software and graphics packages.

5. Connecting a computer to a network

Today, this process can be as simple as wiring the computer to a telephone jack and subscribing to an Internet service provider, although as more powerful communications options become available, this process may become more complex.

6. Using the Internet to find information and resources

Today, locating information on the Internet involves the use of browsers and search engines. The use of search engines and browsers requires an understanding of one's needs and how they relate to what is available and what can be found readily, as well as the ability to specify queries and evaluate the results.

7. Using a computer to communicate with others

Today, electronic mail is a primary mode of computer-based communication. Variants and improvements, as well as entirely new modes of communication, are expected in the future.

8. Using a spreadsheet to model simple processes or financial tables

This skill includes the ability to use standard spreadsheet systems and / or specialized packages (e.g., tax preparation software).

9. Using a database system to set up and access useful information

Today, SQL-based systems[9] are becoming ubiquitous in the workplace, and personal information managers are becoming increasingly common. In the future, different approaches, perhaps Web-oriented, may become the prevalent mode.

10. Using instructional materials to learn how to use new applications or features

This skill involves using online help files and reading and understanding printed manuals. One aspect of this process is obtaining details or features of systems one already comprehends; a second aspect is using the tutorial to grasp the essential models and ideas underlying a new system.

2.7 FITness in Perspective

The intellectual content of FITness is rich and deep. But the depth and richness of this content are determined by the nature of information technology. Although different individuals need different degrees of familiarity with the different elements of FITness, a good understanding of and facility with all of the skills, concepts, and capabilities of FITness are necessary for individuals to exploit the full power of information technology across a range of different applications.

Nevertheless, such depth and richness raise the question of the extent to which it is reasonable to expect that the content of FITness is accessible to a wide range of the citizenry. For perspective on this question, it is useful to consider the National Council of Teachers of Mathematics' (NCTM) standards for mathematics education and the National Research Council's standards for science education.

As described in Appendix B, such organizations focus on the mathematical and scientific education of all students, rather than a special few with previously demonstrated aptitude for mathematics or science. The organizations that produced these standards for mathematics and science education make the case that the intellectual content articulated in the standards is rich, deep, and most importantly not "dumbed down." These organizations believe that learning about science and mathematics is valuable not just for future scientists and mathematicians, but also for a very wide range of the citizenry.

The essentials of FITness are not for the most part dependent on knowledge of sophisticated mathematics. Indeed, the capabilities and concepts, though not the skills, are intellectually accessible even without computers per se. For example,

---

[9] SQL is an acronym for Structured Query Language, a common language used in interactions with databases.

the concept of an algorithm can be expressed and conveyed in an entirely qualitative and non-mathematical manner even to a 4th grader by discussing the rules of a game or following a recipe in the kitchen. Thus, the committee believes that the intellectual content of FITness is no less accessible to citizens than the mathematics and science contained within the NCTM and NRC standards.

A second issue is the following: by design, FITness is a body of knowledge and understanding that enables individuals to use information technology effectively in a variety of different contexts. But does being FIT mean that one will never need to rely on an information technology expert? Put differently, does an individual's consultation of an information technology expert imply a lack of FITness for that individual?

There is certainly some level of FITness at which an individual will not need to rely on an expert to fix an information technology problem or to exploit a new opportunity offered by information technology. But even someone who is FIT enough to not have to rely on an expert may find it advantageous to do so anyway. For example, a highly FIT individual may simply decide that it is not worth his or her time to fix a problem, even if he or she could do so. Furthermore, even if an individual with more basic levels of FITness may still need to consult with an information technology expert to solve a technology problem or to describe a technology solution, that basic understanding and knowledge will help him or her to interact constructively with the expert (e.g., to recognize that a problem is indeed solvable; to explain the problem or solution requirements more precisely; or to understand, implement, or dispute an approach that the expert proposes).

Appendix I

Information Literacy Competency Standards for Higher Education

Prepared by the Association of College and Research Libraries

Reproduced by permission of the Association of College and Research Libraries, a division of the American Library Association from *Information Literacy Competency Standards for Higher Education.* Copyright ©2000 Association of College and Research Libraries.

ASSOCIATION OF COLLEGE AND RESEARCH LIBRARIES

INFORMATION LITERACY COMPETENCY STANDARDS FOR HIGHER EDUCATION STANDARDS, PERFORMANCE INDICATORS, AND OUTCOMES

STANDARD ONE

The information literate student determines the nature and extent of the information needed.

Performance Indicators:

1. The information literate student defines and articulates the need for information.

    Outcomes Include:

    a. Confers with instructors and participates in class discussions, peer workgroups, and electronic discussions to identify a research topic, or other information need

    b. Develops a thesis statement and formulates questions based on the information need

    c. Explores general information sources to increase familiarity with the topic

    d. Defines or modifies the information need to achieve a manageable focus

279

    e.   Identifies key concepts and terms that describe the information need

    f.   Recognizes that existing information can be combined with original thought, experimentation, and/or analysis to produce new information

2.   The information literate student identifies a variety of types and formats of potential sources for information.

Outcomes Include:

    a.   Knows how information is formally and informally produced, organized, and disseminated

    b.   Recognizes that knowledge can be organized into disciplines that influence the way information is accessed

    c.   Identifies the value and differences of potential resources in a variety of formats (e.g., multimedia, database, website, data set, audio/visual, book)

    d.   Identifies the purpose and audience of potential resources (e.g., popular vs. scholarly, current vs. historical)

    e.   Differentiates between primary and secondary sources, recognizing how their use and importance vary with each discipline

    f.   Realizes that information may need to be constructed with raw data from primary sources

3.   The information literate student considers the costs and benefits of acquiring the needed information.

Outcomes Include:

    a.   Determines the availability of needed information and makes decisisons on broadening the information seeking process beyond local resources (e.g., interlibrary loan; using resources at other locations; obtaining images, videos, text, or sound)

    b.   Considers the feasibility of acquiring a new language or skill (e.g., foreign or discipline-based) in order to gather needed information and to understand its context

    c.   Defines a realistic overall plan and timeline to acquire the needed information

4. The information literate student reevaluates the nature and extent of the information need.

Outcomes Include:

    a. Reviews the initial information need to clarify, revise, or refine the question

    b. Describes criteria used to make information decisions and choices

STANDARD TWO

The information literate student accesses needed information effectively and efficiently.

Performance Indicators:

1. The information literate student selects the most appropriate investigative methods or information retrieval systems for accessing the needed information.

Outcomes Include:

    a. Identifies appropriate investigative methods (e.g., laboratory experiment, simulation, fieldwork)

    b. Investigates benefits and applicability of various investigative methods

    c. Investigates the scope, content, and organization of information retrieval systems

    d. Selects efficient and effective approaches for accessing the information needed from the investigative method or information retrieval system

2. The information literate student constructs and implements effectively-designed search strategies.

Outcomes Include:

    a. Develops a research plan appropriate to the investigative method

    b. Identifies keywords, synonyms and related terms for the information needed

    c. Selects controlled vocabulary specific to the discipline or information retrieval source

    d.   Constructs a search strategy using appropriate commands for the information retrieval system selected (e.g., Boolean operators, truncation, and proximity for search engines; internal organizers such as indexes for books)

    e.   Implements the search strategy in various information retrieval systems using different user interfaces and search engines, with different command languages, protocols, and search parameters

    f.   Implements the search using investigative protocols appropriate to the discipline

3.   The information literate student retrieves information online or in person using a variety of methods.

Outcomes Include:

    a.   Uses various search systems to retrieve information in a variety of formats

    b.   Uses various classification schemes and other systems (e.g., call number systems or indexes) to locate information resources within the library or to identify specific sites for physical exploration

    c.   Uses specialized online or in person services available at the institution to retrieve information needed (e.g., interlibrary loan/document delivery, professional associations, institutional research offices, community resources, experts and practitioners)

    d.   Uses surveys, letters, interviews, and other forms of inquiry to retrieve primary information

4.   The information literate student refines the search strategy if necessary.

Outcomes Include:

    a.   Assesses the quantity, quality, and relevance of the search results to determine whether alternative information retrieval systems or investigative methods should be utilized

    b.   Identifies gaps in the information retrieved and determines if the search strategy should be revised

    c.   Repeats the search using the revised strategy as necessary

5. The information literate student extracts, records, and manages the information and its sources.

Outcomes Include:

    a. Selects among various technologies the most appropriate one for the task of extracting the needed information (e.g., copy/paste software functions, photocopier, scanner, audio/visual equipment, or exploratory instruments)

    b. Creates a system for organizing the information

    c. Differentiates between the types of sources cited and understands the elements and correct syntax of a citation for a wide range of resources

    d. Records all pertinent citation information for future reference

    e. Uses various technologies to manage the information selected and organized

STANDARD THREE

The information literate student evaluates information and its sources critically and incorporates selected information into his or her knowledge base and value system.

Performance Indicators:

1. The information literate student summarizes the main ideas to be extracted from the information gathered.

Outcomes Include:

    a. Reads the text and selects main ideas

    b. Restates textual concepts in his/her own words and selects data accurately

    c. Identifies verbatim material that can be then appropriately quoted

2. The information literate student articulates and applies initial criteria for evaluating both the information and its sources.

Outcomes Include:

    a. Examines and compares information from various sources in order to evaluate reliability, validity, accuracy, authority, timeliness, and point of view or bias

    b. Analyzes the structure and logic of supporting arguments or methods

      c.   Recognizes prejudice, deception, or manipulation

      d.   Recognizes the cultural, physical, or other context within which the information was created and understands the impact of context on interpreting the information

3.   The information literate student synthesizes main ideas to construct new concepts.

Outcomes Include:

      a.   Recognizes interrelationships among concepts and combines them into potentially useful primary statements with supporting evidence

      b.   Extends initial synthesis, when possible, at a higher level of abstraction to construct new hypotheses that may require additional information

      c.   Utilizes computer and other technologies (e.g. spreadsheets, databases, multimedia, and audio or visual equipment) for studying the interaction of ideas and other phenomena

4.   The information literate student compares new knowledge with prior knowledge to determine the value added, contradictions, or other unique characteristics of the information.

Outcomes Include:

      a.   Determines whether information satisfies the research or other information need

      b.   Uses consciously selected criteria to determine whether the information contradicts or verifies information used from other sources

      c.   Draws conclusions based upon information gathered

      d.   Tests theories with discipline-appropriate techniques (e.g., simulators, experiments)

      e.   Determines probable accuracy by questioning the source of the data, the limitations of the information gathering tools or strategies, and the reasonableness of the conclusions

      f.   Integrates new information with previous information or knowledge

      g.   Selects information that provides evidence for the topic

5. The information literate student determines whether the new knowledge has an impact on the individual's value system and takes steps to reconcile differences.

    Outcomes Include:

    a. Investigates differing viewpoints encountered in the literature

    b. Determines whether to incorporate or reject viewpoints encountered

6. The information literate student validates understanding and interpretation of the information through discourse with other individuals, subject-area experts, and/or practitioners.

    Outcomes Include:

    a. Participates in classroom and other discussions

    b. Participates in class-sponsored electronic communication forums designed to encourage discourse on the topic (e.g., email, bulletin boards, chat rooms)

    c. Seeks expert opinion through a variety of mechanisms (e.g., interviews, email, listservs)

7. The information literate student determines whether the initial query should be revised.

    Outcomes Include:

    a. Determines if original information need has been satisfied or if additional information is needed

    b. Reviews search strategy and incorporates additional concepts as necessary

    c. Reviews information retrieval sources used and expands to include others as needed

STANDARD FOUR

The information literate student, individually or as a member of a group, uses information effectively to accomplish a specific purpose.
Performance Indicators:

1. The information literate student applies new and prior information to the planning and creation of a particular product or performance.

Outcomes Include:

    a.   Organizes the content in a manner that supports the purposes and format of the product or performance (e.g. outlines, drafts, storyboards)

    b.   Articulates knowledge and skills transferred from prior experiences to planning and creating the product or performance

    c.   Integrates the new and prior information, including quotations and paraphrasings, in a manner that supports the purposes of the product or performance

    d.   Manipulates digital text, images, and data, as needed, transferring them from their original locations and formats to a new context

2.   The information literate student revises the development process for the product or performance.

Outcomes Include:

    a.   Maintains a journal or log of activities related to the information seeking, evaluating, and communicating process

    b.   Reflects on past successes, failures, and alternative strategies

3.   The information literate student communicates the product or performance effectively to others.

Outcomes Include:

    a.   Chooses a communication medium and format that best supports the purposes of the product or performance and the intended audience

    b.   Uses a range of information technology applications in creating the product or performance

    c.   Incorporates principles of design and communication

    d.   Communicates clearly and with a style that supports the purposes of the intended audience

STANDARD FIVE

The information literate student understands many of the economic, legal, and social issues surrounding the use of information and accesses and uses information ethically and legally.

Performance Indicators:

1. The information literate student understands many of the ethical, legal and socio-economic issues surrounding information and information technology.

    Outcomes Include:

    a. Identifies and discusses issues related to privacy and security in both the print and electronic environments

    b. Identifies and discusses issues related to free vs. fee-based access to information

    c. Identifies and discusses issues related to censorship and freedom of speech

    d. Demonstrates an understanding of intellectual property, copyright, and fair use of copyrighted material

2. The information literate student follows laws, regulations, institutional policies, and etiquette related to the access and use of information resources.

    Outcomes Include:

    a. Participates in electronic discussions following accepted practices (e.g. "Netiquette")

    b. Uses approved passwords and other forms of ID for access to information resources

    c. Complies with institutional policies on access to information resources

    d. Preserves the integrity of information resources, equipment, systems and facilities

    e. Legally obtains, stores, and disseminates text, data, images, or sounds

    f. Demonstrates an understanding of what constitutes plagiarism and does not represent work attributable to others as his/her own

    g. Demonstrates an understanding of institutional policies related to human subjects research

3. The information literate student acknowledges the use of information sources in communicating the product or performance.

Outcomes Include:

    a. Selects an appropriate documentation style and uses it consistently to cite sources

    b. Posts permission granted notices, as needed, for copyrighted material

References

2002 Campus Computing Survey (2002).*Campus portals make progress; technology budgets suffer significant cuts* [Online]. Available: http://www.campuscomputing.net/pdf/2002-CCP.pdf. (Accessed May 13, 2003).

Access ERIC. (2000). *What should parents know about information literacy?* [Online]. Available: http://www.eric.ed.gov/resources/parent/infoltrcy.html. (Accessed(Accessed June 24, 2003).

America 2000. (1991, December). *Congressional Digest, 70*(12), 294-295.

American Association of School Librarians (AASL). (2003). *Information power: Basic implementation kit* [Online]. Available: http://www.ala.org/aaslTemplate.cfm?Section=Information_Power&Template=/ContentManagement/ Content Display.cfm&ContentID=21111. (Accessed May 7, 2003).

American Association of School Librarians (AASL) & Association for Educational Communications and Technology (AECT). (1988). *Information power: Guidelines for school library media programs.* Chicago: Author.

American Association of School Librarians (AASL) & Association for Educational Communications and Technology (AECT) National Guidelines Vision Committee. (1996, October). *Information literacy standards for student learning* [Online]. Available: http://www.ala.org/aasl/stndsdrft5.html. Accessed March 15, 1998).

American Association of School Librarians (AASL) & Association for Educational Communications and Technology (AECT). (1998). *Information power: Building partnerships for learning.* Chicago: ALA.

American Library Association (ALA). (1998). Information literacy standards for student learning. In *Indicators of schools of quality* [Online]. Available: http://www.ala.org/aasl/news/ indicators1.html. (Accessed February 20, 1998).

American Library Association (ALA) & Association for Educational Communications and Technology (AECT). (1998). Information literacy standards

289

for student learning. In *Indicators of schools of quality, volume 1: Schoolwide indicators of quality.* Chicago: ALA.

American Library Association Presidential Committee on Information Literacy. (1989). *Final report.* Chicago: Author.

Annenberg/CPB Projects. (1997). *Journey north* [Online]. Available: http://www.learner.org/resources/resource.html?uid=127. (Accessed May 7, 2003).

AOL Time Warner Foundation. (2003). *21st century literacy: A vital component in learning.* [Online]. Available: http://aoltimewarnerfoundation.org/. (Accessed September 29, 2003).

Association for Teacher-Librarianship in Canada. (1995). *Students' bill of information rights* [Online]. Available: http://www.atlc.ca/AboutATLC/studrigh.htm. (Accessed May 7, 2003).

Association for Teacher-Librarianship in Canada & Canadian School Library Association. (1997, November). *Students' information literacy needs in the 21st century: Competencies for teacher-librarians* [Online]. Available: http://www.atlc.ca/Publications/competen.htm. (Accessed May 7).

Association of College & Research Libraries (ACRL). (2000). *Information literacy competency standards for higher education* [Online]. Available: http://www.ala.org/Content/NavigationMenu/ACRL/Standards_and_Guidelines/Information_Literacy_Competency_Standards_for_Higher_Education.htm. (Accessed June 4, 2003).

Association of College & Research Libraries. (2001). *Objectives for information literacy instruction: a model statement for academic librarians* [Online]. Available: http://www.ala.org/Content/NavigationMenu/ACRL/Standards_and_Guidelines/Objectives_for_Information_Literacy_Instruction__A_Model_Statement_for_Academic_Librarians.htm. (Accessed June 4, 2003).

Aufderheide, P. (1993). *Media literacy. A report of the national leadership conference on media literacy.* Queenstown, MD: Aspen Institute.

Australian Library and Information Association (ALIA). (1997, March). *Information literacy forum* [Online]. Available: http://www.alia.org.au/groups/infolit/information.literacy.html (Accessed May 7, 2003).

Australian School Library Association. (1994). *Learning for the future: Developing information services in Australian schools.* Carlton, South Victoria: Curriculum Corporation.

Barner, R. (1996, March/April). Seven changes that will challenge managers–and workers. *The Futurist, 30*(2), 14-18.

Barrows, H. S. (1996, Winter). Problem-based learning in medicine and beyond: A brief overview. *New Directions for Teaching and Learning, 68,* 3-12.

Beck, S. E. (2002, October 30). *LSC 311-02 Information literacy* [Online]. Available: http://lib.nmsu.edu/instruction/lsc311/. (Accessed May 1, 2003).

Behrens, S. J. (1994, July). A conceptual analysis and historical overview of information literacy. *College and Research Libraries, 55*(4), 309-322.

Bellingham Schools. (1996, October 23). *Bellingham Schools course outline: Information literacy and the net* [Online]. Available: http://www. bham.wednet.edu/studentgal/onlineresearch/oldonline/literacy.htm. (Accessed April 23, 2003).

Bentley, M. (1997, October). User education at NYPL's new SIBL. *College & Research Libraries News, 58*(9), 633-636.

The Big6. (2003, February 18). *The Big6 for kids* [Online]. Available: http:// www.big6.com/kids/. (Accessed April 24, 2003).

Bloom, B. S. (1956). *Taxonomy of educational objectives: The classification of educational goals: Handbook I: Cognitive domain.* New York: McKay.

Braden, R. A., & Hortin, J. A. (1982). Identifying the theoretical foundations of visual literacy. *Journal of Visual/Verbal Languaging, 2,* 37-42.

Brandt, D. S. (2002, Spring). Syllabus. In *Information strategies* [Online]. Available: http://www.lib.purdue.edu/gs175_02/index.html. (Accessed May 1, 2003).

Breivik, P. S. (1998). *Student learning in the information age.* Phoenix, AZ: Oryx Press.

Breivik, P. S., & Gee, E. G. (1989). *Information literacy.* New York: Macmillan.

Breivik, P. S., Hancock, V., & Senn, J. (1998). *A progress report on information literacy: An update on the American Library Association Presidential Committee on Information Literacy: Final report* (pp. 1-10). Chicago: ALA, Association of Research Librarians.

Breivik, P. S., & Senn, J. A. (1994). *Information literacy: Educating children for the 21st century.* New York: Scholastic.

Breivik. P. S., & Senn, J. A. (1998). *Information literacy: Educating children for the 21st century* (2nd ed.). Washington, DC: National Education Association.

Breivik, P. S., & Wedgeworth, R. (1988). *Libraries and the search for academic excellence.* Metuchen, NJ: Scarecrow Press.

Bruce, C. (1997). *The seven faces of information literacy.* Adelaide (AU): Auslib Press.

Burchinal, L. G. (1976, September 24). The communications revolution: America's third century challenge. In *The future of organizing knowledge.* Papers presented at the Texas A & M University library's centennial academic assembly, September 12, 1976. College Station, TX: Texas A & M University.

California Academic and Research Libraries Task Force. (1997, September 29). *Recommended texts for consideration related to information literacy* [Online]. Available: http://www.carl-acrl.org/Archives/DocumentsArchive/Reports/rectoWASC.html. (Accessed May 7, 2003).

California Department of Education. (1994). *Information literacy guidelines.* Denver, CO: Author.

California Media and Library Educators Association. (1997). *From library skills to information literacy: A handbook for the 21st century* (2nd ed.). San Jose, CA: Hi Willow Research and Publishing.

California State Polytechnic University Pomona. (1999). *Information competence assessment* [Online]. Available: http://www.csupomona.edu/~library/InfoComp/. (Accessed June 24, 2003).

Callison, D. (1993). The potential for portfolio assessment. In C.C. Kuhlthau (Ed.), *School library media annual* (pp. 30-39). Englewood, CO: Libraries Unlimited.

Callison, D., McGregor, J. H. & Small, R. (Eds.). (1997). Instructional intervention for information use. In *Research papers of the sixth Treasure Mountain research retreat for school library media programs.* March 31-April 1. San Jose, CA: Hi Willow Research and Publishing.

Candy, P. C., Crebert, G., & O'Leary, J. (Eds.). (1994). *Developing lifelong learners through undergraduate education.* Commissioned Report No. 28, National Board of Employment, Education and Training. Australian Government Publishing Service.

Carpenter, J. P. (1989). *Using the new technologies to create links between schools throughout the world: Colloquy on computerized school links.* (Exeter, Devon, United Kingdom, 17-20 October 1988).

Carrier Library, James Madison University Library. (Undated). *Welcome to go for the gold* [Online]. Available: http://www.lib.jmu.edu/library/gold/modules.htm. (Accessed May 1, 2003).

Center for Applied Special Technology. (2000). *The role of online communications in schools: A national study* [Online]. Available: http://www.cast.org/stsstudy.html. (Accessed May 13, 2003).

Center for Civic Education. (1994). *National standards for civics and government.* Calabass, CA: Center for Civic Education.

Colorado Department of Education. (1994). *Model information literacy guidelines.* Denver, CO: Author.

Colorado Educational Media Association. (1994). *Model information literacy guidelines.* Denver: Colorado State Department of Education, State Library and Adult Education Office.

Colorado State Department of Education. (1996, revised 1998). *Rubrics for the assessment of information literacy* [Online]. Available: http://www.cde.state.co.us/cdelib/download/pdf/inforubr.pdf. (Accessed May 8, 2003).

Commission on Higher Education. Middle States Association of Colleges and Schools. (1995). *Information literacy, lifelong learning in the middle states region. A summary of two symposia.* Philadelphia: Middle States Association.

Computer Science and Telecommunications Board, National Research Council. (1999). *Being fluent with information technology.* Washington, DC: National Academy Press.

Consortium of National Arts Education Associations. (1994). *National standards for arts education.* Reston, VA: Music Educators National Conference.

Corporation for Public Broadcasting. (2003). *Connected to the future: A report on children's Internet use from the Corporation for Public Broadcasting* [Online]. Available: http://www.cpb.org/ed/resources/connected/. (Accessed May 7, 2003).

Cortes, C. E. (1992, August). Media literacy: An educational basic for the information age. *Education and Urban Society, 24*(4), 489-497.

Costa, A. L. (1993, February). How world-class standards will change us. *Educational Leadership, 50*(5), 50-51.

Cowles, S. K. (1997). *Warming up: Summary information* [Online]. Available: http://www.nifl.gov/susanc/warmind.htm. (Accessed May 7, 2003).

CTAP Region VII Information Literacy Task Force. (Undated). *CTAP information literacy guidelines K–12* [Online]. Available: http://ctap.fcoe.k12. ca.us/ctap/Info.Lit/Guidelines.html. (Accessed April 24, 2003).

CTAP Region VII Information Literacy Task Force. (Undated). *Information literacy development* [Online]. Available: http://ctap.fcoe.k12.ca.us/ ctap/Info.Lit/Benchmarks.html. (Accessed April 24, 2003).

Cuban, L. (1990). Four stories about national goals for American education. *Phi Delta Kappan, 72*(4), 264-271.

Curzon, S. (1997). *Information competence. Memorandum* [Online]. Available: http://library.csun.edu/susan.curzon/infoprop.html. (Accessed May 1, 2003).

Dalbotten, M. S. (1998). Inquiry in the national content standards. In D. Callison, J. McGregor, and R. Small, *Instructional interventions for information use.* Proceedings of the Treasure Mountain Research Retreat VI, Troutdale, OR, March 31-April 1, 1997.

Division of Reference Services, Olin*Kroch* Uris Libraries, Cornell University Library. (1997, September 1). *Library research at Cornell: A hypertext guide* [Online]. Available: http://www.library.cornell.edu/okuref/research/ tutorial.html. (Accessed May 1, 2003).

Doyle, C. S. (1992). Outcome measures for information literacy within the National Educational Goals of 1990. In *Final report to National Forum on Information Literacy.* Flagstaff, AZ: National Forum on Information Literacy.

Doyle, C. S. (1994). *Information literacy in an information society: A concept for the information age.* Syracuse, NY: ERIC Clearinghouse on Information and Technology.

Drucker, P. (1992, December 1). Be data literate–know what to know. *Wall Street Journal*, A16.

Drucker, P. F., in Harris, T. G. (1993, May/June). The post-capitalist executive: An interview with Peter F. Drucker. *Harvard Business Review, 71*(3), 114-122.

Eisenberg, M. B. (1996, September). Take the Internet challenge: Using technology in context. *Technology Connection, The Book Report, Library Talk*, (Special supplement).

Eisenberg, M. B., & Berkowitz, R. E. (1988). *Curriculum initiative: An agenda and strategy for library media programs.* Norwood, NJ: Ablex.

Eisenberg, M. B., & Berkowitz, R. E. (1996, June). *Helping with homework: A parent's guide to information problem-solving.* Syracuse, NY: ERIC Clearinghouse on Information & Technology.

Eisenberg, M. B., & Brown, M. K. (1992). Current themes regarding library and information skills instruction: Research supporting and research lacking. *School Library Media Quarterly, 20*(2), 103-109.

Eisenberg, M. B., & Johnson, D. (2002). *Computer skills for information problem solving: Learning and teaching technology in context.* ERIC Digest. (Report no. EDO-IR-2002-04). Syracuse, NY: ERIC Clearinghouse on Information and Technology.

Eisenberg, M. B., & Lowe, C. A. (1997). The Big6™ Skills: Looking at the world through information problem-solving glasses. In D. Callison, J. McGregor, and R. Small, *Instructional interventions for information use.* Proceedings of the Treasure Mountain Research Retreat VI, Troutdale, OR, March 31-April 1, 1997.

Farber, E. (1995). Bibliographic at Earlham College. In L. Hardesty, J. Hustreiter, & D. Henderson (Eds.), *Bibliographic instruction in practice: A tribute to the legacy of Evan Ira Farber* (pp. 1-26). Ann Arbor: Pierian.

Florida International University. (2000, February 6). *Information literacy across the curriculum* [Online]. Available: http://www.fiu.edu/~library/ili/ililoex.html. (Accessed May 1, 2003).

Fulton, K. (1997). *Learning in the digital age: Insights into the issues. The skills students need for technological fluency.* Santa Monica, CA: Milken Family Foundation.

Gallagher, S. A., & Stepien, W. J. (1996, Spring). Content acquisition in problem-based learning: Depth versus breadth in American studies. *Journal for the Education of the Gifted, 19*(3), 257-275.

Gardner, H., in Brandt, R. (1993, April). On teaching for understanding: A conversation with Howard Gardner. *Educational Leadership, 50*(7), 4-7.

Geography Education Standards Project. (1994). *Geography for life: National geography standards 1994.* Washington, DC: National Geographic Research & Exploration.

Gilster, P. (1997a). *Digital literacy.* New York: Wiley and Computer Publishing.

Gilster, P. (1997b). *A primer on digital literacy* [Online]. Available: http://www.ibiblio.org/cisco/noc/primer.html. (Accessed June 16, 2003).

Goodin, M. E. (1991). The transferability of library research skills from high school to college. *School Library Media Quarterly, 19*(1), 33-42.

Gratch, B., et al. (1992). *Information retrieval and evaluation skills for education students.* Chicago: Association of College and Research Libraries.

Griffith University. (1994, September). *Information literacy blueprint* [Online]. Available: http://www.gu.edu.au/cgi-bin/frameit?http://www.gu.edu.au:80/ins/training/computing/web/blueprint/content_blueprint.html. (Accessed May 7, 2003).

Haeckel, S. H., & Nolan, R. L. (1993). The role of technology in an information age. In *Annual review of the institute for information studies, the knowledge economy* (pp. 1-24). Queenstown, MD: Aspen Institute.

Hamilton, M. A., & Hamilton, S. F. (1997, May). When is work a learning experience? *Phi Delta Kappan, 78*(9), 682-689.

Hancock, V. E. (1993). *Information literacy for lifelong learning.* ERIC Digest. (Report no. EDO-IR-93-1). Syracuse NY: ERIC Clearinghouse on Information Resources.

Hashim, E. (1986). Educating students to think: The role of the school library media program, an introduction. In *Information literacy: Learning how to learn. A collection of articles from School Library Media Quarterly, 15*(1), 17-18.

Haycock, C. A. (1991, May). Resource-based learning: A shift in the roles of teacher, learner. *NASSP Bulletin, 75*(535), 15-22.

Humboldt State University Library. (2002) *The digital literacy closet* [Online]. Available: http://library.humboldt.edu/dlc/. (Accessed June 16, 2003).

Illinois State Board of Education. (1996). *K–12 information technology plan.* Springfield: Illinois State Board of Education.

Information competence in the CSU: A report submitted to the Commission on Learning Resources and Instructional Technology (CLRIT) by the CLRIT Information Competence Work Group; revised: 1/97. In *A set of core competencies* [Online]. Available: http://library.csun.edu/susan.curzon/corecomp.html. (Accessed May 7, 2003).

Information literacy: A position paper on information problem-solving. (1995, Nov/Dec). *Emergency Librarian, 23*(2), 20-23.

Institute for Information Literacy. (2003). *Institute for information literacy* [Online]. Available: http://www.ala.org/Template.cfm?Section=ACRLs_Institute_for_Information_Literacy. (Accessed May 1, 2003).

International Reading Association & National Council of Teachers of English. (1996). *Standards for the English language arts.* Newark, DE: International Reading Association.

International Society for Technology in Education (ISTE). (2002). *National educational technology standards for students* [Online]. Available: http://cnets.iste.org/students/s_stands.html. (Accessed June 22, 2003).

Irving, A. (1985). *Study and information skills across the curriculum.* London: Heinemann Educational Books.

Ives, B., & Jarvenpaa, S. L. (1993). Information: Empowering knowledge networks with information technology. In *Annual review of the Institute for Information Studies, the knowledge economy* (pp. 53-88). Queenstown, MD: Aspen Institute.

Jacobs, V. (1995). All alone and lost in cyberspace: Closing the gap between the local village and the global village through teaching Namibian children information skills and technology. In *Sustaining the vision. Selected papers from the Annual Conference of the International Association of School Librarianship* (24th, Worcester England, July 17-21, 1995).

Jay, M.E. (2003). *Information literacy: Unlocking your child's door to the world* [Online]. Available: http://www.ala.org/Content/NavigationMenu/AASL/School_Libraries_and_You/Parents_and_Community/Information_Literacy__Unlocking_Your_Childs_Door_to_the_World.htm. (Accessed June 24, 2003).

Joint Committee on National Health Standards. (1997). *National health education standards: Achieving health literacy.* Atlanta, GA: American Cancer Society.

Kanter, J. (1996, Spring). Guidelines for attaining information literacy. *Information strategy: The Executives' Journal, 12*(3) 6-11.

Kasowitz-Scheer, A. and Pasqualoni, M. (2001). *Information literacy instruction in higher education: trends and issues.* ERIC Digest. (Report no. EDO-IR-2002-01). Syracuse, NY: ERIC Clearinghouse on Information and Technology.

Kent State University Libraries & Media Services. (2003). *Project SAILS* [Online]. Available: http://sails.lms.kent.edu/index.php. (Accessed June 24, 2003).

Kentucky Department of Education. (2001). *Beyond proficiency: Achieving a distinguished library media program* [Online]. Available: http://www.kentuckyschools.net/KDE/Instructional+Resources/Curriculum+Documents+and+Resources/Beyond+Proficiency.htm. (Accessed May 7, 2003).

Kindred Public School. (Undated). *Rain forest portfolio* [Online]. Available: http://www.kindred.k12.nd.us/CyLib/rainf.html. (Accessed May 7, 2003).

Kluger, J. (1997, August 11). Calling all amateurs. *Time, 150*(6), 68.

Krovetz, M., Casterson, D., McKowen, C., & Willis, T. (1993, April). Beyond show and tell. *Educational Leadership, 50*(7), 73-76.

Kuhlthau, C. C. (1987). *Information skills for an information society: A review of research.* Syracuse, NY: ERIC Clearinghouse on Information Resources.

Kuhlthau, C. C. (1993). *Seeking meaning: A process approach to library and information services.* Greenwich, CT: Ablex.

Kuhlthau, C. C. (1995). The process of learning from information. *School libraries worldwide, 1*(1).

Kunde, D. (1997, August 12). Workers struggling to deal with e-mail overload. *Syracuse Herald Journal,* A9.

Lance, K. C., Hamilton-Pennell, C., & Rodney, M. J. (1999). *Information empowered: The school librarian as an agent of academic achievement in Alaska schools* [Online]. Available: http://www.library.state.ak.us/dev/ infoemp.html. (Accessed May 27, 2003).

Lance, K. C., Rodney, M. J., & Hamilton-Pennell, C. (2000a). *How school librarians help kids achieve standards: The second Colorado study.* San Jose, CA: Hi Willow Publishing.

Lance, K. C., Rodney, M. J., & Hamilton-Pennell, C. (2000b). *Measuring up to standards: The impact of school library programs & information literacy in Pennsylvania schools* [Online]. Available: http://www.statelibrary. state.pa.us/libraries/lib/libraries/measuringup.pdf. (Accessed May 27, 2003).

Lance, K. C., Welborn, L., & Hamilton-Pennell, C. (1992). *The impact of school library media centers on academic achievement.* Denver: Colorado Department of Education.

Lenox, M. F., & Walker, M. L. (1992). Information literacy: Challenge for the future. *International Journal of Information and Library Research, 4*(1), 1-18.

Loertscher, D. V., & Woolls, B. (2002). *Information literacy: A review of the research.* San Jose, CA: Hi Willow Publishing.

Mancall, J. C., Aaron, S. L., & Walker, S. A. (1986). Educating students to think: The role of the library media program. A concept paper written for the National Commission on Libraries and Information Science. *School Library Media Quarterly, Journal of the American Association of School Librarians, 15*(1), 18-27.

Mankato Area Public Schools. (2003). *Mankato Schools information literacy curriculum guidelines* [Online]. Available: http://www.isd77.k12.mn.us/resources/infocurr/infolit.html. (Accessed September 29, 2003).

McClure, C. R. (1993). Network literacy in an electronic society: an educational disconnect? In *Annual review of the Institute for Information Studies, the knowledge economy* (pp. 137-178). Queenstown, MD: Aspen Institute.

Ministry of Education, Helsinki (Finland). (1995). *Education, training, and research in the information society: A national strategy.* Helsinki (Finland): Author.

Moore, D. M., & Dwyer, F. M., (Eds.). (1994). *Visual literacy: A spectrum of visual learning.* Englewood Cliffs, NJ: Educational Technology Publications.

Murray, J. *Applying Big6™ skills, information literacy standards and ISTE NETS to Internet research* [Online]. Available: http://www.surfline.ne.jp/janetm/big6info.htm. (Accessed September 29, 2003).

National Association for Sport and Physical Education. (1995). *Moving into the future: National standards for physical education.* St. Louis, MO: Mosby Year Book.

National Center for History in the Schools. (1996). *National standards for history.* Los Angeles: Author.

National Commission on Excellence in Education. (1983). *A nation at risk: The imperative for educational reform.* Washington, DC: U.S. Government Printing Office.

National Council for Social Studies. (1989). *From information to decision making: New challenges for effective citizenship.* Washington, DC: Author.

National Council for Social Studies. (1993). *Curriculum standards for the social studies, draft 2.* Washington, DC: Author.

National Council of Teachers of Mathematics. (2000). *Principles and standards for school mathematics.* Reston, VA: Author.

National Council on Economic Education. (1997). *Voluntary national content standards in economics.* New York: Author.

National goals for education. (1990). Washington, DC: Executive Office of the President.

National Research Council. (1993). *National science education standards: An enhanced sampler.* A working paper of the National Council on Science Education Standards and Assessment. Washington, DC: Author.

National Standards in Foreign Language Education Project. (1999). *Standards for foreign language learning in the 21st century.* Lawrence, KS: Allen Press.

New South Wales Department of Education. (Undated). *Information skills in the school.* Ryde, NSW: Author.

Newmann, F. M., & Wehlage, G. G. (1993, April). Five standards of authentic instruction. *Educational Leadership, 50*(7), 8-12.

North Carolina State University Library. (Undated). *Library online basic orientation (LOBO)* [Online]. Available: http://www.lib.ncsu.edu/lobo1/. (Accessed May 1, 2003).

Norton, B., & Gotts, S. (1991). The events of October 1987. In F. W. Horton Jr. & D. Lewis (Eds.). *Great information disasters: Twelve prime examples of how information mismanagement led to human misery, political misfortune and business failure* (pp. 107-124). London: ASLIB.

Oberlin College Library. (2000, April 7). *Winter term 1997 faculty workshop on information literacy* [Online]. Available: http://www.oberlin.edu/library/programs/WT97/. (Accessed May 1, 2003).

Office of the Superintendent of Public Instruction (OSPI) and Washington Library Media Association (WLMA). (1996). *WLMA and OSPI essential skills for information literacy* [Online]. Available: http://www.wlma.org/Instruction/wlmaospibenchmarks.htm. (Accessed May 7, 2003).

Olen, S. (1995). A transformation in teacher education: Or how can disadvantaged teachers become information literate? In *Literacy: Traditional, cultural, technological. Selected papers from the Annual Conference of the International Association of School Librarianship* (23rd, Pittsburgh, Pennsylvania, July 17-22, 1994).

Oregon Educational Media Association. (2000). *Information literacy guidelines: Scientific inquiry* [Online]. Available: http://www.oema.net/infolit/infolit.html. (Accessed May 3, 2003).

Owens, M. R. (1976, January 1). The state government and libraries. *Library Journal, 101*(1), 19-28.

Partnership for 21st Century Skills. (2003). *Learning for the 21st century: A report and MILE guide for 21st century skills* [Online]. Available: http://www.21stcenturyskills.org. (Accessed June 30, 2003).

Peck, K. L., & Doricott, D. (1994, April). Why use technology? *Educational Leadership, 51*(7), 11-14.

Pitts, J., et al. (1995). Mental models of information: The 1993-1994 AASL/Highsmith research award study. *School Library Media Quarterly, 23*(3), 177-184.

President's Committee of Advisors on Science and Technology Panel on Educational Technology. (1997, March). *Report to the president on the use of technology to strengthen K–12 education in the United States* [Online]. Available: http://www.ostp.gov/PCAST/k-12ed.html. (Accessed May 27, 2003).

Prologue and major recommendations of Carnegie Foundation's report on colleges. (1986, November). *Chronicle of Higher Education, 33*(10): 21.

Rader, H. B. (1996). User education and information literacy for the next decade: An international perspective. *Reference Services Review, 24*(2), 71-75.

Randhawa, B. S., & Coffman, W. E. (1978). *Visual learning, thinking, and communication.* New York: Academic Press.

Ratteray, O. M., & Simmons, H. L. (1995). *Information literacy in higher education: A report on the middle states region.* Philadelphia: Middle States Association of Colleges and Schools.

Report to the president on the use of technology to strengthen K–12 education in the United States [Online]. Available: http://www.agiweb.org/hearings/pcastedu.html. (Accessed May 13, 2003).

Rodney, M. J., Lance, K. C., & Hamilton-Pennell, C. (2002). *Make the connection: Quality school library media programs impact academic achievement in Iowa* [Online]. Available: http://www.aea9.k12.ia.us/aea_statewide_study.pdf. (Accessed May 27, 2003).

Russell, S. (Undated). *The Big6-Dig it!* [Online]. Available: http://home.earthlink.net/~s.russell/bigsixdigit.html. (Accessed May 27, 2003).

Savery, J. R., & Duffy, T. M. (1995, September/October). Problem based learning: An instructional model and its constructivist framework. *Educational Technology, 35*(5), 31-38.

Schack, G. D. (1993, April). Involving students in authentic research. *Educational Leadership, 50*(7), 29-31.

School of Information Studies, Syracuse University. (2002). *The center for digital literacy* [Online]. Available: http://istweb.syr.edu/research/Digital%20Literacy.asp. (Accessed June 16, 2003).

SCORE—History-Social Science. (Undated). *Information literacy* [Online]. Available: http://score.rims.k12.ca.us/infolit.html. (Accessed April 24, 2003).

Secretary's Commission on Achieving Necessary Skills (SCANS). (1991). *What work requires of schools: A SCANS report for America 2000.* Washington, DC: U.S. Government Printing Office.

Shapiro, J. J., & Hughes, S. K. (1996, March/April). Information literacy as a liberal art. *Educom Review* [Online]. Available: http://www.educause. edu/pub/er/review/reviewarticles/31231.html. (Accessed May 1, 2003).

Smith, R. L. (1997). *Philosophical shift: Teach the faculty to teach information literacy* [Online]. Available: http://www.ala.org/Content/NavigationMenu/ ACRL//Events_and_Conferences/ACRLs_8th_National_Conference.htm. (Accessed May 1, 2003).

South Carolina Department of Education, Office of Technology, School Library Media Services. (2003). *South Carolina K–12 information literacy and technology education integration guide.* [Online]. Available: http://www. myscschools.com/offices/technology/ms/lms/getpage.cfm?ID=1354. (Accessed September 29, 2003).

State University of New York (SUNY). (1997, October 2). *Information literacy initiative.* [Online]. Available: http://www.sunyconnect.suny.edu/ili/ Default.htm. (Accessed May 1, 2003).

Steinke, S. (1997). *Information literacy guidelines: Introduction and context.* Oregon Educational Media Association (OEMA). [Online]. Available: http://www.oema.net/infolit/Infolit_Intro.html. (Accessed May 1, 2003).

Stripling, B. K. (1993). Practicing authentic assessment in the school library. In C.C. Kuhlthau (Ed.), *School library media annual* (pp. 40-55). Englewood, CO: Libraries Unlimited.

Stripling, B., & Pitts, J. (1988). *Brainstorms and blueprints: Teaching library research as a thinking process.* Littleton, CO: Libraries Unlimited.

Task Force of the Pre-College Committee of the Education Board of the ACM. (1997). *ACM model high school computer science curriculum* [Online]. Available: http://www.acm.org/education/hscur/index.html. (Accessed May 13, 2003).

Temple University Libraries. (2002). *Library skills workbook* [Online]. Available: http://www.library.temple.edu/libinst/lsw.htm. (Accessed May 1, 2003).

Todd, R. (1995). Integrated information skills instruction: Does it make a difference? *School Library Media Quarterly, 23*(2), 133-139.

Todd, R. (2002). School librarian as teacher: Learning outcomes and evidence-based practice. In *68th IFLA Council and General Conference* (August 18-24, 2002) [Online]. Available: http://www.ifla.org/IV/ifla68/papers/084-119e.pdf. (Accessed May 13, 2003).

Todd, R. (2003). Irrefutable evidence: How to prove you boost student achievement. *School Library Journal Online* [Online]. Available: http://slj.reviewsnews.com/index.asp?layout=articleArchive&articleid=CA287119. (Accessed May 13, 2003).

Tri-County Technical College. (Undated). *About the program* [Online]. Available: http://www.appnet.org/infolit/text/tprogram.htm. (Accessed May 1, 2003).

United States Department of Education. (Undated). *No child left behind* [Online]. Available: http://www.nochildleftbehind.gov/. (Accessed June 23, 2003).

United States Department of Education. (1994). *Sec. 102* [Online]. Available: http://www.ed.gov/legislation/GOALS2000/TheAct/sec102.html. (Accessed May 13, 2003).

United States Department of Education, National Center for Education Statistics. (2001). *Homeschooling in the United States* [Online]. Available: http://nces.ed.gov/pubs2001/2001033.pdf. (Accessed June 24, 2003).

University Library–Cal Poly Pomona. (Undated). *CSU work group on information competence* [Online]. Available: http://www.csupomona.edu/library/InfoComp/home.html. (Accessed May 13, 2003).

University Library–Cal Poly Pomona. (1995). *Information competence in the CSU: A report* [Online]. Available: http://www.csupomona.edu/library/InfoComp/CLRIT.html. (Accessed May 1, 2003).

University of Arizona Library. (1996). *Information literacy project: Project charge* [Online]. Available: http://dizzy.library.arizona.edu/infolit/CHARGE.HTM. (Accessed May 1, 2003).

University of Arizona Library. (Undated-a). *Descriptions of information literacy efforts at other universities* [Online]. Available: http://dizzy.library.arizona.edu/infolit/DESCRIPT.HTM. (Accessed May 1, 2003).

University of Arizona Library. (Undated-b). *Librarian–faculty teaching technology partnerships* [Online]. Available: http://www.library.arizona.edu/partnerships/. (Accessed May 1, 2003).

University of Arizona Library. (Undated-c). *Librarian–faculty teaching technology partnerships. History 436* [Online]. Available: http://dizzy.library. arizona.edu/partnerships/hist436sf.htm. (Accessed May 1, 2003).

University of Calgary Information Literacy Group. (Undated). *Information literacy definition* [Online]. Available: http://www.ucalgary.ca/library/ILG/ workdef.html. (Accessed May 13, 2003).

University of California at Berkeley Library, (2002). *Internet guides* [Online]. Available: http://library.berkeley.edu/TeachingLib/Guides/Internet/. (Accessed May 1, 2003).

University of Louisville Office of Information Literacy. (Undated). *Information literacy program* [Online]. Available: http://www.louisville.edu/ infoliteracy/. (Accessed May 1).

University of Massachusetts, Dartmouth. (2000). *Information literacy project: Defining competencies* [Online]. Available: http://www.lib.umassd. edu/infolit/infolit.html. (Accessed May 1, 2003).

University of Texas System Digital Library. (2002). *TILT* [Online]. Available: http://tilt.lib.utsystem.edu/. (Accessed June 24, 2003).

University of Washington. (2001). *Assessment of information and technology literacy* [Online]. Available: http://depts.washington.edu/infolitr/. (Accessed June 24, 2003).

University of Washington. (2003). *The Information School: Informatics* [Online]. Available: http://www.washington.edu/students/crscat/info.html. (Accessed June 24, 2003.

University of Wisconsin-Parkside Library/Learning Center. (2003). *Welcome to the information literacy program* [Online]. Available: https://uwp. courses.wisc.edu/public/Infolit3/index.html. (Accessed May 1, 2003).

Utah State Office of Education. (1996). *Library media/information literacy core curriculum for Utah secondary schools.* Salt Lake City, UT: Author.

Walster, D. (1995). Student-centered information literacy programs: The Colorado vision. In B. J. Morris, J. L. McQuiston, & C. L. Saretsky (Eds.), *School library media annual* (pp. 45-53). Englewood, CO: Libraries Unlimited.

Wileman, R. E. (1980). *Exercises in visual thinking.* New York: Hastings House.

Wisconsin Department of Public Instruction. (1998). *Wisconsin's model academic standards for information and technology literacy.* Madison: Author.

Wisconsin Educational Media Association. (1993). *Information literacy: A position paper on information problem-solving.* Appleton, WI: Author.

Wolff, R. A. (1994). Rethinking library self studies and accreditation visits. In Edward D. Garten (Ed.), *The challenge and practice of academic accreditation: A sourcebook for library administrators* (pp. 125-138). Westport, CT: Greenwood Press.

Work Group on Information Competence. Commission on Learning Resources and Instructional Technology Task 6.1. (1995, December). *Information competence in the CSU: A report* [Online]. Available: http://library.csun.edu/susn.curzon/infocmp.html. (Accessed October 3, 2003).

Zurkowski, P.G. (1974). *The information service environment relationships and priorities.* Washington DC: National Commission on Libraries and Information Sciences.

Annotated ERIC Bibliography

Journal Articles (Elementary–Secondary)

Aaron, S. L. (1995). Bridges, windows, and frameworks: A 21st-century school library media education curriculum. *School Library Media Annual (SLMA) 13*, 24-30. (EJ 516 577)

 Discusses future education for library media specialists that will reflect the changes being brought about as a result of school restructuring. Topics include an educational model based on instructional specialization, realigned staffing patterns, a global perspective, information literacy, and helping students construct effective mental frameworks for learning.

Adams, S., & Bailey, G. (1993). Education for the information age: Is it time to trade vehicles? *NASSP Bulletin, 77*(553), 57-63. (EJ 463 900)

 Traditional instruction employs text/talk vehicle focused on basic literacy, with little effort to engage students in information literacy, or accessing, analyzing, synthesizing, applying, and creating information with electronic media. This article provides Information Age Teaching-Learning Audit to help principals assess their schools' progress in understanding and using emerging instructional technologies (computers, CD-ROMs, videodiscs, scanners, e-mail, and other audiovisual aids).

Anderson, M.A. (1999). Creating the link: Aligning national and state standards. *Book Report, 17*(5), 12-14. (EJ 589 892)

 Discusses the role of the library media specialist in promoting information literacy, focusing on aligning national information literacy guidelines to state and content area standards. The integration of information literacy guidelines into a Minnesota middle school curriculum is described. A sidebar presents an outline that aligns national information literacy guidelines with Minnesota graduation standards.

Bailey, J. P. (1999). Quantifying library quality: A homework center report card. *American Libraries, 30*(8), 59-62. (EJ 608 409)

Discussion of information literacy focuses on the homework help centers developed by the County of Los Angeles Public Library. Describes a study conducted in partnership with the University of Southern California that investigated the cost effectiveness; success; and student, teacher, and parent perceptions of the centers to justify funding.

Barron, D. (1996). Families, technology, and literacy: Roles and research resources for school library media specialists (Part 1). *School Library Media Activities Monthly, 13*(4), 47-50. (EJ 534 523)

Families need to become involved with their children's development of information literacy skills. Statistics on television and home computer ownership and online access for families and schools are presented, and resources that school library media specialists can use to promote family involvement are described.

Barron, D. D. (1996). Recent dissertation research and the individual school library media specialist. *School Library Media Activities Monthly, 12*(9), 49-50. (EJ 523 198)

Describes the role and responsibilities of the school library media specialist as identified in 1994–1996 dissertation research. Highlights include media specialists as collaborative workers, the importance of leadership, commitment to a media literacy skills program and student needs, professional development, the need for principal support, curriculum-integrated library instruction, and personal characteristics.

Barron, D. D. (2001). Thanks for the connections . . . Now are we information literate? *School Library Media Activities Monthly, 18*(3), 49-51. (EJ 637 567)

Discusses Internet access in public schools, home access to computers, and the role of libraries in promoting information access and information literacy. Includes useful Web sites that contain information and resources to help libraries implement "Information Power" and information literacy standards.

Barron, D. D. (2002). The library media specialist, "Information Power," and social responsibility: Part III (effective group processes). *School Library Media Activities Monthly, 18*(8), 48-51. (EJ 649 244)

Discusses how to encourage students to participate effectively in groups, both in the classroom and in extracurricular activities, and relates this participation to information literacy. Topics include learning communities, collaborative learning, task-oriented versus process-oriented support, and running effective meetings.

Barron, D. D. (2002). The SLMAM information literacy series. *School Library Media Activities Monthly, 19*(1), 26, 31 (EJ 656 110)

Provides an introduction to a series of articles that will review nine information literacy models for library media specialists. Topics will include integrating information literacy into the K–12 curriculum, whether the model has been tested in a controlled research environment and in the actual schools, developmental levels, and advice to media specialists.

Berkowitz, B. (1998). Assessment: Big6 scoring guides for diagnosis and prescription. *Big6 Newsletter, 1*(3), 14-15. (EJ 562 892)

Presents Big6 scoring guides that focus on the process of solving information problems as well as the final results; the guides are useful for both formative and summative assessment. Examples are given for elementary and secondary school projects, and a general template is also provided.

Berkowitz, R. (1998). Helping with homework: A parent's guide to information problem-solving. *Emergency Librarian, 25*(4), 45-46. (EJ 565 458)

Summarizes the Big6 Skills information problem-solving approach: (1) Task Definition; (2) Information Seeking Strategies; (3) Location and Access; (4) Use of Information; (5) Synthesis; and (6) Evaluation. Discusses parent and student roles in information problem solving, the value of assignments, and technology and the Big Six.

Breivik, P. & Senn, J. A. (1993). Information literacy: Partnerships for power. *Emergency Librarian, 21*(1), 25-28. (EJ 469 235)

Describes the partnerships between teacher-librarians and principals, teachers, community members, public librarians, and businesses that are necessary to help school children gain information literacy skills. Descriptions, which are adapted from the forthcoming book *Information Literacy: Resources for Elementary School Leaders*, include the rationale for partnership and concrete examples.

Brock, K. (1994). Developing information literacy through the information intermediary process: A model for teacher-librarians and others. *Emergency Librarian, 22*(1), 16-20. (EJ 491 450)

Reports on a study designed to formulate a literature-based model describing what teacher-librarians do as they help students involved in information search and use (ISU). Whether teacher-librarians work with students in all phases of the ISU process and the extent to which their intermediary activities can be related to other models are considered.

Burdick, T. (1998). Pleasure in information seeking: Reducing information aliteracy. *Emergency Librarian, 25*(3), 13-17. (EJ 564 188)

Defines information aliteracy (ability to read without the desire) and proposes that desire be considered a component of information literacy.

Experiences of a group of information aliterate students are examined, opportunity for pleasure through involvement is discussed, and suggestions for teachers and teacher-librarians for reducing the problem are presented.

Cahoy, E. S. (2002). Will your students be ready for college? Connecting K–12 and college standards for information literacy. *Knowledge Quest, 30*(4), 12-15. (EJ 643 527)

Suggests how to implement information literacy standards at all education levels. Discusses two sets of information literacy standards for K–12 and post-secondary education, K–12/academic library cooperation, comparing Association of College and Research Libraries (ACRL) Information Literacy Competency Standards with American Association of School Librarians (AASL) and Association for Educational Communications and Technology (AECT) standards.

Callison, D. (1993). Expanding the evaluation role in the critical-thinking curriculum. *School Library Media Annual (SLMA), 11*, 78-92. (EJ 476 208)

Discussion of the evolving role of the school library media specialist focuses on a model of the teaching role in the development of a critical thinking curriculum. Topics addressed include literacy redefined, restructuring media programs, collection development and information access, staffing changes, and intervention and evaluation strategies.

Callison, D. (1993). The potential for portfolio assessment. *School Library Media Annual (SLMA), 11*, 30-39. (EJ 476 204)

Describes the use of mapping and portfolio assessment by school library media specialists to document changes in student reading, writing, and information use patterns. Topics discussed include new curriculum designs in language arts and social studies, information literacy, comparing earlier and later work, and student reflection.

Callison, D. (1995). Restructuring pre-service education. *School Library Media Annual (SLMA), 13,* 100-12. (EJ 516 587)

Describes steps for improving preservice teacher education, including the training of school library media specialists. Highlights include behavioral aspects, including imitation, isolation, transfer, and technique; technological aspects; and the evolution of library and information literacy skills of the school media specialist.

Callison, D. (1998). Schema and problem solving. *School Library Media Activities Monthly, 14*(9), 43-45. (EJ 565 466)

Presents a revised working definition of schema, lists four types of knowledge that individuals have (i.e., identification, elaboration, planning, and execution), and outlines issues in schema theory. The usefulness of schema in problem solving and information problem solving is discussed, and implications for teachers of information literacy are considered.

Callison, D. (2000). Key words in instruction assignment. *School Library Media Activities Monthly, 17*(1), 39-43. (EJ 618 334)

Discusses library-based assignments for information literacy and suggests the focus needs to change from information location to information use. Topics include online searching, reporting facts, more thoughtful research projects to develop skills, pitfalls of library assignments, and how to make information sources play a secondary role.

Callison, D., & Tilley, C. (1998). Information and media literacies: Towards a common core. *School Library Media Activities Monthly, 15*(2), 25-28. (EJ 577 804)

Discusses the evolution of literacy in American society and considers the importance of information and media literacies. Bloom's Taxonomy of Educational Objectives is used as a framework to describe a set of intellectual skills and abilities that students are expected to master, and examples of activities are included.

Davis, L., et al. (1996). The state of the nation: Teacher-librarianship across Canada. *School Libraries in Canada, 16*(3), 21-24, 26-28. (EJ 536 250)

Compiles reports from school librarians throughout Canada on library activities and the issues affecting them. For each province, the initiatives of its individual school library and media specialists association are highlighted. Discusses various conferences, advocacy, professional development, education, training, information literacy, library funding, and school cutbacks.

Dishnow, R. E. (1994). Updating a library and information skills guide. *School Library Media Activities Monthly, 10*(6), 27-28,47. (EJ 477 976)

Describes the revision of the 1987 edition of *The Wisconsin Library Media Skills Guide* to emphasize information skills rather than library skills. Topics discussed include cooperation between library/media specialists and classroom teachers, including curriculum development and flexible scheduling; new technology; literature use; and suggested activities and resources.

Doyle, C. S. (1995). Telementoring takes off in California: The Telemation project develops integrated curriculum. *Internet Research, 5*(1), 40-45. (EJ 505 457)

Describes the Telemation project, a California grant-funded training project for teachers that used training institutes and telementors to develop information literacy. Highlights include collaboration; peer coaching;

curriculum development; examples; and the TeleLearning Mobile Unit, a mobile learning center with computer workstations.

Eisenberg, M. (1998). Big Six TIPS: Teaching information problem solving. #4 Use of information: Where the rubber meets the road. *Emergency Librarian, 25*(4), 43-44. (EJ 565 457)

Discusses "Use of Information," the fourth stage in the Big6 Skills information problem-solving process. The focus is on the first component of this stage, that is, to engage (read, hear, view) information in a source. Suggests strategies for helping students learn effective use of information skills and addresses recognizing relevance.

Eisenberg, M. (1998). Big6 TIPS: Teaching problem solving. #3: Location and access=think index, keywords and Boolean. *Emergency Librarian, 25*(3), 28. (EJ 564 190)

Focuses on stage three of the Big6 process for teaching information problem solving: location and access. This stage has two components: locate sources and find information within sources. Highlights include the concept of index, keyword search strategy, and Boolean searching.

Eisenberg, M., & Spitzer, K. (1991). Skills and strategies for helping students become more effective information users. *Catholic Library World, 63*(2), 115-20. (EJ 465 828)

Addresses the implications for education of the expansion of information technology and proposes a model for teaching information skills within the context of an overall process. A model called the "Big6™ Skills" is presented, and its application to information problems related to school, life, and work are explained.

Farmer, L-S. J. (1999). Making information literacy a schoolwide reform effort. *Book Report, 18*(3), 6-8. (EJ 601 809)

Presents a case study of how educational reform can improve the library media program, based on experiences at one high school that was assisted by the Bay Area School Reform Collaborative (BASRC) project and its spin-off project, the Bay Area National Digital Library (BANDL). Discusses methods for increasing schoolwide information literacy, development of educational products, successful outcomes, and benefits of partnership projects.

Harada, V., & Donham, J. (1998). Information power: Student achievement is the bottom line. *Teacher Librarian, 26*(1), 14-17. (EJ 582 163)

Focuses on the student-centered *Information Power: Building Partnerships for Learning* mission for school library media programs, and the corresponding information literacy standards. Discusses examples of content-area standards; instructional roles; and three strategies for developing an integrated library media program: collaborating with teachers and administrators, leading, and using technology.

Harada, V. H., & Nakamura, M. (1994). Information searching across the curriculum: Literacy skills for the 90s and beyond. *Catholic Library World, 65*(2), 17-19. (EJ 538 020)

In 1991, a partnership of three public schools in Hawaii received an Elementary and Secondary Education Act grant to develop a K–12 information skills curriculum and purchase electronic resources. Discusses installing the hardware and software, creating the information search framework, and developing the K–12 guide. Evaluates the two-year project and outlines the information search steps.

Harada, V., & Tepe, A. (1998). Information literacy: Pathways to knowledge. *Teacher Librarian, 26*(2), 9-15. (EJ 582 300)

Discussion of the new information literacy standards authored by the American Association of School Librarians (AASL) and the Association for Educational Communications and Technology (AECT) focuses on a new information process model, "Pathways to Knowledge: Follett's Information Skills Model." Topics include the role of teacher-librarians, and other information literacy models.

Harris, J. (1996). Telehunting, telegathering, teleharvesting: Information-seeking and information-synthesis on the Internet. *Learning and Leading with Technology, 23*(4), 36-39. (EJ 518 455)

Presents five plans to assist students in information seeking on the Internet and provides examples of activities. Highlights include practicing search skills, learning about a topic of inquiry and/or question answering, reviewing multiple perspectives on an issue, solving authentic problems, and publishing synthesized and/or critiqued information overviews for other students to use.

If we had information standards, what would they be? Information and library media skills documents. (1994). *School Library Media Activities Monthly, 10*(5), 49-50. (EJ 476 338)

Discussion of the development of educational standards and the impact on school library media programs focuses on what constitutes information skills, or information literacy. Documents for 27 states are listed that outline the information skills actually taught in the various states.

Johnson, D., & Eisenberg, M. (1996). Computer literacy and information literacy: A natural combination. *Emergency Librarian, 23*(5), 12-16 (EJ 526 333)

Teacher-librarians must prepare students to use technology and information effectively. An outline for a curriculum entitled "Computer Skills

for Information Problem-Solving" is presented. Specific desired competencies are listed in the following areas: (1) Task Definition; (2) Information Seeking Strategies; (3) Location and Access; (4) Use of Information;
(5) Synthesis; and (6) Evaluation.

Haycock, K. (1998). Information power: Building partnerships for learning.
Book Report, 17(1), 26-27. (EJ 589 842)
Discusses the guidelines for school library media programs in *Infor-
mation Power* and explains the new Information Literacy Standards for
Student Learning. Topics include independent learning, social responsibil-
ity, performance indicators, and the roles of the library media specialist.

Herro, S. J. (2000). Bibliographic instruction and critical thinking. *Journal of
Adolescent and Adult Literacy, 43*(6), 554-558. (EJ 601 066)
Addresses the value of integrating critical thinking and information
literacy in library instruction for students at all grade levels. Sites specific
examples of successful implementation of critical thinking and library instruction and how these promote information literacy.

Johnson, D. (1999). A curriculum built not to last. *School Library Journal,
45*(4), 26-29. (EJ 586 404)
Describes the development of an information literacy curriculum that
incorporates media and technology by media specialists in the Mankato
Area Public Schools (Minnesota). Topics include identifying current skills,
the Big Six information-processing model, grouping skills within the
model, curriculum integration, projects to replace traditional written reports, identifying necessary resources, assessment tools, record-keeping
systems, and revising.

Johnson, D. (1999). Implementing an information literacy curriculum: One district's story. *NASSP Bulletin, 83*(605), 53-61. (EJ 585 576)
A committee of media specialists, librarians, teachers, parents, and administrators in a Minnesota district devised an information literacy curriculum. They identified current skills and software; learned an
information-processing mode; identified curriculum integration areas;
brainstormed projects; identified needed resources; and developed assessment, record-keeping, and reporting systems

Koch, M. (2001). Information literacy—where do we go from here? *TECHNOS,
10*(1), 1-8. (EJ 633 174)
Defines information literacy and discusses ways that teachers can integrate it into the curriculum. Topics include education policy; funding for
technology; standards, particularly state standards; separate standards for
library media programs; assessment; and using the Big6 program.

Kuhlthau, C. (1993). Implementing a process approach to information skills: A study identifying indicators of success in library media programs. *School Library Media quarterly; 22*(1), 11-18. (EJ 473 063)

Describes a study that evaluated implementing a constructivist process approach to learning information skills in school library media programs. Training institutes for media specialists, a longitudinal case study, and the identification of inhibitors and enablers of successful programs are discussed.

Kuhlthau, C. (1995). The process of learning from information. *School Libraries Worldwide, 1*(1), 1-12. (EJ 503 404)

Presents the process of learning from information as the key concept for the library media center in the Information Age school. The Information Search Process Approach is described as a model for developing information skills fundamental to information literacy, and process learning is discussed.

Langford, L. (2001). Critical literacy: A building block towards the information literate school community. *TeacherLibrarian, 28*(5), 18-21. (EJ 633 164)

Considers the definition of critical literacy as a subset of information literacy and discusses how schools can become information literate with the rise of communications technologies. Highlights include continuous learning, metacognitive processes, critical and creative thinking, and learning communities

Limberg, L. (1993). Swedish school libraries for education 2000: Fears, hopes, and expectations in Swedish school librarianship. *School Library Media Annual (SLMA), 11*, 59-64. (EJ 476 206)

Presents an overview of libraries in Swedish schools. Topics addressed include restructuring Swedish education motivated by new principles for governing schools, economic recession, and a government proposal for a new national curriculum; cooperation with public libraries; district coordination; school libraries as change agents; information skills programs; and future plans.

Loertscher, D.V. (1994). Treasure mountain IV. The power of reading: The effect of libraries and reading promotion on reading competence. *School Library Media Annual, 12*, 198-199. (EJ 495 193)

Describes two Treasure Mountain IV conferences. The first conference brought practitioners together with researchers Stephen Krashen and Keith Lance to discuss evidence that school library media programs make a difference in academic achievement. The second conference focused on the possibility of measuring the impact of library media programs on resource-based teaching and information literacy.

Mancall, J. (1993). The changing library landscape: Impact on student instruction and use. *School Library Media Annual (SLMA), 11*, 66-76. (EJ 476 207)

Discusses changes in school libraries and their impact on student instruction and use. Highlights include national guidelines, the National Goals for Education, educational research and reporting, global patterns, information delivery and storage, the projected configuration for libraries and information services, skills for information literacy, and instructional considerations for achieving skill development.

McFadden, A.C., et al. (1993). Trends and issues in the 1992 professional education literature. *School Library Media Annual (SLMA), 11*, 178-85. (EJ 476 219)

Identifies the main topics addressed in the professional education literature during 1992, including cooperative learning, multicultural education, portfolio assessment, constructivism, adolescence, occupational education, educational management, counseling and personnel services, reading and communication skills, handicapped students, language instruction, information resources, computers, and teacher education.

McKenzie, J. (2000). Winning with information literacy. *TECHNOS, 9*(1), 28-32. (EJ 613 389)

Information literacy is the key to a successful technology initiative. Two scenarios are presented that demonstrate the need for and benefits of addressing teachers' inclinations as well as preparation in terms of instructional technology use. Adult learning possibilities for literacy and technology are identified, and the importance and examples of scaffolding are noted. Lists the 10 myths behind the software trap.

Montgomery, P. (1993). Information skills at the national level: A report on the activities of the information skills task force of the American Association of School Librarians. *School Library Media Annual (SLMA), 11*, 186-188. (EJ 476 220)

Reports on activities of the Information Skills Task Force of the American Association of School Librarians, which addressed three main issues: (1) student competencies required to access, use, and apply information; (2) preparing an information skills curriculum; and (3) ensuring the integration of information skills into the elementary and secondary school curriculum.

Niinikangas, L. (1995). An open learning environment—New challenges for the Finnish School Library. *Scandinavian Public Library Quarterly, 4*, 1-11. (EJ 513 824)

Discussion of the role of Finnish school libraries in supporting learning focuses on the development work and further education provided by the Further Education Centre for Vocational Institutes and Administration in

Finland. Highlights include school libraries in comprehensive schools and vocational institutes, resource-based learning, and information skills and information literacy.

Oberg, D., Hay, L., & Henri, J. (2000). The role of the principal in an information literate school community: Cross-country comparisons from an international research project. *School Library Media Research, 3*. (EJ 618 497)

An international research project investigated the role of principals in developing and supporting information literate school communities. Principals and teacher-librarians completed three surveys examining their perceptions/beliefs about their current and future roles, and views on such concerns as strengths and challenges of the school library, contributions of teacher-librarians, the nature of information literacy, and barriers to integration of information skills. Explores findings and presents cross-country comparisons.

Oberg, D., Hay, L., & Henri, J. (2000). The role of the principal in an information literate school community: Design and administration of an international research project. *School Library Media Research, 3*. (EJ 618 496)

An international study of the principal's role in developing and supporting information literate school communities was conducted in Australia, Canada, Finland, France, Japan, Scotland, and South Korea. The study sought to inform the efforts of principals and teacher-librarians throughout the world seeking to develop such communities. Researchers describe the design and administration of the study and explore the methodological issues involved.

Ohlrich, K. B. (1996) What are we? Library media information specialists, computer technology coordinators, teacher instructional consultants, school-based management team members, or what? *School Library Media Activities Monthly, 12*(9), 26-28, 32 (EJ 523 194)

Discusses four areas in school library media programs that media specialists are expected to develop. Topics include promoting information literacy among students, knowing how to evaluate and use various information technologies, consulting with teachers to strengthen student learning and outcomes, and serving on school-based management committees.

Pappas, M. (1993). A vision of school library media centers in an electronic information age. *School Library Media Activities Monthly, 10*(1), 32-34, 38 (EJ 469 122)

Discusses trends evolving in schools and library media centers as a result of electronic information technologies, including the shift from acquisition to access, the storage of information, the growth of image-based technologies, technology and management, information skills needed for electronic resources, information networks, impact on curriculum, and "hyperlearning."

Pappas, M. (1998). Evaluating the inquiry process. *School Library Media Activities Monthly, 14*(8), 24-26. (EJ 562 953)

Discusses the importance of evaluating the inquiry process of learners to develop independent learners who are information literate. Highlights include national and state evaluation standards; school districts' curriculum documents that reflect information literacy with a focus on process; learner evaluation criteria; and assessment tools and strategies, including librarian, teacher, and student roles.

Pappas, M. L. (1995). Information skills for electronic resources. *School Library Media Activities Monthly, 11*(8), 39-40. (EJ 499 875)

Discusses the importance of developing strong skills in electronic searching and stresses the importance of teaching these skills across the curriculum. Several skill models are suggested, and components of search strategies are briefly outlined.

Plotnick, E. (2000). Information literacy. *Educational Media and Technology Yearbook, 25,* 66-69. (EJ 605 277)

Defines the concept of information literacy, based on the American Library Association (ALA) Presidential Committee on Information Literacy report. Highlights include information literacy research, an economic perspective, national and state standards, elementary and secondary education restructuring, information literacy in higher education, and technology and information literacy.

Rader, H. B. (1994). Library orientation and instruction—1992. *RSR: Reference Services Review, 22*(2), 79-95. (EJ 486 753).

This annotated list of materials dealing with information literacy includes publications on user instruction in academic libraries (140 titles), public libraries (4 titles), school libraries (56 titles), and special libraries (11 titles) and for all levels of users (6 titles). Statistics regarding the numbers of publications are discussed.

Rader, H. B. (1998). Library instruction and information literacy—1997. *RSR: Reference Services Review, 26*(3-4), 143-160. (EJ 601 874)

This annotated bibliography of titles published in 1997 (in English) lists materials dealing with information literacy, including instruction in the use of information resources;, research; and electronic skills related to retrieving, using, and evaluating information. Titles are presented in the categories Academic Libraries, Public Libraries, School Libraries, Special Libraries, All Levels, and Web Sites.

Ryan, J., & Capra, S. (2001). Information literacy planning for educators: The ILPO approach. *School Libraries Worldwide, 7*(1), 1-10. (EJ 643 409)

Describes the ILPO (Information Literacy Planning Overview), which combines facets of information literacy including critical thinking, problem solving, and information technology in a planning document to support teachers and teacher-librarians. Discusses the whole-school approach to integrating information literacy into the curriculum that has been used in Australia.

Simpson, C., et al. (1996). Full speed ahead on the Internet. *Book Report, 15*(2), 3, 5-7, 9-11, 13-14. (EJ 529 710)

This supplement assembles six articles covering Internet usage in the library media center, including selecting and evaluating Internet resources, developing information literacy skills to reach educational goals, and citing Internet resources. It examines demographic profiles of schools that are connected to the Internet and provides tips and guidelines for teachers on using and teaching Internet skills.

Spitzer, K. I. (1999). Information literacy: Facing the challenge. *Book Report, 18*(1), 26-28. (EJ 589 883)

Discusses planning for the implementation of the Information Literacy Standards in schools. Provides a list of resources that focus on the history and development of the concept of information literacy. Discusses the importance of learning about local and state standards. Lists issues to work through when collaborating on a plan.

Taber, M. (2002). Rite of passage: A visit to a university library. *Knowledge Quest, 30*(4), 29-30. (EJ 643 531)

Describes a research project in the social studies curriculum at St. Paul Academy and Summit School (Minnesota) during which students visit a university library. Objectives for student research are to select a topic, design a thesis statement, locate pertinent primary and secondary resources, and write a well-documented, analytical research paper; and to gain information skills necessary for college and university library research.

Thompson, H., & Henley, S. (2001). Implementing a schoolwide information literacy program. *School Library Media Activities Monthly, 17*(6), 24-25, 27. (EJ 625 164)

Discusses how library media specialists can get teachers' support and cooperation to implement a schoolwide information literacy program. Highlights include national or state curriculum standards in language arts, social studies, science, and math; and an example of a poetry unit for language arts that includes information literacy and language arts objectives.

Walster, D., & Welborn, L. (1996). Writing and implementing "Colorado's information literacy guidelines": The process examined. *School Library Media Activities Monthly, 12*(6), 25-28, 36. (EJ 516 616)

> Describes how Colorado's *Model Information Literacy Guidelines* were written and implemented and provides suggestions for developing similar guidelines. Discusses drafting parameters, revisions and community participation, final editing and distribution, and three projects that are contributing to successful implementation.

Willard, N. (2002). Complying with federal law for safe Internet use. *School Administrator, 4*(59), 30. (EJ 642 973)

> School districts are required to comply with the Children's Internet Protection Act (CIPA) mandating that they monitor how students are using the Internet. Although elementary school students need to be supervised, blocking technologies are inappropriate for teenagers. Secondary school students need to know about safe communication skills and have a clear understanding of the expectations for their behavior when using the Internet in school and be held accountable for such use.

Elementary-Secondary ERIC Documents

ACCESS ERIC. (2000). *What should parents know about information literacy?* ACCESS ERIC, Rockville, MD. 6p. (ED 460 787)

> This brochure explains the concept of information literacy, showing why information literacy is important for children, describing how parents can help children become information literate, and directing parents to additional resources. Information literacy is defined as the ability to access, evaluate, and use information effectively. The brochure explains that school-aged children can use information literacy skills to manage their time effectively, make informed decisions, maximize employment opportunities, and increase job success. Suggestions for encouraging information literacy in children include encouraging, supporting, and guiding children in exploring their interests; showing them how to evaluate information; teaching them about authors, and instructing them to consider the reliability of information from the Internet. The brochure explains what parents should know about information literacy in the schools and lists organizations offering information literacy resources.

ACCESS PENNSYLVANIA curriculum guide. (1991). 54p. (ED 355 963)

> This curriculum guide was prepared as a tool for teaching students the purpose and function of the ACCESS PENNSYLVANIA database in the total concept of information literacy. The database, on laser CD, contains information about the holdings of hundreds of school, public, academic,

and special use libraries. The database can be searched at the local level using a microcomputer and two laser disc readers, by title, author, subject, location, type of material, publication date, keyword, or a combination of these reference points. Students must learn to analyze their information needs and evaluate the information source itself. The guide encourages integration of database use into the total curriculum. There are 16 lesson plans, each with the lesson objective, the expected level of student achievement, activities that must be performed by the media specialist and the student, resources needed to teach the lesson, and an evaluation process. The lessons include knowledge of computer hardware and software, as well as how to use the system. Six handouts and a 46-item glossary are included.

Adler, R. P., & Breivik, P. S. (1999*). Information literacy: Advancing opportunities for learning in the digital age. A report of The Aspen Institute Forum on Communications and Society.* Queenstown, MD: Aspen Institutes. 55p. (ED 433 005)

This report is an informed observer's interpretation of the discussions that took place at the 1998 annual meeting of the Aspen Institute's Forum on Communications and Society (FOCAS). It summarizes the inquiry made by FOCAS members into the many issues surrounding information literacy, including what information literacy is; why we need an information literate society; measuring information literacy; and how schools, business, and governments can work together to promote information literacy. Following the summary of deliberations, the report outlines six initiatives suggested by FOCAS members that might be developed further to advance the cause of information literacy: (1) take idea leadership to promote awareness of information literacy, (2) assess and hold educators and political leaders at all levels accountable for students' proficiency in information literacy, (3) give teachers the preparation and support they need to do a better job, (4) involve parents more deeply in their children's education, (5) develop a dramatically different technology-based educational alternative, and (6) increase funding for research in education and information literacy. The appendix includes an "Information Literacy Background Paper," a list of conference participants, author biographies, and a brief description of the Aspen Institute Communications and Society Program.

Australian Library and Information Association. (1994). *Learning for the future: Developing information services in Australian schools.* (Australian School Library Association, Goulburn). Carlton, Australia: Curriculum Corp. (ED 377 826). Document not available from EDRS.

This guide is intended to set a context for the development of library and information services in Australian schools. The focus reflects recent changes in Australian education, in particular the development of national curriculum statements. These changes emphasize the processes of learning and the consequent need for information and information literacy, as well as the shift to collaborative school development planning, decision making, and management. To achieve the desired changes, it is important to develop information literate teachers and students and to use collaborative strategies among teachers, library staff, and administrators to integrate the processes of learning, especially resource-based learning, across the curriculum. Resource-based learning is a methodology that allows students to learn from their own confrontation with information resources. Factors that should be considered in developing the school and library resource center as a positive information environment are outlined, and benchmarks against which schools can evaluate current provisions for developing information literacy are presented.

Barron, A., & Ivers, K. (1996). An Internet research model. In *Call of the north, NECC '96. Proceedings of the annual National Educational Computing Conference* (17th, Minneapolis, Minnesota, June 11-13, 1996). 6p. (ED 398 880).

Meaningful Internet activities should take advantage of the distance, multiple resources, and speed that telecommunications can offer. They should also require K–12 students to synthesize, analyze, and evaluate the information, rather than simply collecting facts. This paper focuses on basic, advanced, and original research activities on the Internet. Basic research refers to retrieving information from a single, often preselected, online source; advanced research includes a wider variety of sources and involves high-order thinking skills; and original research focuses on using the Internet to conduct investigations through surveys and collaborative experiments. Alternatives to online research are examined and a six-step procedural model is proposed for conducting relevant and meaningful Internet activities. The online research model consists of (1) questioning, (2) planning, (3) gathering (online), (4) sorting and sifting, (5) synthesizing, and (6) evaluating.

Breivik, P. S. (2000). Information literacy for the skeptical library director. In *Virtual libraries: Virtual communities. Abstracts, fulltext documents and presentations of papers and demos given at the International Association of Technological University Libraries (IATUL) Conference* (Brisbane, Queensland, Australia, July 3-7, 2000); see IR 057 942. (ED 447 823)

This paper begins by providing background on the information literacy movement, including the educational reform efforts of the 1980s, a higher education summit conference, and the 1989 American Library Association (ALA) Presidential Committee on Information Literacy Final Report. Other highlights include the information literacy triangle; providing universal access by getting the Internet into all schools and public libraries, the need for funding to educate people to take advantage of technological advancements, definitions of information literacy, a UNESCO report addressing the importance of lifelong learning, the Global Knowledge Partnership, and the efforts of the National Forum on Information Literacy. The following practical steps for academic library directors are suggested: (1) Take time to think through the concept of information literacy, (2) ask questions about information literacy on campus, (3) find out what the barriers to information literacy are, and (4) celebrate successes.

Breivik, P. S., & Senn, J. A. (1994). *Information literacy: Educating children for the 21st century.* 198p. New York: Scholastic. (ED 373 801). Document not available from EDRS. (Note: second edition published 1998, ED number pending.)

This book is about resource-based learning, a means by which educators can teach their students to be lifelong learners. The eight chapters contain information to help students learn how to find, process, and evaluate the information they need to handle the task at hand. (1) "Surviving in an Information Age" examines the information explosion and its effects on education; (2) "A Commonsense Approach" identifies methods of instructing information literacy; (3) "Specific Concerns" discusses specific problems that educators will encounter when changing the curriculum; (4) "Overcoming Barriers" pinpoints barriers to the new curriculum and discusses methods of overcoming them; (5) "Your Investment" considers how to reallocate resources to pay for resource-based learning without additional funds; (6) "Connecting with Community Resources" covers how to form partnerships in the community to ensure the successful implementation of the new curriculum; (7) "Assessment of Resource-Based Learning" considers evaluation procedures; and (8) "Moving Forward" gives examples and hints for actually implementing the new curriculum. A reading list is also included.

Burnheim, R. K. (1993). *The questions that they ask.* 19p. (ED 368 379)

This paper discusses the competencies required to work effectively with information. It examines the nature of the information resources and how students interact with them. The discussion moves to the types of questions students have asked and suggests that the predominant types may not be assisting students in developing information usage skills, thus not improving their mastery of a skill set. Reviews of research have indicated that teachers often do not ask questions that require students to work with information resources, relying instead on questions that merely ask for the recall of knowledge. The challenge is for teachers to more frequently pose questions that encourage students to use the problem-solving approaches they will need in the world of the future. The rapid redundancy of information means that no institution can give its students all the knowledge they will need, but students can be given the skills to update and refine their knowledge. Two figures illustrate the discussion.

Caffarella, E. P. (1998) The new information literacy standards for student learning: Where do they fit with other content standards? In *SITE 98: Society for Information Technology & Teacher Education international conference (9th, Washington, DC, March 10-14, 1998) proceedings*; see IR 018 794. (ED 421 076)

The Association for Educational Communications and Technology (AECT) and the American Association of School Librarians (AASL) have formed a committee to write a new edition of the *Information Power* guidelines and to investigate the information literacy needs of K–12 students over the next 20 years. The following nine information standards for student learning have been developed: (1) accesses information efficiently and effectively, (2) evaluates information critically and competently, (3) uses information effectively and creatively, (4) pursues information related to personal interests, (5) appreciates and enjoys literature and other creative expressions of information, (6) strives for excellence in information seeking and knowledge generation, (7) recognizes the importance of information to a democratic society, (8) practices ethical behavior in regard to information and information technology, and (9) participates effectively in groups to pursue and generate information. These standards are divided into three broad categories: information literacy (standards 1–3); independent learning (standards 4–6); and social responsibility (standards 7–9). Each standard is written as a lifelong skill and is therefore not grade specific. This paper examines the standards and the interface of these standards with other subjects typically taught in schools

Carr, J.A. (1998). *Information literacy and teacher education.* ERIC Digest. 4p. (ED 424 231)

Teachers cannot prepare their students to be information literate unless they themselves understand how to find and use information. This Digest discusses the concept of information literacy (the ability to access, evaluate, and use information from a variety of sources) and its relevance for teachers. Professional associations for K–12 and higher education have recognized the importance of information literacy to the teaching-learning process. Two major associations for librarians who work with preservice and inservice teachers have developed guidelines on what information literate teachers need to know. The guidelines emphasize skills for searching, retrieving, and evaluating information, and developing strategies for locating databases, Internet resources, and print materials. Existing models for teachers' information literacy include individual workshops for both preservice and inservice teachers, course-related and course-integrated instruction, and the use of case studies of teaching and learning situations. Teacher educators, teachers, and others interested in preparing K–12 students to be information literate can move forward by reflecting on and adapting existing models.

Champelli, L. (2002*). The youth cybrarian's guide to developing instructional curriculum-related, summer reading, and recreational programs.* New York: Neal-Schuman. 189p. (ED 464 648). Document not available from EDRS.

This guide provides examples of how youth service librarians in school and public libraries have responded to their patrons' interest in and need to know about the Internet. Chapter 1, "Instructional Programs," presents creative programs and Web sites that public libraries have developed to teach children and their parents about the Internet and how to use it. Chapter 2, "Curriculum-Related Programs," describes interesting programs and Web sites developed by youth service librarians in school and public libraries for teaching children effective searching skills, as well as Web sites that librarians have developed to support curriculum-related research units. Chapter 3, "Summer Reading Programs," profiles some of the Web sites and methods librarians have created to enhance traditional summer reading programs for young people. Chapter 4, "Recreational Programs," describes resourceful programs and Web sites youth service librarians have developed that enable young people to use the Internet for creative expression or recreational exploration. Chapter 5, "The Youth Cybrarian's Source Box," suggests Web sites that provide helpful tools to use when teaching young people how to use the Web. Includes a glossary and an index.

Colorado Educational Media Association. (1994). *Model information literacy guidelines.* (Colorado State Department of Education). Denver: State Library and Adult Education Office. 10p. (ED 373 797)

This document contains information literacy standards developed for the state of Colorado. The purpose of the standards is to provide all students with a process for learning that is transferable among subjects and from the academic environment to real life. Its goal is to have all students using information and ideas effectively. The five standards follow: (1) The student constructs meaning from environment, (2) the student creates a quality project, (3) the student learns independently, (4) the student participates effectively as a group member, and (5) the student uses information and information technologies responsibly and ethically. The rationale behind the need for information literacy standards and the standards themselves is presented. Finally, the components of each standard are outlined. A list of

"Information Literacy Standards Writing Project Team" members is also included.

Dame, M. A. (1993). *Serving linguistically and culturally diverse students: Strategies for the school library media specialist.* 175p. New York: Neal-Schuman. (ED 375 650). Document not available from EDRS.

This book provides a framework for expanding the school library's function to meet the needs of the linguistically and culturally diverse students, outlining specific strategies that librarians can use to advocate information literacy and information access equality. Six chapters focus on (1) the emerging role of the proactive librarian and the establishment of the library as a key center for information access; (2) promoting a love of reading among students through storytelling, shared composition, and other literacy activities; (3) library literacy activities that teach and reinforce language; (4) adapting collection development and cataloging systems to meet the needs of linguistically diverse students; (5) collecting multicultural and foreign-language materials; and (6) collecting and using picture files. A directory of resources provides sources and listings of materials relevant to teacher education; library training; grant writing, foreign-language publishers, distributors, and bibliographies; acquisition; picture books; nonprint and multimedia resources; reference works; and organizations.

Danley, E. B., Forde, J. L., Lahmon, J. A., & Maddox, B. K. (1999). Unleashing the yheory: Connecting learning theory to building information seeking skills. In *Unleash the power! Knowledge-technology-diversity: papers presented at the third international forum on research in school librarianship, annual conference of the International Association of School Librarianship (IASL)* (28th, Birmingham, AL, November 10-14, 1999); see IR 057 588. (ED 437 062)

This study surveyed 126 school librarians in 18 countries, representing 131 schools serving more than 113,260 students. The survey instrument requested respondents to describe techniques they used to facilitate information literacy, their perceptions of their functions in the development of independent learners, and the training they received that enabled them to mediate information-seeking and use skills. Survey data revealed that the respondents relate information skills instruction to students' interests, work with other teachers to place information-seeking skills within the context of students' course work, and encourage students to share ideas and skills with each other as they build their own search strategies. Results indicate that the creation of independent, self-directed, lifelong learners is the goal of school librarians over the world. Data also reveal that most of the respondents spend less than one-quarter of their time working with teachers to plan connected programs, and that many school libraries are understaffed.

Doyle, C. S. (1994). *Information literacy in an information society: A concept for the information age.* Syracuse, NY: ERIC Clearinghouse on Information and Technology. 82p. (ED 372 763)

Information literacy is the ability to access, evaluate, and use information from a variety of sources. This document traces the history of the development of the term "information literacy" and discusses the emergence of information literacy as an important concept in contemporary society. Two major events are examined that have driven information literacy into the forefront of educational reform: the Secretary's Commission on Achieving Necessary Skills (SCANS) Report and the National Educational Goals. The impact of technology on the concept of information literacy is discussed. Finally, recent revisions in national curriculum standards that imply recognition of information literacy skills are examined, including mathematics, social studies, and science standards. An annotated bibliography is included.

Dreher, M. J. (1995). *Sixth-grade researchers: Posing questions, finding information, and writing a report.* Reading Research Report No. 40. Summer 1995. 17p. (ED 384 014)

In two sections of a world history class, 43 sixth graders, all considered competent readers, participated in two sets of tasks. First, they used a familiar textbook to locate the answers to six questions, all of which contained terms that could be found in the book's index. Second, they participated in a report-writing project in which they were asked to generate research questions, locate information to answer those questions using multiple sources, take notes, and write a research report conforming to their teacher's expectations. Despite being competent readers who had instruction relevant to finding information and who had completed several reports during the year, these students exhibited a wide range of performance and many difficulties. The results are discussed in relation to their implications for helping children develop independent, flexible strategies for finding and using information.

Eisenberg, M. B., & Berkowitz, R. E. (1999). *The new improved Big6 workshop handbook.* Professional growth series. Worthington, OH: Linworth. 158p. (ED 433 012). Document not available from EDRS.

This handbook is intended to help classroom teachers, teacher-librarians, technology teachers, administrators, parents, community members, and students learn about the Big6 Skills approach to information and technology skills, use the Big6 process in their own activities, and implement a Big6 information and technology skills program. The handbook is designed as a collection of workshop materials for continuing professional education programs. It contains tried and tested exercises, activities, and information that help participants learn the process, approach, and power of the Big6. Parts I and II help the reader identify the need for information and technology skills and develop a working understanding of the Big6. Part III focuses on technology and how to use technology in a meaningful way through integration within the Big6 framework. Part IV turns to implementing the Big6 on the micro (lesson and unit) level. Part V offers specific approaches to assessment using the Big6 steps, and part VI shows the importance of collaboration and partnerships. Part VII prepares readers to integrate Big6 Skills with the curriculum by using curriculum-mapping techniques. The final sections, parts VIII and IX, provide exercises for including parents and the school district (macro level) in the overall plan for success.

Eisenberg, M. B., & Berkowitz, R. E. (2000). *The Big6 collection: The best of the Big6 newsletter.* 216p. Worthington, OH: Linworth. (ED 439 681). Document not available from EDRS.

　　The Big6 is a complete approach to implementing meaningful learning and teaching of information and technology skills, essential for twenty-first-century living. Including in-depth articles, practical tips, and explanations, this book offers a varied range of material about students and teachers, the Big6, and curriculum. The book is divided into 10 main parts: (1) Information Literacy; (2) Big6 Skills; (3) Big6 Practical Approaches: K–Adult; (4) TIPS (Teaching Information Problem Solving); (5) Assessment; (6) Teaching Aides; (7) Big6 in Action; (8) Virtual Wisdom; (9) Parent Connection; and (10) Final Notes. These parts are further subdivided into chapters that represent individual newsletters. Authors and Big6 creators Mike Eisenberg and Bob Berkowitz focus on different scopes of concern or styles of presentation, including a comprehensive treatment of the concept of information literacy; specific guidance on Big6 integration with the real, classroom curriculum; a compilation of TIPS for each Big6 stage; creative and fun ways to present the Big6 process; a focus on assessment, one of the most asked-about aspects of the Big6; and questions and answers about the Big6. More information can be obtained at http://www.Big6. com. Directly addressing the need of libraries, classrooms, and special education areas, this collection will allow library media specialists and teachers to get immediate, practical help on the most extensively used information process model in the world.

Eisenberg, M. B., & Johnson, D. (1996). *Computer skills for information problem-solving: Learning and teaching technology in context.* ERIC Digest. 6p. (ED 392 463)

　　Over the past 20 years, library media professionals have worked to move from teaching isolated library skills to teaching integrated information skills. Effective integration of information skills has two requirements: (1) The skills must directly relate to the content area curriculum and to classroom assignments, and (2) the skills themselves need to be tied together in a logical and systematic information process model. Schools seeking to move from isolated computer skills instruction also need to focus on these requirements. Library media specialists, computer teachers, and classroom teachers need to work together to develop units and lessons that will include computer skills, general information skills, and content-area curriculum outcomes. The "Big6™ Skills Approach to Information Problem Solving" is an information literacy curriculum, an information problem-solving process, and a set of skills that provide a strategy for effectively and efficiently meeting information needs. This model is transferable to school, personal, and work applications, as well as all content areas and the full range of grade levels. The Big6 Skills include (1) Task Definition, (2) Information Seeking Strategies, (3) Location and access, (4) Use of Information, (5) Synthesis, and (6) Evaluation. An addendum is included that presents skills and knowledge related to technology that are not part of the computer and information technology curriculum.

Eisenberg, M. B., & Johnson, D. (2002). *Learning and teaching information technology—computer skills in context.* ERIC Digest. 6p. (ED 465 377)

This digest describes an integrated approach to teaching computer skills in K–12 schools. The introductory section discusses the importance of integrating information skills into the curriculum. "Technology Skills for Information Problem Solving: A Curriculum Based on the Big6 Skills Approach" (Michael B. Eisenberg, Doug Johnson, and Robert E. Berkowitz), a curriculum guide, lists specific technology skills in the following areas (1) Task Definition, (2) Information Seeking Strategies, (3) Location and Access, (4) Use of Information, (5) Synthesis, and (6) Evaluation. A sidebar summarizes the Big6 skills approach to information problem solving.

Ercegovac, Z. *Information literacy: Search strategies, tools & resources.* Los Angeles: InfoEN Associates. 140p. (ED 414 975)

This book was created to teach information literacy. It takes a user-centered perspective in using information technology as a tool to accomplish a variety of tasks and is divided into a series of nine interrelated yet independent chapters. Chapter 1 is an introduction to basic concepts, focusing on fundamental models of information sources and the use of library terminology. Chapter 2 teaches how to cite sources in a work, evaluate information, and use library vocabulary. Chapter 3 explains how to search digital libraries on the Internet and learn the language of Web sources and authoring tools. Chapter 4 explores information access tools such as subject searches and classification systems, like those of the Library of Congress. Chapter 5 provides various search strategies and terminology. Chapter 6 discusses the use of online library catalogs. Chapter 7 teaches how to search for periodical indexes and abstracts and seek online "help." Chapter 8 discusses different types of factual reference sources such as dictionaries and encyclopedias. Chapter 9 covers evaluating and using biographical sources, reviews, and criticism.

Eshpeter, B., & Gray, J. (1989). *Preparing students for information literacy. School library programs and the cooperative planning process.* Alberta, BC: Calgary Board of Education. 120p. (ED 357 766)

This report discusses the development of a school library program for Canadian schools that departs from tradition by focusing on the instructional role as the most significant work of the teacher-librarian and presents a new program model paradigm. The paradigm is examined under three main headings: (1) the instructional component, (2) student information profiles, and (3) cooperative planning. The focus of the instructional component of the model is its information segment, in which five phases are explored: the pre-search phase, information retrieval, information processing, information organizing and creating, and information sharing. The report then discusses what student information profiles are, the importance of having profiles in strengthening library value by building student skills and problem-solving behaviors, and how these profiles are developed for each phase of the information/instructional component. Finally discussed is the cooperative planning and teaching function, in which there is integration of information strategies and skills into the curricular programs of the classroom. Reproducible presentation masters on school library programs and the model paradigm are provided.

Eyre, G. (2001). The role of works of imagination in preparing young people for the information society. In *Libraries and librarians: Making a difference in the knowledge age. Council and general conference: Conference programme and proceedings* (67th, Boston, MA, August 16-25, 2001); see IR 058 199. (ED 459 717)

This paper examines the place of reading in the acquisition of information capability among young people and considers the extent to which this is nurtured and aided by works of the imagination, whether in print or electronic form. Information capability presupposes a range of skills that, in addition to technological skills and the knowledge to use information sources, includes general literacy. The growing literature on information literacy tends to stress the first two requirements. A world of information may be physically and politically available, but this is of no value if it cannot be accessed because an individual lacks the ability to read. Today, works of the imagination are not just confined to print; there are many excellent World Wide Web sites providing works of imagination. Works of imagination in electronic format and the use of electronic facilities in accessing and discussing works also make a valuable contribution to achieving information capability. There is evidence in Australia, for example, that such facilities are encouraging more boys to read. A study in the United Kingdom and Australia is proposed to look at the issues outlined and to link these with provision in school and public libraries.

From library skills to information literacy: A handbook for the 21st century. (1994). Englewood, CO: Libraries Unlimited. (ED 369 415). Document not available from EDRS.

This handbook is designed to help classroom teachers, library media specialists, and others who wish to integrate information literacy into their curriculum. It provides models and strategies that encourage children and young adults to find, analyze, create, and use information as they become productive citizens. The following topics are addressed: information literacy defined, stages of the research process, instructional planning for information literacy, instructional strategies for developing information literacy, sample scenarios of integrated units, and integrating information literacy into local or state frameworks. Included in the appendixes are a report on integrating information literacy into national agendas and a planning guide for research process competencies.

Giguere, M., et al. (1995). Enhancing information literacy skills across the curriculum. In *Literacy: Traditional, cultural, technological. Selected papers from the Annual Conference of the International Association of School Librarianship* (23rd, Pittsburgh, Pennsylvania, July 17-22, 1994); see IR 056 058. 5p. (ED 399 951)

Information literacy is a set of acquired skills and strategies encompassing the abilities to recognize a need for information, retrieve the required information, and evaluate and utilize it effectively. Teaching students how to structure, acquire, analyze, and synthesize information must start much earlier than at the post-secondary level. The paper provides a brief review of the history and development of the information literacy project and describes the resource-based approach that the model utilizes. The information literacy model strives to be an effective tool designed to help students and teacher-librarians in elaborating their research paths. A fundamental assumption upon which the model is based is that the presentation of a rich variety of information resources as well as suggested paths to retrieve these resources will improve the quality of search strategies used and, as a consequence, the research produced. The model is composed of two major components: an inventory and analysis of identified categories of resources and the individual research paths designed for each category, which outline the process one might follow to rapidly and efficiently utilize a resource. The process fosters independent, cooperative, and resource-based learning.

Grassian, E. S., & Kaplowitz, J. R. (2001). *Information literacy instruction: Theory and practice. Information literacy sourcebooks.* Edison, NJ: Neal-Schuman. 468p. (ED 432 065). Document not available from EDRS.

This book discusses the theory and practice of information literacy instruction. Part I provides background, including the definition and history of information literacy instruction. Part II covers information literacy instruction building blocks, including a brief introduction to learning theory; an overview of learning styles; library anxiety, mental models, and conceptual frameworks; and critical thinking and active learning. Part III addresses planning and developing information literacy instruction, including program planning; selecting modes of instruction; the instructional menu; basic copyright and design issues; designing instructional modes and materials; and assessing, evaluating, and revising information literacy instruction programs. Part IV discusses delivering information literacy instruction, including teaching—preparation, performance, and passion; designing information literacy instruction programs for diverse populations; delivering information literacy instruction in various environments; teaching technology; and using technology to teach. Part V discusses the future of information literacy instruction. The book comes with a CD-ROM, which includes tables describing various instructional modes, an interactive Web form and Web pages to aid in selecting among them, handouts for in-house training or personal use, and more.

Hancock, V. E. (1993). *Information literacy for lifelong learning.* ERIC Digest. Syracuse, NY: ERIC Clearinghouse on Information & Technology. 4p. (ED 358 870)

Information literacy requires that the learner recognize the need for information, be able to identify and locate it, gain access to it, and then evaluate the quality of the information received before organizing it and using it effectively. In an information literate environment students engage in active and self-directed activities. Information literacy thrives in a resource-based learning environment in which students and teachers make decisions about appropriate sources of information and how to access them. Information literacy benefits students by counteracting the information dependency created by traditional schooling and sets the teacher free to become the facilitator of interaction at the small-group or individual level. Information literate students are more effective consumers of information resources and become better-prepared citizens, who know how to use information to their best advantage in work and everyday life. The workplace of the future will also demand information literate workers. An early commitment to learning as a process will enable the worker of the future to function effectively.

Haycock, K, et al. (1998). *Foundations for effective school library media programs.* Englewood, CO: Libraries Unlimited. 331p. (ED 428 776). Document not available from EDRS.

This collection of 38 articles, reprinted from *Emergency Librarian,* addresses critical elements of school library media program development and implementation, organized by seven areas: foundations, the school context, role clarification, information literacy, collaborative program planning and teaching, program development, and accountability. The following articles are included: (1) "Strengthening the Foundations for Teacher-Librarianship" (Ken Haycock);(2) "Research in Teacher-Librarianship and the Institutionalization of Change" (Ken Haycock);(3) "Leadership for School Improvement" (Jean Brown); (4) "The School Library Program and the Culture of the School" (Dianne Oberg); (5) "Libraries, Learning and the Whole School" (Michael Marland); (6) "The School Librarian as a Professional Teacher" (Ken Haycock); (7) "Navigating the 90s—The Teacher-Librarian as Change Agent" (Jean Brown); (8) "Developing Information Literacy through the Information Intermediary Process" (Kathy Thomas Brock); (9) "Teacher-Librarians" (Jean Brown & Bruce Sheppard); (10) "Students' Information Literacy Needs" (Association for Teacher-Librarianship in Canada & Canadian School Library Association); (11) "Information Literacy in an Information Society" (Christina Doyle); (12) "Media Literacy" (Mary Megee); (13) "Student Access to the Internet" (Doug Johnson); (14) "Misinformation on the Internet" (Mary Ann Fitzgerald); (15) "Information Skills in the Curriculum" (Carol-Ann Page); (16) "Developing a School-Based Research Strategy K–7" (Sharon Straathof); (17) "Computer Literacy and Information Literacy" (Doug Johnson & Mike Eisenberg); (18) "All that Glitters May Not Be Gold" (David Loertscher); (19) "Curriculum Encounters of the Third Kind" (Ray Doiron); (20) "The School Librarian and the Classroom Teacher" (Antoinette Oberg); (21) "Changing Teaching Practice To Meet Current Expectations" (Jean Brown); (22) "Expanding the Collaborative Planning Model" (Patti Hurren); (23) "Collaborative Planning" (Carol-Ann Page); (24) "Developing the School Resource Center Program" (Carol-Ann Page); (25) "From Library Program to Learning Resources Program" (Mary Tarasoff & Sonya Emperingham); (26) "Prerequisites to Flexible Scheduling" (Jean Donham van Deusen); (27) "Secondary School Assignments" (Liz Austrom); (28) "A Stations Approach to Learning" (Debra Simmons); (29)

"Connecting Writing and Research through the I-Search Paper" (Julie Tallman); (30) "Designing Thematic Literature Units" (Jean Donham van Deusen & Paula Brandt); (31) "What Do You Believe about How Culturally Diverse Students Learn?" (Rita Dunn, Mark Beasley & Karen Buchanan); (32) "Principals and Teacher-Librarians" (Patricia Wilson, Martha Blake & Josette Lyders); (33) "Communication Skills and Strategies for Teacher-Librarians" (Barbara Howlett); (34) "School Libraries—Definitely Worth Their Keep" (Bev Anderson); (35) "Using Evaluation To Bring School Library Resource Center Programs into Closer Alliance with Information Power" (Doris Epler); (36) "Evaluation" (Linda Rafuse & Ruth Law); (37) "Evaluation of the Teacher-Librarian" (Ken Haycock); and (38) "Theory—Where Is My Reality?" (Susan Casey).

Humes, B. (1999). *Understanding information literacy.* Published as a six-panel, two-fold brochure. Washington, DC: National Institute on Postsecondary Education, Libraries, and Lifelong Learning (ED/OERI). 7p. (ED 430577)

    This document defines information literacy (i.e., the ability to access, evaluate, organize, and use information from a variety of sources) and outlines reasons to be concerned about information literacy. It then summarizes the implications of information literacy for teaching, learning, schools, libraries and librarians, the workplace, and society and culture.

Information literacy in an information society. (1994). ERIC Digest. Syracuse, NY: ERIC Clearinghouse on Information and Technology. 4p. (ED 372 756)

    Information literacy is the ability to access, evaluate, and use information from a variety of sources. This Digest defines the information literate person and describes the evolution of the concept. Information literacy is examined in the context of existing practice, and the impact of technology on the storage and dissemination of data, resulting in the need for information literacy in telecommunications, is considered. Finally, information literacy is discussed in relationship to educational reform and to curriculum standards in mathematics, social studies, and science.

Jukes, I., Dosaj, A., & Macdonald, B. (2000). *NetSavvy: Building information literacy in the classroom* (2nd ed.). Thousand Oaks, CA: Corwin Press. 159p. (ED 450 685)

    Presents a manual for effectively imbedding information literacy skills across all grade levels and subject areas. At the book's core is the Skills Framework, a 33-page listing of all the skills needed for addressing information needs using the Internet as the main information source. For any teacher the Framework serves as a set of instructions for the teaching of information-processing skills. The proper use of the Framework for lesson planning is prompted by the use of NetSavvy's complete set of Teacher Tools and Student Tools. NetSavvy is also built around a core process called "the 5As process of information literacy." Although most useful in project-based learning, this five-stage process also can be used to address any information need: Stage 1: Asking (key questions to be answered); Stage 2: Accessing (relevant data); Stage 3: Analyzing (the acquired data); Stage 4: Applying (the data to the task); Stage 5: Assessing (both the result and the process) This logical and useful process forms the basis of the Skills Framework itself as well as all the NetSavvy Tools. Within each of the five stages, the NetSavvy Tools assist teachers and students in checking for necessary prerequisites, in considering a broad range of possible information literacy methods and types of equipment, and in planning assessment techniques that measure process and content. The book is divided into four parts. Part 1, "The Internet, InfoWhelm, and InfoSavvy," consists of three chapters. Chapter 1 considers the emergence of the Internet and its impact on society and education; chapter 2 discusses information overload and its subsequent dysfunctions and proposes a solution; in chapter 3 the 5As of information literacy are presented, and InfoSavvy and NetSavvy are defined. Part 2, "Setting Up the NetSavvy Classroom," is made up of chapters 4–9, which present tools for teachers and students designed for and aligned to work with an organized list of information-processing skills for the Internet: the NetSavvy Skills Framework. Chapter 4 introduces the Ten-Minute Lesson Planner, which offers a quick and efficient way of creating NetSavvy lesson plans using the 5As approach to help integrate information literacy skills into any content area of the curriculum. Chapters 5–9 present lesson planners for each stage of the 5As NetSavvy process and student tools that articulate with each of the five lesson planners. Part 3, "The NetSavvy Skills Framework," covers the complete framework. Part 4, "Overcoming Educational Obstacles and Assumptions," consists of chapters 10–14, presenting five commonly held assumptions about education. Appendixes contain reproducible blank versions of all the NetSavvy teacher and student tools. Includes a reading list.

Kasowitz, A.S. (2000). *Teaching and learning with the Internet: A guide to building information literacy skills.* Syracuse, NY: ERIC Clearinghouse on Information and Technology. 189p. (ED 449 796)

This book is designed to prepare information mentors-educators, parents, educational concept developers, subject-matter experts, and others who guide K–12 students to information literacy to provide instruction, guidance, and services to teach K–12 students how to solve information problems using a variety of information tools and resources. The introduction describes the challenges involved in learning and teaching in a technology- and information-rich society, and presents the Big6 information problem-solving process as a vehicle for information mentors to help students develop information literacy skills. Chapter 1, "Planning Instruction Using the Internet," provides a background on using the Internet in instruction, and guidelines for planning instructional opportunities that incorporate the use of the Internet within an information problem-solving approach. Sample lesson plans and projects are given. Chapter 2, "Coaching K–12 Students with the Internet," presents issues involved when using the Internet with K–12 students and offers suggestions for successful information mentoring experiences. Chapter 3, "Communicating with Students on the Internet," provides background on the role of telecommunications activities in education, particularly Ask-an-Expert services and telementoring projects, and offers suggestions for promoting the use of information problem-solving through online communications. Chapter 4, "Designing and Providing Content on the Internet for K–12 Students," describes some different types of Internet resources designed for K–12 students and offers guidelines and examples for designing content that enhances learning and promotes an information problem-solving approach. Each chapter includes a summary, annotated list of resources, and a worksheet for applying the principles of the chapter. Appendices provide information on: getting started on the Internet (courses and resources); searching on the Internet; evaluation of Internet sites; academic standards on the Internet; locating and designing school Web pages; citing Internet sources; online safety; and designing Web sites. Includes an index.

Keenan, N., et al. (1994). *The Montana library and information skills model curriculum guide*. Montana State Office of Public Instruction, Helena. Dept. of Vocational Education Services. 106p. (ED 382 216)

This document presents a model curriculum for library media skills programs. The first and second sections provide a library and information skills mission statement and an introduction. The collaborative planning process is covered in the third section, including a description of collaborative planning, assessing the process and a collaborative unit, and sample collaborative planning guides. In the fourth section, the problem-solving process is defined and six main skills are highlighted; examples and an assessment of the process and a guide to research planning are also provided. The fifth section defines literacy, and discusses components and assessment of a literacy program. The sixth section contains position statements on the following: technology, flexible scheduling, appropriate staffing for school library media centers, and the role of the school library media program. Appendices provide a list of information and library media skills, 10 ways to analyze children's books for racism and sexism, examples for content area reading, assessment models, and model lessons.

Kirk, J. (1987). *Information skills: An educational perspective for tomorrow.* Paper presented at the Biennial Meeting of the Australian School Library Association (10th, September 3-7, 1987). 19p. (ED 359 981)

Features of the information society are discussed, and implications for education are reviewed. The information society is dominated and even overwhelmed by information. Its future is uncertain, but regardless of the eventual potential for good or harm, information literacy is a precondition of the information society. Young people in Australia are becoming more computer literate, and education authorities are developing new educational agendas for the information society. Resource-based learning is an approach that is particularly appropriate in fostering the development of individual students. The shift in emphasis from the content of what students learn to the processes of learning depends on the use of information and the development of information skills that define the purpose of an information task, locate data, select and interpret data, and use the information to complete the task. A look at information skills as they are taught in other countries highlights developments, with implications for teachers, teacher-librarians, and principals. Effective information skills programs depend on a wide range of resources. Information technology in all its forms must be an integral part of the school curriculum.

Lamb, L. & Todd, R. (1994). *The challenge of information literacy: A Catholic secondary school's response.* Paper presented at the Convention and Exposition of the National Catholic Educational Association on Unity in Diversity: Embracing the Challenge (91st, Anaheim, CA, April 4-7, 1994). 19p. (ED 374 807)

This paper focuses on a program at Marist Sisters' College, Woolwich (MSCW), an Australian secondary school, that integrates information skills into subject curriculums. A description of the school which includes its philosophy and ethnic makeup is presented to give a context for the program. The research project investigated the impact of information skills on learning and teaching. An interdisciplinary planning team was established to help teachers develop information skills in the classroom. The team found that there were four levels of commitment in regard to the program: resistance, curiosity, acceptance, and commitment. The team implemented two strategies to help teachers progress through the stages: a demonstration program was set up so that teachers could observe the process; and teachers were involved in negotiating lesson planning. Both qualitative and quantitative data were gathered to evaluate the program. Both teachers and students found the addition of information skills to the curriculum to be beneficial. These skills had an impact on students' self perception, learning processes, learning outcomes, and on the learning environments. The paper concludes by discussing the role of school administrators in integrating information skills into the curriculum.

Lance, K. C., & Rodney, M. J., & Hamilton-Pennell, C. (2000). *Measuring up to standards: The impact of school library programs & information literacy in Pennsylvania schools.* Pennsylvania Citizens for Better Libraries, Greensburg. Pennsylvania. (ED 446 771)

This document reports on a project that examined the impact of school library media centers on academic achievement in Pennsylvania. The project also determined the impact on academic achievement of: specific activities of certified school librarians; principal and teacher support of school library programs; and information technology, particularly licensed databases and the Internet/World Wide Web. A sample of 500 school libraries was surveyed. Findings in the following areas are presented: (1) presence of adequate school library staffing linked to higher PSSA (Pennsylvania System of School Assessment) reading scores; (2) PSSA reading scores increase as school library staffing increases; (3) school library staffing linked to library expenditures, information resources and technology, and integrating information literacy; (4) school library expenditures linked to information resources; (5) information resources linked to integrating information literacy; (6) information technology linked to integrating information literacy; (7) PSSA reading scores linked directly to school library staffing, information technology, and integrating information literacy; and (8) how highest and lowest scoring schools compare on school library predictors of academic achievement. A copy of the questionnaire is included.

Langhorne, M. J., And Others. (1998). *Developing an information literacy program K–12. A how-to-do-it manual and CD-ROM package. How-to-do-it manuals for librarians, Number 85.* New York, NY: Neal-Schumann Publishers, Inc. 294p. (ED 423 908) Document Not Available from EDRS.

This book, developed by the Iowa City Community School District, recipient of the National Library Media Program of the year Award in 1997, provides a complete K–12 curriculum, with details on when key basic information, research, and production skills should be introduced, expanded, and reviewed. The book is divided into four parts: Part I: "Developing an Information Literacy Program"; Part II: "Model Lessons and Units for Elementary Classes"; Part III: "Model Lessons and Units for Secondary Classes"; and Part IV: ""Additional Instructional Resources for Use Throughout the Year." Problem-solving activities that are integrated with the classroom curriculum include: logic searches; evaluating sources; narrow research topics; database creation; graphs; and diagrams. Over 100 pages of model lesson plans and units for specific curricular areas supplement the guide. Also provided are assessment tools; in-service and policy documents; sample forms; a complete information literacy model with a matrix for recording which units cover which skills; collaborative planning resources; and suggestions for over 100 possible student products. The accompanying CD-ROM contains all the forms, handouts, and transparencies needed to teach the lesson plans and units, formatted for Microsoft Word 6.0 (for Macintosh and Windows).

Lemke, C. (2002). *enGauge 21st century skills: Digital literacies for a digital age.* A guide from the North Central Regional Educational Lab, Naperville, IL. (ED 463 753)

The North Central Regional Educational Laboratory's (NCREL) "enGauge" is a Web-based framework that describes six essential conditions, or system-wide factors critical to the effective use of technology for student learning. In addition to the framework, the "enGauge" Web site includes an online survey instrument that allows districts and schools to conduct online assessments of system-wide educational technology effectiveness. This publication describes a set of 21st century skills that will be increasingly important to students entering the work force. These skills are not at odds with traditional educational skills, but are, in fact, extensions of those skills, adapted to new technologies and new work environments. The educational system will be challenged to encourage the development of these 21st century skills in relevant and meaningful ways. The publication consists of five main sections, following an introduction. The first section, "Digital-Age Literacy," discusses basic, scientific and technological literacies; visual and information literacies; and cultural literacy and global awareness. The second section, "Inventive Thinking," focuses on adaptability/ability to manage complexity; curiosity, creativity, and risk-taking; and higher-order thinking and sound reasoning. Section three, "Effective Communication," deals with teaming, collaboration, and interpersonal skills; personal and social responsibility; and interactive communication. The fourth section, "High Productivity," discusses the ability to prioritize, plan, and manage for results; effective use of real-world tools; and relevant, high-quality products. Section five, "Information Technology," identifies possible social effects with regard to information technology.

Lighthall, L., & Howe, E., And Others. (1999). *Unleash the power! Knowledge-technology-diversity: Papers presented at the third international forum on research in school librarianship, annual conference of the International Association of School Librarianship (IASL)* (28th, Birmingham, Alabama, November 10-14, 1999). 237p. (ED 437 052)

Papers presented at this forum were grouped under the following four broad themes: "Unleash the Power!," "Powerful Roles," "Powerful Partnerships," and "Powerful Technologies." Also included is the paper that won the Takeshi Murofushi Research Award, "Implementing Flexible Scheduling in Elementary Libraries" (Joy H. McGregor). Titles and authors of the papers are as follows: (1) "Connecting Marketing and Implementation Research and Library Program Development: A Case Study of the Implementation of National [U.S.] Guidelines and Standards" (Ken Haycock and Pat Cavill); (2) "The United States National Library Power Program: Research, Evaluation and Implications for Professional Development and Library Education" (Dianne McAfee Hopkins and Douglas L. Zweizig); (3) "Authentic Learning and the Research Processes of Gifted Students" (Kay Bishop); (4) "Treasure Hunt or Torture: Student's Perspectives on Research Projects" (Denise Streitenberger and Joy McGregor); (5) "Meeting Diverse Information Needs: Students with Disabilities" (Jan Murray); (6) "The Impact of Whole Language on Four Elementary School Libraries: Results from a Comparative Case Study" (Sandra Hughes); (7) "Images of Poverty in Contemporary Realistic Fiction for Youth: Preliminary Results of a Content Analysis Using a Social Psychological Conceptual Framework" (Shirley A. Fitzgibbons and Carol L. Tilley); (8) "Young People's Reading and Information Use at the End of the Century" (Sandra Olen, et al.); (9) "Unleashing the Theory: Connecting Learning Theory to Building Information Seeking Skills" (Elizabeth B. Danley, et al.); (10) "Revealing Thinking: Teachers Working Together on Information Literacy" (Penny Moore); (11) "University/School Library Collaborations To Integrate Information Technology into Resource-Based Learning Activities" (Roy H. Doiron); (12) "Assessing Pre-Service Teachers' Beliefs about the Role of the Library Media Specialist" (Linda L. Wolcott, et al.); (13) "The Role of the Principal in an Information Literate School Community: Findings from an International Research Project" (Dianne Oberg, et al.); (14) "The Changing Powers of Readers in a Time of New Technology" (Margaret Mackey); (15) "Students and the World Wide Web: Issues of Confidence and Competence" (Jinx Stapleton Watson); (16) "Evaluating Web Sites: A Critical Information Skill" (Ruth V. Small and Marilynp. Arnone); (17) "Web-Based Instruction for School Library Media Specialists: Unleash the Power of the World Wide Web" (Mary Ann Hindes); (18) "The Use of the Internet in School Libraries: An International and Comparative Survey" (James E. Herring); and (19) "The School Library Web Site: On the Information Highway or Stalled in the Carpark?" (Laurel A. Clyde).

Manitoba Dept. of Education. (1994). *Resource-based learning: An educational model*. 67p. (ED 372 736)

This document was prepared as a guide for educators in Manitoba (Canada) to facilitate the implementation of the resource-based learning model implicit in the province's curriculum guides from kindergarten through Senior 4 and to integrate the instructional programs of the classroom and the school library as specified by the provincial department of education. The guide will facilitate the implementation of the educational reform set out in recent department publications. Resource-based learning is an educational model that actively involves students, teachers, and teacher-librarians in the meaningful use of appropriate print, nonprint, and human resources. The model requires the services of a qualified teacher-librarian to assist teachers in integrating the use of school-library learning resources into their classroom programs in order for the model to be successful. This guide includes a description of the model and an outline of its implementation. (Contains 32 references, a set of learning goals, a glossary, suggestions for student presentations and learning units, 155 resources for classroom teachers, and a 23-item supplementary reading list.)

McKenna, M. (1994). *Libraries and the internet*. ERIC Digest. 4p. (ED 377 880)

The Internet is an international computer network encompassing thousands of smaller interconnected networks. This digest describes various uses of the Internet and its impact on libraries, as well as Internet-related library issues. The Internet applications of electronic mail (E-mail), telnet, and file transfer protocol (FTP) are briefly described. The impact of the Internet on libraries includes: leadership opportunities; cost and time savings; question answering services; international interlibrary loans; document delivery services; online transactions; government information; information sharing; and increased librarian visibility and value to the community. Internet-related issues are discussed with respect to academic, public, special, and school libraries. It is recommended that librarians take an active role in the formulation of national policy and legislation, creation and organization of services and resources, and be properly trained in network literacy in order to provide programs for patrons to become network literate.

McKenzie, J. (2000). *Beyond technology: Questioning, research and the information literate school*. Bellingham, WA: FNO Press. 168p. (ED 450 686). Document Not Available from EDRS.

This collection of previously published essays and articles by the author outlines an approach to school research that is meant to prepare students to explore the most demanding and essential questions of life with independence, skill and confidence. The book describes strategies to make student questioning and research central to schooling, and proposes a campaign to move past technology bandwagons to information literacy. The book is divided into three parts. Part One, "The Primacy of Questioning," includes the following seven chapters: "Questions as Technology"; "Research for an Information Age"; "Questioning Toolkit"; "Students in Resonance"; "The Information Literate School Community"; "Acing the Standards"; and "Strategic Teaching." Part Two, "The Research Cycle," includes the next nine chapters: "The Research Cycle"; "Planning the Voyage"; "The Hunt"; "More Hunting"; "Needles from Haystacks"; "Regrouping Findings"; "Information to Persuasion"; "Searching for the Grail"; and "The New Plagiarism." Part Three: "Research Modules," includes the last four chapters: "Building Research Modules"; "Levels of Modules"; "Scaffolding for Success"; and "Modules and Standards."

McKenzie, J. (2001). *Planning good change with technology and literacy.* Bellingham, WA: FNO Press. 161p. (ED 453 822). Document Not Available from EDRS.

This book describes strategies to put information literacy and student learning at the center of technology planning. Filled with stories of success and with models of good planning, the book shows how to clarify purpose, involve important stakeholders, and pace the change process to maximize the daily use of new technologies. The following chapters are included: (1) "Making Good Change"; (2) "First Things First"; (3) "Future Perfect Planning"; (4) "Beyond IT"; (5) "The New New Thing"; (6) "Beware the Wizard"; (7) "Beware the Gray Flannel Trojan Horse"; (8) "Beware the Shallow Waters"; (9) "Network Starvation"; (10) "The Unplugged Classroom"; (11) "What's the Story Here?"; (12) "How Teachers Learn Technology Best"; (13) "The Research Gap"; (14) "Beyond Edutainment And Technotainment"; (15) "Strategic Deployment"; (16) "Waste Not, Want Not"; (17) "Pacing Change"; and (18) "Managing Quandaries." Appendices include a technology self-assessment form and a scenario of what learning might be like in the future with intelligent hand-held computers acting as tutors and learning assistants.

McNicholas, C. & Nelson, P. (1994). *The virtual school library: Moving toward reality.* Paper presented at the Annual Convention of the National Catholic Educational Association (91st, Anaheim, CA, April 4-7, 1994). 19p. (ED 375 837)

The response of Marist Sisters' College, Woolwich, New South Wales (Australia), to the challenges of teaching information literacy is described. Marist Sisters' College is a high school enrolling approximately 750 girls representing diverse cultures and socioeconomic backgrounds in grades 7 through 12. An integrated information-skills program, described elsewhere, has been developed across the curriculum, and networked computer terminals and CD-ROM towers have become the foundation for an information-technology program aimed at information literacy. The concept of the virtual library serves the College's aspirations for the information environment. The virtual library as it is being developed at Marist Sisters' College gives access to more information than is contained in four walls through electronic access to internal resources and external services, including catalogs and local area networks that enable remote access. Part of the virtual library approach is focusing on the skills needed to use technology as a tool. The virtual library is providing a dynamic and diverse information environment that supports the entire school curriculum. A detailed outline of the information process—defining, locating, selecting, organizing, presenting, and assessing—in terms of skills and outcomes is presented in tabular format. (Contains 12 references.)

Mendrinos, R. (1994). *Building information literacy using high technology: A guide for schools and libraries*. 190p. Englewood, CA: Libraries Unlimited, Inc. (ED 375 820). Document Not Available from EDRS.

This guide to using the tools of online databases, telecommunications, and CD-ROM technology in the educational environment provides a practical introduction to the concepts and importance of information literacy and high technology resource-based learning. It also describes the drawbacks and advantages of these tools from an educator's viewpoint. The book provides procedures for going online and gives guidelines for using CD-ROM technology and networking. Chapter 1 focuses on developing information literacy within a resource-based learning environment using high-tech tools and their affinity with instructional theory and student achievement. Chapter 2 provides a background for online databases, utilities, and telecommunications networks. It covers getting started, advantages and disadvantages of online searching, database vendors, electronic mail, concerns in using telecommunications in the classroom, and the Internet. Chapters 3 and 4 examine CD-ROMs and education, including planning, local area networks, and CD-ROM networks. Case studies of schools using information technology are presented in Chapter 5, and Chapter 6 outlines a model for a research strategy using online technology. Finally, Chapter 7 contains sample lesson plans to serve as models to integrate curricula and high-tech tools to stimulate student motivation and achievement. A glossary and an index are included.

Milam, P. S. (2002). *InfoQuest: A new twist on information literacy.* Worthington, OH: Linworth Publishing, Inc. 225p. (ED 464 639) Document Not Available from EDRS.

This book is a comprehensive guide to implementing the InfoQuest program in libraries, schools, and school library media centers. In the InfoQuest program, a research question is posed each week, and students have all week to come to the media center and use a variety of reference tools and media to research the answer. Small prizes are awarded to the students who have researched the answer correctly. The book is arranged in three parts: Perspective, Philosophy, and Practice. The Perspective section deals with what information literacy is, why it should be taught, information literacy standards, and the current state of information literacy in education. The Philosophy section describes the how-to's: how to teach information literacy more effectively, how to ask higher-order questions, and how to teach InfoQuest itself. The Practice section provides questions and answers by subject (i.e., words, mathematics, science, quotations, literature, geography, history, and biography) and level as well as assessment tools for tracking the progress of the participants. Each chapter in this section includes additional references for individualizing InfoQuest programs.

Montgomery, P. K., & Thomas, N.p. (1999). *Information literacy and information skills instruction: Applying research to practice in the school library media center. Library and information problem-solving skills series.* Englewood, CO: Libraries Unlimited, Inc. 187p. (ED 431 404) Document Not Available from EDRS.

This book brings together the literature on information skills instruction with particular reference to models related to information seeking and the information search process, including representational, instructional/teaching, and facilitation models. Chapter 1 provides an overview of the development of the library curriculum as it has evolved from more traditional forms of reference services. Chapter 2 summarizes the development of school libraries as centralized facilities, the introduction of library skills as a primary focus of library instruction, and approaches to information skills instruction. Chapter 3 focuses on the Information Search Process and intervention models. In chapter 4, conceptual models for teaching information skills are described. Chapter 5 examines instruction in terms of a model for diagnosing information needs and relates information needs to theories of information seeking, learning, and individual differences. In chapter 6, the literature related to information skills instruction is reviewed. Chapter 7 considers the impact of technology on the teaching of information skills, while chapter 8 provides an overview of contemporary approaches to assessment. In chapter 9, research related to interpersonal communication within the context of the school library is presented, and the social nature of information seeking and instruction is explored. An epilogue considers issues of professionalism, service, and leadership for school library media specialists.

National Commission on Libraries and Information Science. (1993). *Open forum on children and youth services: Redefining the federal role for libraries* (Boston, Massachusetts, May 4-5, 1993). 231p. (ED 368 371)

The U.S. National Commission on Libraries and Information Science (NCLIS) conducted an open forum May 4-5, 1993 on the changing role of the federal government in support of library and information services and literacy programs for children and youth. The following topics were addressed: current status of library and information services for elementary and secondary school students; role of school library media centers in achieving the six National Education Goals; future federal roles in support of library media programs and services for children and youth from public libraries; nature of federal support for school library media programs and public library services for students; nature of federal support of technology for school and public library programs for children and youth; role of public and school libraries in promoting resource-based learning, information skills, and instructional activities; how school and public library partnerships should be developed; how libraries can develop intergenerational demonstration programs for latchkey children and young adults and outreach programs for youth at risk; and the community library's role in offering parent/family educational programs for early childhood services. Includes 4 appendices.

New Hampshire State Dept. of Education. (1992). *Information skills: A report from the ad hoc committee.* 25p. (ED 368 358)

In 1990 a committee was formed to develop a list of information skills that could be used by New Hampshire library media professionals to help them develop plans for integrating such skills within their schools. Information skills are processes needed to access, evaluate, organize, communicate, and apply information efficiently and effectively. The following core objectives, which are considered important for all grade levels even though implementation differs according to grade, were developed: (1) understanding the function of information in contemporary society; (2) using libraries and information systems as sources of information and recreation; (3) demonstrating responsible and ethical use of information technologies; (4) recognizing strengths, weaknesses, and impacts of information sources; (5) clarifying information needs and developing search strategies; (6) using a variety of skills and strategies to record and organize information; (7) constructing meaning from information; (8) using a variety of methods and formats to communicate information; and (9) evaluating the effectiveness of search strategies and information use. Four appendixes provide examples of determining levels of emphasis, information skill plans, a sample unit, and a sample planning form.

North Dakota State Department of Public Instruction. (1993). *North Dakota curriculum frameworks, volume I: Language arts, library media, mathematics, science, social studies.* Bismarck, ND: Author. 101p. (ED 370 175)

Curriculum frameworks for North Dakota elementary secondary education are presented in this document. These frameworks are voluntary and serve to promote interdisciplinary learning, active learning, and student diversity. They are part of a larger systemic approach to improve instruction in the state's schools and to identify content outcomes and student performance standards. Each section contains a list of North Dakota educators involved in the framework development; a mission statement for that particular subject area; the graduation outcomes for the state; a list of content outcomes; content outcomes and performance standards for each outcome at grades 4, 8, and graduation; a glossary of terms; and a bibliography. Curriculum frameworks are provided for the following areas: language arts; library media (access to information, information literacy, promotion of lifelong learning); mathematics; science; and social studies.

Olen, S. (1995). A transformation in teacher education: Or how can disadvantaged teachers become information literate? In *Literacy: traditional, cultural, technological. Selected papers from the annual conference of the International Association of School Librarianship* (23rd, Pittsburgh, Pennsylvania, July 17-22, 1994); see IR 056 058. 7p. (ED 399 948)

In a developing country such as South Africa, many teachers enter initial teacher education with little or no experience of libraries and information sources. These students need to become information literate during their initial teacher education; otherwise they will not have the knowledge of information sources and skills they will need if they are going to be role models for their pupils and help them to become information literate. The paper describes a project to improve the media and information skills of underqualified teachers through inservice workshops. The process could also be used as a model for initial teacher education with students from disadvantaged or more privileged backgrounds. It is important for pupils to become information literate, but before this can happen, their teachers must themselves become information literate. Teaching style influences student learning and must follow a clearly formulated process, like the one described. This is one way to help transform the prevailing teacher-centered and textbook-centered teaching style into an interactive teaching and learning process based on available information sources.

Orr, M., & Fankhauser R. (1996). Approaches to research in a digital environment—Who are the new researchers? In *Learning technologies: prospects and pathways*. Selected papers from EdTech '96 Biennial Conference of the Australian Society for Educational Technology (Melbourne, Australia, July 7-10, 1996). 8p. (ED 396 739)

The research process has been a constant feature of the curriculum in primary and secondary schools for many years. The purpose of this process has traditionally been to develop student research skills and to enhance their knowledge within a particular area. The Information Process diagram, developed by the Australian School Library Association in conjunction with the Curriculum Corporation, places the research process within the context of generic learning skills. The advent of the digital information era has challenged and changed many of the traditional research sources, tools, and practices and the premises on which they operate, although the essential process still depends on critical thinking, problem solving, and communicating. The digital information environment is dynamic; multimedia sources combine several media such as text, graphics, animation, audio, and video in an integrated format that is accessed by computer. Related technologies are having an impact on Australian education. Digital cameras, notebook computers, and other devices have aided secondary students in recording observations during an expedition to the Snowy River. Primary students have also used educational technology to enhance information gathering on a trip to a botanical garden. Students can create personalized "knowledge webs," with their assignments hyperlinked to each other and to Internet resources. Each new resource format requires the development of new skills or extensions of old ones to enhance student learning. Students must become competent researchers and information managers with a well-developed capacity to critically evaluate information for accuracy, relevance, and usefulness as well as to search and manage huge quantities of information available through the Internet and other electronic sources. Information literacy within a digital environment uses many of the information skills already identified in the literature, but new skills must be taught if the potential of a digital world is to be exploited. The digital environment has allowed students and teachers to become part of a global research community that is premised on information sharing and individual and collective discovery.

Plotnick, E. (1999). *Information literacy*. ERIC Digest. 4p. (ED 427 777)

Although alternate definitions for information literacy have been developed by educational institutions, professional organizations, and individuals, they are likely to stem from the definition offered in the *Final Report* of the American Library Association (ALA) Presidential Committee on Information Literacy: "to be information literate, a person must be able to recognize when information is needed and have the ability to locate, evaluate and use effectively the needed information." This ERIC Digest describes the evolution of the concept of information literacy and discusses the three predominating themes in research on information literacy, the new workplace of the future, national and state standards, K–12 educational reform and restructuring, information literacy efforts in K–12 and higher education, and information technology as the enabler of information literacy.

Potter, C. J., Lohr, N. J., Klein, J., & Sorensen, R. J. (2000). *Information & technology literacy standards matrix.* Milwaukee: Wisconsin Department of Public Instruction. 346p. (ED 445 663)

Intended to help library media specialists, technology educators, and curriculum planning teams identify where specific information and technology competencies might best fit into the assessed content areas of the curriculum, this document presents a matrix that identifies the correlation between Wisconsin's Information and Technology Literacy (ITL) Standards and English language arts, mathematics, science, and social studies standards. An introductory section describes the Matrix Project, the Matrix Project Advisory Group, academic standards definitions, the matrix models, and the list of integration resources. The second section presents Matrix Model 1, which correlates content standards for each of the four curriculum areas with the ITL Standards. The third section presents Matrix Model 2, which separates the four content standards of the ITL Standards (i.e., media and technology, information and inquiry, independent learning, and the learning community) and arranges them by three grade ranges: K–4, 5–8, and 9–12. The final section provides a listing of resources and resource providers for those educators desiring additional information or ideas on how to integrate information and technology competencies into curriculum and classroom instruction; several World Wide Web sites that contain evaluated lesson plans, many of which incorporate information and technology skills, are included.

Ryan, J., & Capra, S. (2001). *Information literacy toolkit: Grades kindergarten-6 [and] information literacy toolkit: Grades 7 and up [and] research projects: An information literacy planner for students [with CD-ROM].* Chicago: American Library Association. 165p. (ED 454 876). Document not available from EDRS.

The three guides in the new Information Literacy Toolkit Series can help school library media specialists and teachers promote and teach information literacy skills to young library users and collaborate in curriculum planning so that students will develop a cohesive skill set; teach the critical thinking and problem-solving skills that lead to information literacy; and use a step-by-step process, in line with curriculum standards yet flexible enough to adapt to school and district settings. The first two guides, "Information Literacy Toolkit: Grades Kindergarten-6" and "Information Literacy Toolkit: Grades 7 and Up," present skill-level appropriate tools that foster collaboration between libraries and schools, and school library media specialists and teachers. The accompanying student workbook, "Research Projects: An Information Literacy Planner for Students," provides in-class support materials. "Information Literacy Toolkit: Grades Kindergarten-6" is organized into three parts—process overview, planning organizer, and teaching tools—to help library media specialists and teachers introduce information literacy concepts and skills and link literacy to standard subject areas (includes a CD-ROM and an index of blackline masters). "Information Literacy Toolkit: Grades 7 and Up" covers more advanced skills in a broader context, applicable less to defined subject areas than to curricula as a whole (Includes a CD-ROM, a glossary, and an index). "Research Projects: An Information Literacy Planner for Students" challenges students to put the information literacy skills they have acquired to work: analyzing a research topic, brainstorming for ideas, actively taking notes, creating bibliographies, and conducting focused research.

Semali, L.M. (1995). Teaching media: English teachers as media and technology critics. In *Eyes on the future: Converging images, ideas, and instruction.* Selected readings from the Annual Conference of the International Visual Literacy Association (27th, Chicago, IL, October 18-22, 1995). 10p. (ED 391 500)

This paper discusses the role of media in presenting information to society and emphasizes the need for English teachers to incorporate critical media awareness into education. Four postulations are identified that are at the core of teaching media as a form of textual construction: (1) All media are a construction, which represents conscious and unconscious decisions about what knowledge is valid and valued; (2) audiences negotiate meaning; (3) the curriculum represents ideology and values and has social and political implications; and (4) the nature of media messages can affect social attitudes and behavior. Twenty teachers attending a media literacy workshop at Pennsylvania State University in the summer of 1994 were asked to rate the frequency with which they undertook certain core critical media literacy activities; results revealed that teachers were not aware of what they could do about media in their language arts classrooms and that nonprint media are still an isolated phenomenon in schools. The workshop encouraged teachers to work toward integrating forms of media literacy into their teaching and covered analysis of codes and conventions, personal experience, cultural and ideological meanings, and commercial overtones and economic strategies. A table depicts the teachers' ratings on media practice in the classroom.

Simpson, C. (1996). *The school librarian's role in the electronic age.* ERIC Digest. 4p. (ED 402 928)

      The dawn of the electronic age has altered the role of the school librarian. The position is less of a warehouse manager and more of a reference consultant; the emphasis is on access to information rather than collection development; and the librarian is an information center manager, specialist, and teacher of information technology. School restructuring, more student-centered teaching methods, and the change from a passive learning environment to an active one all require collaboration between librarians and classroom teachers to meet the information needs of students. Librarians must become proficient in the use of the new technologies to promote them and instruct students and teachers in their use. As access to information overtakes ownership of information, librarians seek out and evaluate online and other electronic sources to meet the information needs of patrons. Librarians must teach students and teachers to be discriminating users of information, teach ethical use of the materials received, and form access policies and acceptable use agreements. The expanding functions of the library necessitate that the librarian become an information center manager, developing skills to manage the different groups of people who will work in the library. The librarian is the campus expert in information location and management and thus in the best position to be on the forefront of information technology and to train others in its use. The school librarian in the electronic age expands the services available from the library to include computer-based data and sophisticated information-seeking strategies. Working in concert with classroom teachers and curriculum experts, librarians form a comprehensive team designed to enhance student academic achievement and critical thinking skills necessary for success in lifelong endeavors.

Spitzer, K. L., Eisenberg, M. B., & Lowe, C. A. (1998*). Information literacy: Essential skills for the information age.* Syracuse, NY: Information Resources Publications. 349p. (ED 427 780)

      This monograph traces the history and development of the term "information literacy." It examines the economic necessity of being information literate and explores the research related to the concept. Included are reports on the National Educational Goals (1991) and on the report of the Secretary's Commission on Achieving Necessary Skills (SCANS, 1991). Also examined are recent revisions in national subject matter standards that imply a recognition of the process skills included in information literacy. The book outlines the impact information literacy has on K–12 and higher education and provides examples of information literacy in various contexts. Appendixes include Information Literacy Standards for Student Learning (prepared by the American Association of School Librarians and the Association for Educational Communications and Technology), definitions of SCANS components; a chronology of the development of information literacy, correlation of information literacy skills with selected National Subject Matter Standards, Dalbotten's Correlation of Inquiry Skills to National Content Standards, and an explanation of rubrics and their application in standards education. Contains an extensive annotated ERIC (Educational Resources Information Center) bibliography and information about ERIC.

Texas Education Agency. (1993). *The library media center: A force for student excellence.* Austin: Texas Education Agency. 96p. (ED 366 345)

The mission of today's school library media center is to help prepare students to enter the Information Age of the twenty-first century. To carry out this mission, library media specialists, administrators, and teachers must ensure that students can effectively locate, access, interpret, evaluate, and communicate information. The school library media center can offer assistance if it is adequately staffed and funded to develop a program that reaches all students in meaningful ways. This publication is intended to help districts develop library media programs that meet the needs of students and teachers. The following areas are addressed: (1) the library media center program, (2) library media center staff, (3) resources, (4) facilities, (5) financial support, (6) the library media center and the curriculum, and (7) the library media center and technology. Included in the appendixes are state requirements for school library media centers; automation standards for school library media centers; position statements of the American Association of School Librarians; documents relating to material selection, censorship, and copyright issues; a planning guide; and a library media center appraisal checklist.

Thompson, H. M., & Henley, S. A. (2000). *Fostering information literacy: Connecting national standards, Goals 2000, and the SCANS report. Information literacy series.* 257p. Englewood, CO: Libraries Unlimited. (ED 439 667). Document not available from EDRS.

This book focuses on information literacy and facilitating change in schools. Chapters include "What Is Information Literacy?"; "Why Information Literacy?"; "How Information Literacy Relates to National Curriculum Standards"; "Essential Components of Information Literacy"; "The Necessary Reforms and Changing Responsibilities"; "The Problem-Solving Component"; and "Creating All the Parts." Each of these chapters incorporates a summary, notes, and additional readings. The last three chapters include a checklist of information goals, objectives, and strategies, along with additional readings; four sample lesson plans; and World Wide Web resources. Separate appendixes include national standards for math, science, history, English language arts, and fine arts, as well as transparency masters and an Information Literacy handout. Includes an index and a computer disk containing: (1) Hyperlink Document—this file contains a short summary of each chapter of Fostering Information Literacy: Connecting National Standards, Goals 2000, and the SCANS Report, followed by hyperlinks to the Web sites mentioned in that chapter; (2) Information Literacy In-service Transparencies—the transparencies for the Information Literacy In-service may be printed as is, enhanced with graphics, modified, personalized, or adapted to particular situations; (3) Information Literacy PowerPoint Presentation—the PowerPoint presentation may be used as is, enhanced with graphics, modified, personalized, or adapted to particular situations; (4) Information Literacy In-service Handout—the handout may be printed as-is, enhanced with graphics, modified, personalized, or adapted to particular situations; (5) Lesson Plan Model—the blank lesson plan model may be completed by teachers and library media specialists as they work together to develop authentic learning experiences and integrated units of study; and (6) Checklist of Information Literacy Goals, Objectives, and Strategies—the checklist may be filled in and modified as teachers and library media specialists use the strategies mentioned and add some of their own.

Todd, R., et al. (1991). *Evolution, not revolution: Working to full school participation with information skills.* Paper presented at the Biennial Meeting of the Australian School Library Association (Levra, New South Wales, Australia, September 29-October 3, 1991). 19p. (ED 354 909)

An action research project underway at Marist Sisters' College (a secondary school) in Woolwich (New South Wales, Australia) is the first phase in the evolution of an across-the-school commitment to Cooperative Program Planning and Teaching (CPPT). Project goals include establishing an infrastructure to develop a dynamic methodology for CPPT in the school, facilitating the achievement of the individual teacher's goals for CPPT, and widening the CPPT base in the school to establish a schoolwide commitment to information skills. To establish an infrastructure, a school-based interdisciplinary management team was formed. The team identified characteristics of the school, teachers, and administrative staff that could act as catalysts and change agents. Barriers to program development were identified. Understanding the attitudes of teachers toward information skills was a necessary step prior to development of the project planning model. The model was applied to a year 7 science unit to demonstrate the teacher's use of the CPPT approach. The program emphasizes the dynamic role of the teacher-librarian as a teaching partner and change agent for educational innovation.

Todd, R. J., et al. (1992). *The power of information literacy: Unity of education and resources for the 21st century.* Paper presented at the Annual Meeting of the International Association of School Librarianship (21st, Belfast, Northern Ireland, United Kingdom, July 19-24, 1992). (ED 354 916)

Information literacy is the ability to use information purposefully and effectively. It is a holistic, interactive learning process encompassing the skills-based phases of defining, locating, selecting, organizing, presenting, and evaluating information from sources that include books and other media, experiences, and people; being able to consider information in light of knowledge; adding information to current knowledge; and applying this knowledge to solve information needs. An approach for promoting information literacy and establishing an integrated information skills program in a school is described. At Marist Sisters' College, a secondary school in Sydney (Australia), an action research project has attempted to place information literacy at the center of the curriculum. Using R. G. Havelock's model of the change agent, a range of change agent activities has been used. Qualitative evaluation through interviews with eight teachers and 110 students in grades 7, 9, and 11 has demonstrated the positive impacts of the approach on student self-concept, the learning process, the view of information, learning outcomes, and the learning environment. Three appendixes contain a summary of the information process, change agent activities, and a diagram of the planning model.

Utah State Office of Education. (1991). *Elementary and secondary core curriculum standards. Levels K–12.* Library Media. Salt Lake City: Utah State Office of Education. 48p. (ED 371 720).

The Utah State Board of Education established a policy requiring the identification of specific core curriculum standards that must be completed by all kindergarten through grade 12 students as a requisite for graduation. The core curriculum consequently represents standards of learning that are essential for all students. This document presents the core curriculum standards for the state's library media program. The library media skills core curriculum is based on four essential activities: (1) identifying and locating information and resources, (2) selecting and using information and resources, (3) evaluating information and resources, and (4) appreciating and evaluating children's literature. Core standards are identified for each grade level. Specific objectives are listed for kindergarten through grade 6. Beginning with grade 7, library media skills are infused into the language arts core curriculum and will be infused into other curriculum areas as the supporting documents are revised. Standards for grades 7 through 12 that relate to library media skills are listed, along with objectives for each standard, which are to be implemented in a series of projects and papers students will write.

Vandergrift, K. E. (1994). *Power teaching; A primary role of the school library media specialist.* School library media programs: Focus on trends and issues No. 14. 171p. Chicago: American Library Association. (ED 369 419). Document not available from EDRS.

This book illustrates the roles of the school library media specialist as instructional consultant and teacher as well as information specialist and frames these roles in a background of relevant educational concerns. Chapter 1 surveys current efforts to restructure the education system and stresses the importance of the school library media specialist in promoting the use of multiple technologies for educational reform. Chapters 2 and 3 present a variety of teaching models and explain how a school library media specialist may work with classroom teachers to present a range of different learning opportunities for particular subjects made possible by library resources. In this connection, semantic webbing is also discussed, as well as issue- and materials-centered research. Chapter 4 discusses critical thinking and focuses on the necessity of teaching critical evaluation of information to children of all ages. Chapter 5 elaborates on webbing, discussing pre-webs, literary webs, and complete webs. Chapter 6 discusses informal library staff development and includes teaching content for workshops on a variety of topics and for different grade levels. Chapter 7 overviews media center evaluation and presents two evaluative instruments. The first emphasizes time allocation and priorities in general library activities. The second includes a set of paired questionnaires to encourage school and public libraries to study their working relationships together.

Wesson, C. L., & Keefe, M.J. (Eds.). (1995). *Serving special needs students in the school library media center. Greenwood professional guides in school librarianship.* Westport, CT: Greenwood Press. 269p. (ED 385 999)

This collection of papers considers how the school library media specialist serves special needs students and classroom teachers in multiple roles as teacher, information specialist, and instructional consultant or collaborator. Included are the following papers: "Teaching Library and Information Skills to Special Needs Students" (Caren L. Wesson and Margaret J. Keefe); "Assessing Library and Information Skills of Special Needs Students" (Margaret J. Keefe and Caren L. Wesson); "Fostering an Appreciation of Literature in Special Needs Students" (Margaret J. Keefe and Caren L. Wesson); "Vocational Instruction in the Library Media Center" (Deborah Jilbert); "Selection of Materials for Special Needs Students" (Lula Pride and Lois Schultz); "The School LibraryMedia Specialist's Role in Bibliotherapy" (Robertp. King); "Accessibility of School Library Materials for Special Needs Students" (William J. Murray); "Instructional Technology and Students with Special Needs in the School Library Media Center" (Ann Higgins Hains and Dave L. Edyburn); "An Active Role for School Library Media Specialists in the Identification and Placement Procedures for Special Needs Students" (Deborah L. Voltz); "School Library Media Specialists as Partners with Classroom Teachers in Generalizing the Skills of Students with Special Needs" (M. Lewis Putnam); "Fostering Relationships among Special and General Education Students in the School Library Media Center" (Caren L. Wesson and others); "The Special Needs of Gifted and Talented Students in the School Library Media Center" (Caren L. Wesson and Margaret J. Keefe); "Libraries as Laboratories for Learning: Integrating Content, Learner's Needs, and Experience into the Curriculum" (Amy Otis-Wilborn and Terry McGreehin); and "School Library Media Specialists and Professional Development" (Caren L. Wesson). A 35-item annotated bibliography is also provided.

Wisconsin Educational Media Association. (1993). *Information literacy: A position paper on information problem-solving.* 6p. Appleton, WI: Author. (ED 376 817).

Key elements of information literacy are identified, and a rationale is presented for the integration of information literacy in all aspects of the kindergarten through grade 12 and post-secondary curricula. Many aspects of the school restructuring movement and library media programs relate directly to information literacy and its impact on student learning. The basic elements in an information literacy curriculum are (1) defining the need for information, (2) initiating the search strategy, (3) locating the resources, (4) assessing and comprehending the information, (5) interpreting the information, (6) communicating the information, and (7) evaluating the product and the process. Three scenes illustrate students demonstrating information literacy problem-solving skills.

Yaacob, R. A., & Seman, N.A. (1993). Towards achieving a critical thinking society in Malaysia: A challenge to school libraries and educational systems. In *Dreams and dynamics. Selected papers from the Annual Conference of the International Association of School Librarianship* (22nd, Adelaide, South Australia, Australia, September 27-30). 15p. (ED 399 933)

One of the challenges facing Malaysia amidst its economic development is the achievement of a critical thinking society. This would enhance and guarantee the success of research and development programs in addition to having other socioeconomic effects. This paper covers the following topics: Vision 2020, Malaysia's goal to reach developed nation status by the year 2020; Malaysia's educational system; the role of the government/educational system, school libraries, teachers and schools, public libraries, parents, and schools of library and information science; methods of achieving a critical thinking society; information literacy and systematic information skills; characteristics of a critical thinker; and recommendations for the educational system, information skills program, curriculum, and research. Two appendixes consist of considerations for critical thinking skills for school and classroom management and a diagram of issues related to the implementation of the information skills program.

ERIC Journal Articles (Higher Education)

Atton, C. (1994). Using critical thinking as a basis for library user education. *Journal of Academic Librarianship, (20)*5-6, 310-313. (EJ 497 986)

Critical thinking exercises incorporated into an undergraduate course of bibliographic instruction encourage students to analyze and evaluate information and retrieval methods, thus enabling them to become more effective information users.

Baldwin, G. D. (1994). Designing computer mediated communication into the classroom: The virtual social science laboratory project. *ED-Education at a Distance, (8)*1, J5-J12. (EJ 503 446)

Evaluates the use of computer-mediated communication in a sociology course at Henderson State University (Arkansas). Highlights include information literacy and liberal arts education, critical thinking, computer conferencing on campus networks, online teaching methods and evaluation, student characteristics, electronic mail, privacy and freedom of expression, and future possibilities.

Behrens, S.J. (1994). A conceptual analysis and historical overview of information literacy. *College and Research Libraries, (55)*4, 309-322. (EJ 486 800)

Analyzes definitions of information literacy by reviewing library and information science literature of the 1970s and 1980s. The response of the information profession to the expanding range of skills and knowledge required for information literacy is noted. Three main trends in information literacy from the literature of the early 1990s are identified.

Benson, L. D. (1995). Scholarly research and reference service in the automated environment. *Reference Librarian, (48)*, 57-69. (EJ 508 684)

Discusses the challenges and opportunities facing social science academic reference librarians working with researchers in a rapidly changing technological environment. Highlights include faculty relations and training needs; assistance to graduate students, such as suggestions for bibliographic instruction; information products and user expectations; and problems with information overload.

Bruce, C. S. (1995). Information literacy: A framework for higher education. *Australian Library Journal, (44)*3, 158-170. (EJ 518 344)

Discusses information literacy and presents a theoretical framework for higher education. Highlights include characteristics of an information literate person, including independent self-directed learning and the use of information technology, information literacy education strategies in the academic curriculum, evaluating information literacy education, university administration, staff development, and information services.

Cooper, T., & Burchfield, J. (1995). Information literacy for college and university staff. *Research Strategies, (13)*2, 94-106. (EJ 507 071)

Explores the advantages and difficulties of offering information literacy programs to academic staff who work outside the classroom and the feasibility of integrating sessions into the workplace. Topics include the library's role, the institution's role, exploring user needs, and suggestions for promoting staff information literacy.

Daragan, P., & Stevens, G. (1996). Developing lifelong learners: An integrative and developmental approach to information literacy. *Research Strategies, (14)*2, 68-81. (EJ 528 069)

Describes the first component of a four-year, course-integrated library instruction program based on William Perry's developmental model, which was developed at the U.S. Coast Guard Academy. Results of evaluations comparing pre- and post-test scores show increased student levels of information literacy. An appendix presents a year-by-year outline of program goals.

Dennis, N. (2001). Using inquiry methods to foster information literacy partnerships. *Reference Services Review, (29)*2, 122-131. (EJ 633 187)

Discusses the role of academic librarians in expanding information literacy to teach critical thinking; describes the New Media Classroom (NMC) that teaches how to use primary sources on the Web; and shows applications of NMC inquiry activities in a library setting, including a case study that involved collaboration between the librarian and faculty.

Donaldson, K.A. (2000). Library research success: Designing an online tutorial to teach information literacy skills to first-year students. *Internet and Higher Education, (2)*4, 237-251. (EJ 639 522)

Reports on a collaborative effort between librarians and faculty at Seneca College (Toronto) to develop and implement an online, interactive tutorial for first-year business students that used Web-based technology. Discusses objectives, including increasing student knowledge of library resources to increase levels of information literacy and basic research skills.

Dorner, J. L., Taylor, S. E., & Hodson, C. K. (2001). Faculty-librarian collaboration for nursing information literacy: A tiered approach. *Reference Services Review, (29)*2, 132-140. (EJ 633 188)

Describes a collaborative program between librarians and faculty at Ball State University (Indiana) that designed a tiered approach to building nursing students' research skills to ensure that students have the necessary information literacy skills. Highlights include information literacy competencies, Web-based courses, electronic resources for distance education, and future directions.

Dunn K. (2002). Assessing information literacy skills in the California State University: A progress report. *Journal of Academic Librarianship, (28)*1-2, 26-35. (EJ 656 080)

Describes an information literacy skills assessment project by California State University as part of an accountability process. Highlights include information competence, a qualitative study using information scenarios, capturing what students do when they search for information, and ethnographic data.

Ercegovac, Z. (1998). Information literacy: Teaching now for year 2000. *Reference Services Review, 26*(3-4), 139-142. (EJ 601 873)

Focuses on information literacy (IL), specifically the design of a college course and its high school version intended to equip students with essential IL skills. Discusses current problems in information seeking that correspond to each of the phases of the information life cycle: asking a question, accessing and retrieving information, evaluating, keeping relevant items, and putting them to use.

Eisenberg, M., & Spitzer, K. (1998). The Big6: Not just for kids! Introduction to the Big6: Information problem-solving for upper high school, college-age, and adult students. *Big6 Newsletter, 1*(3), 1, 8-10. (EJ 562 891)

Explains the Big6 approach to information problem solving based on exercises that were developed for college or upper high school students that can be completed during class sessions. Two of the exercises relate to personal information problems, and one relates Big6 skill areas to course assignments.

Forys, M., Foyrs, J., Ford, A., & Dodd, J. (2000). Information literacy program for student athletes at the University of Iowa. *Research Strategies, 17*(4), 353-358. (EJ 656 080)

Describes the goals, content, and history of a program at the University of Iowa libraries for teaching library and information literacy skills to incoming men and women student athletes. Provides an assessment of the value of the librarians' work with student athletes.

George, R., & Luke, R. (1996). The critical place of information literacy in the trend towards flexible delivery in higher education contexts. *Australian Academic & Research Libraries, 27*(3), 204-212. (EJ 532 952)

Higher education is responding to the various learning needs of students through the flexible delivery approach, which focuses on student-centered activities, multiple resources, and lifelong learning. Technology and information literacy enable students to deal with information independently, so they are pivotal for flexible delivery. The role of academic libraries in enhancing student skills is also discussed.

Hawes, D. K. (1994). Information literacy and the business schools. *Journal of Education for Business, 70*(1), 54-61. (EJ 490 532)

Examines information, the information society, information overload, and information literacy and establishes a rationale for why universities—particularly business schools—should be teaching the skills that form the foundation of an information literate person. Concludes that business schools are not doing enough, perhaps because of the lack of attention to this issue by accrediting agencies.

Higgins, C., & Cedar-Face, M. J. (1998). Integrating information literacy skills into the university colloquium: Innovation at Southern Oregon University. *Reference Services Review, 26*(3-4), 17-22. (EJ 601 861)

Outlines the Information Literacy Program at Southern Oregon University (SOU), designed to develop information literacy among freshman enrolled in SOU's new university colloquium. Discusses accomplishments and unresolved problems and issues of this model of a learner-centered, supportive, collaborative program.

Iannuzzi, P. (1998). Faculty development and information literacy: Establishing campus partnerships. *Reference Services Review, 26*(3-4), 97-102. (EJ 601 868)

Addresses the connections between faculty development and information literacy and presents strategies for establishing campus partnerships. Discusses five related topics: information literacy and campus culture, campus initiatives, strategies for partnerships, a faculty development model, and the Florida International University Model for Information Literacy.

Kester, D. D. (1994). Secondary school library and information skills: Are they transferred from high school to college? *Reference Librarian, 44* 9-17. (EJ 488 269)

Discussion of secondary school library and information skills focuses on a study at East Carolina University that was conducted to determine what library skills first-year college students had. Highlights include instruction on library usage in high school, actual library usage, and identification of standard reference terms.

Klavano, A. M., and Kulleseid, E. R. (1995). Bibliographic instruction: Renewal and transformation in one academic library. *Reference Librarian, 51-52* 359-83. (EJ 518 320)

Examines the impact of institutional evaluation on Mercy College (New York) library's bibliographic instruction program and its evolution into an information literacy program responsive to changes in student demographics, curriculum content, assessment methods, and communication technologies. Topics include course-integrated instruction, information literacy assessment, peer tutors, and future directions.

Lawson, M.D. (2000). Reaching the masses: Marketing a library instruction course to incoming freshmen. *Research Strategies, 17*(1), 45-49. (EJ 656 061)

Explains the redesign of a freshman-level course in information literacy, information technology, and library research skills at Central Missouri State University that resulted in an increase in student enrollment. Supports the conclusion that marketing and promotion resulted in higher enrollment figures.

Leckie, G. J. (1996). Desperately seeking citations: Uncovering faculty assumptions about the undergraduate research process. *Journal of Academic Librarianship, 22*(3), 201-208. (EJ 526 298)

Faculty often overestimate the scholarly communication experiences, critical thinking abilities, and information-seeking skills of the undergraduates to whom they assign papers. A stratified methodology is suggested for teaching information retrieval skills in the classroom. A strong curriculum-integrated approach could ease the burden on students and academic librarians.

Leckie, G., & Fullerton, A. (1999). Information literacy in science and engineering undergraduate education: Faculty attitudes and pedagogical practices. *College and Research Libraries, 60*(1), 9-29. (EJ 582 317)

Discusses results of a survey and interviews of science and engineering faculty at two Canadian universities regarding their perceptions of students' information literacy skills and their own pedagogical practices. Faculty awareness of, and support for, bibliographic instruction methods and the perceived role of science and engineering librarians were also investigated.

Macdonald, J., Heap, N., & Mason, R. (2001). "Have I learnt it?" Evaluating skills for resource-based study using electronic resources. *British Journal of Educational Technology, 32*(4), 419-433. (EJ 635 531)

Discussion of electronic information resources and information literacy in higher education focuses on the information handling skills students need and the factors influencing their acquisition in two networked re-source-based courses at the United Kingdom Open University. Offers guidelines for course designers incorporating electronic resources.

Maughan, P. (2001). Assessing information literacy among undergraduates: A discussion of the literature and the University of California-Berkeley assessment experience. *College and Research Libraries, 62*(1), 71-85. (EJ 629 890)

Since 1994, the Teaching Library at the University of California-Berkeley has conducted an ongoing Survey of Information Literacy Competencies in selected academic departments to measure the "lower-order" information literacy skills of graduating seniors. The survey reveals that students think they know more about accessing information and conducting library research than they can demonstrate when put to the test.

Milne, P. A. (1996). Generic skills, group work and the World Wide Web: Ingredients for a creative teaching and learning experience. *Education for Library and Information Services: Australia, 13*(3), 21-36. (EJ 536 205)

To teach generic skills, including communication, information literacy, problem solving, teamwork, professionalism, and lifelong learning, University of Canberra's (Australia) Library and Information Science Program developed Network Information Sources (NIS), a group-based project using technology as the content and facilitator of study. NIS consists of World Wide Web learning modules, home page creation, and group work assessment. Evaluates NIS's outcomes and acceptance.

Nichols, J. (1999). Building bridges: High school and university partnerships for information literacy. *NASSP Bulletin, 83*(605), 75-81. (EJ 585 579)

Since most undergraduates at Wayne State University are from the Detroit area, staff decided to communicate with area schools about expectations for incoming freshmen and provide high-school/university curriculum articulation. Four schools successfully participated in a pilot project investigating how a university library/high-school partnership could achieve these goals

Orr, D., et al. (1996). Teaching information literacy skills to remote students through an interactive workshop. *Research Strategies, 14*(4), 224-233. (EJ 538 032)

A program was designed at the Central Queensland University (Australia) Library to teach on- and off-campus students how to access and explore databases, to encourage skill development through learning exercises, and to facilitate peer interaction and discussion of search strategies and techniques. Student evaluation indicated that the program offered distinct benefits.

Otero-Boisvert, M. (1993). The role of the collection development librarian in the 90's and beyond. *Journal of Library Administration, 18*(3-4), 159-170. (EJ 476 169)

   Explores the changing role of the collection development librarian in relation to the issues of budgetary constraints and the impact of electronic technology on academic research. The characteristics, skills, and knowledge required on the job are defined, and different approaches to acquiring them are offered.

Page, M., and Kesselman, M. (1994). Teaching the Internet: Challenges and opportunities. *Research Strategies, 12*(3), 157-167. (EJ 493 295)

   Describes distinctions between networked and traditional information resources, explains how these affect user education, and discusses how to transform traditional library instruction into meaningful network education. The nature of the Internet, the librarian's role, staff training, user instruction, using the network to teach, and opportunities for collaboration are covered.

Pennycook, A. (1996). Borrowing others' words: Text, ownership, memory, and plagiarism. *TESOL Quarterly, 30*(2), 201-230. (EJ 529 487)

   Considers some of the complexities of text, ownership, memorization, and plagiarism. The article suggests that plagiarism needs to be understood in terms of complex relationships between text, memory, and learning as part of an undertaking to explore different relationships between learning, literacy, and cultural difference.

Rader, H. B. (1994). Library orientation and instruction—1992. *Reference Services Review, 22*(2), 79-95. (EJ 486 753)

   This annotated list of materials dealing with information literacy includes publications on user instruction in academic libraries (140 titles), public libraries (4 titles), school libraries (56 titles), and special libraries (11 titles) and for all levels of users (6 titles). Statistics regarding the numbers of publications are discussed.

Rader, H. B. (1995). Information literacy and the undergraduate curriculum. *Library Trends, 44*(2), 270-278. (EJ 513 796)

   Discusses the integration of information and technological skills into the undergraduate curriculum. Topics include information literacy; the role of the academic library in higher education reform; information literacy criteria for undergraduates; and examples of successful curriculum integration programs at Earlham College, the University of Wisconsin-Parkside, and Cleveland State University.

Rader, H. B. (1998). Library instruction and information literacy—1997. *Reference Services Review, 26*(3-4), 143-160. (EJ 601 874)

This annotated bibliography of titles published in 1997 (in English) lists materials dealing with information literacy, including instruction in the use of information resources, research, and electronic skills related to retrieving, using, and evaluating information. Titles are presented in the categories of Academic Libraries, Public Libraries, School Libraries, Special Libraries, All Levels, and Web Sites.

Rieh, S.Y. (2002). Judgment of information quality and cognitive authority in the Web. *Journal of the American Society for Information Science and Technology, 53*(2), 145-161 (EJ 643 518)

Describes a study conducted at Rutgers University that examined the problem of the judgment of information quality and cognitive authority by observing users' searching behavior on the Web, and the effects of those judgments on selection behaviors. Discusses implications for Web design and suggests future research.

Rosen, J., & Castro, G. M. (2002) From workbook to Web: Building an information literacy OASIS. *Computers in Libraries, 22*(1), 30-35. (EJ 645 619)

Describes a Web-based information literacy tutorial, OASIS (Online Advancement of Student Information Skills), developed at San Francisco State University. Discussion includes core competencies identified, design structure and content, planning and marketing, problems and partnerships in the pilot year of OASIS, restructuring the OASIS tutorial, and future plans.

Roth, L. (1999). Educating the cut-and-paste generation. *Library Journal, 124*(18), 42-44. (EJ 599 802)

Discusses teaching information literacy in academic libraries and describes programs developed at California State University that considered new technologies; changing student characteristics, enrollment patterns, and skills; determining authenticity and quality of information sources, particularly on the Internet; curriculum development; faculty-librarian partnerships; assessing information competency; information outreach; and fostering critical thinking.

Ruess, D. E. (1994). Library and information literacy: A core curriculum component. *Research Strategies, 12*(1), 18-23. (EJ 483 735)

Reviews the literature on library and information literacy and describes the development of an undergraduate core course on library and information skills at the University of Alaska, Fairbanks. The bibliographic instruction component is explained, and assessment of the course after the first year is discussed.

Scholz-Crane, A. (1998). Evaluating the future: A preliminary study of the process of how undergraduate students evaluate Web sources. *Reference Services Review, 26*(3-4), 53-60. (EJ 601 865)

Examines current practices among students in an entry-level university composition class to gain insight into how students evaluate Web information and what implications this might have for teaching students to enhance their existing evaluation skills.

Sonntag, G., & Ohr, D. M. (1996). The development of a lower division, general education, course integrated information literacy program. *College & Research Libraries, 57*(4), 331-338. (EJ 537 864)

Presents a model for a course on information literacy that was developed by librarians at California State University at San Marcos. Topics include the role of the library in higher education reform, active learning activities, convincing faculty and administrators of the need for information literacy courses, and future implementation.

Stoffle, C. J. (1998). Literacy 101 for the digital age. *American Libraries, 29*(11), 46-48. (EJ 582 146)

Discusses information literacy and information technology literacy, focusing on the responsibility of academic libraries to impart necessary skills. A sidebar by Kimberley M. Donnely, "Learning from the Teaching Libraries," gives examples of four models of information literacy development by colleges and universities.

Tiefel, V. (1993). The gateway to information: The future of information access . . . today. *Library Hi-Tech, 11*(4), 57-65, 74. (EJ 476 240)

Describes a microcomputer program that serves as a front end to an online library catalog and other information sources and provides guidance to students on searching for and evaluating information. Funding, technology, evaluation, impact on other libraries, and future plans are discussed. Sample screens are included.

Tompkins, P. (1996). Quality in community college libraries. *Library Trends, 44*(3), 506-525. (EJ 520 152)

Examines indicators of quality in academic and research libraries, especially community college libraries. Topics include standards of the Association of College and Research Libraries; standards of the business community, including Total Quality Management; quality management as systemic change; impediments to quality; and information literacy.

Tompkins, P., Perry, S., & Lippincott, J. K. (1998). New learning communities: Collaboration, networking, and information literacy. *Information Technology and Libraries, 17*(2), 100-106. (EJ 577 928)

Discusses the New Learning Communities (NLC) program developed by CNI (Coalition for Networked Information) to support pioneers in education who use networking and networked information to support student-centered teaching and learning. Highlights include computer networks in higher education, especially the Internet; information literacy skills; and collaborative learning and teaching.

Wallace, M. C., Shorten, A., & Crookes, P.A. (2000). Teaching information literacy skills: An evaluation. *Nurse Education Today, 20*(6), 485-489. (EJ 612 533)

Comparison of 55 nursing students who completed an information literacy program integrated into the curriculum with 72 who did not showed that participating students improved library and information skills from pre- to post-test. No significant differences between participants and nonparticipants were found.

Wallace, M. C., Shorten, A., Crookes, P. A., McGurk, C., & Brewer, C. (1999). Integrating information literacies into an undergraduate nursing programme. *Nurse Education Today, 19*(2), 136-141. (EJ 581 080)

Information literacy learning is integrated into a nursing curriculum in Australia to ensure incremental development resulting from learning experiences. A series of learning activities is related to multidimensional assessment tasks, building on each level of skill.

Walter, S. (2000). Engelond: A model for faculty-librarian collaboration in the information age. *Information Technology and Libraries, 19*(1), 34-41. (EJ 616 716)

Reports on the success of a pilot program at the University of Missouri-Kansas City library in course-integrated information literacy instruction in the field of medieval studies that stresses critical thinking skills to properly evaluate Web sites. Discusses faculty-librarian collaboration and future collaboration possibilities.

Whitmire, E. (2001). Factors influencing undergraduates' self-reported satisfaction with their information literacy skills. *Libraries and the Academy, 1*(4), 409-420. (EJ 647 524)

Investigated factors influencing undergraduates' self-reported satisfaction with their information literacy skills at the University of Wisconsin-Madison. Regression analysis revealed that students of color, students satisfied with campus library facilities, and students engaged in interactions with faculty reported greatest satisfaction with their progress. Considers implications for the redesign of academic library services.

Wilson, V. (1994). Developing the adult independent learner: Information literacy and the remote external student. *Distance Education, 15*(2), 254-278. (EJ 501 725)

Analyzes current opinion on the development of information literacy skills among adult higher education students. Highlights include lifelong learning; information literacy and the role of the academic librarian; adult learning theory; defining information skills; and information literacy and the external student, including continuing education, open learning, and distance education.

Wilson, V. (1994). Information literacy and remote external students: Exploring the possibilities offered by new communications technologies. *Australian Academic and Research Libraries, 25*(4), 247-252. (EJ 499 899)

A study was conducted at Edith Cowan University on providing information literacy education to remote students through communication technology. Highlights include educational theory, information literacy, and the role of the library; attitudes to external study and library use; attitudes and access to technology; confidence levels in information seeking tasks; and future directions.

Winkler, S., & Abramson, G. (2001). Organization of the first information literacy workshop. *Journal of Instruction Delivery Systems, 15*(2), 6-9. (EJ 637 549)

Describes the Infolit (Information Literacy) Internet Workshop, designed to discuss information literacy and to stimulate interaction between the public and private sectors. Highlights include workplace requirements; new training, assessment, and support systems that will be needed; business, college, and government roles; information technology use; and the role of teachers.

Zhang, W. (2001). Building partnerships in liberal arts education: Library team teaching. *Reference Services Review, 29*(2), 141-149. (EJ 633 189)

Examines the framework for library bibliographic instruction, analyzes current information literacy initiatives, and reviews efforts of the library at Rollins College (Florida) in promoting active learning and critical thinking skills through partnerships with classroom faculty and professionals of information technology and services, including team teaching and using the Web for research.

Zhang, W. (2002). Developing Web-enhanced learning for information fluency: A liberal arts college's perspective. *Reference and User Services Quarterly, 41*(4), 356-363. (EJ 656 093)

Describes the development of a one-credit Web-enhanced course at Rollins College (Florida) library that encompasses information literacy, basic computer literacy, and critical thinking skills. Topics include benefits to students, including learning at their own pace and communication with students and instructors, and the need to keep educational objectives in mind.

ERIC Documents (Higher Education)

Abbott, W., & Peach, D. (2000) Building info-skills by degrees: Embedding information literacy in university study. In *Virtual libraries: Virtual communities*. Given at the International Association of Technological University Libraries (IATUL) Conference (Brisbane, Queensland, Australia, July 3-7, 2000); see IR 057 942. (ED 447 821)

This paper provides an overview of a project at Griffith University (Queensland, Australia). The Griffith Graduate Project was conceived in 1999 as a student-centered process that would facilitate the development of generic and professional skills over the life cycle of an undergraduate degree program. The first strategy involved a series of workshops with approximately 110 first-year students in the School of Applied Psychology. Students were asked to rate themselves across nine generic skills areas: self-management, interpersonal, problem-solving and decision-making, analysis and critical evaluation, adaptability and learning, teamwork, oral communication, information, and written communication. Following this awareness-raising process, approximately half the students signed up for voluntary library research workshops on catalog, database, and Internet searching; very few of these students availed themselves of the self-paced World Wide Web-based Library Research Tutorial. The second strategy of the project was the development of a Web-based resource directory. The third student-centered strategy was the Professional Portfolio, an electronic resource file that will enable students to organize and track their experiences and achievements and to critically reflect on their current level or stage of development. The integration and development of information literacy as a generic attribute in the curriculum, as well as future directions for the project, is also discussed.

American Library Association. (1995). *Information for a new age: Redefining the librarian.* A Library Instruction Round Table (LIRT) 15th anniversary publication. Compiled by the Fifteenth Anniversary Task Force. Chicago: Author. (ED 379 006). Document not available from EDRS.

Bibliographic instruction (BI), which focuses on the need to make library patrons become more proficient in locating and using information, is a major contributor to information literacy. The 14 papers and essays in this volume describe approaches to proactive interaction with library users with the single goal of achieving an information literate society. The articles included are "Information for a New Age: Fantastic Technology or Institutionalized Alienation?" (Robert Silverberg); "Librarians or Technicians? Which Shall We Be?" (Deanna B. Marcum); "The Death of the Librarian in the (Post) Modern Electronic Information Age" (Robert K. Kieft); "Bibliographic Instruction, Briefly" (Evan Ira Farber); "Information Literacy and Public Libraries: A Community-Based Approach" (Susan Jackson); "The Instructional Role of the Library Media Specialist in the Information-Age School" (Carol C. Kuhlthau); "Education for the Academic Library User in the Year 2000" (Virginia Tiefel); "Library Instruction for Special Libraries: Present and Future" (Mignon Strickland Adams); "Information Literacy" (American Library Association); "Avoiding the Cereal Syndrome; or, Critical Thinking in the Electronic Environment" (Cerise Oberman); "Building Coalitions for Information Literacy" (Abigail Loomis); "Conversation 101: Process, Development, and Collaboration" (Janice A. Sauer); "Expanding the Evaluation Role in the Critical-Thinking Curriculum" (Daniel Callison); and "BI and the Twenty-First Century: An Opinion" (Leigh A. Kilman). A 31-item annotated bibliography is organized around the following themes: technology, libraries, and the future; technology and information literacy; technology and remote users; and the human-machine interface (social and psychological factors). A list of Library Instruction Round Table (LIRT) 15th Anniversary Task Force members and an index are also provided.

Baintin, T. (2001) Information literacy and academic libraries: The SCONUL approach (UK/Ireland). In *Libraries and librarians: Making a difference in the knowledge age.* Council and General Conference: Conference Programme and Proceedings (67th, Boston, MA, August 16-25, 2001); see IR 058 199. (ED 459 713)

Discussions of "skills" in higher education often conflate "information technology" (IT) skills and "information skills". The second term is broader and more directly related to the aims and processes of higher education as a "knowledge creation" activity. A clear distinction should be made between information skills and IT skills. Both information skills and IT skills are essential parts of a wider concept of information literacy. A broadly based definition of information skills in higher education reflects twin dimensions of the "competent student" and the "information literate" person. For the development of the information literate person, the United Kingdom's Standing Conference of National and University Libraries (SCONUL) proposes seven sets of skills developing from a basic competence in library and IT skills, which include the ability to (1) recognize a need for information; (2) distinguish ways in which the information gap may be addressed; (3) construct strategies for location information; (4) locate and access information; (5) compare and evaluate information obtained from different sources; (6) organize, apply, and communicate information to others in ways appropriate to the situation; and (7) synthesize and build upon existing information, contributing to the creation of new knowledge.

Baker, B., & Litzinger, M. E. (Eds.). (1992). *The evolving educational mission of the library*. Chicago: Association of College and Research Libraries, Bibliographic Instruction Section. 202p. (ED 365 347)

At the 1989 annual meeting of the American Library Association (ALA), the Association of College and Research Libraries (ACRL) used a think tank as a dynamic mechanism for exploring future directions both in the discipline of library user education and for the Bibliographic Instruction (BI) Section of ACRL. Discussion centered on the following issues: primary user groups and how they have changed during the past decade, how the curricular reform movement affects the content of bibliographic instruction programs, the appropriateness of information literacy as a phrase to characterize BI librarians' instructional programs for the upcoming decade, and how professional education programs in library and information science can respond to changes. The four discussion issues suggested necessary change or transition, particularly for BI, but more broadly affecting reference and public service, library missions and goals, and the educational focus of the library and information science profession. The eight papers included in the collection are (1) "Bridging the Gap between the Think Tanks" (Donald Kenney); (2) "The Think Tank Papers: Are We in the Ball Park?" (Elizabeth Frick); (3) "Changing Users: Bibliographic Instruction for Whom?" (Lizabeth A. Wilson); (4) "The Changing User and the Future of Bibliographic Instruction: A Perspective from the Health Sciences Library" (James Shedlock); (5) "Curriculum Reform: The Role of Academic Libraries" (Maureen Pastine and Linda Wilson); (6) "Information Literacy: One Response to the New Decade" (Hannelore Rader and William Coons); (7) "Education for the Second Generation of Bibliographic Instruction Librarians" (Martha L. Hale); and (8) "The Future of Bibliographic Instruction and Information Literacy for the Academic Librarian" (William Miller). "Educational Roles of Academic Libraries: State of the Art and an Agenda for the Future" (Randall Hensley and Beth Sandore), a summary document from the conference, is appended.

Beaudoin, M., et al. (1993). *Position paper on learning resource centres and their future in the Ontario Community College System: A technology perspective*. Barrie, ONT: Georgian College of Applied Arts and Technology. 21p. (ED 374 801)

The Learning Resource Centres (LRCs) of Ontario (Canada) are in the midst of a technological metamorphosis unprecedented in their 25-year history. The LRCs are becoming centers for independent, self-paced, experiential learning, places in which students actively create, evaluate, experience, and interpret a world of information through technology. LRCs in Ontario are being influenced by national, provincial, and local trends. As they adopt a broader vision of the future, they plan for important roles in (1) information literacy, (2) alternative learning, (3) software, (4) production, (5) instructional telecommunications, (6) distance education, (7) curriculum design and delivery, and (8) classroom design. Few of the Ontario LRCs are structurally, financially, or technologically prepared for their new and expanded roles. A transformed role for the LRCs implies significant change in alternative learning, information literacy, leadership, access, standards, staff training, and funding.

Beaupre, B. (2000, November). Blending cultural, academic, and technological communication: Literacy for the new millennium. *Research in Education.* (ED 441 234)

A combination of traditional reading, media, and Internet information sources is necessary in today's educational sphere to bridge cultural differences, engage students' realms of experience, and promote academic and cultural literacy. A key issue for educators today is to utilize and extend the vehicles students are currently using to enhance critical thinking skills. Students often come to basic writing classes as academic outsiders, literate in their neighborhoods, often technologically socialized, but lacking the literacy of higher learning. The kinds of literacy skills students must have to function in today's world include an understanding of intertextuality, a validation of many kinds of texts, and the ability to sort through positions on a topic. Discussion about contradictory visual images such as in advertisements can show how information affects response and how a range of sources is needed to draw reasonable conclusions. Students must be taught to evaluate the media sources they use in relationship to other printed information.

Book, D., et al. (1999) *Concept, challenge, conundrum: Library skills to information literacy. Proceedings of the National Information Literacy Conference Conducted by the University of South Australia Library and the Australian Library and Information Association Information Literacy Special Interest Group* (4th, Adelaide, Australia, December 3-5, 1999). Underdale, South Australia: Library Publications. (ED 443 439). Document not available from EDRS)

These proceedings from the fourth National Information Literacy Conference (December 1999) include the keynote addresses and the papers presented in workshop sessions throughout the conference. Acknowledgments by Irene Doskatsch, conference convener, precede the introductory piece by Alan Bundy, "Journey Without End . . .", followed by these papers: "Information Literacy and the Foundations for Lifelong Learning" (Denis Ralph); Keynote Address: "What All Librarians Can Learn from Teacher Librarians: Information Literacy a Key Connector for Libraries" (Ken Haycock); Keynote Address: Information Literacy: Concept, Conundrum, and Challenge (Ross Todd); "Teaching Information Literacy Skills to Indigenous Adults" (Joanne Anderson); "The Role of the Library in an Integrated Computer and Information Literacy Program at Swinburne University of Technology" (Julie Badger); "Why Won't They Use Our Library? Implications of a Pilot Study Investigating the Information Seeking Preferences of Secondary School Teachers" (Julia Bale); "Second Thoughts about Information Literacy" (Susan Boyce); "Integrating Information Literacy into the Health Sciences Curriculum: Longitudinal Study of an Information Literacy Program at the University of Wollongong" (Chris Brewer); "Information and Information Technology Use in Undergraduate Legal Education" (Natalie Cuffe and Christine Bruce); "Information Literacy Lessons from EdNA Online" (Jillian Dellit); "Putting It Online: Information Research Skills for Postgraduates" (Anne Douglas and Lynn Murdoch); "Changing the Mindset: Creating Information Literate Engineers" (Anne Draper and Leith Woodall); "Internet Sources for Lifelong Learning: A Model for Incorporating a Web Component into a Course" (Carole Duffill); "The Dream Student...A Case Study of an Information Literacy Model for Higher Education" (Robin Graham and Justine Lester); "Too Easy—"Web-ezy": an Interactive Library Skills Package" (Garry Hall); "Subject Specialist or Information Expert?" (Liz Hartmann and Kerry Matheson); "Improving Information Skills Programs Using Action Research" (Claire Hill); "An Australian Information Literacy Institute Proposal" (Diana Kingston); "Cooperation and Information Skills Resources" (Diana Kingston); "Striking the Right Balance: Information Literacy and Partnerships between Librarian, Lecturer, and Student" (Maureen Nimon); "Getting Information Literacy into the Curriculum: The Ongoing Dilemma, and How To Be Involved When You Are on the Edge" (Graeme Oke and Jenny Cameron); "Information Literacy and Health Science: Developing a Comprehensive and Sustainable Model" (Debbie Orr, Margie Wallin, Leone Hinton); "Profiling an Information Literature Law Firm" (Carmel O'Sullivan); "From Trainers to Educators: Librarians and the Challenge of Change" (Judith Peacock); "Integration of Information Skills into the School Curriculum at Trinity Lutheran College" (Sharon Rushton); "Information Literacy Competency Standards Workshop" (Patricia Iannuzzi); and Panel Session, "What Is the Challenge?" (Ross Todd, Ken Haycock, Carmel O'Sullivan, Linda Langford, Alan Bundy).

Booker, D., (Ed.). (1992). *Information literacy: The Australian agenda.* Pro-
ceedings of a conference conducted by the University of South Australia
Library (Adelaide, South Australia, Australia, December 2-4, 1992).
Underdale: University of South Australia. 193p. (ED 365 336)

   The aims of this conference were to promote information literacy as a
means of personal and national advancement in today's information-de-
pendent society, to emphasize information literacy as an essential competency for lifelong learning, to ensure that all delegates understand
information literacy and its importance for the economic and social
well-being of their community, to develop cross sectoral cooperation in
promoting information literacy, to establish a broad-based national coalition for information literacy, and to identify the agenda for change needed
across education and information sectors to raise the level of information
literacy. The following papers are included: (1) "Information Literacy:
What's It All About" (Patricia Senn Breivik); (2) "Information Literacy:
Why Worry?" (Rodney Cavalier); (3) "What's the Government Saying?"
(Anne Hazell); (4) "The Learning Society" (Philip Candy); (5) "Establishing the Agenda for Change" (Richard Owen); and (6) "What Can We Learn
from the US Experience?" (Patricia Senn Breivik). Also included are the
proceedings of 16 workshops and 76 recommendations from the workshops, which provide the agenda for action on issues relating to information literacy in Australia. These recommendations address social justice,
staff development, preservice training, research, partnerships and networks, economic development, advocacy, curriculum/methodology
change, and supporting informal learning. Most of the papers contain
references.

Breivik, P. S. (2000) *Information literacy for the skeptical library director.* In
Virtual libraries: Virtual communities. Abstracts, Fulltext Documents and
PowerPoint Presentations of Papers and Demos Given at the International
Association of Technological University Libraries (IATUL) Conference
(Brisbane, Queensland, Australia, July 3-7, 2000); see IR 057 942. (ED 447
823)

   This paper begins by providing background on the information literacy movement, including the educational reform efforts of the 1980s, a
higher education summit conference, and the 1989 American Library Association (ALA) Presidential Committee on Information Literacy *Final Report.* Other highlights are discussion of the information literacy triangle,
providing universal access by getting the Internet into all schools and public libraries, the need for funding to educate people to take advantage of
technological advancements, definitions of information literacy, a
UNESCO report addressing the importance of lifelong learning; the Global

Knowledge Partnership; and the efforts of the National Forum on Information Literacy. The following practical steps for academic library directors are suggested: (1) Take time to think through the concept of information literacy, (2) ask questions about information literacy on campus, (3) find out what the barriers to information literacy are, and (4) celebrate successes.

Brown, L. S. (1996). *Development, implementation, and evaluation of an information literacy program for the Undergraduate School at Philadelphia College of Bible.* Ed.D. Practicum Applied Research Project, Nova Southeastern University. 130p. (ED 402 933)

One of the requirements for students majoring in Bible in the undergraduate school of Philadelphia College of Bible (Pennsylvania) is writing research papers. The papers are designed to promote information literacy by developing research skills, sharpening writing skills, encouraging critical thinking, and promoting problem-solving skills. However, students are not adequately prepared to write their research papers—the first-year English composition course spends only limited time on research strategies and the utilization of specific tools in the library, and students lack critical thinking skills. This study details the creation of a curriculumwide information literacy program. A literature review enabled the development of a library committee questionnaire, academic affairs committee proposal, revised student writing guide, information literacy program booklet, and faculty workshop presentation. The study investigated (1) how other institutions of higher education are meeting students' information literacy needs; (2) how faculty members should be prepared to participate in the program; (3) how students will complete research papers while participating in the program; and (4) how the information literacy program should be implemented and evaluated. Appendixes include the questionnaire, responses, proposal to the academic affairs committee, revised student writing guide, information literacy program booklet, faculty workshop outline, and information literacy evaluation packet.

Brown, L. S., & Ryan, G. J. (1994). *Development of an information literacy program for the Degree Completion Program at Philadelphia College of Bible.* Ed.D. Practicum, Nova Southeastern University. 126p. (ED 402 932)

One of the major requirements in the degree completion program at Philadelphia College of Bible (Pennsylvania) is the completion of a major research paper. The paper is designed to develop research skills, sharpen writing skills, encourage critical thinking, and promote problem-solving skills. Students were not adequately prepared by either the writing guide or the curriculum to write their major research paper. The writing guide was too long and complicated, and the curriculum modules were not designed to encourage research skills or complement the writing assignment. This study describes the creation of an information literacy program for the degree completion program. The degree completion program provides an opportunity for full-time working individuals to graduate with a baccalaureate degree after 22 months of study. Three faculty and student guides were written or revised to provide direction for the information literacy program. The faculty guide was written to provide faculty with definitions, guidelines, and instructions for teaching the information literacy program. The student guide was revised to include a section on basic research skills and instruction on how to write the research paper required for graduation. The library research guide was revised to coordinate the instruction of the faculty guide with the research skills necessary for completion of the student project. Appendixes include the student and faculty guides and a library research handbook.

Brown, L. S., & Ryan, G. J. (1995). *The relationship of time to effectiveness in research skills instruction for students at Philadelphia College of Bible.* Ed.D. Practicum, Nova Southeastern University. 164p. (ED 402 931)

One of the many requirements for students majoring in Bible in the undergraduate program at Philadelphia College of Bible (Pennsylvania) is writing papers. The papers are designed to develop research skills, sharpen writing skills, encourage critical thinking, and promote problem-solving skills. However, students are not adequately prepared to write their papers. The first-year English composition course attempts to develop research skills but spends only limited time on research strategy. The director of the Learning Resource Center is given one hour to present a session on research strategies and give a brief library tour. This study compares the results of teaching three hours of research skills with the results of teaching one hour of research skills. Four sections of first-year English composition students were given a pre-test to gauge their research skills. Two sections received one hour of library instruction, and two sections received three hours of library instruction. A post-test was administered to all students. No significant difference was found in the post-test results between students who received one hour of library instruction and students who received three hours of instruction. Possible reasons for the findings are discussed. Appendixes include the pre- and post-test, one- and three-hour curricula, one- and three-hour worksheets, and test scores.

Bundy, A. (1998). Information literacy: The key competency for the 21st century. In *The challenge to be relevant in the 21st century:* Abstracts and Fulltext Documents of Papers and Demos Given at the [International Association of Technological University Libraries] IATUL Conference (Pretoria, South Africa, June 1-5, 1998), Volume 18; see IR 057 503. (ED 434 662)

This paper examines Australian progress in addressing the implications of two certainties about the twenty-first century: Change will be a constant, and it will be a century of data and information abundance. The focus is on the higher education sector, consisting of 36 public and two private universities. Topics discussed include (1) characteristics of Australian higher education; (2) challenges for libraries; (3) Information Fatigue Syndrome, that is, ill health as a result of information overload; (4) education at a crossroads—changes in the role of education because of the information explosion; (5) lifelong learning; (6) changing the educational paradigm, including development of information skills and information literacy as a goal of higher education; (7) the need for research on information literacy; (8) information literacy as the "zeitgeist" of the times, that is, an idea whose time has come; (9) the marketing of information literacy; (10) a strategic response to ensure that, by 2000, every educator, educational administrator, and librarian in Australia has heard of information literacy; (11) Australian information literacy conferences; (12) summaries of two conference papers on information literacy; (13) information literacy and library competencies; (14) highlights of two Australian government reports on information literacy; and (15) response of Australian university libraries to information literacy and their potential role as educational change agents.

Bunz, U. K., and Sypher, H. E. (2001). *The Computer-Email-Web (CEW) fluency scale—Development and validation.* Paper presented at the Annual Meeting of the National Communication Association (87th, Atlanta, GA, November 1-4, 2001). Previous version of paper contributed to the Annual German Online Research Conference (4th, Goettingen, Germany, May 17-18, 2001). (ED 458 657)

Information fluency is generally defined as an ability to express oneself creatively, reformulate knowledge, and synthesize information regarding new information technology. The term has recently gained popularity over "experience," "expertise," "competence," "knowledge," and "literacy." As with other related concepts, there is a great need to accurately assess "information fluency" for research and pragmatic purposes. This study seeks to address this need by developing a self-report instrument to tap this theoretical concept. The paper explores existing computer competence scales (very few of which even include e-mail or Internet components), reviews the emerging literature on information fluency, and reports about the development of a new Computer-Email-Web Fluency instrument. Evidence of the reliability and validity of the instrument is presented, based on data from students enrolled in basic public speaking courses.

Burkhardt, J., MacDonald, M., Rathemacher, A., Kelland, J.L., & Vocina, M. (2000). *Plan for information literacy at the University of Rhode Island.* Submitted by the Library Strategic Planning Task Force for Teaching and Research, University of Rhode Island. (ED 455 849)

The past five years have seen enormous change in the style of reference work that is done by librarians at the University of Rhode Island (URI) Library. Before the arrival of publicly accessible online databases and catalogs, there were clear lines regarding "doing reference" and teaching how to use the library. Now efforts are more directed toward teaching the URI community how to approach the wide array of resources available to them. With this in mind, the Task Force for Teaching and Research recommends a collective shift from thinking of reference and teaching as separate but related activities to restructuring into a Teaching Library where services are actively promoted as the bridge to information empowerment—to be the link between classroom and information resources. The goal of the Information Literacy Plan described in this document is not to undo the current program in library instruction but to expand and fortify it. This Plan outlines the coordination of information literacy efforts, including what the Library Curriculum Committee will be charged with; ways that the information literacy needs of URI students will be addressed; delivery options for addressing the information literacy needs and awareness of URI faculty; objectives of the Information Literacy Program; a chart outlining information literacy concepts that need to be covered throughout the program/curriculum; delivery options through which these concepts can be taught at URI; and suggested implementation at URI for each year of undergraduate study and for graduate students.

Burnheim, R. (1991). *Curriculum influences on reader education in the TAFE environment.* 12p. (ED 356 771)

This paper describes competency-based training and open learning, two methods of teaching/learning that are having a significant effect on the education offered through Australia's Technical and Further Education (TAFE) program. The paper defines competency-based training and open learning and details the broad impact they are having on resource services delivered through the TAFE college library. Two approaches to providing learners with research process skills that will harmonize with these teaching/ learning methods are described. They include developing a team approach to research and developing thinking skills in concert with the processing of information. The last section of the paper describes how the TAFE libraries can promote their role in the development of informed information users.

Burnheim, R. (1993). *Information literacy: The TAFE scene.* Technical and Further Education-TEQ, Queensland (Australia). Library Network Branch. 11p. (ED 368 377)

The concept of information literacy is explored and the major issues to be developed in its pursuit of technical and further education (TAFE) in Australia are considered. Information literate people are those who have learned how to learn because they know how knowledge is organized, how to find it, and how to use it so that others can learn from them. Australia faces strong competition to remain a viable competitor in the international market. The new types of education and education delivery systems that are developing are essential to the nation's preparedness in the age of information literacy. Research has identified competencies that are required for the information literate. Library activities conducted by TAFE college libraries in Australia are summarized. A major accomplishment is the development of teaching modules in the area of information literacy. Pilot versions have been forwarded to all TAFE libraries in Queensland for testing and evaluation.

Burnheim, R. K. (1993). *The questions that they ask.* 19p. (ED 368 379)

This paper discusses the competencies that are required to work effectively with information. It examines the nature of the information resources and how students interact with them. The discussion moves to the types of questions students have asked and suggests that the predominant types may not be assisting students in developing information usage skills, thus not improving their mastery of a skill set such as that proposed by R. J. Marzano and R. W. Ewy (1989). Reviews of research have indicated that teachers often do not ask questions that require students to work with information resources, relying instead on questions that merely ask for the recall of knowledge. The challenge is for teachers to more frequently pose questions that encourage students to use the problem-solving approaches they will need in the world of the future. The rapid redundancy of information means that no institution can give its students all the knowledge they will need, but students can be given the skills to update and refine their knowledge. Two figures illustrate the discussion.

Carr, J. (1998). *Information literacy and teacher education.* ERIC Digest. Washington, DC. ERIC Clearinghouse on Teaching and Teacher Education. 4p. (ED 424 231)

Teachers cannot prepare their students to be information literate unless they themselves understand how to find and use information. This Digest discusses the concept of information literacy (the ability to access, evaluate, and use information from a variety of sources) and its relevance for teachers. Professional associations for K–12 and higher education have recognized the importance of information literacy to the teaching-learning process. Two major associations for librarians who work with preservice and inservice teachers have developed guidelines on what information literate teachers need to know. The guidelines emphasize skills for searching, retrieving, and evaluating information, and developing strategies for locating databases, Internet resources, and print materials. Existing models for teachers' information literacy include individual workshops for both preservice and inservice teachers, course-related and course-integrated instruction, and the use of case studies of teaching and learning situations. Teacher educators, teachers, and others interested in preparing K–12 students to be information literate can move forward by reflecting upon and adapting existing models.

Carstarphen, M. G. (1995). *New media literacy: From classroom to community.* Paper presented at the Annual Meeting of the Conference on College Composition and Communication (46th, Washington, DC, March 23-25, 1995). 12p. (ED 387 842)

Each new media revolution forces adjustments for both the producers of messages and the receivers of those messages. Integral to the communication process is an understanding of what it means to be literate in an eclectic communication environment and of how the new media may enhance or impede literacy. An important premise for this discussion is that there must be a correlation between two concepts: what it means to be "media literate" (savvy to the processes and protocol of the media) and what it means to be "literate through media" (using the media as conduits to achieve heightened proficiencies in the basic literacy skills of reading, writing and comprehension). "Surfing" one of the incarnations of the new media, the Internet, a researcher asked six respondents questions about literacy and computers. The respondents were two university administrators, two media managers/publishers, a corporate librarian, and an independent writer/teacher. Responses, thought not scientifically solicited, were revealing, and in may ways closely reiterated the Electronic Frontier Foundation's co-founder John Barlow's vision of the transformation of information from product to process. Questions ranged from what media the respondents had encountered through their jobs to how they would define literacy and whether they thought it was in need of redefinition in light of the new media. Most significant results showed that the respondents believed that media and literacy, whether old or new, all involve one thing: the transmittal of information. This transmittal calls for basic skills like the ability to read and write and think critically.

The EDUTECH Report. The education technology newsletter for faculty and administrators. *EDUTECH Report, 9*(1-12) (April 1993-March 1994). 97p. (ED 387 127)

This newsletter examines education technology issues of concern to school faculty and administrators. Regular features in each issue include educational technology news, a book review, and a question and answer column. The cover articles during this volume year are "The Build or Buy Decision: No One Right Answer"; "The National Information Infrastructure" (Bernard W. Gleason); "Information Literacy: Liberal Education for the Information Age" (Patricia Senn Breivik and Dan L. Jones); "The Role of the CIO in the Curriculum Change Process" (John Swearingen); "Seven Basic Principles of Dealing With Vendors"; "Hot Issues 1993-94"; "The Many Layers of Reengineering"; "How to Do A Help Desk Right"; "Do Computers Help Students Learn?" (G. Phillip Cartright); "The One Right Answer for Higher Education"; "Focus on the Foundation: Decision Support Will Happen"; and "Campuses Need Not Wait to Enter Cyberspace" (John V. Lombardi).

Fridie, S. (1994). *Information seeking behavior and user education in academic libraries: Research, theory, and practice. A selected list of information sources.* 88p. (ED 371 766)

This document lists sources useful for academic reference and instruction librarians who are concerned with assisting and teaching novice or nonprofessional end-user searchers. The bibliography is organized in two lists: complete bibliographic citations and subject listing of references. The types of sources listed include journal articles, books, conference proceedings, doctoral dissertations, and ERIC documents. The subject listing of references is organized into four parts. Part I, "Information Seeking Behavior," covers information needs, the research process, the search process, and retrieval performance. Part II, "Psychological Aspects of Information Seeking Behavior," includes psychological theories and research methods, affective factors and anxiety, cognitive factors, user needs and user studies, user-intermediary interaction, human-computer interaction, and individual differences and searching styles. Part III, "Characteristics of Searchers," covers academic background and knowledge of subject, searching experience, level of education of searchers, and other characteristics. Finally, Part IV, "User Education for Information Seeking and Retrieving," includes implications of information technology for user education and reference service; the role of academic librarians; information literacy; critical thinking; learning theories and learning styles; cognitive models and mental models; and instructional objectives, teaching methods, and user education program descriptions.

Hepworth, M. (1999). A study of undergraduate information literacy and skills: The inclusion of information literacy and skills in the undergraduate curriculum. In *IFLA council and general conference.* Conference Programme and Proceedings (65th, Bangkok, Thailand, August 20-28, 1999); see IR 057 674. (ED 441 445)

This paper concerns the inclusion of information literacy and skills training in the undergraduate curriculum. Students were studied to determine their strengths and weaknesses in terms of their information literacy and skills. The methods used to study the students included a number of qualitative techniques applied while students conducted a research project. In general, it was found that students had limited skills in the area of information literacy. Major areas of difficulty include defining the problem, defining where to go for information, developing search strategies, finding material in the library, and developing insights and extrapolating. Based on these findings, recommendations were proposed to help develop information literacy and skills and incorporate their delivery in the university curriculum. The paper argues that incorporation in the curriculum is a necessity for their successful delivery. This is in contrast to treating these areas as separate subjects. In addition, the implications of these changes for faculty, staff, and librarians were defined. The initiative took place at the Nanyang Technological University (NTU) in Singapore and involved the NTU Library and the Division of Information Studies.

Homann, B. (2001). Difficulties and new approaches in user education in Germany. In *Libraries and librarians: Making a difference in the knowledge age.* Council and General Conference: Conference Programme and Proceedings (67th, Boston, MA, August 16-25, 2001); see IR 058 199. (ED 459 752)

In the 1970s, German academic libraries discovered user education as a new area of responsibilities, although promising activities at the end of the decade were not continued because of the lack of staff and organizational conditions. Since the beginning of the 1990s, activities in that field have been renewed, especially by large academic libraries. Because of the difficulties users had in the use of CD-ROM databases and OPACs (Online Public Access Catalogs), courses were offered in the handling of these new electronic information systems. Since then, pedagogical problems come up because of the amount and complexity of knowledge and skills that have to be taught in single lessons. This paper presents background on these developments in user education from the 1970s to the 1990s. The impact of new teaching concepts is addressed, including curriculum theory, Anglo-American models of information literacy, activation and learner-centered teaching/learning methods, and online learning techniques. The modular and project-oriented teaching approaches are then outlined, and the dynamic model of information literacy is presented.

Information literacy: Lifelong learning in the middle states region. A summary of two symposia (1995). (Philadelphia, Pennsylvania, March 27, 1995 and Rochester, New York, May 1, 1995). Philadelphia: Commission on Higher Education, Middle States Association of Colleges and Schools. 28p. (ED 386 157)

This report provides a summary of two symposia on information literacy sponsored by the Commission on Higher Education, Middle States Association of Colleges and Schools (CHE), the National Forum on Information Literacy, and the Association of College and Research Libraries. These events brought together institutions of the Middle States region who have made progress toward institutionalizing information literacy so that they could share their expertise and enhance their varied approaches to information literacy initiatives. The need is noted for campuswide commitment to information literacy as an educational strategy that will improve learning experiences. Several approaches that can help establish commitment and then translate it into reality are discussed: demonstrating the importance of information literacy, ensuring a shared vision among administrators, facilitating professional development, restructuring curricula to emphasize information literacy, adapting to student needs, and collaborating with K–12 and graduate programs. A list of symposia participants is provided.

Kallenberger, N. (2000). Taking the initiative: Ensuring an educational role for libraries in the information society stream. Education and information literacy. In *ALIA 2000. Capitalising on knowledge: The information profession in the 21st century* (Canberra, Australia, October 23-26, 2000); see IR 058 109. (ED 452 867)

This paper comprises four case studies that illustrate the State Library of New South Wales' (Australia) commitment to learning. The first section describes a shared learning environment for graduate information studies students that was collaboratively developed by the State Library and the University of Technology, Sydney (Australia). The second section presents the Industry Placement Program, designed to ensure that students from a wide range of disciplines gain real industry experience relevant to their classroom learning and career interests. The third section covers the library's support for researchers and independent learners, including five main areas in which clients need assistance, that is, procedures, research skills, catalogs/indexes, specific subjects/formats, and new services; examples of questions asked by clients; strategies to address these needs; and development and delivery of two courses in research skills offered by the library. The fourth section presents a case study on Infocus, a service that provides students with information for their study of the New South Wales Higher School Certificate curriculum.

Karelse, C.M. (1998). Smarter higher education: Information literacy adds value. In *The challenge to be relevant in the 21st century:* Abstracts and Fulltext Documents of Papers and Demos Given at the [International Association of Technological University Libraries] IATUL Conference (Pretoria, South Africa, June 1-5, 1998), Volume 18; see IR 057 503. (ED 434 670)

This paper explores some of the difficulties encountered in integrating one of SAQA's (South African Qualifications Association) critical outcomes, that of information literacy, into higher education curricula in the hope of developing a framework of flexible learning. The contributions made, both theoretically and in practice, by INFOLIT, an information literacy project in the Western Cape region of South Africa, are described. The first section discusses the context of globalization, information infrastructures, and knowledge systems. Information literacy theories and practices are summarized in the second section. The next section presents preliminary findings of INFOLIT related to integration of information literacy into academic courses, curriculum development expertise, capacity development of librarians, developing coalitions, replication of courses in different contexts, regional collaboration, changing mindsets, and institutionalizing information literacy. The fourth section describes challenges related to changing teaching and learning, the need for effective evaluation studies, replication of projects, integration and mainstreaming of projects, institutionalization and sustainability, endorsement of pilot projects by senior management, collaboration and partnerships, interactive learning, needs assessments, promotion and marketing, human resource development, inclusion of all players in pilot project formulation and delivery, understanding learning, development of higher order cognitive skills and structured domains of knowledge, and school and community information literacy models.

Kasowitz-Scheer, A., & Pasqualoni, M. (2002). *Information literacy instruction in higher education: Trends and issues.* ERIC Digest. Syracuse, NY. ERIC Clearinghouse on Information and Technology. 4p. (ED 465 375)

Students today face a daily explosion of information resources and the challenge of using these resources effectively and responsibly. Information literacy instruction (ILI) requires a shift in focus from teaching specific information resources to a set of critical thinking skills involving the use of information. ILI in an academic setting includes a variety of instructional approaches, such as course-related library instruction sessions, course-integrated projects, online tutorials, and stand-alone courses. Those running formal ILI programs consider curricular objectives, invoking combinations of instructional solutions over a period of time. This ERIC Digest examines characteristics of successful programs, presents specific examples of approaches currently being undertaken by academic libraries to support ILI, and addresses common challenges in developing and maintaining ILI programs.

Koltay, Z. (1996). *Supporting digital instructional technology: The role of the academic library.* 18p. (ED 403 914)

Academic libraries must reevaluate their instructional technology services in order to fulfill their mission of supporting the teaching activities of their parent institution in the current state of technological development. Applying modern approaches to further traditional library goals and making use of the expertise librarians gain while building and supporting electronic libraries can position the library at the center of an active instructional technology program that benefits the whole campus community. Librarians possess many skills—expertise with organizing information; teaching information literacy; creating and maintaining electronic libraries; concern for effective, easy, and equitable access; knowledge of user behavior; and relationship with faculty—that argue for their involvement with instructional technology support. Students benefit from richness added to the learning experience and gain information skills that will help them both during and after their university careers. Instructors benefit because instructional technology can make their teaching more effective and more efficient. Librarians gain updated services, more visibility, close working relationships with faculty, and an expanded electronic library that includes course materials in support of the university's instructional activities.

Lancaster, K., Keiffer, C., Wooldridge, D., Mckee, D. M., King, P., & Venezianl, C. (1998*). Internet research applications in health and human services degree programs: Promises and problems.* Paper presented at the Mid-South Instructional Technology Conference (3rd, Murfreesboro, TN, April 5-7, 1998). (ED 431 391)

As research through the Internet becomes the method of choice by many students, assessment of Internet materials, student motivation to use traditional research methods, and other pedagogical concerns have become issues in the learning process. This paper describes experiences of faculty from several applied disciplines (i.e., social work, human environmental studies, criminal justice, and nursing) in the College of Health and Human Services at Southeast Missouri State University in the use of the Internet as a tool for student research. Information analysis, opinion synthesis, and methodological applications offer common problems and opportunities for the diverse disciplines. Assessment criteria, problems and solutions in the use of the Internet, and suggestions for possible efforts are reviewed.

Lant, K. M. (2002) Flesh and bone: Information literacy, teaching, and the connected classroom. In *Teaching, learning, & technology: The connected classroom.* Proceedings of the Annual Mid-South Instructional Technology Conference (7th, Murfreesboro, TN, April 7-9, 2002); see IR 021 870. (ED 424 624)

This paper discusses information literacy, teaching, and online technology. The first section introduces the split between mind and body that is made possible by the Internet and related resources. The second section discusses distance learning, including the impact of digital environments in teaching, and the power of virtual education to permit a student to transcend physical limitations. The third section addresses the student/teacher body and emergent phenomena, including the use of online technology as an adjunct to the traditional classroom, the impact of the Internet on education and life, and the demands of instructional modeling and student apprenticeship. The third section considers the cultured classroom, including the dialogic quality of education, the role of the teacher, and the importance of physical presence for learning and culture building. The fourth section covers information literacy and the enhanced classroom, including ways that media and the Internet change learning, the objectives of information literacy, and the structure of the new, information-focused educational environment. The fifth section discusses teaching and information literacy, including the following three guidelines: (1) Contextualize all assignments, (2) build the use of information resources into every assignment, and (3) model in every interaction with students the skills of information literacy.

Lemke, C. (2002). *enGauge 21st century skills: Digital literacies for a digital age.* Naperville, IL: North Central Regional Educational Lab. 32p. (ED 463 753)

The North Central Regional Educational Laboratory's (NCREL) "enGauge" is a Web-based framework that describes six essential conditions, or system-wide factors critical to the effective use of technology for student learning. In addition to the framework, the "enGauge" Web site includes an online survey instrument that allows districts and schools to conduct online assessments of systemwide educational technology effectiveness. This publication describes a set of twenty-first-century skills that will be increasingly important to students entering the workforce. These skills are not at odds with traditional educational skills but are, in fact, extensions of those skills, adapted to new technologies and new work environments. The educational system will be challenged to encourage the development of these twenty-first-century skills in relevant and meaningful ways. The publication consists of five main sections, following an introduction. The first section, "Digital-Age Literacy," discusses basic, scientific, and technological literacies; visual and information literacies; and cultural literacy and global awareness. The second section, "Inventive Thinking," focuses on adaptability/ability to manage complexity; curiosity, creativity, and risk-taking; and higher-order thinking and sound reasoning. Section 3, "Effective Communication," deals with teaming, collaboration, and interpersonal skills; personal and social responsibility; and interactive communication. The fourth section, "High Productivity," discusses the ability to prioritize, plan, and manage for results; effective use of real-world tools; and relevant, high-quality products. Section five, "Information Technology," identifies possible social effects with regard to information technology. Two other sections provide a brief summary and references.

Library faculty in California community college libraries: Qualifications, roles, & responsibilities. (1996). Sacramento: California Community Colleges, Academic Senate. 11p. (ED 395 630)

This report presents background information on library issues in California Community Colleges (CCC); identifies the relationship between the mission of the colleges and the library science discipline; and describes the qualifications, roles, and responsibilities of library faculty. Following a brief introduction, the first section of the report discusses the instructional role of library faculty as the primary teachers of research methods, critical thinking skills, and information literacy skills. This section also indicates that library faculty are at the forefront of the information revolution, developing innovative ways of obtaining, delivering, and facilitating the use of information. The next section describes the role of community college library faculty in curricular development, indicating that they must respond to advances in computer technology, the expanded development of communications technologies, and changes in the college student body and financial base. The following section examines their role in college governance through participation in academic senates and curriculum, professional standards, shared governance, budget, planning, hiring, evaluation, tenure, technology, and other committees. The final section describes the qualifications for employment in the CCC as a master's degree in library science and lists the expertise sought in library faculty candidates.

McKenna, M. (1994). *Libraries and the Internet.* ERIC Digest. Syracuse, NY. ERIC Clearinghouse on Information & Technology. 4p. (ED 377 880)

The Internet is an international computer network encompassing thousands of smaller interconnected networks. This digest describes various uses of the Internet and its impact on libraries, as well as Internet-related library issues. The Internet applications of electronic mail (e-mail), telnet, and file transfer protocol (FTP) are briefly described. The impact of the Internet on libraries includes leadership opportunities, cost and time savings, question answering services, international interlibrary loans, document delivery services, online transactions, government information, information sharing, and increased librarian visibility and value to the community. Internet-related issues are discussed with respect to academic, public, special, and school libraries. It is recommended that librarians take an active role in the formulation of national policy and legislation and creation and organization of services and resources, and be properly trained in network literacy to provide programs for patrons to become network literate.

Olen, S. (1995). A transformation in teacher education: Or how can disadvantaged teachers become information literate? In *Literacy: Traditional, cultural, technological. Selected Papers from the Annual Conference of the International Association of School Librarianship* (23rd, Pittsburgh, Pennsylvania, July 17-22, 1994); see IR 056 058. 7p. (ED 399 948)

In a developing country such as South Africa, many teachers enter initial teacher education with little or no experience of libraries and information sources. These students need to become information literate during their initial teacher education; otherwise they will not have the knowledge of information sources and skills which they will need if they are going to be role models for their pupils and help them to become information literate. The paper describes a project to improve the media and information skills of underqualified teachers through inservice workshops. The process could also be used as a model for initial teacher education with students from disadvantaged or more privileged backgrounds. It is important for pupils to become information literate, but before this can happen, their teachers must themselves become information literate. Teaching style influences student learning and must follow a clearly formulated process, like the one described. This is one way to help transform the prevailing teacher-centered and textbook-centered teaching style to an interactive teaching and learning process based on available information sources.

Perspectives and accomplishments, 1993-1994: Annual report of the executive director. (1995). Philadelphia: Commission on Higher Education, Middle States Association of Colleges and Schools. 20p. (ED 378 929)

This annual report by the Commission on Higher Education's Middle States Association of Colleges and Schools details progress toward goals and objectives, annual statistics, and key issues in accreditation and quality assurance. A recurring theme of the report and the year it covers is the changing relationship between accrediting agencies and the federal and state governments, specifically in light of the Higher Education Act amendments of 1992. Following an opening message from the executive director, the first section describes executive and professional staff liaison with institutions in a range of campus visits and office meetings related to self-study, evaluation, and the requirements and expectations for applicant and candidate institutions. A section on annual statistics lists institutions receiving candidate status, reaffirmed accreditation, follow-up reports, candidate reports, visits, or other developments. The next four sections discuss information literacy and library support efforts, policy development work, new policy statements on student transfer and articulation, and accreditation of free-standing American institutions abroad. This section also discusses areas for policy work and development in 1994–1995. The report includes a description of liaison with external organizations and groups, and workshops, conferences, and special events held during 1993–1994. A final page lists Commission members and staff.

Rafaill, W. S., & Peach, A. C. (2001) Are your students ready for college? Technology literacy at Georgetown College. In *Proceedings of the annual Mid-South Instructional Technology Conference* (6th, Murfreesboro, TN, April 8-10, 2001); see IR 021 138. (ED 463 728)

In 1999, Georgetown College (Kentucky) established the Information Technology Literacy Program, which requires new students to demonstrate basic proficiencies in the use of information technology resources in several proficiency areas (i.e., Internet, library Web-based databases and on-line catalogs, e-mail, word processing, spreadsheets, databases, and presentations) as a requirement for graduation. Students are given a task-based technology assessment test within the first three weeks of their first semester. The test results are then used as an advising tool to determine whether the student needs additional technology skills. A summary of the first two years of this testing data as well as specific trends are discussed. A list of schools surveyed for comparative purposes and the assessment test tasks are appended.

Ratteray, O. M. T., & Simmons, H. L. (1995). *Information literacy in higher education: A report on the middle states region.* Philadelphia: Commission on Higher Education, Middle States Association of Colleges and Schools. 10p. (ED 388 136)

A survey of 830 institutions of higher education in the United States explored the status of initiatives to promote information literacy, which is defined as a subset of critical thinking skills that consists of an individual's knowing when he or she has an informational need and how to access, evaluate, and effectively use information. The survey found that, on a national basis, institutions in the Middle States Association of Colleges and Schools

(MSACS) region may be leading other regions of the country in applying information literacy strategies on campus. Of the 259 MSACS respondents, 31 percent indicated that they have a "functional" information literacy program, 27 percent offered a course that focuses on information literacy abilities, and 19 percent integrated information literacy experiences into courses in all majors. The survey also found that 19 percent of MSACS respondents have developed formal assessments of students' information literacy skills, and that 38 percent provided faculty and staff development to support the information literacy program. MSACS institutions were, on average, above the national norms in these areas. Data are provided in six tables.

Rodd, R. (2000). Information literacy in electronic environments: Fantasies, facts, and futures. In *Virtual libraries: Virtual communities.* Abstracts, Fulltext Documents and PowerPoint Presentations of Papers and Demos Given at the International Association of Technological University Libraries (IATUL) Conference (Brisbane, Queensland, Australia, July 3-7, 2000); see IR 057 942. Online title varies slightly. (ED 447 834)

This paper focuses on the concept and practice of information literacy in relation to the virtual information environment. Key challenges for the development of digital information services are identified, and three fundamental components of information literacy (connecting with, interacting with, and utilizing information) and related research findings are summarized. Two tables present models of student research using traditional print-based information and World Wide Web-based information. Each table describes characteristics of the information environment and student responsibilities for six dimensions: starting point of search, document scope, document quality, information relevance, indicators of information quality, and information management. Implications for information literacy instruction related to the following learning principles are summarized: (1) Learning is about making and maintaining connections; (2) learning is an active search for meaning; (3) learning is developmental—a cumulative process involving the whole person; (4) learning is both individual and social; (5) learning is strongly affected by the educational climate; (6) learning requires feedback, practice, and use; (7) much learning takes place informally and incidentally; (8) learning is grounded in particular contexts and individual experiences; (9) learning involves the ability of individuals to monitor their own learning; and (10) learning is enhanced by taking place in the context of compelling situations.

Sarkodie-Mensah, K., et al. (2000*). Reference services for the adult learner: Challenging issues for the traditional and technological era.* Binghamton, NY: Haworth Press. 435p. (ED 447 309). Document not available from EDRS.

This book offers approaches for teaching adult patrons how and where to find information in libraries and through information services. It includes 34 papers, organized in seven sections, expressing the views of faculty, adult students, and administrators as well as librarians on theories of educational psychology that explain how adults learn. The book provides suggestions from adult learners to help reference service personnel understand what these clients need to know about using new technologies and finding information. Section 1, "Information Explosion, Technophobia, and Technostress," includes "Information Explosion: Continuing Implications for Reference Services to Adult Learners in Academia" (Ezzo and Perez); "Information Explosion and the Adult Learner" (Christian, Blumenthal, and Patterson); "Stress Relief: Help for the Technophobic Patron from the Reference Desk" (Harrison); "Overcoming Technostress in Reference Services to Adult Learners" (Quinn); "Technological Mediation: Reference and the Non-Traditional Student" (Grealy); and "Challenges Faced by Reference Librarians in Familiarizing Adult Students with the Computerized Library of Today: The Cuesta College Experience" (Bontenbal). Section 2, "Understanding the Characteristics, Needs and Expectations of Adult Learners to Better Serve Them," includes "Envisioning the Mature Re-Entry Student: Constructing New Identities in the Traditional University Setting" (Given); "A Close Encounter Model for Reference Services to Adult Learners: The Value of Flexibility and Variance" (Baron and Strout-Dapaz); "Helping Adult Undergraduates Make the Best Use of Emerging Technologies" (Moslander); "Understanding the Characteristics, Concerns, and Priorities of Adult Learners To Enhance Library Services to Them" (Veal); and "After-Five Syndrome: Library Hours and Services for the Adult Learner" (Anne Fox). Section 3, "Theories of Adult Learning: Implications for Reference and Instructional Services for the Adult Learner," contains "How Do We Learn? Contributions of Learning Theory to Reference Service and Library Instruction" (Roy and Novotny); "Andragogical Librarian" (Ingram); and "Adult Learning Theory and Reference Services" (Ghaphery). Section 4, "From a Distance: Providing Reference and Instructional Services for the Adult Learner," includes "The Librarian as Bricoleur: Meeting the Needs of Distance Learners" (Jayne); "Interactive Reference at a Distance: A Corporate Model for Academic Libraries" (Ware, Howe, and Scalese); "Reference Provision in Adult Basic and Community Education" (Renshaw); "The University Library's Role in Planning a Successful Distance Learning Program" (Hufford); "Library

Services to External Students from Australian Universities" (Middleton and Peacock); "Facilitating Adult Learning: The Role of the Academic Librarian" (Currie); and "Going the Distance (and Back Again)" (Gibson and Scales). Section 5, "Reference, Instruction, and Information Literacy," includes "Reference Services to Police Officer Students at the School of Police Staff and Command, Traffic Institute, Northwestern University" (Ramachandran); "Library Instruction and Information Literacy for the Adult Learner" (Caravello); "Adult Students: Wandering the Web with a Purpose" (King-Blandford); "Breaking the Mold: Using Educational Pedagogy in Designing Library Instruction of Adult Learners" (Naomi Harrison); "Delphi Method in Web Site Selection" (Green). Section 6, "Serving Diverse Populations: Disabled Patrons and International Students," contains "Reference Services for All: How To Support Reference Service to Clients with Disabilities" (Miller-Gatenby and Chittenden); "Strategies for Providing Effective Reference Services for International Adult Learners" (Kumar and Suresh); "Reference Services to the International Adult Learner" (Brown); "Reference Services: Meeting the Needs of International Adult Learners" (Chattoo); and "Reference Services and the International Adult Learner" (Liestman). Section 7, "From the Horse's Mouth: Views from Faculty, Administrators, Librarians, and Students," includes "Faculty Expectations and the Adult Learner" (Mullins and Park); "Providing Quality Library Service to the Adult Learner: Views of Students, Faculty, and Administrators" (Simmonds); and "Towards an Integrative Literature Search: Reflections of a 'Wild' Adult Learner" (Fisher). Articles contain summaries, references, and keywords; the book is indexed.

Sherratt, C. S., et al. (1992). *Information services study. Final report.* Cambridge, MA: Massachusetts Institute of Technology Libraries. 74p. (ED 366 344)

In 1991–1992, the Massachusetts Institute of Technology (MIT) Libraries conducted an Information Services Study with support from the Office of the Provost. Its purpose was to study how faculty, research staff, and students in three disciplines on campus gather information for their work. Members of the departments of Brain and Cognitive Sciences, Management Science in the Sloan School of Management, and Materials Science and Engineering were asked about the information sources they use and their methods of discovering these. The staff assigned to the study were then expected to formulate preliminary recommendations for library and information services based on the findings. This report contains the summary of responses to the questionnaire, themes, recommendations for services, and suggestions for further research. Included in the appendixes are the organization of the study; a list of sources, including annotated bibliographies of sources consulted for instrument development and sources for alternative methodologies; areas for question development; data gathering instruments, including "MIT Community Survey of Information Acquisition and Usage," the interview guide, and the focus group discussion guide; and a statistical summary of the questionnaire.

Tompkins, P. (1995). *Information literacy: Real writers, real research.* Paper presented at the Annual Meeting of the Conference on College Composition and Communication (46th, Washington, DC, March 23-25, 1995). 13p. (ED 388 996)

The decision to organize English 112 courses around a research project entitled "A Survey of the Freshman Composition Requirement at Richmond Area Colleges and Universities" resulted from concerns as the fall of 1993 approached. English 112 emphasizes the study of literature and the production of a research paper that presents an argument by paraphrasing information in books and periodicals. Since the instructor himself has an aversion to writing this type of perfunctory paper, he assumed that his students would have the same aversion. In an article, Richard L. Larson argues that the concept of a research paper has no substantive identity, that is, it is impossible to differentiate between texts that incorporate and evaluate new information and those that do not. In the composition classroom, a research paper is any attempt by writers to gather information for themselves, the world, or others as they make meaning for a purpose. What is the purpose of freshman English but to prepare students to be self-critically aware as they revise their discourse for a variety of audiences and purposes? With these considerations in mind, a research project was devised that would involve the entire class and serve a real purpose. That project raised important questions such as (1) What qualifies a researcher as competent? (2) What is the role of students as researchers and writers? and (3) How can educators rethink information literacy so that they can kill the mistaken perception of the so-called research or terminal paper?

Warner, M. (1998). *Western Carolina University's model of integrating information literacy: Partnering the first year composition instructor, students and a personal librarian.* Paper presented at the Annual Meeting of the Conference on College Composition and Communication (49th, Chicago, IL, April 1-4, 1998). (ED 424 581)

First-year composition courses (particularly the semester course devoted to exposition, argumentation, and research) were the site at Western Carolina University for an alliance between professors and librarians as they attempted to integrate information literacy. Librarians developed six modules to teach "The Big6 Skills Approach to Information Problem Solving": (1) Task Definition, (2) Information Seeking Strategies, (3) Locating and Accessing Information, (4) Using Information, (5) Synthesis (organizing information from multiple sources and presenting the information), and (6) Evaluation. Each librarian was assigned to a cluster group of four or five English composition instructors, allowing English instructors to identify the most logical sequence for the skills to be presented in their class as well as to inform the librarians of specific paper assignments. Examples use the first three information skills to show how they were integrated into courses, as librarians, in discussion with individual instructors, determined the actual assignments that would allow the students to practice the literacy skill, the topics most applicable to the papers students were required to write, and the time needed for instruction.

Wiggins, M. E. (1994). *Hands-on instruction in an electronic classroom.* A Final Report to the U.S. Department of Education of a Research and Development grant awarded to establish a fully equipped electronic training room and test the effectiveness of hands-on instruction in learning the NOTIS OPAC and SilverPlatter ERIC. Brigham Young University, Provo, Utah. 109p. (ED 369 391)

This document is the final report to the U.S. Department of Education on a research and development grant awarded to establish a fully equipped electronic training room and test the effectiveness of hands-on instruction in learning the NOTIS OPAC (online public access catalog) and the Silver-Platter ERIC database on CD-ROM. The purpose of the study was (1) to identify common errors and problems experienced by students using computer-based research tools; (2) to develop hands-on training modules for specific computer systems; (3) to create a computer-equipped training facility that can serve as a model for other institutions; and (4) to implement the training modules on an experimental basis, evaluate their effectiveness, and further refine them. The study was divided into a NOTIS study and an ERIC study. The NOTIS study found no measurable difference in learning between the hands-on group and the lecture/demonstration group. The ERIC group found that hands-on instruction was slightly more effective than a lecture/demonstration alternative and that student interest is enhanced when taught in a hands-on environment.

About ERIC

Inquiries about ERIC may be addressed to:

ACCESS ERIC
2277 Research Blvd., 6L
Rockville, MD 20850
Telephone: 301-519-5157

Toll free: 800-LET-ERIC (538-3742)
Fax: 301-519-6760
E-mail: accesseric@accesseric.org
URL: http://www.eric.ed.gov

How to Order ERIC Documents

ERIC references with an ED number are typically research papers and other monographs. The least expensive way to obtain these in full text is by seeking out an ERIC microfiche collection; these are housed at more than 1,000 locations worldwide. To locate the ERIC Resource Collection near you, connect to http://www.ed.gov/BASISDB/EROD/eric/SF or check with your local library. Many libraries now offer E*Subscribe, which grants their patrons free electronic access to some ERIC documents. Ask your local librarian if the library offers this valuable service. Otherwise, microfiche, paper, and selected electronic copies may be ordered for a fee from:

ERIC Document Reproduction Service (EDRS)
7420 Fullerton Rd., Suite 110
Springfield, VA 22153-2852
Telephone: 800-443-ERIC (3742) or 703-440-1400
Fax: 703-440-1408
E-mail: service@edrs.com
URL: http://edrs.com

Cost: Depends on format and length.

Information needed for ordering includes the ED number, the number of pages, the number of copies wanted, the unit price, and the total unit cost. Sales tax should be included on orders from Maryland, Virginia, and Washington, DC.

Some commercially produced books cited in the database are not available in full text through ERIC and may have to be obtained through interlibrary loan, a book retailer, or the publisher.

Journal Articles

ERIC references with an EJ number are journal articles. Again, the least expensive way to obtain full text is to consult a library, either to track down the appropriate issue of the originating journal or to try to obtain the article through interlibrary loan. Otherwise, articles may be available from the journal publisher or from one of the following article reproduction services (for a fee). Please be aware that no article reproduction service carries 100 percent of ERIC-indexed journal titles. Ingenta offers a large number of journals.

> Infotrieve
> 41575 Joy Rd.
> Canton, MI 48187
> Telephone: 800-422-4633
> E-mail: service@infotrieve.com
> URL: http://www4.infotrieve.com

Cost per article:

U.S., Canada, and Mexico: $12.00 service fee + copyright royalty + delivery

International: $14.00 service fee + copyright royalty + delivery

> Ingenta
> Telephone: 617-395-4046
> Toll-free: 1-800-296-2221
> E-mail: ushelp@ingenta.com
> URL: http://www.ingenta.com/ (registration required)

Price varies by publisher.

Information needed for ordering includes the author, title of article, name of journal, volume, issue number, page numbers, date, and EJ number for each article. Fax services are available.

Index

395

About the Authors

MICHAEL B. EISENBERG is Dean and Professor of the University of Washington's Information School. He previously worked as Professor of information studies at Syracuse University and as Director of the Information Institute of Syracuse, which includes the ERIC Clearinghouse on Information & Technology, the award-winning AskERIC Internet information service, and the Gateway to Educational Materials (GEM). Mike is a prolific author with numerous books and articles on information science and technology, information literacy, education, and the role of libraries. He is nationally known for his innovative approach information and technology literacy: the Big6. Mike also consults with school  districts, businesses, and government agencies on information resources, services, curriculum, technology, and management. He earned his Ph.D. in Information Transfer at Syracuse University's School of Information Studies and his MLS from the State university of New York at Albany.

 CARRIE A. LOWE is Internet Policy Specialist for the American Library Association. In this position, she analyzes legislation and policy related to library technology issues such as privacy, E-Rate and the digital divide. Prior to her role at ALA, Carrie was Senior Education Associate for the Public Broadcasting Service (PBS). Carrie presents frequently to a variety of audiences on the topics of information literacy, information problem-solving, and educational technology. She has also written articles on the topics for academic and professional journals. Carrie is a graduate of the University of Wisconsin, Madison,

where she earned her bachelor's degree in Education. She earned her MLS at Syracuse University's School of Information Studies in 1998 and was awarded the 1998 Graduate Leadership Award. Carrie is a member of Beta Phi Mu, the National Library Honor Society.

KATHLEEN L. SPITZER is a library media specialist at Cicero–North Syracuse highschool (Cicero, NY). She serves on school level and district level technology and software committees and maintains the school library's web site. A 1991 MLS/School Media graduate of the School of Information Studies at Syracuse University, Kathy has presented workshops on information skills and technology and has authored numerous books and articles on the topic. Kathy is a member of ALA-AASL, NYLA/SLMS, NYSUT, Beta Phi Mu (National Library Honor Society), and is active with the Central New York Media Specialists (CNYMS), an affiliate of NYLA/SLMS.